PAUL *and the* EARLY JEWISH ENCOUNTER *with* DEUTERONOMY

PAUL *and the* EARLY JEWISH ENCOUNTER *with* DEUTERONOMY

DAVID LINCICUM

B
Baker Academic
a division of Baker Publishing Group
Grand Rapids, Michigan

Published in 2013 by Baker Academic
a division of Baker Publishing Group
P.O. Box 6287, Grand Rapids, MI 49516-6287
www.bakeracademic.com

Originally published in 2010 as *Paul and the Early Jewish Encounter with Deuteronomy*, Wissenschaftliche Untersuchungen zum Neuen Testament 2. Reihe, by Mohr Siebeck, Tübingen, Germany.

Printed in the United States of America

Library of Congress Cataloging-in-Publication Data for the original edition is on file at the Library of Congress, Washington, DC.

Baker Academic ISBN 978-0-8010-4910-1

The internet addresses, email addresses, and phone numbers in this book are accurate at the time of publication. They are provided as a resource. Baker Publishing Group does not endorse them or vouch for their content or permanence.

For Julia

My dream thou brok'st not, but continued'st it

Preface

This monograph presents a lightly revised version of a doctoral thesis defended in the Theology Faculty at the University of Oxford in July 2009. The monograph and the underlying thesis together mark the culmination of a long process – a process that would have been impossible without the generous help of a number of people.

Without the patient and persistent guidance, challenging questions, and whole-hearted investment of my supervisor, Professor Markus Bockmuehl, the thesis would have been much poorer; he has proven to be a Doktorvater in the grand tradition. His influence is evident throughout the work in ways ranging from the subtle to the profound. In addition, I benefited from the suggestions of those who read and commented on significant sections of the thesis, including Professor Richard Bauckham, and Drs. John Muddiman and Mark Edwards. My two examiners, Professors William Horbury and Martin Goodman, posed trenchant questions for further reflection. Professor G. K. Beale kindly encouraged my first investigations of Deuteronomy in Paul. A number of colleagues at the Universities of St. Andrews, Oxford and Tübingen, where research for this thesis was carried out, deserve mention for thought-provoking conversations and friendship: Martin Bauspieß, Patrick Egan, Chris Hays, Drew Lewis, Kenneth Liljeström, R. J. Matava, Casey Strine, Tim Stone, and Seth Tarrer. Among these friends, Chris Hays deserves special mention: a fellow sojourner whose warm friendship and probing insights have strengthened me and this work in innumerable ways. Finally, the members of the Theology Faculty in Oxford have generously supported my transition from doctoral student to junior colleague with good humour and grace.

Ideas from some portions of the investigation were aired at various scholarly meetings and conferences, to whose participants I owe thanks for challenging and illuminating responses. Portions of Chapter 2 were presented to the 2008 "Annual Seminar on the Old Testament in the New" chaired by Professor Steve Moyise at St. Deiniol's Library. Some portions of Chapters 3 and 8 were presented as "Paul and the Temple Scroll: Reflections on Their Shared Engagement with Deuteronomy" to the Oxford New Testament Graduate Seminar, 24 January 2008 and to the "Scripture in Early Judaism and Christianity" Unit at the 2008 SBL meeting in Boston. An early version of portions of Chapter 8 was presented in January 2009 as "The Shape of Paul's Deuteronomy" to the German-English New Testament Colloquium at the University of Tübingen in conjunction with the Institut zur Erforschung des Urchristentums. For such opportunities I am grateful to organizers and participants alike.

The underlying thesis was enabled by generous financial help from a number of organizations and individuals. Grants from the Sir Richard Stapley Educational Trust, the Grinfield Bequest, the Faculty of Theology in Oxford, and an Overseas Research Student Award from the University of Oxford relieved financial anxieties and allowed me to focus on my research. A generous Scatcherd European scholarship facilitated a research stay in Tübingen for most of the 2008–2009 academic year, where I also incurred debts to Professor Hermann Lichtenberger and Dr. Scott Caulley for their hospitality and collegial discussion. In addition, I have been fortunate enough to have had significant support in one form or another from numerous friends and family members: Beth and Leon Smart, Christine and Jack Piers, Clem and Mary Lincicum, Steve and Becky Lincicum, Judy Lincicum, Amy Stephens, Brandon Lincicum, Matt and Katie Lincicum, Paul and Laura Piers, Matt Piers, Brent and Lindsay Gosnell, David and Andreea Hoover, Brandon and Denise Walsh, Carmen and Eli Foster, Devin and Larissa Vaughn, Holly and Shawn Duncan, Rick and Rebecca Prenshaw, Walt and Mercy Avra. Each name conceals a debt of gratitude which will not soon be forgotten.

Furthermore, I would like to express my gratitude to Prof. Dr. Jörg Frey for accepting the thesis for publication in this series, and to Dr. Henning Ziebritzki and Ilse König at Mohr Siebeck for their excellent help in guiding the thesis to publication.

Finally, my most significant human debt is cheerfully acknowledged: Julia has borne with a distracted husband in a spirit of patient sacrifice and warm support during these nomadic years, and it is only right that my longstanding gratitude and admiration should here be publicly expressed.

Oxford, Good Friday 2010   David Lincicum

For the reprint of this edition, I am grateful to Daniel Driver and Jim West for kindly sending along errata, and to James Ernest and the team at Baker Academic for granting this technical work a wider audience.

Oxford, Advent 2012

Table of Contents

Abbreviations

Abbreviations follow *The SBL Handbook of Style* (Peabody, MA: Hendrickson, 1999). In addition, note the following:

BDAG W. Bauer. 2000. *A Greek-English Lexicon of the New Testament and other Early Christian Literature*. English editions by W.F. Arndt, F.W. Gingrich, and F.W. Danker. 3rd ed. Revised and Edited by Frederick William Danker. Chicago: University of Chicago Press.

BDF F. Blass, F. and A. Debrunner. 1961. *A Greek Grammar of the New Testament and Other Early Christian Literature*. Translated and revised by Robert W. Funk. Chicago: University of Chicago Press.

CCSL Corpus Christianorum Series Latina

CIJ *Corpus Inscriptionum Iudaicarum*

CPJ *Corpus Papyrorum Judaicarum*

DJD *Discoveries in the Judaean Desert*

ESV English Standard Version

ET English translation

EVV English versions

HT Hebrew text

IJO *Inscriptiones Judaicae Orientis*

JIGRE *Jewish Inscriptions of Graeco-Roman Egypt*

JIWE *Jewish Inscriptions of Western Europe*

LCL Loeb Classical Library

LSJ Henry George Liddell, Robert Scott and H. S. Jones with R. McKenzie. 1996. *A Greek-English Lexicon*. 9th ed. Oxford: Clarendon.

MAMA *Monumenta Asiae Minoris Antiqua*

MS(S) Manuscript(s)

MT Massoretic text

NRSV New Revised Standard Version

OTP J. H. Charlesworth, ed., *The Old Testament Pseudepigrapha*. 2 vols. Garden City, NY: Doubleday.

PG J. P. Migne, *Patrologia Graeca*

SEG *Supplementum Epigraphicum Graecum*

Str-B H. Strack and P. Billerbeck. 1926–28. *Kommentar zum Neuen Testament aus Talmud und Midrasch*. 6 vols. Munich: Beck.

TDNT G. Kittel and G. Friedrich, eds. 1964–76. *Theological Dictionary of the New Testament*. Translated and edited by G. W. Bromiley. 10 vols. Grand Rapids: Eerdmans.

Chapter 1

Introduction

> Because all the generations which arose before
> us forever even until now stand here with us this
> day before the Lord our God, and all the genera-
> tions which are to arise after us stand here with
> us this day.
>
> *Targum Neofiti* Deut 29:14

1.1. Inferring an Icon: Paul, Scripture and the Jews

In the twelfth and thirteenth centuries, a number of ornately illustrated Bibles were commissioned by members of the wealthy European aristocracy.
In keeping with the practice of the day, the manuscripts were supplied with
intricately executed pictures at the beginning of each work, the Pauline
epistles being no exception. Striking, however, is the clarity of the statement these historiated initials urge: Paul's letters are a profound repudia-
tion and confutation of Judaism. One twelfth century manuscript, in the
initial of Romans, depicts Paul standing victoriously on a vanquished Lady
Synagoga, herself blindfolded and despondent.[1] Other manuscripts, especially of the so-called *Bibles moralisées*, repeat in variation scenes in
which a nimbed and sainted Paul stands over against his Jewish adversaries, the latter clearly identified by their pointed hats: Paul is perceived as
already fundamentally other than his benighted Jewish contemporaries.[2]
Insofar as the law figures in these illustrations, it is a symbol of a vain
Jewish literalism in opposition to the liberating Christian gospel, at best of
use to Paul in refuting culpably pedantic Jewish interpreters, though not in
any true sense a source of constructive reflection for the apostle.

---

[1] Boulogne, Bibl. Mun., MS 2, Vol. II, fol. 231; see Eleen 1982: 69 and fig. 120; see
also her fig. 328. For other roughly contemporaneous portrayals of Synagoga as blinded,
see Blumenkranz 1966: 61–66.

[2] See, e.g., Eleen 1982, figs. 245–48. On these manuscripts, note esp. Eleen 1982:
118–49; Lipton 1999, who calls them "an unprecedented visual polemic against the
Jews" (1). What is more, in an ironic twist, Lipton suggests that the monarch may have
had the manuscript made for himself in keeping with the laws of the King in Deuteronomy 17 (10–11).

Iconographic illustrations often function in manuscripts of the Pauline epistles as heuristic statements through which the epistle is to be read, that is, as a sort of holistic indication of what to look for in the letter, a visual act of interpretation.[3] Clearly, to the degree that contemporary scholarship on Paul may be said to operate with its own implicit "iconography" of the apostle, it stands at a far remove from these medieval examples. The guiding images that led readers to hear the Corpus Paulinum in a certain way also contributed to the mistreatment and abuse of actual and not just iconographic Jews – though we should be clear that the images are probably symptom more than cause of the underlying political and religious malaise. Nonetheless, the contemporary reader of Paul's letter collection feels rightly chastened by the tragic events of the 20th century: in the shadow of the holocaust, we are more aware than ever that hermeneutical construals of Jews and Judaism can have devastating political consequences. After the *Judenfrage* hinted at by these images was answered so horrifically in the last century, we have rightly abandoned such iconography as interpretative guides. Perhaps equally importantly, and as the argument of this investigation can be taken to suggest, these images do not do justice to the nature of the Pauline epistles themselves. Paul, Scripture, and the Jews: the constituent subjects of the iconography remain the same today, but they have been drastically re-configured with reference to one another.

Of course, now it is *de rigueur* (if also something of a truism) to say that Paul himself is among the Jews and operated within the time before a clear distinction between Judaism and Christianity. This is so whether one chooses to describe the early Christian movement as one form of "Middle Judaism" (so Boccaccini 1991), as a sibling locked in rivalry with an emerging Rabbinic Judaism (so Segal 1986; similarly Hengel 2005), or as a movement engaged on a journey whose "way" has not departed from that of other Jewish movements (so, e.g., Becker and Reed 2003; cf. Boyarin 2004). Now, however, when we are accustomed to hearing of the sheer pluriformity of Second Temple Judaism, the precise form of Paul's debt to his ancestral tradition may yet be susceptible to further definition. If we wish to describe this Jewish apostle to the Gentiles, we might do worse than to begin with the presupposition of Paul's Jewish identity (firmly established especially over the past 30 years or so) and seek further specificity in one aspect of this identity. Answering this desideratum, the present study offers a reading of Paul as a Jewish interpreter of Deuteronomy among other Jewish interpreters of Deuteronomy.

---

[3] See Eleen 1982: 45–46, 149, etc. The evidence Eleen marshals of the influence of the so-called Marcionite prologues on Pauline iconography in biblical manuscripts supports this hermeneutical function.

1.2. Paul and Deuteronomy

Presented as a series of Moses' final speeches to Israel as she is about to cross the Jordan and "inherit" the land of promise, Deuteronomy already represents itself as a re-visioning of the law and rings with a contemporizing quality that seeks to collapse the distance between generations in its telescopic address. A broad tradition of subsequent interpretation and re-appropriation of Deuteronomy was virtually assured in light of two factors: Deuteronomy served as a fundamental and normative text expressing the will of God, and the conditions in which Deuteronomy later came to be read and heard no longer aligned with those to which it originally addressed itself.[4] Thus, if Brevard Childs is correct in claiming that Deuteronomy "instructs future Israel on the manner in which past tradition is properly made alive in fresh commitment to the God of the covenant" (1979: 224), it is equally true that the manner in which these instructions were followed varied widely among those who considered themselves addressed as Israel. We might say that Deuteronomy was therefore encountered as both constraint and possibility – as constraint, in that its normativity was granted as binding; as possibility, in that its very consciousness of resourcing posterity lent itself to multiple and irreducibly diverse interpretations.

This dual aspect of Deuteronomy's reception, therefore, makes possible the comparative venture of the present investigation. If all interpreters agree on the sheer givenness of Deuteronomy's authority as Torah, the precise interpretative goals with which they approach the end of the Pentateuch differ in intriguing ways. This study seeks to delineate the range of approaches to the "last book of Moses" in Jewish literature spanning from approximately the third century BCE to the third century CE, with a special focus on the relief into which such delineation casts the apostle Paul. The nature of this question, then, naturally entails a consideration of the construal of texts as wholes. What it might mean to look for a holistic rendering of a text will, I hope, become apparent as we proceed.

To be concerned with Deuteronomy as in some sense a whole corresponds in important ways to the *realia* of its encounter in antiquity (see § 2

---

[4] Cf. Fishbane 1985: "…the two following factors which may be isolated as necessary *historical* components in the development of post-biblical Jewish exegesis: on the one hand, authoritative texts or teachings whose religious-cultural significance is fundamental; on the other, conditions to which these texts or teachings do not appear to be explicitly pertinent" (3; cf. also 15). Fishbane's student, B. Levinson (1997), suggests that Deuteronomy itself has already performed an act of hermeneutical transformation in appropriating and refining earlier traditions, though he casts this in much more agonistic form than Fishbane (e.g., 148–53, etc.), sometimes, however, by means of extreme suspicion.

below). Nevertheless, at one time it was perhaps customary, at least in certain circles of English-speaking scholarship, to blithely dismiss Paul's scriptural quotations as mere flights of atomistic imagination. Paul, it was argued, seized upon the wording of individual verses that could perpetuate his argument, wrenched them from their context, and smuggled the fragments into his letters in an act of hermeneutical baptism – in the best light, an embarrassing, if also perhaps apostolically authorized, indiscretion which we sensible modern readers would do best to avoid. After all, hadn't Paul indicated his contempt for context when he wondered aloud, "What does God care for oxen?" And it has to be conceded that, judged according to historical-critical standards, Paul showed nothing like the modern exegete's concern to understand Scripture in its original historical setting.

Nevertheless, if this position, admittedly overdrawn here, could once claim something like a consensus, all that has now changed. Following on from the work of C. H. Dodd in the 1950s, and especially in the wake of Richard Hays's epochal 1989 study, *Echoes of Scripture in the Letters of Paul*, an increasing number of voices in recent scholarship has claimed the apostle Paul as a consummate interpreter of Scripture. Much of this work has drawn on insights from literary and theological criticism to suggest that Paul and other early Christian authors approached Scripture with reading strategies that, while certainly not akin to modern historical criticism, display their own internal logic and respect for context. Some examples of this trend, to be sure, tend to abstract Paul's reading of Scripture from his own historical situation, and critics have highlighted this a-historical tendency. But it is clear that we have seen a significant shift in emphasis: exit Paul the purveyor of pithy, free-floating axioms, enter Paul the reader. While much of the interest in seeing Paul as engaged in some form of holistic biblical interpretation has so far centered on his appropriation of Isaiah, increasing attention is also being paid to the other books in his functional canon – and Deuteronomy features among Paul's favorites. Nevertheless, consideration of Paul's recourse to Scripture in terms of such holistic construals has not often been undertaken.

Elsewhere I have offered a more detailed history of research on the question of Paul's recourse to Deuteronomy, and it need not be repeated *in extenso* here.[5] Nevertheless, this work stands indebted to the several significant studies that have recently addressed aspects of the role Deuteronomy plays in Paul's letters. Individual monographs have been largely or wholly devoted to Paul's engagement with Deuteronomy in Galatians 3 (Wisdom 2001), 1 Corinthians 8 (Waaler 2008) and Romans 10 (Bekken 2007). Some have proposed that Paul operates within a Deuteronomic pat-

---

[5] See Lincicum 2008a; note also 2008c. To the works there surveyed should be added esp. Moyise and Menken 2007; Bekken 2007; Waaler 2008.

tern of thought (e.g., Scott 1993a; 1993b), though this position has not gone unchallenged (e.g., Waters 2006). The roles played by the Song of Moses (Bell 1994) and Deut 27–30 and 32 more broadly (Waters 2006) in Paul have also been subjected to enlightening scrutiny. Others have examined Paul's ethical teaching in light of his appeals to Deuteronomy (Rosner 1994; Perona 2005). As this brief paragraph is already sufficient to suggest, however, most major studies have been concerned *either* with Paul's ethical appeals to Deuteronomy *or* with his theological readings.[6] The major exception, and thus the most important study to mention in this regard, is Francis Watson's *Paul and the Hermeneutics of Faith* (2004), which concludes that the two aspects are fundamentally incompatible.[7] In light of the significance of his work and the fact that my own conclusions differ from his, it is worth here considering how Watson views Deuteronomy as functioning in Paul's letters.[8]

Watson's discussion of Deuteronomy is found in the final chapters of his study of Paul's engagement with Scripture. Paul, as an exegetical theologian, Watson argues, had a comprehensive scriptural hermeneutic by which he read the Pentateuch as a complex narrative unity – a narrative unity that both discloses and resolves major tensions in its own self-presentation as law and promise. The metaphor of a three-way conversation is key to Watson's presentation: Paul engages with Scripture, but also engages with his fellow Jews who likewise read the sacred text – even when that engagement must be characterized as tacit (2004: 78–79). In a series of juxtaposed readings, Watson presents Paul as an exegete who reads Scripture in light of God's action in Christ and God's action in Christ in light of Scripture, and so definitively stresses "the hermeneutical priority of the promise" (2004: 15 n. 5 and *passim*). Watson labors to demonstrate that "Paul cites individual texts not in an *ad hoc* manner but on the

---

[6] The other four major conclusions of the survey in Lincicum 2008a are: (1) Compared to the relatively high number of studies concerned with the reception of Isaiah in Paul, Deuteronomy has received little attention. While some of this can surely be attributed to the greater frequency of Isaiah citations in Paul, Deuteronomy also functions as an important theological and ethical resource for the apostle, and should be examined accordingly. (2) Recent studies on the *Vorlage* of Paul have set the stage for a more intensive investigation of the types of engagement Paul makes with individual books and sections of Scripture. (3) Many contributors have suggested that Paul's understanding of the 'curse of the law' is explicable by recourse to Deuteronomy, but there is as yet no agreement as to either how much of Deuteronomy provides the context for the assertion or what theological import recourse to Deuteronomy has for one's construal of the 'curse of the law'. (4) Systematic study of Paul's ethical engagement with Deuteronomy has not been carried out beyond 1 Corinthians 5–11.

[7] In response to Watson, note also Martyn 2006; Engberg-Pedersen 2006; Campbell 2006; Stanley 2006; Watson 2006a, 2006b, 2007; Hays 2007.

[8] The following paragraphs largely rely on Lincicum 2008a: 53–56.

basis of a radical construal of the narrative shape of the Pentateuch as a whole, highlighting and exploiting tensions between Genesis and Exodus, Leviticus and Deuteronomy" (2004: 3).

Having argued that Paul's doctrine of justification functions as a hermeneutical key to scripture, and that his doctrine, in turn, is derived from a reading of Hab 2:4 in its context and in light of Christ, Watson turns to construe the shape of Paul's narrative reading of the Pentateuch. In the end, from Paul's perspective, so Watson argues, readings of the law fall on either side of the fault line of human agency: does the Torah ultimately teach the way to live righteously before God in faithful fulfillment of the covenant commandments, or does it rather (as Watson's Paul believes), in a complex narrative, ultimately subvert human agency to suggest that only divine action in fulfillment of the promise can bring life?

Deuteronomy, Watson proceeds to argue, bears for Paul a dual function in this complex narrative: on the one hand, he can cite its commandments as precepts for the Christian community to follow; on the other hand, he reads the book as both disclosing and resolving the second great tension in the Pentateuch. As alluded to above, Watson devotes a mere ten pages to the former category before dismissing the problem of Paul's appeal to the law he is criticizing:

There is a striking discrepancy between this parenetic use of texts from Deuteronomy and the motif of 'the curse of the law', which likewise appeals to Deuteronomy. How can it be that laws which continue to guide individual and communal conduct are at the same time the bearers of a curse? This is one of the more obvious examples of a real 'contradiction' within Paul's understanding of the law (Watson 2004: 425; note Watson's explicit agreement with H. Räisänen's position: 426 n. 24).

Paul's main theological appeal to Deuteronomy, Watson suggests, is twofold: in chs. 27–30, the curse of the law is set forth – not simply as a contingent possibility, but in the fusion of horizons as a historical actuality realized within Israel's history (as told in the deuteronomistic history) and in Christ's death. This historical actuality effectively eviscerates an appeal like that of the author of Baruch for a return to the law with renewed zeal. Secondly, then, Paul reads the Song of Moses (Deut 32) as foretelling the failure of the law, the future inclusion of the Gentiles, and the ultimate salvation of Israel by divine action – thus foreshadowing the victory over the curse of the law. In questioning the adequacy of the law, Paul in this respect demonstrates an affinity to the author of *4 Ezra*. With this, Watson has completed his creative reconstruction of Paul's reading of Torah.

The scope and penetration of Watson's reading of Deuteronomy are exemplary. The overall thesis of his work blends creativity, boldness, and theological concern – unfortunately less common than it should be in Pauline exegesis. On the whole, his contention that "Paul engages with these texts by way of representative narratives and individual texts which are supposed to articulate the fundamental dynamics of the Torah as a whole" (2004: 275) must be regarded as having received solid substantiation.

At times, however, one wonders whether Watson oversteps the evidence. Occasionally Watson appears to present Paul almost as a proto-deconstructionist reader, subverting the dominant interpretation of the Torah by looking for the *aporiai*, reading at the margins of the Pentateuch, finding and exploiting the loopholes like Gen 15:6 in the Abraham narrative or the death associated with the giving of the law in Exodus. This is fine in so far as it goes – we know that Paul's readings were forged in controversy. Watson's construal, however, focuses almost exclusively on the theological instances in Paul's citations, but marginalizes Paul's *ethical* appeals to the law as a source of ongoing moral formation for the Christian church (so rightly Eastman 2006). While it is a crucial corrective for Watson to argue that "Paul's 'view of the law' is his reading of a text" (2004: 514 and *passim*), the text which Paul reads in turn makes both moral and existential demands. These demands are not reducible to suggestions under the loose guidance of the Spirit, but still perceived as, in some sense, commands reflecting the will of God, and so sharing something in common with ethical appeals to the law by other Jews of the period. We noted above, for example, Watson's dismissal of Paul's ethical appeals to Deuteronomy (2004: 416–26) and his quick recourse to the category of "contradiction" to explain these. Watson's approach deserves to be supplemented by approaches that focus on the use of Scripture in ethical contexts and the presence of halakhic argument in Paul's letters. We might ask whether Paul has a "second" reading of the law, beyond the curse, given back to the church through Christ's death and resurrection and the presence of the Spirit, so that Christians now "fulfill" the law (e.g., Rom 8:1–4).

Clearly one of the strongest points of Watson's presentation, and one of the most promising for future investigation, is his attempt to produce a "big-picture," holistic reading of Paul's reception of Deuteronomy. While his reading is less integrated and so less comprehensive than is ideal (so Hays 2007: 130), he has demonstrated the value of examining the presence of Deuteronomy in Paul, even as others have done for Isaiah in Paul. Incidentally, it is striking to note Watson's complete silence with regard to Isaiah in Paul (Hays 2007; but see Watson 2007: 136), as well as a number of other specific texts that do not fit within Watson's proposed schema (see also Stanley 2006: 359).[9] The fundamentally antithetical nature of the

---

[9] While this will be an issue for any account purporting to give the shape of Paul's overall hermeneutic, it is especially problematic for such a strong reading as Watson's

reading of the Pentateuch he posits, moreover, does not do justice to the texture of the apostle's thought. Though this claim must be borne out in the course of subsequent study, we here note that where Watson may be correct that Paul discovers two major tensions in the Torah, namely, "between the unconditional promise and the Sinai legislation" and "between the law's offer of life and its curse" (2004: 23), any such tensions are arguably resolved *diachronically* for the apostle – in the unfolding story of the old covenant and the gospel (2004: 24). At times Watson transposes this into starkly synchronic categories to posit an absolute dichotomy between law and promise. This also partially explains why Watson never explores precisely *why* the law failed in Paul's view, beyond stating the law's claim to be operative at the level of human agency (though note 2004: 518).

In short, Watson has offered a rich and stimulating presentation of Paul as a holistic interpreter of the Pentateuch in general, and Deuteronomy in particular. Nevertheless, such a strong thesis inevitably overlooks important evidence, and the results of this investigation seek, *inter alia*, to query the adequacy of the polarizing excesses to which Watson's Paul tends.

1.3. Locating the Present Study's Approach

Scholarship on Paul and Scripture is, like other areas of New Testament study, marked by a plurality of irreconcilable methods. This is not necessarily a lamentable state, and each method lays claim to the fruit borne from its unique perspective.[10] I wish neither to suggest that the approach of the current study represents the only valid approach to Paul and Deuteronomy, nor to engage in that *forschungsgeschichtliche* temptation to portray all predecessors as thieves and robbers, or, to change the metaphor, as mired in the darkness of ignorance only now to be dispelled by the light of my own conclusions. I do suggest, however, that an approach to Paul via the broader effective history of Deuteronomy draws attention to an overlooked aspect of Paul's engagement with Scripture. The following specific elements serve to locate the approach of the present investigation in the spectrum of current approaches.

(see, e.g., Hos 1–2 in Rom 9; the Adam-Christ parallels in Rom 5 and 1 Cor 15; the catena at 2 Cor 6:16–18; Ps 112:9 in 2 Cor 9:9; Exod 16:18 in 2 Cor 8:15; Prov 25:21–22 in Rom 12:20; and all of the major prophets and the writings).

[10] So also, e.g., Moyise 2008a, and more fully, with a sort of *sic et non* approach, in 2008b.

1.3.1. The Search for Holistic Construal

To lend more precision to the question at hand, it is worth pausing first to consider in more depth what it might mean to ascertain the shape of an author's construal of a particular biblical book. In speaking of such a construal, I rely on a point made by David Kelsey in his examination of "the uses of Scripture in modern theology."[11] He writes, "Close examination of theologians' actual uses of scripture in the course of doing theology shows that they do not appeal to some objective text-in-itself but rather to a text construed *as* a certain kind of whole having a certain kind of logical force" (1999: 14).[12] In this case, we are interested not in Scripture as a whole but in the book of Deuteronomy. Even to pose the question is to acknowledge that Deuteronomy is not always the same Deuteronomy to each of its readers, but that one can speak meaningfully of Josephus's or the Temple Scroll's or the Gospel of Matthew's Deuteronomy as much as Paul's Deuteronomy. In this sense, the shape of a particular author's construal of the book must be ascertained differentially and deictically, and so inevitably in a somewhat discursive fashion. At the beginning of Part II, I will propose a set of questions to put to the texts under investigation in order to ascertain aspects of their approach to Deuteronomy. Here it should be noted that intertextuality, one of the dominant *modi operandi* of studying Paul's engagement with Scripture, makes only a partial contribution to the task.

1.3.2. On Intertextuality and Effective History

The term intertextuality (*intertextualité*) was apparently first coined by Julia Kristeva,[13] before being developed by Roland Barthes and Harold Bloom, among many others. The most influential proponent of intertextuality in the study of Paul and Scripture has arguably been Richard Hays. He employs a "soft" version of intertextuality in his work *Echoes*, more strongly influenced by John Hollander's work on the figure of echo than the post-structuralist notion of intertextuality *per se*.[14] But intertextuality,

---

[11] Kelsey (1999 [1975]), though in fact there may be certain analogues in the patristic notion of the σκοπός of Scripture, whether in its entirety or in discrete parts (on this notion, see Young 1997). Francis Watson's work, *Paul and the Hermeneutics of Faith* (2004) makes use of a similar concept (he himself makes reference to Kelsey), though my application of it differs from his.

[12] In contrast to the claim of Vanhoozer (2008: 191–92), Kelsey does in fact allow for theologians to have multiple interlocking construals of Scripture, but focuses on one for the sake of his presentation (1999: 15–16).

[13] See Kristeva 1969: 143–73 (originally written in 1966); ET, 1980: 64–91; 1986: 34–61. Cf. also Kristeva 1974: 57–61; ET 1984: 57–62; 1986: 109–112.

[14] Note Hays 2005: 174, where Hays distances himself from an ideological application of intertextuality and writes, "Nothing is at stake for me in the use of the term."

at least in its most theorized versions, is not so much a theory of literary influence as it is a theory of the semiotic construction of all our perceptions of reality – and to claim that the genealogical pedigree of 'intertextuality' has no bearing on its subsequent meaning is surely not without irony.[15] In this vein, Kristeva complains in her later writing that intertextuality "has often been understood in the banal sense of 'study of sources'" (1986: 111). It is admittedly most often employed in Pauline studies in this latter, more "banal sense,"[16] but even in this under-theorized form it tends toward an abstraction from history. By approaching Paul's encounter with Scripture as the interplay of two texts, one is sometimes presented with a Paul who bears a strange resemblance to his narrative critics, engaged in a virginal act of interpretation apart from the pesky prejudices of corporeality and temporality as a first-century Jew. One may also sense a certain interpretative exhaustion as the quest for fainter and fainter echoes of Scripture in Paul's letters is met with diminishing returns. Intertextual interpretation of Paul and Scripture has yielded unmeasured gains in our recovery of Paul as a thoughtful appropriator of Israel's sacred texts, but such an approach deserves to be supplemented by more historical considerations. In this context, I suggest that approaching Paul from the horizon of Deuteronomy's broader effective history[17] may go some way toward redressing the imbalance in intertextual presentations of the apostle and answering the question of how Deuteronomy as a whole is (or is not) perceived and (re)appropriated.

There can be no question of an absolute or fundamental contrast between these approaches, but the differences in emphasis are significant. Where intertextuality tends to approach the issue from Paul's stance as an interpreter, an effective-historical approach may consider Paul as one instantiation of Deuteronomy's broader effects, and so restore a sense of the productive temporal and historical distance between Paul and Deuteronomy. This distance, however, should be conceived not as an isolating factor but as an aspect enabling a richer understanding of Deuteronomy.[18]

---

[15] Note the remarks by Culler 1981: 100–18 on the plasticity of the term. In further critique, note Irwin 2004 and within biblical studies, Tuckett 1997: 3–6; Rese 1997 (though Rese overstates the atomistic nature of early Christian exegesis); Hatina 1999.

[16] For example, Berkley 2000 recognizes the tension in appealing to intertextuality in a historical study, but persists in adopting a position like that of Hays, which he calls a "minimalist intertextuality" (48–49).

[17] On "effective history" (*Wirkungsgeschichte*) note also Luz 1985; 1994; Räisänen 1992b; Bockmuehl 1995, esp. 57–63; Gnilka 1998; etc. All of this work is ultimately indebted to H.-G. Gadamer (see, e.g., Gadamer 1989: 277–307; 2006).

[18] "Understanding is to be thought of less as a subjective act than as participating in an event of tradition, a process of transmission in which past and present are constantly mediated" (Gadamer 1989: 290, italics removed).

Deuteronomy itself is a book that opens into the future – a future, indeed, that it has a hand in shaping. In this sense, Deuteronomy in the very contemporaneity of its address functions for those who later come to encounter it as both a resource and a challenge for subsequent reflection and "use". Without the long tradition of viewing Deuteronomy as divinely authorized Torah, recited in synagogue, affixed to one's very body in the *tefillin* and the doorposts of one's house in the *mezuzah*, debated in scribal circles, actualized for legal guidance, supplying lenses for the interpretation of Israel's history – without some consideration of the long pre- and post-history of Paul's encounter with Deuteronomy, we are bound to miss what is distinctive in the apostle's reception of the book. Within the contours of this broader history, then, to note the aspects of Deuteronomy that are significant for each author is an illuminating procedure and supplies the differentiation I suggested was important for ascertaining an author's construal of a book. This, in fact, aligns with what Steven Fraade has recently suggested ought to be undertaken. He writes,

in addition to considering discrete interpretive traditions, we need to look more broadly at which biblical books, or parts of books, attracted the interpretive attentions of different interpretive authors/communities (even if only at the editorial level of the extant texts). Presumably, such differences of scriptural focus do not simply reflect differences regarding what was considered to be canonically authoritative, but also which parts of shared scriptures were of particular significance to the rhetorical/ideological self-defining interests of the respective authors and their textual communities (Fraade 2007: 104).

Perhaps somewhat fancifully, then, we might conclude that the characteristically German concern for history (*Wirkungsgeschichte*) must supplement and correct the French fascination with theory (*l'intertextualité*). More to the point, the interpretative solipsism toward which theories of intertextuality sometimes tend can be redressed with reference to the long communal tradition of receiving Deuteronomy in liturgy as a message divinely addressed to the present: the authors considered in this study considered themselves part of the Israel whose response to the delivery of the law was, "We will hear and we will do it" (Deut 5:27).

1.3.3. A Polyphonic Conversation

Therefore, in focusing on the broader effective history of Deuteronomy, this study seeks to sketch a succession of engagements with Deuteronomy, ranging chronologically from Tobit and the Temple Scroll to the Targums. This line of interpreters effectively comprises an ongoing conversation with Deuteronomy and, implicitly, with one another – a metaphor that Watson has helpfully suggested. In contrast to Watson, however, it may be urged that to some degree the partners whom one chooses to include in the conversation will bias the voices one comes to hear. Watson contrasts

Paul's appeal to Deuteronomy with that of Baruch, and compares it to 4 Ezra, and so ends up with a Paul who effectively rejects the law as a failed project. No doubt such choices are based on prior judgments about the type of interpretative endeavor in which Paul is engaging, and the same charge could be leveled at this study. Nevertheless, in seeking to broaden the conversation as much as possible, this study investigates in turn those who evince a significant interest in the interpretation or use of Deuteronomy. Inevitably the choice will be somewhat subjective, and some may complain that by selecting authors who display a holistic construal of Deuteronomy the interpretative strategy of Paul has been determined in advance. To some degree, of course, this is a fair charge. But it is also worth suspending judgment to see whether interesting results are achieved from proceeding on a supposition that Paul's recourse to Deuteronomy is not incommensurable with that of his Jewish contemporaries. Thus, in order to chart the polyphonic conversation over Deuteronomy, each major text will be examined on its own ground before rushing to comparison. This may in fact provide some intriguing gains that are screened out when comparisons are limited to individual verses or interpretative traditions. In this sense, like the almost mythical category of scholastic commentaries on Aquinas's commentary on Aristotle, the present study could be described as a meta-commentarial endeavor – a study of the study of Deuteronomy.[19]

1.3.4. Is It Legitimate to Isolate Deuteronomy?

Deuteronomy is, of course, the final book of the Pentateuch, the last fifth of the "five fifths of Torah" known from Rabbinic literature. Is it legitimate to isolate Deuteronomy and consider its interpretation as a separate book?[20] Is not to do so to run the risk of distortion? Clearly Deuteronomy is not independent of the preceding books of Torah, nor do its ancient interpreters ignore the constant connections (and contradictions) with what has come before. But, in fact, Deuteronomy stands in some relief from the preceding books, and the question might be more severe for other "fifths" of Torah than for Deuteronomy. As Rolf Rendtorff writes, "it is obvious that Deuteronomy is a separate book. It is clearly framed by a new beginning and a definite end; it has its own style, its own topics, and its own

---

[19] Although in fact most of the texts to be examined are not strictly speaking in commentary format (the works of Philo and the *Sifre* perhaps being exceptions). Cf. Fraade: "Although today we might take for granted the commentary form as a way of interpreting a text, especially of Scripture, in postbiblical but prerabbinic varieties of Judaism, if we may judge from the extant literary evidence, it does not appear to have been the favored mode of scriptural interpretation" (1991: 2).

[20] Cf. Rendtorff 1996 who poses the question to Mary Douglas, "Is it possible to read Leviticus as a separate book?"

theology" (1996: 24). Indeed, the sheer distinctiveness of its tone and repetitive vocabulary often enable one to identify its presence in other
works.[21] Even in the heyday of source-critical approaches to the Pentateuch, the individuality of the "D" source was recognized.[22] As I shall suggest, in antiquity the distinctive character of Deuteronomy was recognized
as well.[23] What is more, the fact that the work was most likely encountered
as a single scroll may also have contributed to a recognition of its self-
standing character. So we shall proceed by limiting ourselves chiefly to the
role played by Deuteronomy, but aware of the hermeneutical pressure exercised by the other books of Torah as well.

1.3.5. Some Matters of Definition

Before proceeding to the reception of Deuteronomy, we must first clarify a
few matters of definition. First, in this study the adjective "Deuteronomic"
is used to denote that which relates to the book of Deuteronomy itself,
while "Deuteronomistic" is reserved for that which relates to the so-called
Deuteronomistic History (Judges–2 Kings) and the tradition flowing from
it.[24]

A more disputed area of definition, however, concerns how one describes the various levels of textual engagement seen in a range of Second
Temple Jewish interpreters. There have been repeated and prolonged terminological discussions, some of which have genuinely advanced our ability to describe and recognize strategies of textual engagement.[25] Without
endorsing the need for a universally agreed upon vocabulary, in the present
study the following categories are employed. A quotation or explicit quotation is a verbatim repetition of a scriptural text that is also marked for the
reader or hearer with an introductory formula or interpretative comments

---

[21] Note esp. Weinfeld 1972: 320–65 for a list of Deuteronomic phraseology.

[22] See Nicholson 1998. Of course, there have also been arguments to distinguish between various levels of redaction of Deuteronomy, notably between the Deuteronomic
Code (Deut 12–26) and later exilic or post-exilic frame narratives, though these do not
substantially alter the individuality of the book as a whole.

[23] In addition to the evidence garnered for the distinctiveness of Deuteronomy
throughout this investigation, note also the titles used for Deuteronomy in antiquity, discussed in Cohen 1997b; 2007; Berthelot 2007.

[24] Thus, no attempt is made to distinguish a Deuteronomistic redaction of Deutero-
omy itself, nor does this study concern itself with the existence or possible effects of a
"Deuteronomic school" – to which has been ascribed, it should be noted, an ascending
amount of redactional activity (for a critical response to this phenomenon of "pan-
Deuteronomism," see esp. Schearing and McKenzie 1999).

[25] See, e.g., Koch 1986: 11–20; Hays 1989: 29–33; Stanley 1992: 33–37; Porter
1997b, 2006, 2008; Moyise 2008; Ciampa 2008; cf. also the related discussion in
Thompson 1991: 28–36.

signaling the presence of a foreign body of text.[26] An implicit citation supplies a verbatim or near verbatim section of a scriptural text but without the introductory formula or interpretative comments to signal its presence to the reader or hearer. An instance of paraphrase or rewriting occurs when the substance of the original scriptural account is rendered in other words.[27] Allusions and echoes both refer to a scriptural precursor text in a manner that is less explicit than a citation, the difference between them being a matter of assertorial weight and intention – though distinguishing between them is not always possible or necessary.[28] Finally, it may occasionally be possible to discern the presence of scriptural concepts or ideas which are not directly supported by a high volume of verbal resonance.[29]

These categories clearly operate along a sliding scale of explicitness, and most of the engagements with Deuteronomy that will concern us in this study function at the more explicit end of the scale. Nevertheless, it should also be kept in mind that arguments for the presence of less explicit reminiscences of Deuteronomy (echoes, allusions, concepts) are cumulative and probabilistic in nature. The fact that an author elsewhere explicitly cites and interprets other texts from Deuteronomy renders more likely, though not ineluctable, a proposed reference to Deuteronomy that is less explicit. This suggests a certain dis-analogy to the comparisons sometimes offered between the influence of Shakespeare's language and phraseology on modern English speech and writing, and the influence of the language of Scripture on Second Temple Jewish speech and writing. While no doubt

---

[26] This especially follows Koch 1986 and Stanley 1992.

[27] See also the discussion of "rewritten Bible" in § 3.2.2 below. Here it should be stressed that the paraphrase or rewriting need not be of a narrative text, as is sometimes suggested.

[28] This corresponds roughly to Porter's five categories: "formulaic quotation; direct quotation; paraphrase; allusion; and echo" (2008: 29). Without entering into the discussion here, I take it that Hays's well-known seven criteria for discerning an echo, while not intended to be scientifically rigorous (note Wagner 2002: 11 and n. 44), provide a helpful set of guidelines for evaluating the presence, though not necessarily the import, of a proposed echo.

[29] Compare Ciampa 2008: "Concepts and ideas are more likely to be 'scriptural' if: (1) Paul and/or other early Jewish or Christian authors associate them with scriptural quotations, allusions, and/or echoes elsewhere in their writings; (2) they have a distinctive background in the Jewish Scriptures and are typically introduced in Jewish (and early Christian) discourse as Jewish or scriptural concepts; (3) they reflect dissimilarity (in some significant aspect) to Greco-Roman ideas or concepts while also demonstrating similarity to a distinctive (generally known) Jewish concept that has roots in Scripture; or (4) they reflect dissimilarity (in some significant aspect) to Greco-Roman and Jewish ideas or concepts but are explicable in terms of new or alternative interpretations of Scripture inspired by Jesus or by the context and needs of the early church (especially if explicit scriptural support is given for the idea within early Christianity)" (48).

such influence is sometimes purely stylistic in nature, each instance needs to be evaluated on a case-by-case basis.

Finally, it will be noted that these categories of inquiry locate the present study's interest in a relatively "author-oriented" direction, or at least in the direction of an implied or constructed author. This is not to deny the usefulness of studies that concentrate their energies on the rhetorical effects of quotation or on consideration of the original audience's capacity to understand and evaluate the presence of Scripture in Paul's letters or other texts.[30] It is, however, to recognize that what we might call authorial effects comprise precisely the sort of information that is most available to us.[31]

1.4. The Plan of the Present Study

Standard dissertation format has long been to proceed in a two-step fashion: first, survey works of the Second Temple period as "Jewish background" to Paul; second, background now firmly in hand, address (the implicitly Christian) Paul himself. While of course this approach retains certain merits, recent discussion of the Jewishness of Paul has in fact problematized this method. If it is possible to see Paul as in some sense a radical Jew, then the line separating the background from the foreground appears more arbitrary. Paul is not a later Christian author who has rejected Judaism and yet has some shadowy obligations to a now-distant past. Rather, he is a Jew among Jews, standing as one member of a spectrum, one particular instantiation of one particular people. Simply identifying Paul as Jewish, however, does not yet say very much, for it is clear that Paul must be sought in a particular dynamic of radicalism and fidelity with reference to his ancestral tradition.

Compare the incisive comments of Peter Schäfer, offered in honor of Martin Hengel but with a broader applicability:

---

[30] Most notably, this has been undertaken by Stanley 2004. The chief problem in this type of study is the speculative nature of the conclusions. In response, see Lincicum 2006; Abasciano 2007 (who, however, may overstate the reader competence of Paul's first audiences).

[31] This should not be confused with the now universally defamed quest for an authorial intention, at least if conceived as a mental intention standing behind the text. In the time after the high days of Theory, however, we may be returning to a certain "rehumanization of the humanities" that makes the question of an author once more congenial – though not of course susceptible to naïve description. See, e.g., Cunningham 2002; Eagleton 2003; Zimmerman 2004.

The phrase 'the Jewish background of Christianity,' more often than not, has the pejorative overtone which is only too well known to all of us: Judaism as the background, the dark foil against which the bright light of Christianity shines all the more gloriously and triumphantly. There is no need in this circle to emphasize that Martin Hengel doesn't fit this cliché with all its unfortunate and tragic results. He is miles away from such a view – but he is also miles away from the naïve approach which has become fashionable among some New Testament scholars and according to which all problems can be solved, all history mended, if only the 'Jewishness' of the New Testament were recognized. This is not to say that the New Testament is not a Jewish source; it certainly is, but its relation to Judaism is a historical question which can be adequately dealt with only historically and not through some well-meaning but vague feelings (Schäfer 2005: 25).

In this light, it may not be enough simply to ask what Judaism can tell us about Paul; rather, we should also ask what Paul may tell us about Judaism. This investigation also, then, serves as a small contribution to the re-integration of New Testament study with the study of Second Temple Judaism which has been called for recently by a number of voices (*inter alia*, Stemberger 2008; Müller 2008). Here it is instructive to listen to the words of the late Martin Hengel himself:

It is generally recognized that a knowledge of Judaism at this period is essential for scholarship on the beginnings of Christianity and for the interpretation of the New Testament. Furthermore, relating the beginnings of Christianity to the context of Jewish history of that period constitutes an essential enrichment that allows us better to understand the creative energy of Jewish thought at that time: for even an illegitimate daughter has decisive features in common with her mother... Next to Josephus, Philo, Qumran, and the early rabbinic tradition, the New Testament could become the most important source for Judaism of the first century CE. Viewed historically, it was the most effective offspring of Judaism and, as I see it, represented one of several real possibilities within the development of Judaism in antiquity (2005: 98–99).

In light of these two voices, then, this book seeks to examine the reception of Deuteronomy in Paul's letters not simply by conducting sideways glances at how Jewish authors had interpreted the same texts that end up in his letters, but by examining how a broad stream of Jewish authors received Deuteronomy as a whole, both before and after Paul. To see Paul as one member in this chain of tradition thus enables us to view Paul as a Jewish reader of Deuteronomy but also casts light on the Jewish reception of Deuteronomy. These are not so much mutually interpretive realities as an instance of the specific and the general, or perhaps better, many specific instances of a general phenomenon.

Thus, the investigation proceeds in two parts followed by a conclusion. First, I survey "the Liturgical Deuteronomy in the Second Temple Period" (§ 2) to provide insight into the sort of cultural koine that in one form or another stands behind all of the engagements with Deuteronomy here surveyed. The material exigencies of books and reading, the public recitation of the Torah in worship, the practices of *tefillin* and *mezuzot*, all contribute to the basic force Deuteronomy comes to bear in this period. The section concludes with an indication of the influence this context may have had in preparing Paul for his reception of Deuteronomy. In Part II, then, the specific Jewish authors who exhibit an interest in Deuteronomy are surveyed in roughly chronological fashion, moving from the texts from the Judean desert to the Apocrypha and Pseudepigrapha, Philo, Paul, Josephus, and finally to some later Jewish interpretations in the *Sifre to Deuteronomy* and the Targums (§§ 3–8). In this way, a trajectory of interpretation (perhaps better, a series of trajectories) is charted in which Paul's recourse to Deuteronomy can be understood and which, in turn, allows Paul's reception of Deuteronomy to shed light on that of his Jewish rough contemporaries. Finally, Chapter 9 draws some conclusions from this material and suggests its import for both Pauline studies and how we conceive of Paul in reference to Second Temple Judaism (§ 9).

In one sense, then, this book is involved in positing new icons, or at least in making explicit the contours of the iconography with which Pauline scholarship has been recently laboring: instead of Paul triumphing over a defeated, ashamed and blinded Synagoga, we might picture a scene in which a maternal Lady Synagoga hands to Paul the scroll of Deuteronomy, which Paul reverently receives from her (§ 2). Rather than Paul simply preaching over the Jews in a monological act of proclamation, we might picture a scene in which several Jewish interpreters gather around the scroll of Deuteronomy, each arguing for his or her own construal, alternately expressing agreement or disagreement with one another in an irreducibly polyphonic encounter (§§ 3–8). And rather than present a Paul who is already simply other than his interlocutors, nimbed and sainted, we might glimpse Paul in his own knobbed hat, perhaps the glimmer of his halo only beginning to be visible, as he points with one hand to the scroll of Deuteronomy and with the other to the crucified Christ (§ 9).[32]

---

[32] Of course there is an important sense in which individuals or movements can only be known through their effects in a retrospective evaluation, and this re-imagining should not be read as another variation on the tired tune that historical-critical exegesis, administered by practitioners lately wakened from their dogmatic slumber, can now finally free the New Testament from the theological sclerosis to which it has been forcibly subjected. It is rather to recognize that each age has to wrestle with Paul anew, to see that the sheer persistence of his apostolic presence necessitates a certain non-finalizable engagement with his person and legacy: *defunctus adhuc loquitur.*

Part I

The Ancient Encounter with Deuteronomy

Chapter 2

The Liturgical Deuteronomy
in the Second Temple Period

2.1. Introduction

Morna Hooker once quipped that B. H. Streeter's fault in forming his hypothesis of Gospel origins was to suppose the evangelists to be just like him: Oxford professors in spacious offices, surrounded with books, meticulously dissecting and reassembling pericopes with surgical precision.[1] Scholars of the reception of Scripture (i.e., the Christian Old Testament) in the Second Temple period have sometimes been guilty of similar self-projections, imagining a Paul or a Qumran sage or the author of *Jubilees* to be fastidious academics like themselves, untouched by the popular fads of *Volksreligion*, virginally happening upon some choice scriptural text to employ in their latest research project while thumbing through the volumes of their own or perhaps an institutional library. Many studies of the reception of the Old Testament have in fact been ahistorical in their orientation to a troubling degree.

It is the purpose of this chapter to move toward redressing that lack by examining some neglected aspects of engaging with Deuteronomy during the Second Temple period. In the first place, then, I will devote attention to what might be called the "material *realia*" of reading and hearing Deuteronomy: its dual existence in Greek and Hebrew, its concrete form in manuscripts, the circles of its influence among the literate and illiterate. This consideration of Deuteronomy's material remains leads to the suggestion that one of the primary *loci* of encounter would have been in that nexus of practices that we might term "liturgical." The next three sections, therefore, examine the presence and function of Deuteronomy in public synagogal Torah readings, in *tefillin*, *mezuzot* and excerpted texts, and in the regular recitation of the *Shema'*. Finally, I suggest, in light of Paul's background and education, the influence such liturgical praxis may have had on Paul's pattern of engagement with the book of Deuteronomy in his letters.

---

[1] Hooker 1975: 29; cf. also Neill and Wright 1988: 363.

2.2. Encountering Deuteronomy: The Material *Realia*

Before discussing the literary reception of Deuteronomy, certain prior questions present themselves: In what languages, in what physical form, in what contexts was Deuteronomy encountered? The purpose of this section is to enumerate some such historical considerations in order both to describe the limitations within which study of Paul's engagement with Deuteronomy must operate, but also to highlight interpretative options arising from these historical considerations.

In speaking of Deuteronomy in the Second Temple Period, one might immediately face the question: which Deuteronomy? Even apart from and prior to the issue of sharply divergent interpretations, one encounters flatly different texts. After all the critical edition is a distinctively modern concern, and the phenomenon of translation, especially that into Greek, must have created a sort of second Deuteronomy, almost unknown in its distinctive Grecian garb. If translation is always already interpretation, then what sort of reality does that deceptively singular concept, "Deuteronomy," actually possess?

There is, clearly, some force to this imaginary interlocutor's set of questions. Research in semantics has repeatedly shown that, while languages do not mechanistically determine one's range of possible thoughts (as, for example, in the hoary – and false – adage, "Hebrew thought is concrete, Greek thought is abstract"[2]), it is probably true that new possibilities of signification and connotation arise when translations are made: the target language always exerts some pressure on the translated text. In the course of our investigation, we will have occasion to note some instances when Paul (whether consciously or not) exploits such occurrences (see esp. § 6.5.4).

At another level, however, the conclusions to which our questioner presses should be resisted. Apart from the fact that text-critical work actually *was* performed in antiquity (instance the Alexandrian scholars of Homer), the difference between the Greek translation of Deuteronomy and its Hebrew mother is a matter of degree, not of kind (and even more so for the hebraizing revisions). Unlike some other books of the Septuagint which diverge sharply from their known Hebrew *Vorlage*, for example, parts of Exodus, Jeremiah or Proverbs,[3] the translator of Deuteronomy has

---

[2] Classically critiqued in Barr 1961.

[3] Although at times this may more likely be explained by an alternative, non-extant Hebrew *Vorlage* than by loose translation (Proverbs perhaps being an exception). In general, note Aejmelaeus 1987.

repeatedly been described as "restrained."[4] It is true, of course, that the text that, say, Paul knew in the first century would not have been strictly identical to the original translation of Deuteronomy in the third century BCE (or the Göttingen edition by John William Wevers which is our best approximation to it). Rather, as the manuscripts from the Judean desert have made clear,[5] almost immediately after the translation a number of revisions toward the original Hebrew began.[6] Although because of Greek Deuteronomy's relative fidelity to its Hebrew *Vorlage* these changes are less drastic than in some other books, this should be kept in mind in considering the textual state of affairs in Paul's quotations, as well as in those of other authors. Further mention should be made of the tendency of manuscripts of Deuteronomy, whether in Hebrew or in Greek, to be somewhat expansionistic or affected by parallel passages, no doubt due to the repetitive nature of the book itself.[7] That small variations in the textual status of Deuteronomy existed was apparently not seen to threaten its widespread popularity; at times such revisions probably even existed side-by-side within the same community, as in the one that used the recension-

---

[4] See esp. the works of John William Wevers. Note Wevers 1977a: 500–01: "Jerome is interested in clarity; Deut is more obsessed by faithfulness to the parent text sometimes to the point of obscurity"; Wevers goes on to speak of the "convervatism" of Deut (501). Cf. also Wevers 1994: 280: "As a general rule the translator is faithful to his parent text."; see Wevers 1977b; Wevers 1978; Wittstruck 1976. Aejmelaeus (1996), however, makes a distinction between Deut's quantitative fidelity (it rarely introduces elements not represented in the Hebrew text) and Deut's sometimes qualitative freedom (especially with respect to semantic renderings of individual words). Also, Wevers 1997 draws attention to dozens of slight differences that reflect varying degrees of interpretational modification on the part of the translator.

[5] See Tov 2001b, who suggests that all of the early Greek biblical manuscripts found at Qumran reflect the text of the Old Greek with varying degrees of revision toward the Hebrew (as 8HevXIIgr most markedly shows). Cf. Tov 2003a; 2004: 299–302. Further on the Greek manuscripts from Qumran and the surrounding areas, note Leaney 1976 (who especially places the phenomenon of Greek Jewish scriptures in broader historical perspective); Ulrich 1984; 1992; Greenspoon 1998. It should also be noted that the LXX/OG of Deuteronomy has received some support among the Hebrew texts from Qumran as well (see 4QDeut^q; and, to a lesser degree, 4QDeut^{c, h, j}). See further Greenspoon 1998: 120–21.

[6] Here I presuppose the dominant view of Septuagint origins as single (associated with P. de Lagarde) rather than the alternative theory of a Targum-like plural origin (suggested by Paul Kahle). These revisions were probably the occasion for the 2nd c. BCE pseudepigraphical defense of the Septuagint, *The Letter of Aristeas* (on which see, e.g., Müller 1996: 46–58). On the general state of the LXX in the period of NT formation, note Hanhart 1984.

[7] So, e.g., Wevers 1978: 86: "[t]he most obvious characteristic of the text of Deuteronomy is its repetitive style" and so "parallel passages have played havoc with the textual transmission" (cf. 86–99). Cf. also Wevers 1994. For harmonizing Hebrew manuscripts of Deuteronomy, note, e.g., Crawford 2005.

ally distinct manuscripts known as 847 and 848.[8] Given the focus of our investigation on Paul, the attention of this study is necessarily centered on Deuteronomy in Greek, though we will certainly have occasion (e.g., in our discussion of the Judean desert texts in § 3 below) to return to the Hebrew.

If, then, Deuteronomy was not a radically fluid text, in which physical form might it have been encountered? Because the codex did not arise until the 2nd century,[9] most Second Temple encounters with Deuteronomy as a book would have been in roll form, and the surviving evidence bears this out: all four of the extant manuscripts of Greek Deuteronomy before the 2nd century CE are in roll form.[10] Of course, as our investigation of *tefillin*,

---

[8] See, e.g., Aly and Koenen 1980: 8–9: "In fact, 847 and 848 [a.k.a. the 2nd c. BCE manuscripts P. Fouad Inv. 266b–c] represent different recensions. Nevertheless, both rolls were apparently used by the same Jewish community and witness the early, occasionally the original form of the text of *Deuteronomy*" (italics original). They also mark the tendency toward harmonization in both texts (9).

[9] On the rise of the codex in the 2nd century, see Kenyon 1951: 87–120; and esp. Roberts and Skeat 1983. A broad survey of ancient codices, Jewish, Christian and pagan, can be found in Turner 1977; cf. Llewelyn 1994. A helpful quantitative analysis can be found in Hurtado 2006: 43–93. In a number of publications, T. C. Skeat has examined this rise of the codex and a selection of the theories invoked to explain it. Among the numerous suggestions by Skeat and others, the most promising are (1) a slight savings in cost (10–25%; on which see Skeat 2004c; 2004f); (2) the early precedent of a Christian collection such as the four Gospels (Skeat 2004a; 2004d) or Paul's letters (Gamble 1995: 49–66); and (3) as a more remote possibility, the mobility required by the new Christian movement and the precedent this set (McCormick 1985). The supposed inconvenience of the scroll as opposed to the codex is an anachronistic conception which fails to explain the persistence of the scroll for three centuries among pagan writers (indeed, longer for Jewish biblical manuscripts) and should not be invoked to explain the rise of the codex (so Skeat 2004b; 2004e; contra, e.g., Knox and Easterling 1985: 18). Joseph van Haelst (1989) has argued convincingly that the origins of the codex are more probably pagan (i.e., Roman: cf. Martial, *Epigr.* 1.2; *P. Oxy.* 1.30), though it owes its success to early Christian usage. Needless to say, the factors contributing to both the birth and the rise of the codex are many and complicated.

[10] For early rolls with Greek Deuteronomy note 4Q122=4QLXXDeut (parchment, 2nd century BCE; Ulrich 1992: 195–97, pl. 43; on the date, note the comments by P. J. Parsons in Ulrich 1992: 11–12); P. Ryl. Gk. 458 (papyrus; ca. 2nd century BCE; Roberts 1936: 9–46; Wevers 1977b); P. Fouad, Inv. 266b (papyrus; 1st century BCE) and P. Fouad , Inv. 266c (papyrus; late 1st century BCE; both in Aly and Koenen 1980 [i.e., 847 and 848]; note the initial edition by F. Dunand (1966, 1971), on which see Kilpatrick 1971; cf. also Aly 1971; Turner 1987: no. 56; Wevers 1978: 64–85). For early examples of 2nd or 3rd century CE papyrus codices containing Deuteronomy, note Rahlfs MS 963 (see Kenyon 1935; cf. Roberts 1979: 78–81; Pietersma 1974; Wevers 1978: 52–63); and P. Baden 4.56 (see van Haelst 1976: no. 33; Bilabel 1924: 24–27, no. 56). For indication of other slightly later papyrus MSS of Deuteronomy, see van Haelst 1976: nos. 52, 54, 55, 58, 59 (cf. also nos. 241, 299, 906); more broadly, see Rahlfs and Fraenkel 2004: 475–76. On the textual history of Greek Deuteronomy, see esp. Wevers 1978.

mezuzot, and excerpted texts below will indicate, Deuteronomy did circulate in various degrees of excerption (§ 2.4; cf. also § 3.4). Nonetheless, arguably even such smaller sections in some sense presuppose the whole, and it may be plausibly suggested that both share a common liturgical derivation. Furthermore, the size and weight of rolls demands that some consideration be given to how one conceives of Paul or another author having recourse to the book: rolls were certainly not pocket editions. Every model of an ancient author's interpretative activity implicitly presupposes some manner of encounter with the original text; physical considerations indicate some of the constraints within which such imaginative judgments must operate.

Although Deuteronomy existed physically in book (i.e., roll) form, encounter with it as written text was limited by social conditions – notably poverty and the lack of compulsory education – that prohibited widespread literacy. Recent studies have suggested that the literacy rate in the Roman Empire probably did not exceed 10–15%,[11] Roman Palestine probably displaying a similar rate.[12] In a society with such limited literacy, the mediation of sacred truth through the text ensured that a certain amount of prestige and power accrued to those who could read[13] and, even more, to those who could write.[14] Indeed, the intrigue and assumed potency of writing may have contributed to its prowess in *tefillin* and *mezuzot*, in inscriptions, and in magical contexts.[15]

---

[11] Harris 1989; A. Bowman 1991; Hopkins 1991; Botha 1992; Gamble 1995: 1–41.

[12] That the literacy rate in Palestine was considerably lower than in the broader Empire has been argued by Hezser 2001: 496–504; cf. Bar-Ilan 1988: 21–38. The suggestions of high levels of literacy by some earlier scholars now appear exaggerated (e.g., Harnack 1912: 27–31; Richardson 1914: 183), but the considerations of P. Alexander 2003 tell against conceiving of the literacy rate as abysmally low. With specific reference to Hezser, see also Snyder 2002, who stresses especially that her heavy emphasis toward material culture and Rabbinic sources renders her book less useful for the earlier period, especially pre-70 CE. For this period, the work of Millard 2000 should be consulted. He contends that "The literacy situation in Jewish society differed from that in the Graeco-Roman in a notable way because there was a strong tradition of education in order that men, at least, should be prepared to read from the Scriptures in synagogue services" (157). He goes on to note (158) the difference in Jesus's appeal to "Have you never read" when talking to Pharisees, priests, scribes and Sadducees (Matt 12:3, 5; 19:4; 21:16, 42; 22:31; Mark 2:25; 12:10, 26; Luke 6:3; 10:26) in contrast to his addresses of mixed audiences with "You have heard it was said" (Matt 5:21, 27, 33, 38, 43; cf. John 12:34). Note also the contention of Evans (2001) that Jesus was most likely literate.

[13] Beard 1991; Bowman and Woolf 1994.

[14] Goodman 1994.

[15] On which see § 2.4 below and Lincicum 2008b; 2008d. Cf. Harris 1989: 219, 325, etc.

Nevertheless, the fact that Deuteronomy was a written text did not automatically exclude the illiterate majority of the population from its range of influence. Rather, its influence would have been experienced in various modes of orality or aurality. The boundary between orality and textuality, rather than comprising a strict line of division, resembles that between illiteracy and literacy: both nebulous and permeable. Although there may be some benefit from contrasting primary orality with textuality as ideal types,[16] theories that assume a radical discontinuity between literate and illiterate or textual and oral modes of cognition have been rightly questioned.[17] Such a stark contrast is rendered unlikely for the Greco-Roman period when one considers the significant degree of interpenetration between the two modes, seen, for example, in the wide popularity of rhetoric.[18] Functionally, this suggests that the influence of a written text, especially one as prominent as Deuteronomy, would not have been confined to the circles of the literate.

On the other hand, the upsurge of interest in orality since the mid-20th century, especially when de-coupled from the romantic ideology with which it is sometimes freighted (i.e., that a once-pristine orality then underwent a "fall" into the constrictive technology of writing),[19] provides a helpful corrective to an anachronistically "typographic" or even electronically-centered mindset. In both the Greco-Roman and the Jewish worlds (which were, of course, hardly as separable as such heuristic labels imply), texts were written for the ear (e.g., Isocrates, *Phil.* 25–27), and reading was almost always reading aloud.[20] Oral patterns of composition, often at-

---

[16] Note, e.g., Goody 1986; Ong 1986; 2002. The application of such orality – literacy dynamics to biblical studies has been most famously achieved in Kelber 1997. See also Kelber 1987; Ong 1987; Farrell 1987; J. Dewey 1987.

[17] See, e.g., Street 1984: 44–65; Halverson 1992. In critique of Kelber, see Halverson 1994; Hurtado 1997; and (in part) A. Dewey 1987: 110–13. Paul J. Achtemeier (1990: 27 n. 156) warns against "a too-hasty application of the change from the oral medium to the written medium to the time the NT was written." Note further Bowman and Woolf 1994; Jaffee 1994.

[18] Rightly Achtemeier 1990; Talmon 1991; Beard 1991: 138–39; Boomershine 1994; A. Bowman (1991: 22) writes, "the interesting thing is not that there was no mass literacy in the ancient world but that ancient society could be profoundly literate with a reading-and-writing population of, let us say, less (perhaps much less) than 20%, the precise figure being insignificant." This interpenetration of orality and literacy is not sufficiently accounted for in Stanley 2004; see esp. Abasciano 2007.

[19] So esp. the works by Kelber mentioned in n. 16 above.

[20] Cf., e.g., Acts 8:30. On reading aloud as the normal practice in antiquity, the classic work is Balogh 1927; though note the important correctives offered by Knox 1968 (whose arguments also stand against Achtemeier 1990: 15). For further discussion (in which the passage from Augustine's *Confessions* 6.3 runs like a scarlet thread) note Hen-

tributable to the pervasive cultural influence of ancient rhetoric, have left their mark on the New Testament documents and elsewhere.[21] Further-more, this interplay between the oral and the written ensured that memory often served as a middle ground mediating between textual and oral modes of encounter. As William Harris concludes:

> Thus there occurred a transition away from oral culture. This was, however, a transition not to written culture (in the sense in which modern cultures are written cultures) but to an intermediate condition, neither primitive nor modern...But some of the marks of an oral culture always remain visible, most notably a widespread reliance on and cultivation of the faculty of memory.[22]

Especially when considered in light of the practice of synagogue reading to be examined below (§ 2.3), these factors grant an *a priori* likelihood that Deuteronomy's influence extended far beyond those encounters recover-able to us now through literary remains. At one level this is simply to state the obvious: the total effects of any text swell beyond our ability to con-sider them. Alternatively considered, however, such a fact suggests that examination of some neglected encounters with Deuteronomy in the an-cient world, for example in liturgical contexts, may well throw light on its literary reception as well.

In fact, the physical manuscript remains from the first centuries lend a striking confirmation to the suggestion that Deuteronomy was encountered orally or aurally as well as in written form. Many of the early manuscripts preserve various markers for sense-division, widely assumed to facilitate public reading – especially when these are found in biblical texts.[23] In

---

drickson 1929; Clark 1931; McCartney 1948; Starr 1991; Slusser 1992; Gilliard 1993; Gavrilov 1997; Burnyeat 1997. Cf. Saenger 1997: 6–13, who is probably correct in sug-gesting, however, that "no classical author described rapid, silent reference consultation as it exists in the modern world" (9). On the importance of orality more generally, note Graham 1987; L. Alexander 1990; Achtemeier 1990; Ward 1994; Cox 1998.

[21] The bibliography surrounding ancient rhetoric and the New Testament is massive; see, e.g., Watson and Hauser 1994: 101–206.

[22] Harris 1989: 327; cf., e.g., Small 1997. See further § 2.6.1 below.

[23] See, e.g., Korpel 2000, who stresses that the unit divisions are ancient and show at least some widespread agreement across manuscripts and translations; cf. also Tov 2000: 335: "it stands to reason that some kind of sense division was embedded in the original manuscripts of the Bible," although his account of this differs from Korpel's. Tov also suggests that the earliest Greek manuscripts bear more signs of such divisions than later ones (342–46). For a connection of sense divisions and liturgical reading, see esp. Perrot 1969; 1973: 107–16; cf. also Revell 1971–72; 1976; contra, e.g., Tov 2000: 337. For ex-ample, of P. Ryl. Gk. 458, Revell writes, "For the Septuagint, it provides, in combination with the other Greek texts discussed here, definite evidence that this version was used for formal lections in the Synagogue" (1971–72: 222). For the argument that the paragraph marker originated in Greek texts to facilitate reading aloud, note Johnson 1994. See also Jastram 1994: 209–11: 4QNum[b] preserves both paragraph-divisions and the employment

Greek manuscripts, these range from spaces between (what later came to be) verses or sentences, the use of the *paragraphos* (a line or mark written in the margin to indicate a new section) or *ekthesis* (a large initial letter protruding into the margin) to other general indications of sense division.[24] According to Emanuel Tov, early Jewish rolls of Greek Scripture sometimes employ spaces to indicate verses (P. Ryl. Gk. 458; P. Fouad. Inv. 266a–c, 4QpapLXXLev[b]; 4QLXXNum; 8HevXIIgr; P. Oxy. 3522; P. Yale 1); show evidence of sense divisions (4QLXXLev[a]; P. Fouad Inv. 266a–b; 4QpapLXXLev[b]; 8HevXIIgr); use the *paragraphos* (4QLXXLev[a]; P.Fouad Inv. 266b; 4QpapLXXLev[b]; 8HevXIIgr hand A; cf. also 1QS) or, in one case, *ekthesis* (8HevXIIgr). Deuteronomy 32 is written stichometrically in one early manuscript (P.Fouad 266b). All of this suggests that a properly historical evaluation of a document like Deuteronomy must include its liturgical reception. After all, the purpose for which Deuteronomy (or the other rolls of Scripture for that matter) was copied and kept, studied and memorized, was fundamentally religious. This suggests that, in an important sense, Deuteronomy's "natural habitat" in the first century is in liturgy. Though speaking about a later time period, the conclusion of William A. Graham is apt. He writes,

> to understand the phenomenon of scripture in any fashion that is remotely faithful to historical realities, we must look to its function as a text that above all has been read and recited aloud, repeated and memorized, chanted and sung, quoted and alluded to in the oral and aural round of daily life (1987: 156).

It is to these historical, that is, liturgical realities that we now turn.

2.3. The Synagogue and the Reading of the Law

The liturgical practices hinted at by the material *realia* are perhaps most fully expressed in the public reading of the law in the synagogue. Three aspects of this liturgical action require some clarification: the presence of the ancient synagogue, the public reading of the Torah, and especially the controverted questions of the existence of a reading cycle and of *lectio continua* for the Law before the destruction of the Temple in 70 CE.

---

of red ink in ten places to mark an opening line; the two do not completely overlap, but a liturgical function has been suggested. Cf. also Hurtado 2006: 178, who speaks of "particular efforts to facilitate the public/liturgical usage of texts, especially, of course, those texts treated as scriptures" (here with reference to Christian texts, but equally applicable to Jewish MSS).

[24] These are most readily accessible in Tov 2001a; cf. Tov 2004: 303–15; Kraft 2002; 2003: 66; 2007.

2.3.1. The Synagogue in the Second Temple Period[25]

The precise origins of the synagogue, the subject of much recent discussion, are shrouded in darkness and probably irrecoverable to us now in any specific form.[26] Nevertheless, the tendency of later Jewish authors to ascribe its origin to either Moses or Ezra (likely by means of association with the public reading of Torah to be discussed in § 2.3.2–2.3.3 below; cf. Deut 31:9–13; Neh 8:1–8; Agua Pérez 1983: 344) is some indication of its perceived antiquity, and it was probably in existence by the Persian period.[27] While the functions of the synagogue ranged from providing a court for local justice to serving as a venue for civic assembly, its most explicit purpose, at least by the first century CE, was as a religious institution, although the nature of Jewish law ensured that no fundamental separation between these elements existed.

Our earliest physical evidence for the synagogue consists of papyri from Egypt, beginning in the 3rd century BCE (e.g., *CPJ* no. 129).[28] The Egyptian material, as most of that from the Diaspora, tends to speak of the meeting-place as a *"proseuche"* (προσευχή) rather than a "synagogue" (see, e.g., *CPJ* nos. 134, 138, 432; cf. also more geographically diverse: *CIJ* no. 531 [in Latin transliteration; *JIWE* 2.602], 682 [*IJO* 1.BS1], 683

---

[25] General surveys of the synagogue in the Second Temple period are plentiful; see Schrage 1971; Schürer 1979: 2.423–54; Safrai 1987; Meyers 1992; Urman and Flesher 1995; Bloedhorn and Hüttenmeister 1999; Levine 2005: 45–134; Catto 2007; Runesson, Binder and Olsson 2008.

[26] The conclusion of Bloedhorn and Hüttenmeister (1999: 270) is apt: "Very little can be said about the origin of the synagogue with any certainty."

[27] So Runesson 2003, 2004 who offers a helpful discussion of synagogue origins, especially stressing the need for a multi-faceted approach, irreducible to simply, say, discussions about archaeological discoveries; contra, e.g., Grabbe 1988. In the 1990s, Howard Clark Kee attempted to cast doubt on the existence of the synagogue before the late first century CE, but his arguments have been massively refuted by subsequent discussion; see Kee 1990; 1994; 1995; contra whom, see Oster 1993; Riesner 1995; Atkinson 1997; van der Horst 1999: 18–23; Kloppenborg Verbin 2000. The idea that the synagogue did not arise until the second half of the first century is simply untenable.

[28] Most of the archaeological record in the Diaspora dates from the 2nd century CE and later; for a survey, see Kraabel 1979, updating Sukenik 1934. In Palestine, the number of first century synagogues, though subject to debate, has on any reckoning been expanding over the past several decades. Now first century synagogues have been identified at Gamla, Masada, Herodion, Kiryat Sefer, and possibly, Qumran, Capernaum, Jerusalem and Jericho, although the caution of Meyers (1992: 255) should still be remembered: "The dearth of early Second Temple synagogue remains stands in striking contrast to the large number of synagogues referred to in ancient literary sources; but such an anomaly derives from our modern misunderstanding of the synagogue as a social and religious institution and the synagogue as a distinct and discrete architectural entity." Cf. also Levine 1981.

[*IJO* 1.BS5], 683a [*IJO* 1.BS7], 684 [*IJO* 1.BS4], 690 [*IJO* 1.BS20], 726 [*IJO* 1.Ach65]). This usage agrees with Philo's general tendencies (e.g., *Legat.* 132, 134, 137–38, 148, 152, 156; *Flacc.* 41, 45, etc.) as well as finding support in the description of Diaspora synagogues found in Acts (see 16:11–14 cf. also Josephus, *Vita* 277 [of Tiberias]; Juvenal, *Sat.* 3.296), while Palestinian material tends to employ the term "synagogue" (so, e.g., Matt 4:23; 13:54; Mark 1:21; Luke 7:1; John 6:59; Josephus, *Bell.* 2.285–92; 7.44; and in Philo's discussion of the Palestinian Essenes: *Prob.* 81–82). Though some have sought to press this terminological distinction into the service of denying the existence of synagogues *per se* in the early first century, no essential difference between proseuche and synagogue can be maintained. This is suggested not least by an Egyptian papyrus that speaks of a "synagogue in a proseuche" (συναγωγῆς ἐν τῆι προσευχῆι; *CPJ* 138).[29] One can also see from this example that the term "synagogue" is susceptible to a range of meanings from "assembly" to the building in which such assembly took place. An inscription from Cyrenaica dated to the second year of Nero's reign (i.e., 56 CE) uses the term in both senses.[30] And, in fact, the range of other Greek terms beyond these two to describe both the building and the assembly means that any theory constructed on terminological distinctions is likely to be suspect (see the helpful table in Oster 1993: 186; contra, e.g., Kee 1990).

Nevertheless, the fact that someone could even propose the non-existence of the synagogue in the early first century, however unlikely the theory may be in itself, highlights the relative paucity of our evidence. Much that we would like to know has been lost to the ravages of time.[31] Through all the foggy uncertainty surrounding the forms and practices of the early synagogue, however, one indubitable historical aspect pierces the mist to confront the observer again and again: the synagogue exists for the public reading and learning of the Torah.

---

[29] See esp. Hengel 1971.

[30] *SEG* 17 no. 823; Lüderitz 1983: no. 72. Cf. *CIJ* no. 93 = *JIWE* 2.209; *CIJ* 1447 = *JIGRE* 20.

[31] For example, McKay (1994) has proposed that the early synagogue did not serve as a place of prayer or "Sabbath worship," being restricted to the reading and study of the Law. While her arguments have been plausibly critiqued by van der Horst (1999: 23–37), she has still managed to highlight the problematic state of our knowledge of what actually transpired in the early synagogue. For some indications of prayer in the diaspora setting, see Leonhardt 2001: 141.

2.3.2. The Public Reading of the Law

Our ancient sources are unanimous in ascribing to the synagogue in the first century CE the practice of reading the Law.[32] Although Philo tends to assimilate the synagogue to the model of the philosophical school (so *Spec. Leg.* 2.62; cf. *Prob.* 81–82; *Somn.* 2.127; *Mos.* 2.211–12, 215–16),[33] he is also clear that the learning of wisdom involves hearing and studying the Torah:

> He [i.e., Moses] required them to assemble in the same place on these seventh days, and sitting together in a respectful and orderly manner hear the laws read so that none should be ignorant of them. And indeed they do always assemble and sit together, most of them in silence except when it is the practice to add something to signify approval of what is read. But some priest who is present or one of the elders reads the holy laws to them and expounds them point by point till about the late afternoon, when they depart having gained both expert knowledge of the holy laws and considerable advance in piety.[34]

Thus, in Philo's account of the Jews' pursuit of the "philosophy of their fathers" (*Mos.* 2.215), the synagogue functions as the place where the Torah is not only heard, but learned and explained as well (cf. Leonhardt 2001: 88–95).

The New Testament also confirms Philo's general picture of the synagogue as a place for the reading and exposition of the Torah. In connection with Paul, it is especially striking to note that he refers to the "reading of the old covenant" (ἀναγνώσει τῆς παλαιᾶς διαθήκης) and "Moses being read" (ἀναγινώσκηται Μωϋσῆς), both of which seem to be metonymous expressions for the reading of the Torah (2 Cor 3:14–15). In Acts 15:21, we read "For in every city, for generations past, Moses has had those who proclaim (τοὺς κηρύσσοντας) him, for he has been read aloud (ἀναγινωσκόμενος) every Sabbath in the synagogues." The connection between reading and exposition is further suggested by Acts 13:15 ("After the reading of the law and the prophets, the officials of the synagogue sent them a message, saying, 'Brothers, if you have any word of exhortation for the people, give it'") and Luke 4:16–20 as well (where only the reading from Isaiah is mentioned, the Torah reading being perhaps assumed[?]). Furthermore, Josephus connects the weekly reading in the synagogue with the attainment of a thorough knowledge of the Law, though we should take his apologetic hyperbole *cum grano salis*. He writes that Moses

---

[32] Schrage 1971; Perrot 1973, 1988; Schürer 1979: 2.423–54; Levine 1987: 15; Safrai 1987b; Riesner 1995; Schiffman 1999; Levine 2005: 146–53; Catto 2007: 116–25.

[33] Note also that Philo mentions the four philosophical virtues in this context (*Mos* 2.216: cf. Plato, *Republic* 4.428b; *Laws* 1.631c, etc.).

[34] *Hypoth.* 7.12–13 (in Eusebius, *Pr. Ev.* 8.7.12–13); LCL translation. Cf. Martin 2000.

left no pretext for ignorance, but instituted the law as the finest and most essential teach-ing-material; so that it would be heard not just once or twice or a number of times, he ordered that every seven days they should abandon their other activities and gather to hear the law, and to learn it thoroughly and in detail. This is something that all [other] legislators seem to have neglected.[35]

He goes on to boast, "Were anyone of us to be asked about the laws, he would recount them all more easily than his own name. So, learning them thoroughly from the very first moment of consciousness, we have them, as it were, engraved on our souls" (*C. Ap.* 2.178; Barclay 2007: 270). Other Second Temple voices also offer slightly more oblique testimony to the importance of the reading and exposition of the Torah (see 1QS 6:6–8; 4Q251 1:5; 4Q266 5 ii:1–3 = 4Q267 5 iii:3–5;[36] *T. Levi* 13:2).

This connection between the synagogue and the reading of the Torah is strikingly confirmed by two archaeological discoveries from the Second Temple period. The first is particularly valuable in connection with the present inquiry – a partially-preserved Hebrew scroll of Deuteronomy dis-covered in one of the few first-century synagogues identifiable by archaeo-logical remains, that at Masada. The scroll was discovered, along with a nearby Ezekiel scroll, buried within the synagogue in what either served as a geniza or perhaps a protective hiding place for the sacred documents in light of the impending Roman takeover.[37] This suggests that, even in a possibly makeshift synagogue during the last years of the Zealot resis-tance, the reading of Scripture played an important role. The second find is the well-known Theodotus inscription, found in Jerusalem by Raymond Weill's expedition just before the First World War.[38] The inscription's pre-70 CE date has recently been confirmed on both stratigraphical and paleog-raphical grounds.[39] The inscription states:

Theodotos son of Vettenus, priest and *archisynagogos*, son of an *archisynagogos* and grandson of an *archisynagogos*, built the synagogue for the reading of the Law and for the teaching of the commandments (εἰς ἀν[άγν]ωllσ[ιν] νόμου καὶ εἰς [δ]ιδαχ[ὴ]ν ἐντολῶν), and the guest room, the chambers, and the water fittings, as an inn for those in need from foreign parts, (the synagogue) which his fathers founded with the elders and Simonides.[40]

---

[35] *C. Ap.* 2.175; from Barclay 2007: 269. Compare the similar contention in a some-what less apologetic context: *Ant.* 16.43–45.

[36] On which see Schiffman 1999: 45.

[37] Yadin 1966: 187–89; cf. Hüttenmeister 1977: 314–15; Talmon 1999: 51–58.

[38] See Weill 1920: 186–90; cf. Shanks and Reich 2004: 86–88, 130–32; *SEG* 8 no. 170; *CIJ* 1404.

[39] Riesner 1995: 192–200; Kloppenborg Verbin 2000; Reich in Shanks and Reich 2004: 130–32; contra esp. Kee 1990, 1995.

[40] Kloppenborg Verbin 2000: 244, slightly modified.

Several aspects of the inscription are striking. The fact that the inscription itself dates from before 70 CE makes it an extremely early witness for the synagogue; that this re-foundation of a synagogue by an *archisynagogos* whose grandfather held the same office may well suggest that the synagogue had been functioning for several generations, probably at least from the Herodian period.[41] To identify this inscription with a specific synagogue (e.g., that of the Cilicians; cf. Acts 6:9),[42] is probably to overstep our evidence, but that it is written in Greek within Jerusalem should not be overlooked. This raises the serious possibility that both the reading and exposition of the Torah were undertaken in Greek as well, and that this took place in the general time when the apostle Paul himself was in the city (see § 2.6 below).[43]

In light of this brief survey of evidence, then, the conclusion of Schrage appears fully justified: "The synagogue is undoubtedly many other things, but it is primarily the place of the Torah, which is to be read and taught, heard and learned here."[44] Deuteronomy, of course, is a constitutive aspect of the Torah that was read and heard, expounded and discussed week in and week out. But was Deuteronomy read in part or in whole, in order or at random? Can we press toward a more specific conclusion?

2.3.3. *Lectionary Cycles and* Lectio Continua: *Did They Exist in the First Century?*

The *fact* of readings from the Law is widely attested from the quotations and archaeological evidence adduced above (§ 2.3.2); but what about the *manner*? To ask this sort of question is to venture into dangerous waters; more than one study involving ancient reading practices has been dashed to pieces on the rocky shores of anachronism.[45] Perhaps the most common aspect of such shipwrecked studies, however, is a certain tendency to import the later list of *haftaroth*, readings drawn from the prophets, into the time before the destruction of the Temple, and to seek strict coordinations of these prophetic readings with those drawn from the Torah, usually by

---

[41] It is possible, of course, that the term *archisynagogos* has only an honorific function, in which case the chronological inference from several generations of *archisynagogoi* loses some of its force.

[42] So Jeremias 1969b: 65–66.

[43] Cf. Sevenster 1968: 133–34; Hengel and Deines 1991: 56–57, 137.

[44] Schrage 1971: 821.

[45] Ranging from the more subtle suggestions of Thackeray on Septuagint origins (1923) to the venturesome arguments of Guilding (1960) and Goulder (1974) on the Gospels of John and Matthew, respectively, as closely bound up with specific lectionary cycles. In critique, note, e.g., J. Porter 1963; L. Morris 1964; Crockett 1966; Heinemann 1968. In sympathetic critique of Goulder specifically, see Goodacre 1996: 330–39, 360–62; cf. Chilton 2002.

means of either an annual or a triennial lectionary cycle (for which see Büchler 1892–1894; Mann 1971). Certainly at least some of the *haftaroth* are traditional and may be traced back to influences in the Second Temple period,[46] but on the whole our evidence for the cycles does not pre-date the late second century.[47] This, then, places the vexed question of the annual vs. the triennial reading cycle beyond our chronological purview.[48]

Nevertheless, the evidence just adduced widely presupposes the reading of the Law on the Sabbath. While perhaps the custom may trace its origin to the special Sabbath and festival readings,[49] by the first century the weekly reading of the Law appears to be a universal phenomenon. That such reading was in fact *sequential* may be suggested by the following observations. The Mishnah preserves a discussion about what to do with the normal readings when the readings for the special Sabbaths arise. The anonymous decision is that after the four Sabbaths of special readings, "on the fifth [Sabbath] they revert to the set order. At all these times they break off [from the set order in the reading of the Law (Danby's explanatory note)]: on the first days of the months, at the [Feast of] Dedication, at Purim, on days of fasting, and at *Maamads* and on the Day of Atonement" (*m. Meg.* 3:4; Danby ed.). This apparently preserves the remembrance of a time when there was a set order of normal Pentateuchal readings but these were not yet tied to specific Sabbaths and so had to be interrupted ("bro-

---

[46] Cf. N. Cohen 1997a; 2007; and perhaps Luke 4:16–20; Acts 13:15.

[47] This is not, of course, to claim that the prophets were not read or even that they may not have been read liturgically (though we have no direct knowledge of this); the Qumran *pesharim*, while not liturgical documents *per se*, do presuppose for at least some of the prophets a certain form of *lectio continua* (so Perrot 1984: 126).

[48] Of the two, the so-called triennial reading cycle is possibly the older. In simplified terms, the difference may stem from the early debate about whether readings later conducted on Monday, Thursday and the afternoon of the Sabbath should be "counted" toward the advancement of the reading in the Torah (so the annual cycle) or whether such should simply be an anticipation of the Sabbath readings proper (so the triennial cycle); cf. *m. Meg.* 3:6; *t. Meg.* 3:10 (Neusner ed.). See, e.g., Stemberger 1996: 241–43; Graves 2007: 473 n. 22.

[49] Apart from special Sabbath and regular festival readings, one other public reading of Deuteronomy should perhaps be mentioned, although it may not be immediately relevant to our central concerns: the septennial reading of the Law prescribed in Deut 31:9–13 at the festival of *Sukkot*. Josephus mentions this as a duty fulfilled by the High Priest (*Ant.* 4.209–11), but the Mishnah suggests that, at least once, Agrippa performed the reading (*m. Sot.* 7:8; cf. *Sifre Deut.* § 157, 160). Whether this reflects an actual historical occurrence (so Perrot 1973: 275–76) or not (so Hengel and Schwemer 1997: 468 n. 1295) is difficult to ascertain, though it would not be out of character with Agrippa's political ingenuity (if indeed Agrippa I and not Agrippa II is intended; for the problem, see Schwartz 1990: 157–163).

ken off") to allow for the festal readings.[50] Further, later in the same tractate we find the remains of a different debate concerning the introduction
of mid-week readings: "On Mondays and Thursdays and on Sabbaths at
the Afternoon Prayer they read according to the set order; and these are not
taken into account" (*m. Meg.* 3:6; Danby ed.). Apparently this suggests
that when readings on weekdays were introduced, they proceeded along
the "set order" of the normal course through the Pentateuch, but that such
readings were not allowed to progress the overall standing in the Torah:
their readings had to be recapitulated on the Sabbath meeting ("these are
not taken into account"), perhaps in order not to slight those whose duties
kept them from the weekday assemblies. This arrangement presupposes an
earlier sequential reading course that has been only somewhat awkwardly
accommodated to weekday readings.[51]

So much for the *terminus ante quem*. Can we find any traces of the beginning of such sequential reading? Having devoted more attention to this
particular question than anyone else, Charles Perrot has argued that the
remnants of such sequential reading are preserved in the *petuchot* and
setumot found in early Hebrew manuscripts. Before the introduction of
chapter and verse, such markings served to organize the text into large
sense-units.[52] According to such markings, Perrot has deduced from the
oldest manuscripts and other indications that the following passages from
Deuteronomy would have been read (though the end of each reading is not
marked in the text, he presumes that the sections would not have been
much longer than the twenty-one or twenty-two verse prescription of the
rabbinic period):

1:1; 2:2; 2:31 [2:25]; 3:23 [4:7]; 4:41 [4:25]; 6:4; 7:12 [8:1]; 9:1; 10:1; 11:26 [11:10];
12:20 [12:29 and 13:2]; 14:1 [omit]; 15:7 [14:22]; 16:18; 17:14 [18:14]; 20:10 [20:1];
21:10 [22:6]; 23:10 [23:22]; 24:9 or 19; 26:1 [26:16]; 28:1; 29:9 [29:1]; 30:11 [30:1];
31:1 [31:14]; 32:1; 33:1.[53]

One can immediately surmise that, although this does not include everything in Deuteronomy, most of the book is comprehended by the system.

Also immediately clear, however, is that this reading, while sequential,
cannot be described as *lectio continua*.[54] Though certainty is extremely difficult in such darkly shrouded historical questions, it may be worthwhile to

---

[50] So Safrai 1987b: 927 (though some of his essay engages in anachronistic reconstructions).

[51] So, e.g., Agua Pérez 1983: 353. Cf. Heinemann 1968: 45.

[52] Perrot 1973: 115.

[53] Perrot 1973: 94. These are, according to Perrot, the most ancient readings, with
alternatives judged to be somewhat later variations placed in brackets (see 88–90; cf. also
44).

[54] Cf. Perrot 1973: 115–16; 141–47; Agua Pérez 1983: 355.

test the evidence for an early practice of *lectio continua*. The chief evidence from which Perrot deduces his claim of sequential though not continuous readings from the Torah are the *petuchot* and *setumot*.[55] Because these are derived from Hebrew manuscripts while not found in such systematic fashion in Greek manuscripts, Perrot grants that *lectio continua* may have been practiced in the Diaspora.[56] He further adduces at least six arguments for *lectio continua* as a post-70 CE phenomenon (1973: 141–47):

1. After the year 70 there was a complete reorganization of the synagogue, the synagogue now functioning as a substitute for the Temple: "in these conditions, it was almost inevitable that the methods themselves for public reading would be entirely reviewed" (1973: 43). While this may be true, it is also clear that a *number* of significant changes came about by the second century (e.g., an emerging triennial cycle, midweek readings, developed rules for who may read and in what manner, etc.). We have noted above that a continuous reading pattern was later interrupted (cf. *m. Meg.* 3:4, 6); might this rather have been the change that occurred after the destruction of the Temple? Further, one may sometimes note a tendency to ascribe all significant change from 200 BCE to 200 CE to the effects of the Temple's fall; without denying its importance, one may also call attention to a certain degree of overstatement.[57]

2. Perrot draws attention to *b. B. Qam.* 82a, where it is said that in Ezra's day only a few verses of the Torah were read. Apart from noting the late date of the saying, one may suggest that the reference here is rather to the shortness of some of the pericopae read on special Sabbaths (e.g., Deut 16:9–12 at Pentecost; see *m. Meg.* 3:5) rather than a global statement about readings *per se*. One might also, however, take it as a reference to the earliest synagogue readings, perhaps in use by the third century BCE, in which case the relevance of the saying for the first century CE would be perhaps questionable (the Talmudic text only suggests two different lengths: three or ten verses).

3. Third, Perrot notes that in *m. Meg.* 4:4, the High Priest is said to skip in his reading on Yom Kippur, though the relevance of this text to synagogue reading is negligible.

4. Next, Perrot points to the statement in *m. Meg.* 4:10 that some texts are not allowed to be translated (Gen 35:22; Exod 32:21–25, 35) and asks whether this does not imply that they were not previously read. In fact, however, that such texts are still read may argue for the opposite point: tradition is preserved in their reading, even if their interpretation is hurriedly by-passed (contrast *t. Meg.* 3:34 [Neusner ed.] on "the Chariot," i.e. Ezek 1; cf. *t. Meg.* 3:38–40).

5. Fifth, he suggests that because the Mishnah knows of chosen portions for reading on festal days, earlier readings might also have been such chosen pieces. As in his third ar-

---

[55] Cf. Agua Pérez 1983: 365: "The only criterion which we possess is that of the *petuchot* and *setumot* sections."

[56] Perrot 1973: 116; Perrot 1984. Cf. Perrot 1973: 133: "One might even ask whether the practice of *lectio continua* of the Torah was not already generally accepted in the Diaspora." It is unclear how to reconcile this statement with his claims about Philo's work as a witness to a sequential but not continuous reading cycle (1973: 148–50).

[57] So rightly S. Cohen 1999; Neusner 2005.

gument, the relevance of this is not entirely clear, as most suggest a somewhat different impulse for festal readings than for regular synagogue readings.

6. Finally, he goes on to state, "When the principle of *lectio continua* was admitted, it would forcibly impose a profound reorganization of the order of the readings" (1973: 145). This may be true in part, but only if one envisages a situation in which a significant degree of attachment of certain readings to certain days held true – a situation that may have found some local adherents but was probably not widespread until a later time, if even then. One might also ask whether, if the practice of *lectio continua* was more prevalent in the Diaspora, such reading would have been undertaken in synagogues in Israel that had Diaspora ties and conducted services in Greek (cf. Acts 6:9).

What is the relevance of this somewhat pedantic refutation of Perrot's arguments against an early practice of *lectio continua*? The main upshot is this: everyone agrees that by the late second century, the practice of *lectio continua* for the Torah had been established.[58] Perrot traces its origins to the reorganization of the synagogue after the destruction of the Temple; my examination of his arguments for the chronology of this assertion show that they are less than compelling. That *lectio continua* developed as a *"prolongement"* (Perrot 1973: 151) of the *petuchot* and *setumot* seems reasonable;[59] the evidence has not left us a specific time when such prolongation occurred. In this light, the conclusion of Lawrence Schiffman appears prudent; he writes, "It would seem that these widespread and organized reading rituals in Pharisaic-rabbinic circles so soon after 70 CE lead to the conclusion that the reading of the Torah...would have been practiced in synagogues in the early first century, even before the destruction" (Schiffman 1999: 54).

Of course, even if Perrot is correct, a worshiper at the local synagogue would have heard the majority of Deuteronomy read and explained in sequential order thus, in the more attentive at least, fixing some picture of its overall shape and scope. If the full practice of *lectio continua* was in force, the shape and scope of Deuteronomy in synagogue worship can be extended to its canonical form. While reading cycles *per se* are an anachro-

---

[58] Later rabbis were to say that the reason one does not skip in the Torah is "that Israel should hear the Torah in the proper order" (*y. Meg.* 4:5 [75b]; Neusner ed.).

[59] Note the alternative contention of Elbogen 1993: 132 [120]: "it is quite probable that in the most ancient period the reading was not consecutive, but every Sabbath a passage (עניין) was freely chosen; even when this custom was prohibited 'so that Israel should hear the Torah in order,'[*y. Meg.* 4:5, 75b] there was still no conception of a regular order of readings – that is, a cycle." It should be noted, however, that he himself places the introduction of the Torah readings before the closing of the canon of prophets in the 3rd c. BCE (131–32 [119–20]), so that by the 1st century CE there may have been a regular, though not yet cyclical (i.e., specific readings tied to specific Sabbaths) method of reading.

nistic notion to apply to the first century, the sequential (and possibly continuous) reading of the Torah stands on good ground.

Excursus: Deuteronomy's Place in the Library

To ascertain Deuteronomy's place in the ancient library might have provided a significant insight into how its physical context contributed to its interpretation; unfortunately our information is slender in this realm. It is almost certain that Deuteronomy figured among the scrolls kept in the Temple library (for such scrolls see Josephus, *Ant.* 3.38; 4.303; 5.61; *Vita* 418; *Bell.* 7.150, 162; *m. Mo'ed Qat.* 3:4; *m. Kelim* 15:6; possibly 2 Macc. 2:13–15; cf. also the Arch of Titus in Rome).[60] If Herod's library contained a copy of Deuteronomy, perhaps in Greek translation, it would then have staked its claim alongside volumes of Homer and Hesiod, geographers and historians, polemicists against and defenders of the Jews (Wacholder 1961). There are some slight indications for private ownership of books (cf. 1 Macc. 1:56–57; 2 Macc. 2:13–15; 2 Tim 4:13), but only the very wealthy would have been able to afford more than a handful of scrolls. Probably the most common place for scrolls to have been kept is in the synagogue, where the widespread practice of the reading of the Torah and, later, the Prophets and some of the writings (e.g., Esther at Purim) necessitated having such scrolls on hand. Of course the manuscript finds at Qumran attest a high concentration of Deuteronomy manuscripts (see § 3.3 below), but the characterization of the caves as a "library" is contested (but note Lange 2006). Although we do not have evidence of Deuteronomy employed in pagan writings before the rise of Christianity,[61] if the legends

---

[60] The status of such scrolls as authoritative textual exemplars has been a matter of debate; contrast Klijn 1977 with Blau 1902: 99–106; Talmon 1962; Tov 2003b.

[61] For Deuteronomy in the writings of later pagan opponents to Christianity, see Rinaldi 1989: 289–300 (nos. 150–70). He asks, "How, then, and through what channels were pagans able to become acquainted with the scriptures of the Jews and Christians?" (110). The answer he gives: "The Scriptures were usually brought to the attention of the pagan public by those who had already accepted them" (110), also pointing to the Greek and Roman settlements in Palestine (110–111), and, of course, to the presence of Jews in the Diaspora (111–13) and the popular penetration of Jewish traditions into the magical texts (114). He concludes, however, that "study of the penetration of the biblical texts amongst pagan authors is still at the beginning" (118). The extant quotations of Deuteronomy among such writers really begin with Celsus (probably the latter half of the second century CE), and continue on through Porphyry (who wrote nearly after 270 CE) and the Emperor Julian (wrote in 362–63 CE), along with excerpts preserved in the *Apocriticus* of Macarius of Magnesia (4–5th c. CE) and in Ambrosiaster (wrote ca. 384 CE; see pp. 121–63). Rinaldi further notes the tendency, especially of Julian, to use Deuteronomy's monotheism as an argument against Christological affirmations (contrast 1 Cor 8:4–6!); cf. Rinaldi 1989: nos. 157, 169; Rinaldi 1998: 164. Cf. also J. Cook 2004: "it

connecting the translation of the Septuagint to Demetrius of Phalerum, librarian of Alexandria, are given any credence,[62] then Deuteronomy may have found its place in that great Ptolemaic achievement as well.[63]

Within the synagogue, the Torah later came to be kept within a "Torah shrine," a sort of "architectural stone structure which was the *housing* for the Ark of the Scrolls built on the Jerusalem-oriented wall. The enclosing structure is either an aedicula, niche or apse" (Hachlili 1988: 167), the aedicula being the earliest of these.[64] The Torah shrine and some other symbols (e.g, the *bema* or raised platform for reading), however, probably only enter the synagogue after the destruction of the Temple (Hengel 1971: 179 [166]), and most likely not until the mid-second century at the earliest (Meyers 1999: 202; the synagogue at Dura Europa offers a good example of many of these). Before this time, the Torah was probably kept in a portable wooden case (an "ark": תיבה or ארון or κιβωτός or ἀαρών) brought in from an adjacent room for services (*m. Taʻan.* 2:1–2; *t. Meg.* 2:13, 16; 3:21),[65] though also available for consultation and study during the week. That Paul's reference to a veil lying over the minds of unbelieving Jews when Moses is being read (2 Cor 3:14–16) is, as some older commentators suggested, a cryptic reference to the physical location of the Torah in the synagogue is suggestive, but probably impossible to prove.

2.4. *Tefillin, Mezuzot* and Excerpted Texts

For the faithful Jew of the Second Temple period, encounter with Scripture would have been not only weekly in the Sabbath reading of the Law, but also a daily experience; for those allowed by social position and compelled

---

was the advent of Christianity that seems to have finally generated a close reading of the OT on the part of pagan intellectuals" (p. 1).

[62] The suggestion of a royal initiative for the translation has received more serious attention in recent years; note, e.g., Barthélemy 1978b; Collins 2000; cf. Borgen 1997: 33.

[63] In such a library, Deuteronomy would have lain horizontally on an open shelf, stacked with other rolls and with an identifying tag on its end to facilitate quick recognition. Cf. Sarna 1989: 19–21; more broadly, Casson 2001.

[64] For Torah shrines from the second or third century on, see Wendel 1950; Goodenough 1953–68: 4.99–144; Hachlili 1976, 1988: 166–94; Meyers 1999.

[65] So Levine 2005: 352: "In Second Temple synagogue buildings, it would seem that the Torah chest was mobile and was introduced into the main hall only when it was to be read"; cf. Wendel 1950: 20 (123–24); Goodenough 1953–68: 4.116; Bloedhorn and Hüttenmeister 1999: 292. If the conjectural note of Marcus and Wikgren (LCL) at Josephus, *Ant.* 16.164 (in Josephus' recollection of a decree by Augustus, no less) is correct, this text may also be an early reference to the "ark" in connection with a synagogue.

by religious devotion, the regular wearing of *tefillin* would have provided a powerful enactment and remembrance of the commands of Torah. To bind Scripture to oneself in the *tefillah* and to affix it to one's dwelling in the *mezuzah* created communal mnemonic activities both mediated by and centered on the biblical text. The impact of such regular liturgical practices in shaping the reception of Scripture in the Second Temple period has been underrated; we will here, therefore, highlight the function and content of the *tefillin* and *mezuzot* from the period of New Testament formation.[66]

Tefillin, sometimes also called "phylacteries" under the influence of Matt 23:5, are small leather capsules containing certain passages of Scripture that were bound on the upper forehead and on one's left arm. The passages classically included are those interpreted to prescribe the "binding" of the words as "a sign on your hand" (Exod 13:9; cf. 13:16; Deut 6:8, 11:18; לאות על ידך) and as "an emblem on your forehead" (Exod 13:9; ולזכרון בין עיניך) or as "frontlets between your eyes" (Exod 13:16; Deut 6:8, 11:18; ולטוטפת בין עיניך).[67] Including the paragraphs in which these verses occur, the standard *tefillin* as prescribed by later rabbinic practice were comprised of Exod 13:1–10, 11–16; Deut 6:4–9, 11:13–21.[68] The *mezuzah* consists of a small scroll rolled up and affixed to the doorposts of one's house, bearing the passages that prescribe such an action (i.e., the two Deuteronomy passages from the *tefillin*; note esp. 6:9, 11:20: על מזוזת ביתך ובשעריך).

On a literary level, *tefillin* and *mezuzot* are relatively well-attested. Our earliest clear literary evidence for the use of *tefillin* and *mezuzot* comes from the pseudepigraphical 2nd century BCE *Letter of Aristeas*.[69] In the midst of his appeal for the reasonableness of the Jewish religion and legislation, Eleazar is portrayed as turning his attention to the *mezuzot*: "Furthermore in our clothes he has given us a distinguishing mark as a reminder [i.e., *zizithot*, fringes], and similarly on our gates and doors he has commanded us to set up the 'Words,' so as to be a reminder of God (ἐπὶ τῶν πυλῶν καὶ θυρῶν προστέταχε μὲν ἡμῖν τιθέναι τὰ λόγια πρὸς τὸ μνείαν εἶναι θεοῦ)."[70] He then goes on to describe the wearing of the arm *tefillah*, though no mention is made of the head *tefillah*: "He also strictly

---

[66] For an overview of the *tefillin* and *mezuzot*, see Safrai 1976: 796–800; Schürer 1979: 2.479–81; Fagen 1992; Rabinowitz 2007a, 2007b; Cohn 2008.

[67] On the translation and meaning of טוטפת see Tigay 1982, and note especially his "appendix" on the interpretive translations rendered in the versions (330–31).

[68] See, e.g., *b. Men.* 34b–35a *bar.*

[69] An earlier, though uncertain, reference may be from late 4th century BCE Egypt: Cowley 1923, published an Aramaic statement of accounts from ca. 300 BCE that speaks of a "*tefillah* of silver" (תפלה זי כסף). He asks, "Can it be used in the ordinary sense, a 'phylactery' in a silver case?" (198–99).

[70] § 158; translation from Shutt 1985: 23; Greek text from Pelletier 1962a: 176–78.

commands that the sign (τὸ σημεῖον) shall be worn on our hands, clearly indicating that it is our duty to fulfill every activity with justice, having in mind our own condition, and above all the fear of God."[71] It is striking that the mention of these rituals comes in the midst of a discussion of memory (cf. §§ 153–57), and is preceded by the employment of a mixed quotation of Deut 7:18 and 10:21: "You shall remember the Lord, who did great and wonderful deeds among you."[72]

Philo of Alexandria, the Gospel of Matthew, and Josephus also mention the *tefillin* and *mezuzot*. Philo refers to them in a discussion of justice, although, at least for the *tefillin*, it is not entirely clear that he envisages a literal observance (*Spec. Laws* 4.137–42).[73] In a passage that has garnered some notoriety, Matthew portrays Jesus as denouncing the Pharisees because "they make their phylacteries broad" (πλατύνουσιν τὰ φυλακτήρια αὐτῶν), rendering *tefillin* by the Greek word also meaning "amulet" (23:5).[74] As others have argued persuasively, however, such an identification need not be the case, and, at any rate, the charge is directed against the hypocritical abuse of *tefillin*, not against *tefillin* as such.[75] Within his paraphrastic retelling of Deuteronomy, Josephus testifies to the existence of the *mezuzot*[76] and also provides a clear reference to both the arm and head *tefillin* (*Ant.* 4.213).

Before the manuscript discoveries at Qumran and the surrounding areas in the mid-20th century, most of our information was derived from later rabbinic sources, where *tefillin* and *mezuzot* are both discussed extensively.[77] These sources made it clear that there was some controversy over

---

[71] § 159, Shutt 1985: 23. Cf. Pelletier 1962a: 178–79 n. 2 where he detects a reticence on the part of Greek authors to name the *tefillin* with a substantive noun for fear of identification with amulets (as, he suggests, Matt 23:5).

[72] § 155, Shutt 1985: 23. Compare Justin Martyr's later connection of *tefillin* with remembrance (*Dial.* 46).

[73] But note N. Cohen 1986.

[74] For examples, see, e.g., Daniel 1977; Kotansky 1994: 126–54: "The Phylactery of Moses."

[75] See esp. Tigay 1979; Davies and Allison 1988: 1:17–19; contra, e.g., Fox 1942, who argues that this is a malicious association; and contra J. Bowman 1959, who argues that Matthew was actually talking about Pharisaic amulets.

[76] Perhaps as part of his apologetic strategy, Josephus employs language reminiscent of the public monumental honor shown to a benefactor in casting Moses as commanding the people to "inscribe" (ἐπιγράφειν) on their doors the "greatest of the benefits which God has bestowed on them" (τὰ μέγιστα ὧν εὐεργέτησεν αὐτοὺς ὁ θεὸς) when describing the *mezuzot* (*Ant.* 4.213; Greek text from LCL, translation mine).

[77] For *mezuzot*, see, e.g., *b. Men.* 32b–34a; for *tefillin*, see esp. *b. Men.* 34b–37b, 42a–b; cf. *b. Sanh.* 48b. Note also the two minor tractates of the Talmud, *Tefillin* and *Mezuzah*.

the order of the passages in the *tefillin*,[78] but by and large the picture was rather straightforward and uncontroversial. The discovery of the manuscripts in the Judean desert, however, revealed a broader degree of diversity not only in order, but also in the content of the *tefillin* and *mezuzot*.[79]

The appendix below lists the biblical passages in *tefillin* and *mezuzot* found at Qumran and the surrounding areas, together with certain manuscripts that have been identified as "excerpted texts" (see further § 3.4 below). Conclusions drawn from that material are presented here. The most striking aspect of the *tefillin* and *mezuzot* from the Judean desert is the broader range of pentateuchal passages they employ, though still in identifiable continuity with the later rabbinic prescriptions. While *tefillin* found at Murabba'at (MurPhyl) and Nahal Se'elim (XHev/Se Phyl), as well as some of those from Qumran (4QPhyl C; 8QPhyl Group I), contain the same four passages prescribed in the Mishnah and Talmud, most of those found at Qumran display more diversity, suggesting that the process of standardization had reached a fairly widespread effect by the beginning of the 2nd century when the former caves were used and abandoned in the Bar Kochba revolt.

Often the Qumran *tefillin* preserve the paragraph preceding that which later came to be prescribed. For example, 4QPhyl I preserves not simply Exod 13:1–10, but in fact Exod 12:43–13:10. The same type of extension may be observed in 1QPhyl, 4QPhyl B, 4QPhyl H, 4QPhyl M, 4QPhyl Q, 8QPhyl, and XQPhyl 1, and among the *mezuzot* in 4QMez C and 8QMez. Other texts, however, are found in the *tefillin* which go beyond simple extension, the first and most striking of which is the Decalogue in Deuteronomy 5.

The Decalogue or its frame are attested in 1QPhyl (Deut 5:1–21, 23–27), 4QPhyl A (Deut 5:1–14), 4QPhyl B (Deut 5:1–6:5), 4QPhyl G (Deut 5:1–21), 4QPhyl J (Deut 5:1–32), 4QPhyl L (Deut 5:7–24), 8QPhyl Group III (Deut 5:1–14), and XQPhyl 3 (Deut 5:1–21), and also in one *mezuzah*, 4QMez A (Exod 20:7–12//Deut 5:11–16?). This amounts to a presence in at least one quarter of all of the *tefillin* and *mezuzot* from the Judean Desert, a fact more striking when allowance is made for the fragmentary condition of the manuscripts. The presence of the Decalogue appears even

---

[78] See *b. Men.* 34b *bar.* (Soncino ed.): "Our Rabbis taught: What is the order [of the four Scriptural portions in the head-tefillah]? 'Sanctify unto Me' [Exod 13:1–10] and 'And it shall be when the Lord shall bring thee' [Exod 13:11–16] are on the right, while 'Hear' [Deut 6:4–9] and 'And it shall come to pass if ye shall hearken diligently' [Deut 11:13–21] are on the left." The ambiguity inherent in the description of the two passages "on the left" gives rise to the differing interpretations that later emerge in the disagreement between Rashi (the biblical order) and Rabbenu Tam (Deut 6 last). See the pre-Qumran discussion in Greenstone 1905.

[79] For a helpful overview, see Schiffman 2000b.

more significant when one considers its attestation in excerpted texts, widely believed to have served a liturgical purpose: from Qumran, note 4QDeut[n] (Deut 5:1–6:1) and 4QDeut[j] (Deut 5:1–11, 13–15).[80]

That the inclusion of all or part of the Decalogue in the *tefillin* or *mezuzot* should not be considered a mere sectarian oddity but enjoyed a more widespread currency is suggested by at least three observations. First, while all of those manuscripts written in the "Qumran scribal practice"[81] differ from the limited selection of the four later texts, the extra portions of Scripture, including the Decalogue, are not confined to such *tefillin* and *mezuzot*.[82] Nor do the additions seem to be limited to either arm or head *tefillin*.[83] Second, the Nash Papyrus, a 2nd century BCE Egyptian papyrus,[84] while probably not itself a *tefillah* or *mezuzah*, bears marks of being a liturgical text and contains some striking similarities to the Qumran material.[85] The papyrus presents what is most likely the text of Deut 5:6–21 with substantial harmonizations toward Exod 20:2–17,[86] and directly following this, Deut 6:4–5.[87] This especially recalls the Qumran *tefillin* 4QPhyl B, G–I, and perhaps also 4QPhyl J and O. The small size and harmonizing tendency of the papyrus together with its excerpting of significant passages suggest that it was used for liturgical purposes; its geographical separation from Qumran suggests that it provides an independent and roughly contemporaneous witness to the inclusion of the Decalogue in the liturgy of the time.

These suggestions are confirmed, third, by later rabbinic statements discussing the prohibition of the Decalogue in Jewish liturgy. While *m. Tamid* 5:1 recalls the Temple-era liturgical service which included the De-

---

[80] See esp. Tov 1995; Duncan 1997.

[81] See esp. Tov 1992: 107–11; cf. Brooke 2003: 57.

[82] Emanuel Tov has noted that the Cave 4 *tefillin* that reflect the Qumran scribal practice also contain alternative portions of Scripture, and argues on this basis that they reflect a different origin than the other *tefillin* from Cave 4 not written in the Qumran scribal practice. While this may be true for Cave 4, the fact that the *tefillin* from Caves 1, 8, and X are not written in the Qumran scribal practice and do contain alternative portions of Scripture (as Tov himself notices) minimizes the significance of these results. See Tov 1997.

[83] Contra Yadin 1969: 34–35; so rightly, Baillet 1970: 414.

[84] On the Nash Papyrus generally, see S. Cook 1903; Burkitt 1903; Albright 1937. Albright's proposed date of the second half of the 2nd century BCE on paleographical grounds has been widely accepted.

[85] The Nash Papyrus has been employed in Qumran comparisons by, *inter alia*, White 1990a, 1990b; Eshel 1991.

[86] So S. Cook 1903; Albright 1937.

[87] Deut 6:4–5 is prefaced by a statement similar to that found in the LXX: "And these are the statutes and the judgments that Moses [LXX: κύριος] commanded the sons of Israel when they went forth from the land of Egypt." See Burkitt 1903: 407.

calogue,[88] the Babylonian Talmud on this passage, ascribed to third and fourth generation Tannaites, comments:

Rab Judah said in the name of Samuel: Outside the Temple also people wanted to do the same, but they were stopped on account of the insinuations of the *Minim*. Similarly, it has been taught: R. Nathan says, They sought to do the same outside the Temple, but it had long been abolished on account of the insinuations of the *Minim* (*b. Ber.* 12a; Soncino ed.).[89]

The Talmud Yerushalmi provides an interpretation of the "insinuations of the *Minim*": the Decalogue is not recited "On account of the claims of the heretics. So that people should not have any cause to say that only these [Ten Commandments] were given to Moses on Mount Sinai" (*y. Ber.* 1:4; Neusner ed.). Whether the *Minim* were a group of quasi-Judaizing Christians,[90] antinomian Hellenistic Jews akin to Gnostics,[91] or simply a sect no longer identifiable,[92] the Rabbis agreed that the Ten Commandments should be de-emphasized in order to safeguard the revelatory status of the entire Torah. Judging from the testimony of *m. Tamid* 5:1, it seems safe to assume that this happened after the destruction of the Temple in 70 CE, and was widespread enough to leave its imprint on the *tefillin* discovered at Wadi Murabba'at from the beginning of the 2nd century CE reflecting the standard rabbinic practice mentioned above. Although the Mishnah is aware of sectarian practices with regard to *tefillin* (*m. Meg.* 4:8) and the reference to the prohibited "five partitions" in the *tefillin* probably reflects this dispute (*m. Sanh.* 10:3), the fact that the Decalogue was recited in the Temple suggests that in the Second Temple Period the inclusion of the Ten Commandments in liturgy and in *tefillin* was unlikely to have been solely a sectarian practice.[93]

Thus far the Decalogue. Other variant texts, however, are also found in the Qumran *tefillin* and *mezuzot*. Deuteronomy 32:14–20, 32–33 appears in a *tefillah* text (4QPhyl N) that was apparently bound in the same case as

---

[88] "The officer said to them, 'Recite ye a Benediction!' They recited a Benediction, and recited the Ten Commandments, the *Shema'* [Deut 6:4–9], and the *And it shall come to pass if ye shall hearken* [Deut 11:13–21], and the *And the Lord spake unto Moses* [Num 15:37–41]" (Danby ed.).

[89] Cf. also *Sifre Deut.* §§ 34–35 with specific reference to the prohibition to place the Decalogue in *tefillin*, on which see Urbach 1990: 164–66.

[90] Compare the attempt in the *Kerygmata Petrou* to distinguish between the true law of Moses and the "false pericopes" that later intruded (H III 47; H II 38; Strecker 1992: 533–34).

[91] Vermes 1959, 1975; cf. the stance taken in Ptolemy's *Letter to Flora* 5.1–15 (in Epiphanius, *Panarion* 33).

[92] Urbach 1990.

[93] This conclusion was anticipated before the Qumran discoveries by Mann 1927: 287–99; note also Schneider 1959; Stemberger 1989; Doering 2005: 21–26.

the more usual texts (4QPhyl L–M). Although this is the only instance of Deuteronomy 32 in a *tefillah*, another manuscript preserves the end of the Song followed by a long margin, suggesting that this was an excerpt and not a full scroll of Deuteronomy (4QDeut^q).[94] A second manuscript of excerpted texts also bears Deut 32:7–8, found after other liturgically significant passages (e.g., portions of Deut 5, 6, 8, 11; Exod 12–13; see 4QDeut^j). Moshe Weinfeld has suggested that the prominence of Deuteronomy 32 may be due to its recitation by the Levites in the Temple on the Sabbath, pointing to *b. Roš Haš.* 31a; *y. Meg.* 3:6, 74b.[95] While such texts clearly date from a much later period and so cannot shed definitive light on the period of time in question, they do attest the perceived fittingness of Deuteronomy 32 and Temple liturgy in that later time. Deut 8:5–10, while not appearing in the *tefillin*, is found in two excerpted text collections (4QDeut^n, 4QDeut^j), in the former of which it actually precedes the text of the Decalogue (Deut 5:1–6:1).[96] Again, Weinfeld has offered the anachronistic, if not implausible suggestion that its presence is due to its use as the blessing after meals (cf. *b. Ber.* 44a).[97]

The impression that begins to emerge from the *tefillin* and the *mezuzot*, especially in light of the excerpted texts also found at Qumran (see further § 3.4 below), is one of intense liturgical interest in certain portions of Deuteronomy and Exodus, especially chapters 5–6, 8, 10–12, and possibly 32 of the former, and 12–13 of the latter.[98] This impression is further confirmed by the unusually high degree of harmonization present in these texts,[99] which may suggest a knowledge of broader or at least parallel contexts beyond what one might expect in a written *Vorlage*, perhaps reflecting a practice of writing these texts from memory.[100] Further, it seems that

---

[94] See Skehan 1954.

[95] Weinfeld 1992a: 428.

[96] On 4QDeut^n note Stegemann 1967: 217–27; White 1990a; Eshel 1991.

[97] See Weinfeld 1992b: 251–52; Weinfeld 1992a: 428. In light of 4QDeut^j, however, Weinfeld's contention that the space in 4QDeut^n between v. 8 and v. 9 reflects a halakhic judgment about the mandatory benedictions for certain foods (1992a: 429) appears somewhat doubtful; rather, it may simply be due to a patch of unusable leather (White, 1990b: 194 n. 5); cf. esp. Duncan 1992: 202–03.

[98] J. T. Milik speaks of the maximum choice of biblical pericopes ("le choix maximum des péricopes bibliques") in the *tefillin* and *mezuzot* as Exod 12:43–13:16; Deut 5:1–6:9; 10:12–11:21, and sometimes Deut 32 (1977: 38). If we include the excerpted texts, we might extend this by adding Deut 8:5–10.

[99] See esp. the discussions in White 1990a; 1990b; Eshel 1991; Duncan 1992; 1997; Tov 1995; Brooke 2003.

[100] Cf. *b. Meg.* 18b: "R. Jeremiah says in the name of our Teacher: *Tefillin* and *mezuzoth* may be written out without a copy, and do not require to be written upon ruled lines. The law, however, is that *tefillin* do not require lines, but *mezuzoth* do require lines, and

a marked preference for Deuteronomy over Exodus can be discerned both in the choice of Deuteronomy for the text of the Decalogue and in the fact that most of the "extensions" are drawn from Deuteronomy rather than from Exodus or from another book.

Though our evidence from the Second Temple Period for the actual practice of wearing *tefillin* is still somewhat sketchy, in light of the lack of statements to the contrary basic points of continuity with later tradition may probably be assumed. The men of the community,[101] especially the very devout, would have "laid" *tefillin* during morning prayer, perhaps wearing them all day if their work allowed for the ritual purity required.[102] The daily recitation of the *Shemaʿ* included at least Deut 6:4–9 and 11:13–21, and this may have been said as the *tefillin* were put on (see § 2.5 below).[103] The laying of *tefillin* was widely understood to be a fulfillment of the imperative to remember: affixing the very words of Deuteronomy and Exodus to oneself in the *tefillah* or one's dwelling in the *mezuzah* was a powerful anamnetic act that could scarcely have failed to shape the broader reception of those books in liturgy and literature, in synagogue and school. An awareness of the content and practice of the *tefillin* and *mezuzot* will grant our understanding of the reception of Deuteronomy in literary texts of the Second Temple period an element of depth that would otherwise be lacking. They provide a glimpse into a daily act of remembrance called forth by and executed by means of the words of Scripture themselves. To ignore such an identity-shaping act can only impoverish our understanding of Deuteronomy's reception in the Second Temple era.

We have noted above that the Gospels depict the Pharisees as specially concerned about their *tefillin* (cf. Matt 23:5). Of course, the practice of wearing *tefillin* was not confined to the Pharisaic party or any specific sect of ancient Judaism, as their attestation among the Dead Sea Scrolls is sufficient to suggest. The fact that *tefillin* are specifically mentioned chiefly in contexts of apologetic explanation of Judaism to outsiders (cf. *Aristeas*, Philo, and Josephus above) also suggests that they may have been a widespread and relatively uncontroversial practice during the Second Temple

---

both may be written without a copy. What is the reason? – They are well known by heart" (Soncino ed.).

[101] Whether women in the Second Temple period would have worn *tefillin* is difficult to say, though they were later either "exempt" from so doing (*m. Ber.* 3:3) or prohibited (*Tg. Ps.-J.* Deut 22:5).

[102] Cf. *b. Men.* 36a–36b.

[103] According to *Sifre Deut.* § 34, the injunction to repeat (שנן) "these words" (Deut 6:7) applies only to the paragraphs in Deuteronomy, and not the other paragraphs in the *tefillin* (on which see Urbach 1990: 165–66); there was apparently a sense in which Deuteronomy, itself a repetition or a *deuterosis* of the law, was thought to commend its own repetition, its own *deuterosis*.

period, common among the several sects and non-sectarian strands of Judaism (the later rabbinic disputes notwithstanding). If the passages included in the *tefillin* were perceived at the time as straightforwardly commanding the observance of the wearing of *tefillin*, this would have been palatable to the Sadducean party as well (cf. Josephus, *Ant.* 13.297).

Whether or not this was the case, however, for a Pharisee like Paul the observance of *tefillin* would almost surely have been considered a requirement of the "traditions of the fathers" to which Paul was so zealously devoted (Gal 1:14; cf. also Mark 7:3).[104] Though, of course, we have no direct evidence from his letters, written years later, that Paul once wore such *tefillin*, there may be some heuristic usefulness in examining his appeals to Deuteronomy in light of them.[105]

2.5. The Recitation of the *Shema'* (*Qiriath Shema'*)

We have just had occasion to note the connection between the passages in the *tefillin* and the *mezuzot* with the central confession of Israel: the *Shema'* (from esp. Deut 6:4: שמע ישראל: "Hear, O Israel"), and it is worth pausing briefly to consider the recitation of the *Shema'* in daily prayer. The title came to denote three of the passages just discussed, Deut 6:4–9, 11:13–21, and Num 15:37–41.[106]

Texts from the Mishnah connect this act of recitation with both the Temple (*m. Tamid* 4:3–5:1) and the synagogue (*m. Meg.* 4:5–6; cf. Str-B 4/1: 205–07). In fact, the first sentence of the first tractate of the Mishnah is concerned with regulations for the recitation of the *Shema'* (*m. Ber.*

---

[104] Cf. Schnelle 2005: 66–67: "As the distinguishing mark of his past life as a Pharisee, Paul names his zeal for the traditions of the fathers (Gal. 1:14, "I advanced in Judaism beyond many among my people of the same age, for I was far more zealous for the traditions of my ancestors")....The goal of the Pharisaic movement was the sanctification of everyday life by a comprehensive program of Torah observance in which the keeping of ritual purity laws had particular significance not only within the temple confines but in every realm of life. Thus the Torah was extended in some cases in order to apply it to the multiplicity of everyday situations (cf., e.g., Aristobulus 139ff.; Josephus, *Ant.* 4.198; Mark 2:23–24; 7:4)." See further Lührmann 1989: 76.

[105] Would Paul have later considered such observances as part of "the works of the law" (τὰ ἔργα νόμου) to be suspended for the sake of Gentile contact because of the associated purity requirement? Or would he have continued in them in connection with his ongoing concern for the Jewish festal calendar and Temple-related observances? It is difficult to say, and the nature of the case is such that one would not expect positive evidence one way or the other.

[106] To use the designation, "the *Shema'*" to refer to all three passages as a unit may be something of an anachronism as they are still named individually in the earliest sources (so Hammer 1991: 310), but their traditional connection with each other is clear.

1:1),[107] and that tractate clearly envisages a twice-daily recitation, once in the morning and once in the evening (cf. *m. Ber.* 1–2). This pattern is most likely confirmed by Josephus, who mentions prayer twice each day ("both at its beginning and when the time comes for turning to sleep"; Feldman 2000: 406) in close connection with his discussion of the *mezuzot* and *tefillin*, thus suggesting that he refers to the recitation of the *Shema'* (*Ant.* 4.212–13).[108]

The foundational importance of the *Shema'*, especially Deut 6:4–9, is also seen in numerous quotations and allusions in the New Testament and other writings (e.g., Matt 22:37; Mark 12:29–32; Luke 10:27; 1 Cor 8:4–6; James 2:19; see also Gerhardsson 1996: 300–18; Horbury 2000; cf. 1QS 10:13–14; *Apoc. El.* 2:10; *Ps. Orph.* 10 = Aristob. 4:5; *LAB* 23:2, etc.). The influence of Num 15:37–41 (cf. Deut 22:12) may be seen in the practice of making fringes on one's garments (*zizith*; cf. *Let. Arist.* § 158; Matt 9:20; 23:5; Mark 6:56; Luke 8:44). Although the precise relationship between the *tefillin* and the recitation of the *Shema'* is historically obscure, both probably served a similar purpose in general terms to recall and solidify one's fidelity to the one God of Israel. The recitation of the *Shema'* was occasionally understood in later times as a sort of *précis* of the Torah,[109] and especially once the benedictions were firmly attached it was understood to be a submission to the yoke of God's kingdom. But even during the Second Temple period the impulses that led to such later measures were inchoately at work, and we shall have occasion to return to the striking, indeed almost shocking transformation this central confession undergoes in Paul's exegetical hands (cf. 1 Cor 8:4–6; see § 6.4.1 below).

2.6. Paul and the Liturgical Deuteronomy

Everything we have said so far may be considered in broad terms as background to most Second Temple readings of Deuteronomy, though of course in varying degrees of proximity and importance. But now we turn specifically to Paul, and examine his connection with this liturgical tradition in more historical detail. To anticipate our results: Paul probably en-

---

[107] This is the first sentence in at least most recensions of the Mishnah; see Stemberger 1996: 120.

[108] On the possibility of an early form of the *berakoth* accompanying the recitation of the *Shema'* mentioned in this text of Josephus, note Verseput 1997: 183–84.

[109] Note *b. Men.* 99b: "Even though a man but reads the Shema' morning and evening he has thereby fulfilled the precept of ['This book of the law] shall not depart [out of your mouth]'," Soncino ed.; *Midr. Ps.* 1.17: "By the reading of Shema', for when a man reads the Shema' morning and evening, the Holy One, blessed be He, reckons it for him as if he had labored day and night in the study of Torah," Braude ed. Cf. Str-B 4/1.

countered a Septuagintal form of Deuteronomy in a Greek-speaking synagogue during his days of study in Jerusalem, and may have committed it to
memory there. While his reading of Deuteronomy as a whole involves factors beyond the liturgical, the liturgical importance of certain sections of
the book is reflected in his letters as well.

2.6.1. Paul's Background and Education

That the apostle Paul belonged to the Pharisees is one of the striking pieces
of his biography that has come down to us through the testimony of both
Acts (23:6; 26:5) and his own letters (Phil 3:5). Though occasional attempts are made to see Paul as a "diaspora Pharisee" (among whom Paul
would be the only member whose remembrance has survived),[110] recent
studies have persuasively argued that Paul's Pharisaic heritage should be
firmly linked to a Jewish education in *Eretz Israel*,[111] as the *auctor ad
Theophilum* had already suggested (Acts 22:3).[112] To debate whether Paul
was of the Shammaite[113] or Hillelite[114] variety of Pharisaism may or may
not be an exercise in anachronism,[115] but a Pharisee marked by zeal for his
ancestral customs he certainly was (Gal 1:13–14; Phil 3:4–6).

---

[110] See Lentz 1993: 54–55, though he puts this fact to different use.

[111] Note, e.g., Hengel and Deines 1991; Hengel and Schwemer 1997; Riesner 1998.
More broadly, see Lührmann 1989; Tassin 1996; Vahrenhorst 2005. Even, e.g., Lentz
1993, who suggests that Luke presents an idealizing portrait of Paul, and that it is unlikely that one person would have combined in himself citizenship of Tarsus, of Rome,
and good Pharisaic upbringing, concedes, "That Paul came from Tarsus, moved to Jerusalem, and was at home in both the Greek and Jewish world may indeed be true" (26).
Likewise, Stemberger 2005 critiques some excesses of Hengel's historical reconstruction, but still concedes that Paul had roughly the same type of education that Hengel suggests. Tomson (1990: 51–53) can call Paul a "Hellenistic Pharisee" but one who is
"rather much at one with Palestinian, Pharisaic-Rabbinic Judaism." To claim a period of
study in Jerusalem for Paul is not to dismiss Greco-Roman influence on the apostle, for
even in Jerusalem Paul would have had the opportunity to acquaint himself with Hellenic
thought. Note also Porter and Pitts 2008 who, however, suggest a Greek elementary education in Tarsus (including, e.g., progymnasmata).

[112] As especially stressed by van Unnik 1962; 1973. But see du Toit 2000, who suggests that van Unnik has been over-stringent in his interpretation of the evidence, but still
comes to the conclusion that Paul came to Jerusalem in his adolescence; so also Hengel
and Deines 1991: 34–35.

[113] So Townsend, 1968; Hübner 1973; Wright 1997: 26–35: Paul was a zealous
Shammaite Pharisee, "one of the strictest of the strict" (26).

[114] Famously argued by Jeremias 1969a; in critique, note Haacker 1997: 71–77.

[115] Légasse 1995: 377. This debate assumes, of course, that both the Houses of
Shammai and Hillel were 'Pharisees', but that is an assumption that may be open to question, as Professor Martin Goodman has stressed to me in personal conversation.

What, though, can we say about the process by which Paul came to be educated as a Pharisee? We are not interested in psychological speculations about *why* Paul became a Pharisee but in the more mundane (and available) question of how a "Hebrew of Hebrews" who speaks such proficient Greek and evinces a profound debt to the Greek translation of the Old Testament might be explained given what we know of Jewish education in the first century.

Our knowledge of Jewish elementary education in the first century is, like many of the areas investigated in this chapter, certainly limited. As mentioned briefly above in our discussion of literacy (§ 2.2), compulsory and universal education is an anachronistic conception to apply to the first century (so already N. Morris 1937: 20), but for those who could read and write, the most common purpose mentioned in our sources seems to have been the reading and study of Torah.[116] The *Testament of Levi* urges, "Teach your children letters also, so that they might have understanding throughout all their lives, as they ceaselessly read the Law of God" (13:2; Kee 1983: 792–93).[117] It seems likely that Paul would have learned to read Torah as the beginning of his education, especially if we are to understand the description of him in Acts as a "son of Pharisees" (23:6) in a genealogical sense. It is even possible that he attended a Greek school in Jerusalem (so Hengel 1991: 54–62, 135–38; cf. Hock 2003); if so, this would likely have been a Jewish institution, with the Septuagint taking the role played by Homer in Greco-Roman education.[118]

But the content and occasionally the style of his letters together with the testimony of Acts (22:3) suggests that Paul also received "higher education" in Jerusalem. Our knowledge of the "house of study," so well-attested in later rabbinic literature, is sparse indeed for the first century. It had already been mentioned by Ben Sira (בית מדרש; MS B at 51:23; Beentjes 1997: 93), and possibly would have been a locus for the scribal activity of which the Gospels speak. Architecturally, the study house, especially in its earliest manifestations, was probably not often a separate facility, but more an activity pursued within local synagogues or private

---

[116] Even Hezser (2001: 68) draws attention to this: "The focus on the reading of the Torah in Jewish elementary education seems to have been customary at least since the last centuries of the Second Temple." Cf. Safrai 1987a; Byrskog 1994: 96–98; Gerhardsson 1998: 56–66 (with some anachronism).

[117] On Torah education as a parental duty, note further e.g., Deut 4:9; 6:7; 11:19; Philo, *Legat.* 210; Josephus, *Vita* 7–9; *C. Ap.* 1.60; 2.204; *4 Macc.* 18:10–19; and later, *m. Abot.* 5:21; *m. Yoma* 8:4; *t. Qidd.* 1:11; *Sifre Deut.* § 46. Cf. Juvenal, *Sat.* 14.100–106 (= Stern 1980: no. 301).

[118] On the preponderance of Homer in literary school exercises, see the papyrological survey in Cribiore 1997; cf. also Sandnes 2009: 40–58.

residences during the week.[119] Whatever else "sitting at the feet of Gamaliel" might have meant, it is probably safe to think of such education as laying the foundation for Paul's knowledge of Scripture and exegetical facility (Riesner 1998: 268), though of course Paul's convictions about the substance and proper goal of scriptural interpretation were to be heavily revised in the post-Damascus days.[120]

In both Jewish and Greco-Roman educational practices from antiquity, the role of memory and memorization appears to have been a central pillar. The famous saying of the Mishnah, "At five years old [one is fit] for the Scripture, at ten years for the Mishnah, at thirteen for the commandments, at fifteen for the Talmud..." (*m. Aboth* 5:21, Danby ed.), while post-dating Paul in its final redaction by at least a century and a half and reflecting the greater formalization of that time, may still express some basic continuity with the educational priorities of an earlier day: Scripture and traditions of the fathers. Later rabbinic literature abounds with feats of memory, as in the Yerushalmi passage where R. Ishmael b. R. Yosé says, "I am able to write out the entire Scripture from memory" (*y. Meg.* 4:1 [74c]; Neusner ed.). Again the Tosefta recounts that "R. Meir went to Assya to intercalate the year, and he did not find there a Scroll of Esther written in Hebrew. So he wrote one out from memory, and then he went and read [the Scroll of Esther] from it" (*t. Meg.* 2:5, Neusner ed.).[121] Further, it has been suggested that the Mishnah is mnemonically structured for memorization (Neusner 1985), and the term "Mishnah" itself means "repetition" (from שנה; cf. δευτέρωσις in Greek).[122] Likewise, Greco-Roman authors over a long period of time stressed the importance of memorization (e.g., Plato, *Phaedr.* 274e–275a; Xenophon, *Sym.* 3.5). Quintillian suggested that memory played a key role in the art of oratory:

---

[119] For some reflections on why the house of study is so difficult to identify in architectural remains, see Urman 1995; cf. also Hezser 1997: 195–214.

[120] It should be stressed that, even if one discounts the testimony of Acts for the reconstruction of Paul's historical biography, his letters still confirm that he was someone of Pharisaic background (Gal 1:13–14; Phil 3:4–6) who probably knew Hebrew or Aramaic (Phil 3:5; 2 Cor 11:22) as well as Greek, and had a broad-ranging interest in and knowledge of Scripture, presumably the result of intensive study.

[121] Note further Byrskog 1994: 158–60; Gerhardsson 1998: 122–70.

[122] Cf. Justinian's (in)famous *Novella* 146 (conveniently available in Kahle 1959: 315–17): "But we strictly forbid what they call Deuterosis, as it is neither included in the Holy Scriptures nor transmitted of old through the Prophets, but is an invention of men who spoke merely with earthly wisdom and were not divinely inspired" (Chapter I; Kahle 1959: 316). On Deuterosis, see del Valle Rodríguez 2005, who notes that it sometimes applies to the Mishnah proper, and other times is more broadly applied by Christians to denote the Talmud or even "Jewish doctrine"; the concept was studied in the Church Fathers as early as Hody 1705: 238–40.

It is memory which has brought oratory to its present position of glory. For it provides the orator not merely with the order of his thoughts, but even of his words, nor is its power limited to stringing merely a few words together; its capacity for endurance is inexhaustible, and even in the longest pleadings the patience of the audience flags long before the memory of the speaker.[123]

Memory, it seems, was part and parcel of ancient literary culture and education.

More proximate to the first century Jewish milieu, we have repeatedly had occasion to notice the connection of memory with hearing the Torah. Note, for example, Josephus: "For it is good that they [the laws] be inscribed in their souls, able to be guarded in memory and never obliterated....Let your children also, in the first place, learn the laws, the lesson most beautiful and productive of happiness" (*Ant.* 4.210–11; Feldman 2000: 406; cf. *C. Ap.* 2.176–78). The cultivation of the faculty of memory seems to have been one of the most noticeable and enduring aspects of the intersection of orality and literacy to which I have already drawn attention.[124] Thus, when we encounter the frequent quotations in, e.g., Paul's letter to the Romans, recourse to the hypothesis of a pre-formulated collection of *testimonia* to explain the breadth and variety of his choices is unnecessary;[125] rather, this background suggests that the conclusion of Hengel and Deines is more likely to be correct: "Paul knew large parts of his Holy Scripture off by heart" (1991: 35–36). When this educational milieu is placed alongside the liturgical prominence of Deuteronomy in the Second Temple period, together with the frequency of Deuteronomy cita-

---

[123] Quintillian, *Inst. Orat.* 11.2.7–8 LCL; quoted in Small 1997: 126–27. Teresa Morgan suggests that, for Quintillian, memory is one of the key natural faculties employed in education (1998: 246). As Dr. Mark Edwards of Oxford has stressed to me, however, there is a certain dis-analogy with respect to Quintillian's appeal to memory: for the orator, a speech recited verbatim from memory would have defied the proper requirements of the rhetorical occasion. Rather, one should memorize the main points and then extemporize accordingly. At a more general level, however, it is clear that Quintillian upholds the importance of cultivating the capacity to remember as part of one's education. For the whole topic of memory in the Greco-Roman world, see Small 1997: 81–239, who surveys a broad range of ancient mnemotechnic devices, though she notes that"[t]he methods themselves are not as important as the fact that training in memory was an integral part of the educational curriculum by the time of the Romans" (136). Cf. Harris 1989: 327.

[124] One more indication that knowledge of Torah was not limited to the literate may be found in the people whom Josephus includes in the immediate context of the quote just adduced: "let neither woman nor child be excluded from this audience, nay nor yet the slaves" (*Ant.* 4.209), i.e., those people most likely to be unable to read the law for themselves. The account is clearly idealized, but may reflect at least some historical concern for the public promulgation of Torah.

[125] Further note Lincicum 2008c.

tions in Paul's letters, to think of Paul committing the book of Deuteronomy to memory does not stretch the imagination.

Much of the liturgical evidence we have amassed, however, concerns the Hebrew text of Deuteronomy, while Paul was writing in Greek: how are we to account for this?

2.6.2. Paul and the Greek Liturgy of the Synagogue

The phenomenon of bi- or even tri-lingualism among Jews and other ancient peoples under imperial dominion was widespread and well-known,[126] and there is no compelling evidence to doubt Paul's knowledge of Hebrew and/or Aramaic.[127] Nevertheless, Paul's quotations evince an almost exclusive proximity to the Septuagint and in the small number of cases where his wording more nearly approximates the Hebrew, a Greek text that has undergone a hebraizing revision is widely seen to be the most probable explanation.[128] Paul, I will suggest, shared the halakhic view, whether by default or conviction, that the Greek language was an acceptable vehicle to convey the Scriptures and other liturgical actions.

The importance of Greek to Jewish life, not least in Palestine, has been amply documented,[129] and this importance extended to liturgical matters as

---

[126] So Treu 1973; Fitzmyer 1979; Hengel 1991: 136 n. 259; Cotton, Cockle and Millar 1995: 215; S. Porter 1997a.

[127] This is probably one implication of Paul's self-description as Ἑβραῖος (Phil 3:5; 2 Cor 11:22; Tomson 1990: 52; cf. Hengel 1983: 9–10; contra, e.g., Wagner 2002: 7–8 n. 29).

[128] So, e.g., Koch 1986; Stanley 1992. The only serious challenge to this near-consensus in recent years has been Lim 1997. Lim writes, "greater caution must be exercised in describing biblical quotations in the Pauline letters as a whole to be septuagintal, since such a textual characterization assumes that the citations agree with the Septuagint over and against the MT, Samaritan, and all other text-types and recensions. To be distinctively septuagintal, as is often claimed, the cited verse or individual reading should agree with the LXX in those passages where the Septuagint differs from all other text-types. The reasoning should not simply be that a Pauline reading agrees word for word with a printed edition of the Septuagint that is being used for comparison" (141). Although this is true in part, one must also consider that the tendency of an author to quote a Greek text in places where it diverges from other texts may shed light on those places where the major text types are in relative agreement. When Paul's wording agrees verbatim with a "septuagintal" quotation, this actually does hold significance; for there are many ways one might render, even 'literally,' a Hebrew sentence into Greek (on which see esp. Barr 1979). Philo of Alexandria's comments are apt: "who does not know that every language, and Greek especially, abounds in terms, and that the same thought can be put in many shapes by changing single words and whole phrases and suiting the expression to the occasion?" (*Mos.* 2.38; LCL).

[129] See, e.g., Sevenster 1968; Treu 1973; Hengel 1974: 1.58–65; Fitzmyer 1979; Mussies 1987; S. Porter 1997a; Millard 2000; Walser 2001, 2003; Rajak 2002: 46–64; Watt 2003.

well. All of our early synagogue inscriptions are in Greek (Hengel 1971: 172 [159]), and the Theodotus inscription has been called the "clearest reference" for the reading of Greek Scripture in Israel during the Second Temple period (Tov 2003b: 252). The impulse for the translation of the Septuagint itself has also been plausibly ascribed to the liturgical needs of Jewish communities in the Diaspora,[130] but the translation would have been significant for those groups of Diaspora Jews who settled in Jerusalem as well – perhaps after traveling there on pilgrimage (cf. John 12:20; Acts 2:5–11; 6:9). Whatever the truth in the Aristeas legend that the translators came from Jerusalem to Alexandria to undertake the project, it is telling that in Philo's day he can conceive of the translators from Jerusalem as Jews "who had received an education in Greek (τὴν Ἑλληνικὴν ἐπεπαίδευντο παιδείαν) as well as in their native lore" (*Mos.* 2.32; Colson trans. in LCL).[131] Further, an early colophon to the Greek translation of Esther claims that the translation has been made by a Jerusalemite (see Bickermann 1944). Early rabbinic literature recognizes the propriety of reciting, *inter alia*, the *Shema'* and the daily prayer in any language (*m. Sot.* 7:1; though see Str-B 4/1: 196 for debate), while Rabban Simeon b. Gamaliel thought that only Greek was acceptable as a second language for the translation of Scripture (*m. Meg.* 1:8; cf. *Deut. R.* 1.1).[132] While after the second century one may notice a certain "rehebraization" of rabbinic Judaism (*riebraizzazione*; so Colorni 1964: 49; cf. 38–50), coinciding with the virtual disappearance of Jewish literature composed in Greek from the second century onward, Greek continued to play an active, if more sub-

---

[130] Perhaps most famously by Thackeray 1923 (cf. Jellicoe 1968: 64–70), though many ascribe to this general view. Even those who see the impulse as originating in a royal Ptolemaic decree also recognize the sustained success of the translation as due to its liturgical importance (so, e.g., Barthélemy 1978b: 334; cf. also Fernández Marcos 2002 on N. Collins 2000). Indeed, this liturgical importance is probably the *particula veritatis* in Paul Kahle's conception of the Septuagint as arising from a number of Targum-like translations upon which a later standardization was forced (cf. Kahle 1959: 235–39, 264).

[131] Of course, Philo's view of the translation is remarkably rosier than some later rabbinic portraits. He claims that "if Chaldeans have learned Greek, or Greeks Chaldean, and read both versions, the Chaldean and the translation, they regard them with awe and reverence as sisters, or rather one and the same, both in matter and words, and speak of the authors not as translators but as prophets and priests of the mysteries, whose sincerity and singleness of thought has enabled them to go hand in hand with the purest of spirits, the spirit of Moses" (*Mos.* 2.40; LCL).

[132] Of this text, Revell (1971–72: 218), notes that this is in "a context which, from the comparison with *tefillin* and *mezuzot*, clearly indicates that full liturgical usage is under consideration, not just the use of a translation read after the Hebrew text." Cf. also *y. Sot.* 7:1 [21b]; *b. Meg.* 9a, and the later contrasting ruling of *Masseket Soferim* 35a ("Rule 6").

dued role in Jewish liturgy and life (note, e.g., *m. Meg.* 2:1; *t. Meg.* 2:6; cf. Justinian's *Novella* 146, dated 553 CE).

During Paul's day, it has been estimated that 10–15% of the inhabitants of Jerusalem spoke Greek as their mother tongue.[133] Presumably some of these would have been among the frequenters of the synagogue (or synagogues) of the Libertini (i.e., the "Freedmen"), the Cyrenians, Alexandrians, Cilicians and Asians mentioned in Acts 6:9 (ἐκ τῆς συναγωγῆς τῆς λεγομένης Λιβερτίνων καὶ Κυρηναίων καὶ Ἀλεξανδρέων καὶ τῶν ἀπὸ Κιλικίας καὶ Ἀσίας). Paul is said to have moved among the synagogues of Jerusalem (cf. Acts 24:12), and later rabbinic literature knows of multiple synagogues in Jerusalem before the Temple's destruction (*t. Suk.* 2:10; and with hyperbolic exaggeration: *b. Ket.* 105a; *y. Meg.* 3:1, 73d), including one said to be of the Alexandrians (*t. Meg.* 2:17) and another of the Tarsians (טורסיים; *b. Meg.* 26a).[134]

Whatever Paul's precise historical connection might have been with the Greek-speaking Jews of Jerusalem, some of whom were to be among the first converts to the new post-Easter Jesus movement (the so-called "Hellenists" [Ἑλληνισταί]),[135] that he moved among the Greek-speaking synagogues as a young man, perhaps as an aspiring teacher, seems eminently plausible (cf. Riesner 1995: 206).[136] It is in these synagogue gatherings that Paul would have heard the Torah read sequentially in Greek, and perhaps have engaged himself in the sort of "teaching of the commandments" which the Theodotus inscription commemorates. Here Paul may have recited the *Shema'* in Greek, perhaps as he laid *tefillin*.[137]

---

[133] Hengel and Deines 1991: 55. Note also Mussies (1987: 1054–55): "Jerusalem, then, must still have been a centre of Greek learning in the first century C.E., where men like Josephus (who visited the empress Poppaea when he was only 26 years of age), James the brother of Jesus, and Paul might have acquired the command of Greek needed either for their writings or their missions."

[134] See Riesner 1995: 188–89, who also discusses the alternative translation of this word as "metalworkers." Note also Schürer, 1979: 2.445 n. 80.

[135] For contrasting estimations see, e.g., Hengel 1983 and Räisänen 1992a.

[136] Note Hengel and Deines 1991: "on the one hand [Paul] studied Pharisaic scribal learning in the school of Gamaliel and perhaps with some other teachers; on the other he had his spiritual home in some of the Greek-speaking synagogues in Jerusalem (or perhaps there was only one), where he may have seen his task as being that of a teacher communicating the Pharisaic understanding of the law to the Diaspora Jews who streamed to Jerusalem in large numbers" (61).

[137] We have no knowledge of early *tefillin* in Greek or any other language besides Hebrew, but this may reflect the facts that a) our only first century *tefillin* are from the caves of the Judaean desert and b) the ruling on *tefillin* being permitted only in Hebrew is from later rabbinic literature (*m. Meg.* 1:8). Nevertheless, the fact that the Nash papyrus is in Hebrew and was found in Egypt is striking, the vast majority of the Jewish papyri from Egypt being in Greek (though Oxford's Sackler Library has several unedited

2.7. Conclusion

Deuteronomy enjoyed a widespread popularity during the Second Temple period (see §§ 3–8 below; Brooke 1997a; Crawford 2005), a popularity that is probably both occasioned by and reflected in its liturgical prominence. In this chapter I have attempted to give some account of that liturgical prominence, and in this sense these results may be broadly construed as important for many of the various individual engagements with Deuteronomy by Second Temple authors surveyed throughout our study. Nevertheless, Paul's interpretation of Deuteronomy is the goal toward which this work presses, and we have progressively tightened our compass of inquiry to center on him.

What, then, have we gained that might materially enrich an understanding of Paul's recourse to Deuteronomy? First, this liturgical setting provides a viable *Sitz im Leben* for considering Paul's initial encounters with Deuteronomy as a book (i.e., a roll). All of our early Greek manuscripts show evidence of being designed for public reading, and the importance of such an act of public reading is strengthened when approached via the more sociological concerns with low literacy rates and an interpenetration of the oral and the written on the one hand, and from the more particularly archaeological and literary attestation to the synagogue and its activities on the other. Deuteronomy was an emphatically public book, and one which specifically commended its own internalization and memorization. Given Paul's background and what we can surmise of his education, and especially in light of the liturgical setting in which he would have encountered Deuteronomy in the regular rhythm of Sabbath worship, that he had followed Deuteronomy's cues and pondered it deeply, quite possibly committing it to memory in its entirety, seems entirely possible. Indeed, this gains support in the rather broad distribution of his quotations across the book, though admittedly he does have certain preferred *loci*. In contrast to some modern ahistoricizing approaches, then, this sketch provides a more historically responsible account of how Paul came to know Deuteronomy *as a whole*, and indeed suggests that those who would deny such knowledge to the apostle must marshal stronger arguments to support their case.

Indeed, the evidence of this chapter tells definitively against the sufficiency of *testimonia* theories that envision Paul's encounter with Scripture in atomistic form. Such theories suggest either that Paul received

---

Hebrew papyri from Oxyrhynchus, whose eventual publication may change this estimation). If the Nash papyrus perhaps served as a "master copy" from which *tefillin* could be written, this would provide some evidence for an early emphasis on the propriety of Hebrew. This is, of course, a somewhat speculative suggestion, and our evidence allows us no certainty on this point.

as traditional some sort of pre-formulated collection of Christian proof-texts which he then used to his own ends in his letters, or that in the course of his study he jotted down individual texts in notebooks to use in his later letters, and so his primary source for the Old Testament quotations was his collection of decontextualized quotes.[138] Both variations have a common emphasis on texts isolated and removed from their original contexts, though, admittedly, more stress is placed on this in the former. But both forms of the theory, especially when offered as a global theory of Paul's engagement with Scripture, suffer from the weakness of ascribing to Paul a modern individualist's *modus operandi*. This liturgical-anamnetic encounter with Deuteronomy, especially when seen alongside the positive evidence of the Deuteronomy citations in Paul's letters, proves to be a much more viable global option for understanding Paul's encounter with the sacred text.[139]

Second, then, this investigation suggests that liturgical interest was not evenly distributed across Deuteronomy's thirty-four chapters, but especially centered on some key texts. The *tefillin* and the *mezuzot*, along with the recitation of the *Shema'* and the excerpted texts from Qumran, all demonstrate a sustained interest in Deut 5:1–6:9, 10:12–11:21, and 32:1–43. This selection of texts corresponds to a significant portion of Paul's quotations from Deuteronomy (see Rom 7:7; 10:19; 12:19; 13:9; 15:10; 1 Cor 8:4–6; cf. Rom 9:14; Gal 2:6; Phil 2:15). While our actual knowledge of Paul's own liturgical praxis, both before and after his commission as an apostle, is decidedly slim, this suggests that whether Paul abandoned some of his prior liturgical commitments or decided to continue in them as far as possible (as Acts seems to suggest), he shared with the Judaism of his time a penchant for reflection on the texts that were central to the life of the worshiping community. Paul counts himself among those on whom the words of Deuteronomy sovereignly impose themselves as divinely authoritative, received in a liturgical act that constitutes Paul as less an interpreter than a servant of the *viva vox dei*.

Do these two findings, then, reflect contrary impulses? On the one hand, a concern with Deuteronomy encountered in sequential, perhaps continuous reading, building toward some overall picture of the book as a whole; on the other, an excerpting tendency, isolating significant passages from their broader context. Admittedly, the evidence is somewhat ambiguous in this regard, but rather than pit these two impulses against each other, it

---

[138] In this light, it is striking to observe that the *testimonia* hypothesis receives its fullest explication at just the time that form criticism achieved its own ascendancy; surely the common emphasis on an anonymous collective responsible for selecting and preserving authoritative traditions cannot be accidental.

[139] See further Lincicum 2008c.

may be more responsible to see them as interrelated phenomena. As in the later funerary inscriptions whose appeal to the "curses written in Deuteronomy" serves as a legitimizing acclamation,[140] arguably the *tefillin* and *mezuzot*, the excerpted texts, and even the recitation of the *Shema'*, depend for their vitality on a presupposed relation to the scroll of Deuteronomy, itself a constitutive part of Israel's Torah. In this sense, it may be more useful to think of these excerpted texts as less the product of an *atomizing* tendency than of an *epitomizing* tendency. While the former drives toward free-floating isolation, the latter chooses, for instance, key portions of Deuteronomy to recite every morning and evening, not because the original whole is unimportant, but simply because one cannot recite the entire thirty-four chapters twice each day. After all, it is not just any words that end up in the excerpted texts, but words from a book with the recurring *Leitmotiv*: hear, learn, keep, repeat![141] The whole and the part, then, each actualize the impulse of the book in varying, but arguably complementary fashions. In fact, this "whole and part" shape is precisely the sort of imprint Deuteronomy has left on Paul's letters. In this way, such a liturgical-anamnetic model describes the historical preconditions for those who see Paul and other authors as engaged in some sort of holistic or contextual reading of Deuteronomy.

This chapter is more of an exercise in historical prolegomena than in interpretation *per se* – one might say, more concerned with the "given" than the "made" or with the realm of "cultural memory" rather than hermeneutics – but I hope that it is clear that such prolegomena are not without importance in interpreting Paul's use of Deuteronomy itself. For Deuteronomy as a text carries a distinctive momentum, perhaps even a pressure, through the Second Temple period, and any attempt to understand the shape of that momentum and its imprint in Paul's letters neglects the liturgical encounter to its deficit. Paul himself participates in this dynamic, and to keep in mind these liturgical undulations will provide us with a heuristic lens through which to consider Paul's and his contemporaries' engagement with the last book of the Pentateuch. It is to a closer investigation of those engagements that we now turn.

---

[140] For some such 2nd–3rd century CE inscriptions from Roman Phrygia, see *MAMA* 6.335a; 6.335; *CIJ* 760; *SEG* 44 (1994) no. 1075; *IJO* 2.213. Cf. Ramsay 1915a; 1915b: 353–69; Robert 1940–1965: 10.249–56 (with plates XXIX, XXXIII, XXXIV); Kant 1987: 705; van der Horst 1991: 56–57; Trebilco 1991: 61–63; Gager 1992: 191 (no. 91); Strubbe 1994: 115–20; Ceylan and Corsten 1995: 89–92 = Corsten 1997: 192–93 (no. 111).

[141] Cf. Assmann 2007: "Rück-Bindung, Erinnerung, bewahrendes Gedenken ist der Ur-Akt der Religion. Das Deuteronomium hat diese Struktur narrativ entfaltet und zu einer bildkräftigen Erinnerungsfigur gehärtet" (227–28; cf. 212–28).

Part II

Reading Deuteronomy

Introduction to Part II

If Part I of this investigation has explored the givenness of Deuteronomy as a sort of cultural koine appropriated in liturgy as a common possession of all Jews in the Second Temple period, Part II investigates the manifold ways in which Deuteronomy comes to be appropriated, re-contextualized, disputed, cited and put to practical ends in a range of distinct encounters spanning the time from Tobit and the Temple Scroll to the Targums. Alternately expressed, Part I concerns itself with Deuteronomy as given, Part II with Deuteronomy as made. Of course, to use such expressions could give the impression that Deuteronomy is simply an inert substance capable of unbounded differentiation. The unfolding argument of the next six chapters, however, discloses a series of encounters that bear a striking family resemblance, even in their diversity. The fascination of the task lies in precisely that dynamic of familiarity and newness.

The aim in this part of the investigation is not to offer an exhaustive and archival catalogue of every place where a quotation from Deuteronomy appears, but rather to arrive at a representative typology of reading strategies as discerned in various corpora. This then should clarify Paul's own employment of Deuteronomy by supplying not simply parallel instances of citation of the same passage, but also some indication of the overall shape and function of Deuteronomy in authors and texts from a variety of standpoints. To this end preference has been given to authors and texts who demonstrate sustained interest in Deuteronomy as evinced in the repeated attention they devote to it. In order to let each text or author make its own contribution, we proceed here in roughly chronological order to consider first the documents from the caves surrounding Qumran, then moving on to selected texts from the Apocrypha and Pseudepigrapha, Philo of Alexandria, the apostle Paul, and Josephus, as well as some later trajectories of Jewish interpretation of Deuteronomy.

It is important to be clear about the aim and importance of these chapters. If our interest were simply in a conventional "background" to Paul's citations of Deuteronomy, to investigate only those citations of Deuteronomy actually paralleled in Paul's letters would suffice. The intent of these chapters, however, is to approach this question from the advancing horizon of Deuteronomy itself, ascertained through its effective history. I hope that

part of the accomplishment of these chapters is to document that Deuteronomy carries with it a particular force, a shape composed of both mass (in
the givenness of its content) and energy (in the traditions of its interpretation). If something like this is true of texts in general, even more so does it
characterize the text of Scripture which presents itself and is accepted as
divinely authoritative by a broad range of Second Temple Jewish authors,
Paul included. Not only, though, does Deuteronomy retain a broadly defined shape as it is interpreted through the centuries, it also prepares the
hermeneutical space which it subsequently comes to inhabit. By its role in
liturgy, its literary reception, and its own address directed to posterity,
Deuteronomy has already primed Paul and his Jewish contemporaries to
engage with it. This is not, however, to say that specific interpretations are
delivered concretely and incorrigibly in advance, nor that any particular
author's interpretation can be discerned merely by registering contemporary interpretative practice. As these chapters so amply demonstrate, the
singular hermeneutical force of Deuteronomy comes to be actualized and
expressed in a variety of different contexts and ways.[1]

In contrast to some investigations of Paul and his recourse to Scripture,
this study is concerned with the interconnection of both formal and material dimensions of interpretative praxis. Rather than observing a technique
or a method and then seeing whether it is applied by Paul to any specific
text, we are interested to see whether certain formal procedures of interpretation are bound up with a material pressure from Deuteronomy itself. Ascertaining these together should go some way toward disclosing the
"shape" that Deuteronomy comes to have for a variety of interpreters, and
so prepare the way to ask whether and to what extent Paul's letters serve as
an instantiation of a Jewish encounter with Deuteronomy. In order to accomplish this, the following questions will motivate this investigation,
though the nature of the sources means that not every question will be answered by every text. As to the method of engagement, does this text re-
write, quote, allude, or introduce Deuteronomy in a specific way? Does
Deuteronomy appear as a distinctive voice, or is it assimilated to the voice
of Scripture more broadly? Is there a specific interest in one part of the
book over against another, or is it evenly distributed across Deuteronomy's
thirty-four chapters? Is there a legal interpretation, and if so does it display
an actualizing tendency? If the concern tends to be on the final chapters, is
this concern future-oriented and possibly eschatological, or is it rather ret-

---

[1] Compare a point, with a slightly different emphasis, made by Gary Anderson: "In
this sense we can say with some justification that Christian material cannot always be
illuminated by Second Temple sources without first placing those sources in a trajectory
of Jewish development" (1998: 9–10), though this begs the question of what is Christian
and what Jewish in the Second Temple period.

rospective? Finally, is there any evidence of the means by which Deuter-onomy was encountered for the authors involved? Though to pose all of these questions to each text would grow tedious, these concerns should add an analytical precision to our concern with Deuteronomy's *Nachleben* in the Second Temple period.

We begin by considering how Deuteronomy functions in the texts found in the Judean desert in mid-20th century.

Chapter 3

Deuteronomy at Qumran

3.1. Introduction

The fundamental importance of the Torah for the community or communities reflected in the manuscripts found in caves along the Dead Sea has been evident since their earliest publication, even if the striking hermeneutical stance of the *pesharim* meant that some earlier investigations tended to obscure this with a focus on the prophetic. Nevertheless, conceiving of themselves as the "sons of Zadok" (בני צדוק in 1QS 5.9) and undertaking "an errand in the wilderness," the covenanters found deep significance in the priestly traditions, laws and wilderness narratives of Exodus, Leviticus and Numbers.[1] Even more so, however, did the books of Genesis and Deuteronomy captivate them.[2] The former left its impression not only in numerous copies of biblical manuscripts, but also in a number of secondary expansions based on the stories in Genesis, including the Genesis Apocryphon, *Jubilees*, and the Enochic literature. The latter permeated the community in liturgical, legal, and more broadly ideological dimensions.[3] Indeed, there is a "Deuteronomic feel" to much of the sectarian literature, reflected not least in the emphasis on covenant fidelity and radical obedience to Torah. It is the purpose of this section to delineate the shape of this importance, with special reference to those places where explicit dependence on Deuteronomy can be ascertained. What emerges is a multi-faceted recourse to Deuteronomy, congruent with what one might expect of a community concerned with one of its foundational documents.

Of course, one of the difficulties in discussing "Deuteronomy at Qumran" is that of provenance: which caves furnish manuscripts that count as evidence? How do we know which compositions are sectarian in nature and which belong to broader streams of Judaism? Do the caves reflect a single community, or are they deposits of different sects? In what follows, I assume the "Groningen hypothesis" of Qumran origins, which suggests

---

[1] See, e.g., Brooke 1993; Pike 1996; Fabry 1999, 2000.

[2] In this regard, the relative degrees of attention to the individual books of the Torah, as indeed to the books of Scripture more generally (esp. Isaiah and Psalms), is similar at Qumran and in the New Testament. See Brooke 1997a.

[3] Cf. Duncan 2000; Crawford 2005; Lim 2007.

that the manuscripts found near Qumran reflect a sect that is an off-shoot of a broader Essene movement.[4] Although such an Essene identification has been increasingly challenged in recent years, no other interpretative option has yet convinced a majority of scholars, and the Essene hypothesis continues to marshal the evidence of classical sources in its support.[5] Most of the major compositions examined below either stem from Qumran Cave 4 or have other textual exemplars from that cave (e.g., the 4Q524 version of the Temple Scroll or the Cave 4 fragments of the *Serekh ha-Yaḥad*). In one case two manuscripts from different caves may even have been written by the same scribe (1QS and 4Q175; Cross 2002: 308). Whether all of these were originally sectarian compositions is a question that will be left unanswered in this investigation, together with such vexed problems as the relationship between the Damascus Document and the *Serekh ha-Yaḥad*. The aim in this section is chiefly to see how Deuteronomy actually functions in each of these compositions. If it could be proven definitively that some of these compositions stemmed from groups that had no historical connection to one another and so would not have known each other's compositions, this would only weaken our conclusions at the level of their combination, but such evidence does not appear immediately forthcoming.

3.2. The Role of Deuteronomy in Major Compositions

Deuteronomy features in striking ways in a number of major compositions from Qumran. In the following, I suggest that Deuteronomy appears as a document of God's covenant with Israel (1QS 1–3); as an actualized legal authority (the Temple Scroll and CD); and as a judgment on Israel's history (MMT and a number of Moses-pseudepigrapha). While not every cita-

---

[4] See García Martínez 1988; García Martínez and van der Woude 1990 (both now reprinted in García Martínez 2007); García Martínez 1995. The Groningen hypothesis's argument that the Qumran sect is an off-shoot of a larger Essene movement sometime in the mid-2nd century BCE is also shared by G. Boccaccini's hypothesis about Enochic Judaism (1998; see also the essays in Parts 4 and 5 of Boccaccini 2005). Though aspects of the Groningen hypothesis have been challenged (note Lim 1993; Part 4 of Boccaccini 2005), it still retains the best explanatory power for Qumran's origins, though these results are not bound to its conclusions. It may also be that revision will be required in light of Jodi Magness's arguments against the existence of R. de Vaux's "Period Ia" at the Qumran site (2002); the fact that many of the manifestly sectarian writings stem from before the 1st century BCE would imply that the timeline of the founding of the sect should be dissociated from that of the founding of the settlement at Qumran (so Elgvin 2005).

[5] For the classical texts about the Essenes, see Vermes and Goodman 1989; cf. Beall 1988.

tion from Deuteronomy can be brought under one of these umbrella categories, this characterization does cover the most prominent and decisive
among them. To examine the uses of Deuteronomy in this way goes some
distance toward sketching the shape of Deuteronomy's distinctive impact
at Qumran although, as we shall see, certain aspects of their recourse to
Deuteronomy recur in other Jewish authors.[6]

3.2.1. Deuteronomy as Stipulating Entrance to the Covenant: 1QS 1:16–3:12

From the initial publication of the *Serekh ha-Yaḥad*, the programmatic role
of Deuteronomy in its first columns has been noted.[7] While much of the
language of the composition has a Deuteronomic ring to it, this is perhaps
nowhere more clear than in the ceremony described in 1QS 1.16–3.12.[8]
These three columns are suffused with the Deuteronomic language of "entering the covenant" (עבר בברית), not veering from his precepts "to the
right or to the left" (ללכת ימין ושמאול), curse and blessing (ארור and
ברוך), and "this covenant" (ברית הזות) or "the words of this covenant"
(דברי הברית הזות). It is widely agreed that the liturgy preserved in these
columns functioned as a covenant entrance or covenant renewal ceremony,
although, as Philip Alexander points out, the allusive and suggestive portrayal means that it "would be impossible to stage that event on the basis

---

[6] The discussion of how to identify specifically sectarian writings is, of course, a live
one. In my view, both the Temple Scroll and MMT are probably works from the early
period before or during the sect's formation, and so it is difficult to see them as the
unique possession of the Qumran covenanters. Nevertheless, the fact that such writings
are found in the caves in multiple copies does suggest that they were not without interest
for the group, and the distinctive halakhah of the Temple Scroll and MMT tends in general to agree with the Damascus Document in aligning with what later comes to be called
"Sadducean" halakhah, though they are not in agreement at every point.

[7] See, e.g., Brownlee 1951.

[8] The fragmentary preservation of the copies of this composition means that only 1QS
preserves this section, though it may once have been attested in at least 4QS[b], 4QpapS[c],
and 5QS. The redactional and compositional history of the *Serekh* is a controverted one.
S. Metso (1997, 1998, 2002) has argued that the scriptural citations are later additions to
shore up the morale of the community; though she does not include Deut 29:18–20 as an
explicit citation, she does suggest that this liturgical section is "relatively late" (1997:
140, 145). This, then, means that Metso conceives of 1QS as a later edition of the text
whose earlier form is preserved in the palaeographically posterior MSS 4QS[b,d] (so also
Bockmuehl 1998). While this may well be correct, it is worth bearing in mind Philip S.
Alexander's caution that strong evidence is needed to overturn palaeographical priority
to suggest a different order of manuscript filiation as Metso does (Alexander 1996).
Metso does note, however, that "The *Community Rule* alludes to the Old Testament almost constantly. Old Testament phrases and expressions have been worked into the very
fabric of the text without being designated as citations" (1998: 218; cf. 2002: 81).

of this text" (1996: 439). These columns draw on a range of biblical passages in the formation of the ceremony, but most decisive are the priestly blessing in Num 6:24–26 and the description of the covenant ceremony in Deut 27–29.[9]

Two aspects of the *Serekh*'s reliance on Deuteronomy are notable. First is the apparent attempt to re-enact the entrance to the covenant described in Deuteronomy on a yearly basis (1QS 2.19: שנה בשנה). The alternation between curses and blessings and the responsorial acclamations of "Amen, Amen" (1.18–20; 2.1–18) are clearly modeled after the ceremony in Deuteronomy 27.[10] What is more, the formula "those entering into the covenant" (העוברים בברית; 1.24; 2.10; cf. 1.18; 2.19–21) recalls the hapax phrase in Deut 29:11.[11] This may signal that the rationale for their re-enactment of the covenant ceremony is to be found within Deuteronomy. Deuteronomy 29 itself telescopes the future and the present: "It is not with you alone that I am making this sworn covenant, but with whoever is standing here with us today before the LORD our God, and with whoever is not here with us today" (29:14–15 [MT 29:13–14]; contrast Deut 5:3).[12] In this sense to participate in a yearly ceremony of curses on disobedience and blessings for fidelity evidences a typological identification with Israel at Gerizim and Ebal and may suggest that, as many have observed, the sectarians see themselves as the vanguard of a renewed Israel (cf. 2.4–10 and the curse on "all the men of the lot of Belial", i.e., presumably non-sectarian Jews).

The connection to Deuteronomy is evident, second, in the implicit citation of Deut 29:18b–21 in 1QS 2.13–17.[13] The texts run as follows:

Deut 29:18b–21:

Beware lest there be among you a man or woman or clan or tribe whose heart is turning away today from the LORD our God to go and serve the gods of those nations. Beware lest there be among you a root bearing poisonous and bitter fruit, one who, when he hears the words of this sworn covenant, blesses himself in his heart, saying, 'I shall be safe,

---

[9] See Baumgärtel 1953; Leaney 1966: 123–43; Knibb 1987: 84–88; Metso 1997: 141.

[10] Note also 1QM 13.1–6. Cf., e.g., Wernberg-Møller 1957: 51; Weinfeld 1986: 8; 46–47.

[11] Cf. Pouilly 1976: 73; Metso 1997: 141. Elsewhere even within these columns the phrase is בא בברית (e.g., 2.12, 18), thus suggesting that the connection to Deut 29:11 may well be intentional.

[12] Cf. 1QM 13.7–8: "You [est]ablished a covenant with our fathers and ratified it with their offspring for tim[es] eternal."

[13] More fully, see Weise 1961: 104–10; Leaney 1966: 134; Laubscher 1980. Hebrews 12:15 also alludes to the "root of bitterness" and a common recourse to the voluntarist aspect of the covenant in Deuteronomy with the attendant warnings of apostasy may go some way toward explaining some of the apparent similarities between Hebrews and certain texts from Qumran.

though I walk in the stubbornness of my heart.' This will lead to the sweeping away of moist and dry alike. The LORD will not be willing to forgive him, but rather the anger of the LORD and his jealousy will smoke against that man, and the curses written in this book will settle upon him, and the LORD will blot out his name from under heaven. And the LORD will single him out from all the tribes of Israel for calamity, in accordance with all the curses of the covenant written in this Book of the Law (ESV).

1QS 2.13–17:

When he hears the words of this covenant, he will congratulate himself in his heart, saying: 'I will have peace, in spite of my walking in the stubbornness of my heart.' However, his spirit will be obliterated, the dry with the moist, without mercy. May God's anger and the wrath of his verdicts consume him for everlasting destruction. May stick fast to him all the curses of this covenant. May God separate him for evil, and may he be cut off from the midst of all the sons of light because of his straying from following God on account of his idols and obstacle of his iniquity (García Martínez and Tigchelaar 1997: 73).

As this comparison makes clear, the original context in Deuteronomy concerns the secret idolater who considers him- or herself to be safe within the communal covenant. To the contrary, Deuteronomy suggests that the communal nature of the covenant does not negate the individual responsibility of its members, and this individual and voluntarist aspect has been seized upon by the *Serekh* as a warning to those entering the sectarian covenant: God will ensure that the disobedient one (the metaphorically "idolatrous") is rooted out and that the curses of the covenant will rest upon that person.[14] The phrase "stubbornness of heart" (שרירות לב) that occurs in Deut 29:19 and 1QS 2.14 then recurs throughout 1QS as a warning against apostasy (2.26; 3.3; 5.4; 7.19; 9.10; 4QS[d] [4Q258] I.4), suggesting some of the influence that Deuteronomy's conceptualization has had on the composition.

In short, then, the *Serekh ha-Yaḥad* conceives of Deuteronomy as a book of the covenant. As M. A. Knibb has suggested, "the covenant concept is fundamental to the Qumran community, and in this, as in so many other matters, the community was simply appropriating to itself a basic Old Testament idea" (1987: 84). More specifically, it is Deuteronomy that gives definition to the idea of entering and maintaining the covenant, and the *Serekh* implies that Deuteronomy functions as an authoritative vision of God's covenant with Israel and points the way toward fidelity by offering salient warnings against apostasy. Deuteronomy is not so much adduced as an authority in a formal citation as it is rewritten in a way that allows the sectarians to inhabit its world.[15] The terms of the covenant as

---

[14] On the "curses of the covenant" see also 5.12; CD 1.17; Dahmen 2003: 295–96.

[15] Indeed, though there are certainly many instances of Scripture introduced with a citation formula, we do not see among the scrolls the same appeal to genres and titles of books that we find in Philo (see § 5.2 below) or Paul (§ 6.2). Thus, Berthelot is correct in

specified in Deuteronomy 27–29 are crucial regulators of the sectarian quest for renewal.

3.2.2. Deuteronomy as Actualized Legal Authority: The Temple Scroll and Damascus Document

Deuteronomy, however, was not only read to describe entrance to or apostasy from the covenant, but also to detail the way to live in fidelity to that covenant. Along with the other books of Torah (esp. Exod–Num), Deuteronomy provided both explicit and implicit warrant for legal or halakhic decisions about how to live rightly before God. Rather than gather together all of the many references to Deuteronomy in the sectarian legal documents, we shall here focus on the largest single concentration of them in the Temple Scroll, as well as noting some occurrences in the Damascus Document. In both instances we highlight out of the many possible case studies those that have some parallel in Paul's letters in order to facilitate comparative study.

Probably earlier than the Damascus Document, though similar in some respects, is the Temple Scroll from Qumran. The Temple Scroll survives in at least four copies (4Q524; 11Q19–21; possibly also 4Q365ᵃ), the earliest of which, 4Q524 (4QTemple Scroll), has been dated by its editor on paleographical grounds to the third quarter of the second century BCE (150–125 BCE; Puech 1997a: 47–50; 1998: 87–88). The composition's most complete manuscript, 11Q19 (11QTemple^a), is the longest extant scroll from the Judean Desert, and will provide the basis for our comments in this section.[16] The age of the manuscripts, together with a number of detailed points where the *halakhah* of known sectarian documents such as 1QS and CD varies from that found in the Temple Scroll, suggests that it belongs, together with works like *Jubilees*, to that murky period before the foundation of the Qumran community. While some have suggested it is a unified composition (in practice, Yadin 1983; Wacholder 1983: 16–17), perhaps even written by the Teacher of Righteousness himself (Wacholder 1983: 203–04; García Martínez 1993: 94), most scholars rightly see it as a

---

saying "l'usage du titre pour introduire une citation n'est pas la règle" (2007: 131). It is possible that ספר התורה שנית, attested in 4Q177 1–4.14, is a reference to Deuteronomy (cf. Deut 17:17 and the Greek title), though this may also be read adverbially. Note also 1Q30 1.4 which may speak of "five books" (ס]פרים חומשים), a probable reference to the Pentateuch (Berthelot 2007: 139).

[16] See the magisterial edition by Yadin 1983; note also Qimron 1996. Translations are taken from Parry and Tov 2005, which is a slightly revised version of Yadin 1983. Cf. also Maier 1985; García Martínez and Tigchelaar 1998: 1228–89. For a comparison of the Temple Scroll and Paul with reference to Deuteronomy, see Lincicum 2009, on which some of the following paragraphs depend.

composite document whose final redaction incorporates either four or five sources.[17] Our concern with Deuteronomy means that the last two of these sources, the "Deuteronomic paraphrase" (cols. 51.11–56.21; 60–67) and the "Statutes of the King" (cols. 57–59) will be of greatest interest, together with some material from the redactional seams. The first of these sources is, as its name might suggest, a paraphrase drawn from the central law code of Deuteronomy 12–26, for the most part following the order of the biblical text with both minor and major additions and alterations at various points. When the paraphrase reached Deut 17:14–20, the redactor inserted the "Statutes of the King," three columns comprised of a pastiche of commands for the king drawn from all over Scripture, together with a set of curses and blessings for the king and his people.

The Temple Scroll's self-presentation is striking: the third person style of the biblical text has been almost entirely rewritten in first-person discourse, thus casting the Scroll as the direct speech of Yahweh in a daring rhetorical move. For example, Deuteronomy's "For the LORD your God has chosen Levi out of all your tribes, to stand and minister in the name of the LORD, him and his sons for all time" (18:5 NRSV) becomes "for them [i.e., the priests] I have chosen out of all your tribes to stand before me and minister and pronounce blessings in my name, he and all his sons always" (60.10–11) in the Temple Scroll. Despite the change in rhetorical position, however, the Scroll still retains a relative proximity to the biblical text, especially in the Deuteronomic Paraphrase. That the Temple Scroll offers more than a passing engagement with the Torah is further suggested by two observations. First, col. 44.5 speaks of "the sons of Aaron, your brother" while in 51.6–7 the divine voice speaks of the things "which I tell you on this mountain." Thus, the direct speech of Yahweh is still addressed to Moses, as the alternation of second person singular commands and third person plural verbs also suggests: Moses is to hear, promulgate and implement these statutes among the people of Israel (so also e.g., Crawford 2000b: 18). Second, as several scholars have pointed out, the first extant column of the Temple Scroll, probably the second column in the original, paraphrases Exod 34:10–16 along with Deut 7:25–26. The combination of these texts suggests that the setting of the Scroll is the foundation of the second covenant with Israel in the desert, after the first

---

[17] On sources, see Wilson and Wills 1982; Stegemann 1988; 1989; and, in a somewhat different vein, Wise 1990. There may be five or perhaps more likely four main sources: Temple and vicinity (cols. 2.1–13.8; 30.3–47.18); Calendar (cols. 13.9–30.2); Purity Laws (cols. 48.1–51.10 – though whether this is an independent source has been questioned); Laws of Polity or Deuteronomic Paraphrase (cols. 51.11–56.21; 60.1–66.17); Torah of the King or Statutes of the King (cols. 57–59). It has also been proposed that the final redactor is also responsible for the Deuteronomic paraphrase (e.g., Schiffman 1992), which seems quite possible.

tablets had been broken in response to the Golden Calf incident (Exod 32). This, then, may locate the Temple Scroll in the same historical moment that Deuteronomy purports to describe, perhaps filling in the silence of Exod 34:32: "Afterward all the Israelites came near, and he gave them in commandment all that the LORD had spoken with him on Mount Sinai."[18]

This then raises the question of the purpose and genre of the Scroll. For if the Temple Scroll records the second giving of the Law to Moses on Sinai in direct first-person discourse, then this composition subtly presents itself as being the speech of which Deuteronomy is the quotation. That is, while redactional analysis has confirmed that the Temple Scroll presupposes something very similar to our canonical Deuteronomy (Schiffman 1992: 551), the Scroll would apparently have us believe that it is not quoting Deuteronomy, but that Deuteronomy is derivative of it.[19] Is the Temple Scroll, then, involved in an Oedipal conspiracy to kill its own father, to displace and so eliminate its parent-text by appearing to be self-generated, or, more accurately, generated as the product of direct divine revelation?

The question is difficult to answer, and is one that has divided commentators since the scroll's discovery. The two contrasting views offered by Mink and Wacholder are representative of this disagreement. On the one hand, Mink contends that "The Temple Scroll cannot be understood as an attempt to add yet another book to the Law; nor was it intended to replace Deut." (1987: 48). Wacholder, on the other hand, suggests that "The Temple Scroll is not to be characterized as an epitome attempting to paraphrase, conflate, or supplement Moses' legal corpus, but rather as a code of laws uttered by God Himself on Mount Sinai which claims at least equality to and probably superiority over the Mosaic Torah" (1983: 6). The fact that the Scroll is selective in its scriptural harvesting, and does not, for example, reproduce the Decalogue or the *Shema'* has often been taken as evidence that it presupposes other scrolls of Torah.[20] Indeed, the purpose of the Scroll as the recapitulation of the second law given to Moses on Sinai precludes the need to include the Decalogue, as this was already recorded as being delivered publicly by Yahweh to the people of Israel. Whether the Scroll means to displace the original form of those com-

---

[18] For this general understanding, see Mink 1987: 36–38; VanderKam 1994; Crawford 2000b: 18. Cf. Weinfeld 1992c: "Why does the *Temple Scroll* open with the second covenant? The *Temple Scroll* writer is concerned to begin at the covenant that was renewed after the golden calf incident and not in the chapters that describe the preceding covenant which was annulled. This objective already exists in the Book of *Deuteronomy* itself" (178; cf. Deut 5:28; 10:4; 28:69 [29:1]).

[19] This may be similar to the way in which "*Jubilees* employs Deuteronomy as a model for its self-authorization, but goes even further than Deuteronomy in claiming the authority of Moses' revelation at Sinai" (Najman 2003b: 50).

[20] So, e.g., Schiffman 1994: 110.

mandments which it reprises in modified form is more difficult to say. The question may be asked: does the very act of re-presentation, with the implicit claim to correct the original, suggest that, at times, the practical effect sought by the Scroll went beyond supplementing the original to supplanting it? We may here note that the problem is common to the much-discussed genre (if it is appropriate to speak of a "genre" as opposed to an activity) of "rewritten Bible," also sometimes variously called "parabiblical" or "parascriptural" texts.[21] The observation that such rewritten texts are manifestly epiphenomenal does not settle the question of their hermeneutical stance, though arguably their concern for the re-presentation of the original betrays a concern with the importance of the latter – and this in a way before the full development of the emerging commentary tradition. This understanding of such rewritten texts as offering actualizing interpretation rather than patricidal cooptation of the original has been preferred in recent scholarship,[22] and the books of Deuteronomy and Chronicles may provide a certain scriptural pedigree for this understanding (that is, unless their canonical inclusion alongside Exodus and Samuel-Kings is understood to be an ironic blunder, like the social *faux pas* of a party host who unknowingly seats two bitter rivals next to each other at an otherwise pleasant *soirée*). We may find some confirmation of this in the striking inclusion of what look like solemn asseverations to have retained the precepts unaltered in several texts that actually *do* modify the biblical text substantially. So, following Deut 13:1 [ET 12:32], the Temple Scroll reads, "All the things that I command you concerning them today you shall be careful to do; you shall not add to them nor take from them (לוא תוסיף עליהמה ולוא תגרע מהמה; 11Q19 54.5–7). Similar statements are found in the pseudepigraphical defense of the Septuagint known as the *Letter of Aristeas* (310–11) and several times in the biblical retelling of Josephus's *Antiquities* (1.17: οὐδὲν προσθεὶς οὐδ' αὖ παραλιπών; 4.196–97; 10.218; cf. also *1 En.* 104.10–13).[23] The fact that the phrase is included may suggest that the various authors see themselves as rendering the substance of

---

[21] See n. 40 below.

[22] With specific reference to the Temple Scroll, see Yadin 1983; Mink 1987; Callaway 1989; Weinfeld 1992c; Swanson 1995; Crawford 2000b: 27. Contrast Wacholder 1983; Wise 1990.

[23] For further instances, see, e.g., Philo, *Spec.* 4.143–44; *Sifre Deut.* § 82; *Did.* 4:13; Lim 1997: 37–40. On *1 En.* 104:10–13, Nickelsburg suggests, "The nature of these writings is not certain, but it is possible that the author is condemning the kind of rewriting of the Torah that one finds in such books as *Jubilees* and the Qumran Temple Scroll, where divine sanction is claimed for tendentious interpretation of the Torah" (2001: 534), though this can remain no more than a conjecture. Note also Fishbane 1972 for parallels to the formula in ANE literature.

the biblical account in an updated form.[24] In the end, the Temple Scroll can be legitimately described as involved in an act of self-presentation as Torah in some fashion. Even if it is seen as claiming priority over other books of Torah, the Qumran sectarian community apparently held it as worthy of less attention than the biblical Deuteronomy, whose surviving manuscript remains outnumber those of the Temple Scroll in a ratio of almost nine to one.

To say that the Temple Scroll did not displace its scriptural forebears does not imply that its claims to authoritative status need to be downplayed. Indeed, as Hindy Najman has argued, in this period "The only passable roads to textual authority led through the past" (Najman 2003b: 15). She goes on to write:

Works like *Jubilees* and the Temple Scroll, not unlike the earlier work of Deuteronomy, seek to provide the interpretive context within which scriptural traditions already acknowledged as authoritative can be properly understood. This is neither a fraudulent attempt at replacement, nor an act of impiety. It is rather, we may charitably assume, a pious effort to convey what is taken to be the essence of earlier traditions, an essence that the rewriters think is in danger of being missed (2003: 45–46).

This need to convey a new, authoritative interpretation of the earlier Torah is most acute in matters of halakhah, such halakhah providing the catalyst for sectarian division much more prominently than issues of theology *per se*.[25] In fact, however, in halakhic terms, the problem of how to relate contemporary understandings of obedience to Torah to the inscripturated original was common to Second Temple Judaism, though approaches to its resolution differed.[26] What the later pharisaic or rabbinic 'doctrine' of the oral Torah (תורה שבעל פה) accomplished has been approached by our redactor by including contemporary understandings within the biblical text in an interpretative activity that is implicitly understood to be inspired. According to L. H. Schiffman, the redactor "seeks to assimilate extrabiblical traditions by the contention that his new, rewritten *Torah* properly expresses the will of God as revealed in the original document. He asserts that the correct meaning of the divine revelation at Sinai, apparently left vague in the canonical *Torah*, is to be found in the Temple Scroll" (1989: 242). For example, whereas Deuteronomy speaks of the prohibition of

---

[24] Lim suggests that the formula "expresses an impulse to preserve the Mosaic precepts within the context of a contemporary application of the law" (1997: 39).

[25] So García Martínez 1993: "In the pluralistic Judaism of the period, the path of sectarian formation is not marked by ideological differences or by eschatology. Instead, it falls back on the level of the *halakhah* which regulates real life" (92; so almost identically 1988: 121). Cf. Schiffman 2000a.

[26] Schiffman 1989: "All Jewish groups in the Second Temple period endeavored to assimilate extra-biblical teachings into their way of life" (241).

non-sacral slaughter of animals unless "the place where the LORD your God will choose to put his name is too far from you" (12:21), the Temple Scroll specifies this distance as a three-days journey (52.l4). This representation of Deuteronomy is thus also a presentification of it, a making present or actualizing it to respond to the demands of the redactor(s)'s time.

The sheer volume of halakhic material in the Temple Scroll has made it a fascinating document from its initial discovery.[27] Its chief concerns are for purity regulations of the ideal Temple, considered on analogy with the wilderness camp in the Pentateuchal narratives, for the distinctive calendar which is one of the hallmarks of Qumran sectarian documents, and to a somewhat lesser degree for various halakhot about tithes and marriage laws, as well as the Statutes of the King. The judgments of the Temple Scroll often stand in continuity with those that are described as Sadducean in later rabbinic sources (Schiffman 1990; cf. בני צדוק "sons of Zadok" in 1QS 5.9). Much of this material belongs in its conclusions to its sectarian milieu, but other aspects may be common to broader streams of Judaism.

The Temple Scroll's first appearance in modern scholarship was on the question of crucifixion, and this may be its most well-known contribution to the elucidation of a Pauline (and more broadly New Testament) problem.[28] Whereas it was once thought that Paul engaged in exegetical innovation by appealing to Deuteronomy's description of a post-mortem impalement as an act of shame for a warrant of Christ's crucifixion, the Temple Scroll demonstrates that two centuries before Paul penned his letter to the Galatians (cf. § 6.5.1), these verses were understood as referring to crucifixion, or at least to some type of putting to death by suspension. The text reads:

If a man informs against his people, and delivers his people up to a foreign nation, and does harm to his people, you shall hang him on the tree, and he shall die. On the evidence of two witnesses and on the evidence of three witnesses he shall be put to death, and they shall hang him on the tree. And if a man has committed a crime punishable by death, and has defected into the midst of the nations, and has cursed his people and the children of

---

[27] By 'halakhah,' I have in mind "the tradition of formulated rules of conduct regulating life in Judaism" (Tomson 1990: 19). While the Mishnah, the Talmuds and the halakhic midrashim all testify to the ongoing importance and formalization of halakhah in later centuries, the Temple Scroll and 4QMMT (whose halakhah tends to agree with the Temple Scroll) have offered definitive proof of the antiquity of the tradition. While halakhah need not be explicitly tied to the biblical text, here our concern naturally centers on the halakhic employment of Deuteronomy.

[28] See, inter alia, Yadin 1971; 1983: 1.373–79; Baumgarten 1972; Ford 1976; Wilcox 1977: 85–90; Hengel 1977: 84–85; Rosso 1977; Fitzmyer 1978; Puech 1997b; Brooke 2005; O'Brien 2006; Chapman 2008: 125–32. The other well-known contribution of the Temple Scroll centers on the question of divorce and remarriage.

Israel, you shall hang him also on the tree, and he shall die. And their body shall not remain upon the tree all night, but you shall bury them the same day, for those hanged on the tree are accursed by God and men; you shall not defile the land which I give you for an inheritance (11Q19 64.6–13; cf. 4Q524 frag. 14).

It is crucial to note that the word order of the MT has been reversed in two of the three instances in which Deut 21:22–23 is quoted: "he is put to death and you hang him on a tree" becomes "you shall hang him on the tree, and he shall die". Also, the apparent protasis of the MT's sentence becomes the apodosis in the Temple Scroll: crucifixion is now the approved penalty for acts of treason and for those who commit "crimes punishable by death" and flee Israel (cf. 4QpNah 3+4 1.6–8). The potential ambiguity of the MT's "what is hung is a curse of God" (קללת אלהים תלוי) is specified by the Temple Scroll's, "those hanged on the tree are accursed by God and men" (מקוללי אלוהים ואנשים תלוי העץ). This apparently describes the curse as the outcome of the punishment rather than its reason (so also the LXX and Gal 3:13).[29] While the Septuagint may have been the most proximate cause facilitating Paul's understanding of this text, the Temple Scroll shows that there was already some tradition of associating crucifixion with being cursed by God.[30]

The tradition of legal or halakhic exegesis of Deuteronomy is not, of course, limited to the Temple Scroll, but is also found, for example, in the Damascus Document. To take one example of a shared instance of halakhic interpretation may be instructive. In two places the Temple Scroll reprises the "law of witnesses" prescribing the necessity for the testimony of two or three witnesses in agreement in order to condemn an offending party (11Q19 61.6–10; 64.8–9; cf. Deut 19:15). In the first of these, the Temple Scroll treats the law as the paraphrase reaches Deut 19:15 in its progression through Deuteronomy. In the second instance (64.8–9), however, the law of witnesses is introduced in the midst of the passage on crucifixion we have just examined. Ben Zion Wacholder has suggested that the Damascus Document's well-known treatment of the law of witnesses may be dependent on 11Q19 64.6–11 (1989). Wacholder's suggestion stems partially from his somewhat dubious view that the Temple Scroll actually functioned as the authoritative Torah for Qumran, but it is still interesting to examine the Damascus Document in light of the Temple Scroll on this point. In the Damascus Document, the relevant text runs:

---

[29] Cf. two later Jewish traditions: the Targum MS V (Vatican Ebr. 440), at Deut 21:22 reads: "and you shall crucify him on a wood[en gallows]" (Klein 1980: 2:175). *Sifre* considers but rejects crucifixion as the referent of Deut 21:22 (§ 221).

[30] For the differences between Paul's wording and the LXX, see Koch 1986: 124–26; Stanley 1992: 245–48; further, see § 6.5.1 below.

Any matter in which a man sins against the law, and his fellow sees him and he is alone: if it is a capital matter, he shall report it in his presence, with reproach, to the Inspector; and the Inspector shall personally record it, until he does it again in the presence of someone, and he too reports it to the Inspector; and if he is caught again in the presence of someone, his judgment is complete (CD-A 9.16–20; trans. García Martínez and Tigchelaar 1997).

The full explication of this passage is beyond our present purposes (see further Levine 1973; Neusner 1973; Schiffman 1975; 1983: 73–88; Hempel 1998: 93–100; cf. also Matt 18:15–20). Crucial to note here is that this passage is concerned with the "combination of witnesses." That is, in contrast to later rabbinic rulings (see Neusner 1973; Schiffman 1975; 1983: 73–88), this text suggests that an infraction need not be seen by two witnesses simultaneously in order for the offending party to be liable for his or her offense; rather, individual witnesses are recorded and have a cumulative effect (cf. also § 6.3.4 below). This is a halakhic advance on the earlier precept of the Temple Scroll and demonstrates how fidelity to Deuteronomy in legal praxis involved a process of continual reflection on and reinterpretation of the biblical text to respond to the practical exigencies of the community.[31]

Both the Temple Scroll and the Damascus Document, then, conceive of Deuteronomy as of crucial importance for the praxis of life in the covenant, and seek to clarify and extend its precepts in ways appropriate to the new realities faced in their own day. Deuteronomy's importance, strikingly, does not translate into a slavish literalism in its interpretation and obedience, but requires an act of correlation with other sources of authority. In the Temple Scroll, this act of correlation is perhaps more radical and thoroughgoing than anywhere else in Second Temple Jewish literature, but that it was deemed necessary to achieve a rewriting of Deuteronomy in particular should not be overlooked.

3.2.3. Deuteronomy as a Judgment on History: 4QMMT and Apocryphon of Jeremiah

Not only does Deuteronomy provide the Qumran community with an understanding of the covenant and the ethical and legal direction for fidelity to that covenant, it also suggested a theological interpretation of history. Two compositions, each extant in several manuscripts from Qumran Cave 4, preserve multiple references to Deuteronomy as a judgment on Israel's history. One, that of MMT, does so retrospectively; the other, the *Apocry-*

---

[31] For Deuteronomy elsewhere in the Damascus Document, see Deut 32:21 in 4QD[a] frag. 3 ii.3–5; Deut 9:23 in 4QD[d] (4Q269) frag 2.1; Deut 27:18 in 4QD[d] frag 9.2 = 4QD[e] (4Q270) frag 5.15 = 4QD[f] (4Q271) frag 3.9; Deut 23:24 in 4QD[e] (4Q270) frag 6 col ii.19 = 4QD[f] (4Q271) frag 4 ii .7–8; Deut 5:12 in 4QD[e] (4Q270) frag 6 v.3.

phon of Jeremiah, does so proleptically, at least in part, from Jeremiah's standpoint in what we would describe as a *vaticinium ex eventu*.

4QMMT, or *Miqsat Ma'ase ha-Torah* ("Some Works of the Torah") is perhaps more well-known for its distinctive, apparently 'Sadducean' (or at least Zadokite) halakhah and, in Pauline studies, its attestation of the phrase "works of the Law." In fact, however, while MMT does occasionally employ Deuteronomy halakhically,[32] most often it derives its legal rulings from Lev–Num, and the last book of the Pentateuch fulfills a different function. Deuteronomy, rather, functions as a sort of historiographical eschatology or a prophetic interpretation of Israel's history with future implications. The author states one of his purposes in writing the epistolary treatise: "so that you may study (carefully) the book of Moses and the books of the Prophets and (the writings of) David [and the events of] ages past" (C 10–11). Immediately after this, the author gives some indication of what he expects his addressee(s) to find there:

And in the book (of Moses) it is written......that [you will stray] from the path (of the Torah) and that calamity will meet [you]. And it is written, 'and it shall come to pass, when all these things [be]fall you,' at the end of days, the blessings and the curses, ['then you will take] it to hea[rt] and you will return unto Him with all your heart and with all your soul,' at the end [of time, so that you may live] (C 11–16).

This is comprised of two quotations from Deuteronomy 31 and 30 respectively. The first is a quotation from Deut 31:29: "For I know that after my death you will surely act corruptly and turn aside from the path that I have commanded you. And in the last days [באחרית הימים] calamity will befall you, because you will do what is evil in the sight of the LORD, provoking him to anger through the work of your hands." In MMT, however, the phrase "in the last days" has been removed from this quotation and inserted into the second Deuteronomy citation drawn from 30:1–2. This leads M. Bernstein to write, "It is clear that the author of MMT understands the content of 31:29, the misfortune which will befall the people in the end of days, to be the same as the curse of 30:1. Thus that text can also be located at the end of days" (1994: 48; similarly Brooke 1997b: 78).

---

[32] Cf. 4QMMT B 39–41 = Deut 23:2–4 (37–38); C 6–7 = Deut 7:26. I follow the numbering and translation of the composite text of Strugnell and Qimron 1994 which incorporates 4Q394 3–10; 4Q395–399. For helpful surveys of the use of Scripture in the composition as a whole, see Bernstein 1994; Brooke 1997b. Strugnell (1994: 62–63, 67) suggests that the collection of laws is modeled on Deuteronomy. The incipit to Section B (אלה מקצת דברינו), he writes, is "a free-standing introduction to a collection of laws, perhaps consciously modeled on the opening of Deuteronomy" (63). Of the epilogue, he suggests that "Deuteronomy would thus provide a parallel for the ending of this work just as it did for the beginning" (67). This is possible, though the fragmentary state of the text precludes firmer conclusions.

These quotations from Deuteronomy then provide the hermeneutical bridge to a theological interpretation of Israel's history in terms of the partially realized covenant blessings and curses:[33] "And we know that some of the blessings and the curses have (already) been fulfilled as it is written in the bo[ok of Mo]ses" (MMT C 20–21). The blessings, it seems, happened in the days of Solomon (18) while the curses befell Israel "from the days of Jeroboam the son of Nebat and up to when Jerusalem and Zedekiah King of Judah went into captivity," that is, the Babylonian exile (18–19). According to the author, some of the blessings and curses remain for the "end of days" which may now be in the process of being realized, or at least on the imminent horizon (21).[34] This eschatological interpretation of history, however, is probably both occasioned by and at the service of the halakhic vision that comprises the majority of the treatise.[35] The author goes on to urge, "Think of the kings of Israel and contemplate their deeds: whoever among them feared [the To]rah was delivered from troubles; and these were the seekers of the Torah whose transgressions were [for]given" (C 23–25). In other words, the response to the curse is to heed the call to return to Torah and so attain the blessing. Only renewed obedience to Torah can avert the threatened curse of Deuteronomy's covenant.

A similar verdict on Israel's history, though from a different perspective and rhetorical position, is found in a group of pseudepigraphal fragments from Qumran, originally entitled "Pseudo-Moses" by their editor (4Q385a; 4Q387; 4Q387a; 4Q388a; 4Q389; 4Q390),[36] but then re-entitled *Apocryphon of Jeremiah C*. The composition is apparently comprised of a divine foretelling of the events of Israel's history to Moses or, more likely, Jeremiah (Dimant 1992: 410, 432–33; 2001); its judgment on Israel's history is a largely negative one, and so it comes to be in prophetic terms what MMT is in historical review.[37] While much of the composition is

---

[33] Cf. § 6.5.1 below for Paul's stance toward the covenant blessings and curses.

[34] The text is somewhat unclear at this point, though this seems to be the sense of it. Cf. Qimron and Strugnell 1994: 60: "At the end of days, however, the blessings will return, and (if our reconstruction and interpretation of ll. 21–22 are correct) they will last forever and will not be cancelled. The curses will fall upon the wicked and exterminate them." Cf. Bernstein 1994: 49–50; Dahmen 2003: 300–01.

[35] So Qimron (2006: 193): "MMT provides an important witness to the Community members' belief that they were living in the last days of an evil period of history. From the halakhic content of the composition it is apparent that this belief is precipitated by the Community's perception that the rest of Israel was transgressing the Torah. In other words, halakhic concerns are the basis for the Community members' belief that they were living in the 'latter days'."

[36] See Dimant 1992; 2001: 2–3, 89–260.

[37] As Dimant says, "the assumption that the present text is conceived as a pseudepigraphon in which God offers Moses a review of future history, provides a coherent setting for both of the 4Q390 fragments, as well as for fragments from other manuscripts

fragmentary, Deut 31:16–18 has influenced 4Q390 I.8–11: "they will disobey everything and will do what is evil in my eyes. And I will hide my
face from them and deliver them to the hands of their enemies and abandon [them] to the sword. But from among them I will make survivors remain so th[at] [t]he[y will] not [be exter]mi[nated] by my anger [and] by
the concealment [of my face] from them" (García Martínez and Tigchelaar
1998: 785). While the text is too fragmentary to ascertain whether a certain
course of action was recommended or whether a strict blessing and curse
polarity was exercised in its interpretation of Israel's history, this composition agrees with MMT in reading history through the lens of Deuteronomy
and in finding that history lacking.[38]

3.3. Deuteronomy in Biblical and Rewritten Bible Manuscripts

A confirmatory indication of the importance of Deuteronomy at Qumran
may be drawn from the large number of manuscript copies found among
the caves. In fact, the caves produced at least 32 or 33 manuscripts of Deuteronomy, which includes 31 or 32 Hebrew manuscripts and one Greek
manuscript (4Q122), with three additional Hebrew manuscripts recovered
from the surrounding areas (Mur 2; XHev/Se 3; Mas 1c).[39] Deuteronomy,
then, ranks second only to the Psalms in the number of extant manuscripts,
and surely such proliferation of copies offers eloquent testimony to its importance. Although some of these are too fragmentary to be sure whether

---

which also contain sections of a historical review" (1992: 433). In her 2001 DJD edition,
she clarifies that the work offers both historical review and prophetic preview, although
the point of transition between the two has not been preserved in the manuscripts (96–
100).

[38] This may bear some similarity to the role of Deuteronomy in the Admonition of
CD; note Campbell 1995: 184: "What is noticeable about texts drawn from the Torah is
their emphasis upon two interrelated themes: firstly, situations of rebellion in the after-
math of the exodus but before entry into the land, as reflected in Ex 32 and, especially,
passages from Nu (but also Gn 6,7 and 10); secondly, Lv 26 and Dt 27–32, which centre
on the related story of the sin-exile-restoration of the people after initial residence in the
land – what we may characterize as the rebellion *par excellence*."

[39] See Tov 2002; also note Dahmen 2002 for the identification of various fragments in
the Deuteronomy MSS that were originally left unidentified; and Puech 2001: 123–24 for
his proposed identification of *4QDeutéronome'* = *4Q38ᶜ*, two small fragments of Deut
12:31–13:(1)3(?) and 14:28–29. Puech's suggestion accounts for the variation between
32 and 33 MSS. See further García Martínez 1994; Dahmen 2003: 271–73; Lim 2007:
10. For a synoptic list showing the attestation of various verses of Deuteronomy, see
Martone 2001: 48–62. See also, as an addition to the lists of Tov and Dahmen, the an-
nouncement of a new fragment of Deuteronomy, possibly Samaritan, by Charlesworth
2008.

they comprised an entire manuscript of what has come to be the canonical Deuteronomy or were simply quotations of some sort, nevertheless in relative terms the significance of these numbers may be maintained. Deuteronomy, it seems, holds a particular appeal for a sect intent on re-actualizing the covenant and purifying Israel.

Deuteronomy also appears in a number of rewritten Bible compositions. In some such manuscripts, the distinction between variant text type and rewritten Bible is difficult to draw, while others are clearly designed to reconfigure and expand on their scriptural inspirations. Arguably even the most rewritten compositions have as their aim the actualization and re-presentation of the original for a new day.[40] Apart from the Temple Scroll, considered more fully above (§ 3.2.2), Deuteronomy features in part in the so-called "Reworked Pentateuch" (for Deuteronomy, see 4Q158 frags 7–8; 4Q364 [Deut 1–14]; 4Q365 frags. 37–38; 4Q366). These manuscripts occasionally conflate Deuteronomy with other texts from Exodus and Numbers, consistent with an aim to harmonize the Torah in order to make it "live-able".[41] Further, several pseudepigraphic compositions are cast as Moses's speech in ways reminiscent of Deuteronomy (1Q22; 4Q375; 4Q376 = 1Q29; cf. also 2Q21). These have been described as "Pseudo-Deuteronomies or Deutero-Deuteronomies" because they imitate Moses's style of speech and subject matter.[42] For example, 4Q375 concerns the detection of the false prophet and draws explicitly on Deuteronomy 13 and 18. Instead, however, of the means there prescribed, apparently the prophet is to be brought before the priest who performs a rite to test the validity of

---

[40] The term "rewritten Bible" was apparently first coined by Geza Vermes (1973: 95). The term is, as most recognize, problematic due to the lack of a clearly defined canon (i.e., a "Bible") in the late Second Temple period (so Crawford 2000a; Najman 2003b: 7–9; Campbell 2005; Bernstein 2005), though the basic concept of the rewriting of scripturally authoritative documents has been embraced by the same scholars. Whether the rewriting of Scripture should be seen as an activity (so Harrington 1986: 243; Brooke 2000) or as a genre (Alexander 1988b; Bernstein 2005) has been a source of contention. Cf. further Najman 2003b: 1–69; Fernández Marcos 2006; Fraade 2006b; Falk 2007. As a further matter of complication, some use the terms "rewritten Bible" and "parabiblical texts" as roughly synonymous, while others employ the respective terms to denote differences of genre or degree of modification. Hindy Najman, however, can speak of the "general consensus among scholars who work on Second Temple literature that the essential function of Rewritten Bible is interpretive" (2003b: 7; cf. also 43 n. 8), though such a characterization does not preclude the text's claim to likewise be authoritative. Cf. also Brooke 2000: 780; Falk 2007: 140–53.

[41] 4Q158 frags. 7–8: mixed version of the Decalogue from Exodus and Deuteronomy; 4Q364 frag. 23: Deut 2:8–14 + Num 20:14–18; 4Q366 frags. 3–4: Num 29:12–30:1 + Deut 16:13–14. For details, see Dahmen 2003: 297–300.

[42] See Strugnell 1990: 249.

the prophet's message.[43] Strugnell calls Deuteronomy "an early specimen of the genre,"[44] and, indeed, it is likely that Deuteronomy set the precedent for such later re-imaginings. This suggests that Deuteronomy's characterization of Moses has been adopted, a feature we will also see in our discussion of later texts (e.g., the *Testament of Moses* [§ 4.7 below]). These rewritten compositions thus demonstrate the perceived importance of Deuteronomy for understanding present day needs, as well as displaying a marked tendency to harmonize priestly and Deuteronomic traditions.

3.4. Excerpted Texts, *Tefillin* and *Mezuzot*

In the previous chapter I drew attention to the liturgical role of Deuteronomy in the *tefillin* and *mezuzot* (§ 2.4). It is worth recalling here that the bulk of the Second Temple evidence for such liturgical praxis stems directly from remains found in the caves along the Dead Sea. The so-called "plusses" in comparison to the later Rabbinic requirements for these texts include chiefly the Decalogue and sections of Deuteronomy 6 and 10, with Deuteronomy 32 also appearing. Though excerpted texts were noted in passing in connection with the liturgical use of Deuteronomy, to linger over the specific interpretations of Deuteronomy they suggest helps to give a broader picture of Deuteronomy's role.

Emanuel Tov draws a distinction between excerpted texts and rewritten Bible: "Excerpted texts should be regarded as biblical texts, excerpted for a special purpose, and presented without a commentary, while rewritten Bible texts, whose contents are often very close to what we are used to calling biblical manuscripts, do not pretend to present the text of the Bible."[45] Whether this distinction always holds true is perhaps questionable, as the "Reworked Pentateuch" manuscripts mentioned above may indicate (§ 3.3). Nevertheless, among such excerpted text collections, four are comprised of significant passages from Deuteronomy:

4QDeut[j] (4Q37 = Exod 12:46–51; 13:1–5; Deut 5, 6, 8, 11, 30[?], 32)

4QDeut[kl] (4Q38 = Deut 5, 11, 32)

4QDeut[n] (4Q41 = Deut 8:5–10; 5:1–6:1 + Exod 20:11; cf. Nash Pap)

4QDeut[q] (4Q44 = Deut 32:37–43).[46]

---

[43] For discussion, see Strugnell 1990: 224–34.

[44] Strugnell 1990: 249.

[45] Tov 1995: 583; cf. 583–86.

[46] See Tov 1995; Duncan 1997; and the appendix below. Tov includes also 5QDeut (5Q1 = Deut 7:15–24; 8:5–9:2?), though Duncan does not; it does seem to lack some of

The conclusions reached earlier do not need to be repeated here. Suffice it to say that, judging from the significant overlap of these texts with those found in the *tefillin* and *mezuzot*, the widespread conclusion that these texts served a devotional or liturgical function appears justified.[47]

Here, however, an excerpted text collection from Qumran that preserves the only extant "exegetical-ideological anthology"[48] of biblical passages is of interest. *4QTestimonia* (4Q175) quotes, in succession, Exod 20:21b according to the Samaritan Pentateuch (=Deut 5:28–29+18:18–19); Num 24:15–17; Deut 33:8–11; and 4QapocrJoshua (4Q379), a sort of pesher on Josh 6:26.[49] The lack of explicit interpretative comments, however, leaves the significance of these passages in the realm of implication. It has been suggested that the first three texts speak of various aspects of a single Messiah (the prophetic, the royal, the priestly),[50] or three different eschatological figures (i.e., the prophet, the Messiah of Israel and the Messiah of Aaron),[51] while the last quotation identifies three negative eschatological figures.[52] Conversely, the messianic interpretation of the text has been questioned,[53] and it may be that the lack of a fuller context prohibits a definitive decision as to the sense of the excerpted text collection. Nevertheless, to claim that the text concerns itself with eschatological actors is de-

---

the characteristics of other excerpted texts, not to mention providing the sole example of Deut 7 in an excerpted text. On these as excerpted texts, see also White 1990a, 1990b; Eshel 1991.

[47] So Tov 1995; Duncan 1997.

[48] So Tov 1995.

[49] For the text, see Allegro 1956: 182–87; Allegro 1968: 57–60 (pl. XXI); and esp. the important remarks and corrections of Strugnell 1970: 225–29; see further Fitzmyer 1971; Cross 2002.

[50] So Allegro 1956: 187.

[51] See Brooke 1985: 309–10 for a survey of those who hold to the position. Num 24:15–17 is also cited in CD 7:18–21 and 1QM 11.6–7, though in the former it apparently refers to two figures, the "Interpreter of the Law" (דורש התורה) and "the Prince of the whole congregation" (נשיא כל העדה). On the "Messiahs of Aaron and Israel," note 1QS 9.11; CD 12.23–13.1; 14.19; cf. *T.Sim.* 7:1–2; *T.Jud.* 21:1–3.

[52] H. Eshel (1992) suggests that "in *4QTest*, the pesher appears to have been composed for its context and *4Q379* quoted from *4QTest*" (412), and he highlights a possible historical background in John Hyrcanus I and his two sons, Antigonus and Aristobulus I, who died in 103 BCE. This is possible, but it does introduce a certain awkwardness in the character of the document that otherwise consists purely of quotations.

[53] See, e.g., Lübbe 1986, who points to some weaknesses in the messianic interpretation, though his own constructive proposal that the document concerns merely fidelity and apostasy in general terms is hardly more convincing. Note also Joseph Fitzmyer's questioning of his earlier messianic interpretation of 4Q175 (2000: 98–100). But see Zimmermann (1998: 436): "4Q175 ist ‚messianisch‘ in dem Sinne, daß diejenigen Funktionen bzw. Ämter zur Sprache kommen, die in anderen Texten aus Qumran und z. T. im Frühjudentum einem ‚Gesalbten‘ zugeschrieben werden konnten."

fensible in light of the explicit focus on individual figures occurring in forward-looking passages of the Torah, regardless of whether such figures may be described as explicitly messianic. To inquire about the role of Deuteronomy in the text is complicated by the fact that the first text cited is apparently drawn from the traditional association of Deut 5:28 and 18:18–19, which occur together at Exod 20:21b in the Samaritan Pentateuch (cf. also 4Q158 frag. 6). If the text is conceived of as coming from Exodus, the scriptural order is retained in the citations: Exodus, Numbers, Deuteronomy (and Joshua?). But we know that both Deut 5:28 and 18:18–19 occurred in the biblical manuscripts at Qumran in their respective places in Deuteronomy, and to suggest a dichotomy in their derivation (Exodus, not Deuteronomy) may not do justice to the multiplicity of attestation (Exodus and Deuteronomy). At the very least the citation suggests that such description as is also found in Deut 5:28 and 18:18–19 was read as looking forward to a positive prophetic figure. The third citation, that from Deut 33:8–11, provides a similar forward-looking description of a Levitical figure.[54] What is more, the blessing requested for this third figure (19: ברך) functions to offset and call forth the final curse of the negative figure, the foil for the preceding three (22: ארור). In this way, the text participates in the fundamental blessing vs. curse polarity that is one of the pervasive marks of Deuteronomy's influence on the Qumran literature.

What, then, can we infer about Deuteronomy's reception in this excerpted text collection? What conceptualizations inform and suggest the reading evidenced? Deuteronomy, apparently, supplies one or two pages of the eschatological script, and in particular may specify the function if not the precise identity of one or two key positive actors. In addition, perhaps, it provides the binary polarization of blessing vs. curse to separate the divinely favored *dramatis personae* from the disapproved. The text is enormously suggestive, even if its interpretation is not obvious. Deuteronomy was not written for its own day alone, but already discloses the decisive actions and actors of a coming future.

3.5. Conclusion: Deuteronomy at Qumran

Doubtless it would be possible to multiply examples of citations of or allusions to Deuteronomy in various manuscripts, or to find other citations that do not fit comfortably under any of the rubrics we have so far used.[55] Nev-

---

[54] On the textual character of this citation, see Duncan 1995.

[55] For example, 11Q13 2.2–9 is an eschatological interpretation of Deut 15:2 with reference to Melchizedek, and it is not immediately apparent how this would be related

ertheless, the following conclusions can be drawn from the preceding survey. The high number of manuscripts of Deuteronomy at Qumran provides an initial indication of its importance, as does its presence in "rewritten Bible" manuscripts: the last book of the Pentateuch serves as an important resource to the sect, the subject of study and reflection in the liturgical act of Sabbath reading (4Q264a I.4–5) and the constant periods of study devoted to it in order to arrive at correct halakhic judgments (1QS 6). This liturgical setting is further enhanced when note is taken of the expanded *tefillin* and *mezuzot* found among the Qumran manuscripts. Asking about the context of the encounter with the scroll of Deuteronomy at Qumran leads one directly to liturgical and practical spheres.

What is more, the rewritten Bible manuscripts, together with other Moses-pseudepigrapha, display a marked interest in the Deuteronomic characterization of Moses; indeed, their own portrayals of Moses appear to be consciously modeled on the portrait emerging from Deuteronomy. Further, Deuteronomy emerges as a fundamental document regulating the covenant both in terms of entrance to that covenant and in terms of defining apostasy from it. In this sense, it fulfills the function of policing the borders of the covenant, as it were. Deuteronomy also provides rich fodder for sectarian consideration of what it might mean to live in fidelity to their God. This legal authority, however, does not exercise a straightforward constraint, but is accessed through actualizing interpretations of the Torah that seek to clarify the obscure or harmonize with other authoritative texts or traditions.

Moreover, we see an attempt to understand the history of Israel on the basis of Deuteronomy's own diagnosis and prognosis as the blessing and curse polarity reflected in the covenant ceremony is transposed into a diachronic evaluation of Israel's history. At least in the form found in MMT, this strategy is used to urge renewed fidelity to the Torah as the means by which to secure blessing and avoid curse. Finally, Deuteronomy is seen as a word that encompasses the future as it functions as a word to the present. This is seen in varied ways in the eschatological excerpted text collection 4Q175 on the one hand, and the actualizing of the Temple Scroll on the other. In all of these instances, appeal to the authority of Deuteronomy is achieved in various ways: in the act of reading and hearing of the biblical manuscripts, in binding the text to one's body in the *tefillin*, in expanding the text in the Reworked Pentateuch, in writing with the voice of Deuteronomy to express the divine will for today (Temple Scroll), in explicitly appealing to the words that "the Lord spoke to Moses" about an eschatological prophet (4Q175) and in stipulating the re-actualization of the cove-

---

to our developing typology (though perhaps as an eschatological text it does share certain similarities with 4Q175).

nant ceremony in what is understood as a re-promulgation of Deuteronomy's vision for the Israel of their own day (1QS 2). The form of the appeal differs, but the authority and relevance of Deuteronomy remains constant.

From these literary remains from the Judean desert we now turn to consider selected texts from among the Apocrypha and the Pseudepigrapha, and to ask whether in the variety of these works it is possible to discern a fundamentally similar Deuteronomic pattern.

Chapter 4

Deuteronomy in Apocrypha and Pseudepigrapha

4.1. Introduction: A Deuteronomic Pattern?

The varied texts that we have come to call the Apocrypha and Pseudepigrapha range broadly in their dating, authorship, provenance, and theological perspective, often bound together more from a view to convenience than any kind of genetic relationship. Nevertheless, it has been proposed that some of these books display a similar pattern of indebtedness to the final chapters of Deuteronomy, and such works come under examination here. Identifying holistic construals of Deuteronomy in these texts is necessarily a subtle process in light of their form and their method of incorporating Deuteronomy, but a Deuteronomic influence is clearly present in some of these works. Caution must be exercised, however, in recognizing that not every citation of Deuteronomy entails an engagement with the whole.[1] George Nickelsburg has repeatedly highlighted such Deuteronomic influence, going so far as to speak of a "pattern" which is "drawn from Deuteronomy 28–32" (2006: 222). This pattern essentially consists of the following elements: God gives the law to Israel and decrees blessings for obedience and curses for disobedience; Israel sins; the curses fall upon Israel as punishment; in distress Israel repents and returns to the law; God vindicates Israel (Nickelsburg 2006: 222). Before examining some major witnesses to such a pattern – Tobit, Baruch, and the *Testament of Moses* –

---

[1] For example, 4 Maccabees explicitly cites Deuteronomy twice (Deut 33:3 in 4 Macc. 17:19 and Deut 32:39 in 4 Macc. 18:18–19), but that author's aim is more explicitly an act of philosophical apologetics (cf. 1:1–12), and he or she appears less indebted to an overarching reading of Deuteronomy, perhaps approaching Deuteronomy through 2 Maccabees. *4 Ezra* has been cited as an example of a work indebted to a strictly "Deuteronomic" action-and-consequence scenario – in this case a remarkably pessimistic scenario (Hofmann 2003: 332–36; Watson 2004: 474–513). While certain parallels of thought are undeniable (e.g., sin as violation of the law, national disaster as a result of disobedience, etc.), many of these are not specific to Deuteronomy but may be found throughout the Hebrew Bible. It would be possible to demonstrate certain parallels in 4 Ezra especially to Deut 29–30 (e.g., *4 Ezra* 3:20–27; 14:6, etc.) but in general specific textual indebtedness to Deuteronomy is difficult to discern. The same might be said for some of the other texts that Nickelsburg 2006 includes in his typology of Deuteronomic influence, esp. Sirach, Judith, the Psalms of Solomon and 2 Baruch.

it is worth briefly examining three texts in which Deuteronomy functions notably, even if somewhat less prominently.

4.2. *Jubilees*

The book of *Jubilees*, probably composed in the mid-2nd c. BCE, comprises a rewriting of Genesis 1 – Exodus 24.[2] *Jubilees* begins its rewriting with a strikingly Deuteronomic prologue. As in Exod 24:12, Moses is beckoned to the top of Mount Sinai to receive the law (1:1–4a). In *Jub.* 1:4b–25, Moses is provided with an overview of Israel's history with clear departures from Exodus and similarities to Deuteronomy, especially Deuteronomy 30–31 (see Charles 1913: 11–13 nn.; Brooke 1997c: 49; VanderKam 2000: 267; Lambert 2006). Moses is told in advance that once the Israelites enter the land, "they will eat and be satisfied, and they will turn to strange gods who will not save them from any distresses" (*Jub.* 1:7b–8a),[3] clearly echoing Deut 31:20. The Israelites will then hear the account being revealed to Moses "as testimony against them" (*Jub.* 1:8b), rhetorically positioning *Jubilees* in the same position as the Song that Moses receives in Deuteronomy as a testimony against Israel (Deut 32), itself closely associated with the law in their mutual function as "witness" (31:20–29). Though the Lord will send his prophets to warn Israel, she will remain in rebellion and so will be scattered among the nations (*Jub.* 1:13; cf. Deut 4:27). Afterward, however, "they will turn to me from among the nations with all their heart and with all their soul and with all their might. And I shall gather them from the midst of all the nations" (*Jub.* 1:15; cf. 1:15–18),[4] a hope with strongly Deuteronomic roots (e.g., 4:29–30; 30:1–4; cf. Deut 28:13–14 with *Jub.* 1:16b). Moses, however, then interrupts in order to intercede with God for the people (*Jub.* 1:19–21), perhaps remi-

---

[2] Note the survey of scholarly opinion concerning the date in Segal 2007: 35–41 (though note his own demurral in light of his particular redactional theory on pp. 319–22). See also the survey of chief concerns of *Jubilees* in Segal 2007: 6–11; VanderKam 2008. The inclusion of *Jubilees* in this category, rather than under the writings preserved among the Dead Sea Scrolls is admittedly somewhat arbitrary, especially given the fact that the Temple Scroll was considered in the previous chapter. For the sake of convenience, however, it is included in the present chapter, especially in light of the historical consciousness which its author uses Deuteronomy to express.

[3] Translations from Wintermute 1985, slightly modified. Cf. VanderKam and Milik 1994 for fragments of *Jubilees* 1 from Qumran (4Q216, cols. I–IV). Here, with VanderKam and Milik's suggestions:

(4.—II.3) ואכלו ושב‹ע›ו[ופנו] אחד אלהים אחר[ים אשר לא יושיעום מכל מ[צוכית

[4] Only partially preserved in 4Q216 II.17:

ואחרי כן ישובו] אלי מתוך הגוי[ם בכל לבם]

niscent of Deut 9:26–27 (so Lambert 2006). In response, God assures Moses that his divine initiative will ensure that Israel will return to him, though this can only be after they "acknowledge their sin and the sins of their fathers" (*Jub.* 1:22).[5] Once such acknowledgement has been made, however, God will circumcise their hearts in order for Israel to obey the law fully (*Jub.* 1:22–25; cf. Deut 30:6). The movement of the chapter is clear: Israel sins, endures punishment, remembers God and acknowledges her sin, and finally experiences divine blessing once more (so Berger 1981: 314 n. 6a). The ultimate divine blessing, moreover, undergirds their obedience with divine initiative and oversight, thus transcending a mere "return to the law" and the concomitant fragility of human obedience. Thus this overview of history in advance, by now becoming a familiar *topos* from the final chapters of Deuteronomy, stands at the introduction to the book of *Jubilees* as a striking inducement for Israel to remember her God in the midst of distress and to hope for renewed divine action on her behalf.

4.3. Second Maccabees

Next, a case that is worth considering because of the questions it raises as to how we ascertain a holistic reading of or indebtedness to Deuteronomy: 2 Maccabees.[6] Presenting itself as an epitome of Jason of Cyrene's larger work (2:19–32), 2 Maccabees tells the story of the conflicts between To-rah-observant Jews and Hellenizing rulers under the Seleucid kings Antio-chus IV Epiphanes to Demetrius I (Habicht 1976: 167–69; Goldstein 1983). It is fair to say that Deuteronomic influence on the book is less per-vasive than most of the other literature surveyed in this chapter, at least in terms of textual evidence. Deuteronomy is cited explicitly only once, in the description of the torture suffered by one of the seven brothers in 2 Macc 7:5–6:

The body was now completely helpless, but the king ordered that he be brought, still breathing, to the fire and fried. As the odor of frying began to spread widely, the brothers and their mother exhorted one another to die noble, saying, "The LORD God looks on

---

[5] Lambert 2006 argues that *Jubilees* 1 does not evince an interest in "repentance," but shows a singular stress on divine agency. While Lambert has correctly indicated that *Jubilees* emphasizes the priority of divine action, he does not sufficiently account for *Jub.* 1:22 (his argument on pp. 645–46 notwithstanding). In the end, his study serves as a cau-tion against applying an anachronistic account of "repentance" to *Jubilees* (one that lays undue stress on human initiative and autonomy), but does not successfully exclude *Jubi-lees* 1 from exhibiting a Deuteronomic paradigm.

[6] See Williams 2003 for recent approaches to the book.

and truly is relenting concerning us, as Moses declared in the Song Which Confronts as a Witness: "And He will relent concerning His servants" (διὰ τῆς κατὰ πρόσωπον ἀντιμαρτυρούσης ᾠδῆς διεσάφησε Μωυσῆς λέγων Καὶ ἐπὶ τοῖς δούλοις αὐτοῦ παρακληθήσεται).[7]

The most striking aspect of the citation is the identification of Deuteronomy 32 as "the Song Which Confronts as a Witness," a title that clearly acknowledges the broader contextual indications in Deuteronomy that Moses tells the Song to Israel to witness against them (e.g., Deut 31:19, 21; 32:46; cf. 31:26, 28). Others, however, have suggested that the influence of Deuteronomy 32 extends beyond this citation: D. Schwartz has suggested that "anyone familiar with 2 Maccabees who reads Deut. 32 will find it difficult, if not irresponsible, to avoid the conclusion that this song informed our author's thought very thoroughly" (1998: 229), noting a "sin-punishment-reconciliation" theme which he suggests is derived from Deuteronomy 32. Given the widespread influence of the latter chapters of Deuteronomy as documented in this chapter, this is entirely possible, but the evidence is admittedly less straightforward than in some other roughly contemporaneous texts.

4.4. Pseudo-Philo

Pseudo-Philo also provides a proleptic overview of Israel's history in his *Liber Antiquitatum Biblicarum*.[8] In the midst of his sprawling re-telling of Israel's history, Ps-Philo does not tend to favor Deuteronomy explicitly. In one place, however, in *LAB* 19, we find his most concentrated engagement with Deuteronomy. In narrative terms, the chapter comes after the bulk of the first four books of the Pentateuch (with numerous omissions and additions) has been retold. Rather than incorporating material from the legal portions of Deuteronomy or even the Ten Commandments or the *Shema'*,[9]

---

[7] The translation is from Goldstein 1983, the Greek text from Hanhart 1976.

[8] Pseudo-Philo's *LAB* was most likely composed in Palestine during the latter half of the first century CE. It only survives in Latin translation and, while there are occasional dissenting voices, most agree that the text was originally composed in Hebrew, translated into Greek, and subsequently translated from Greek into Latin. See Harrington 1970; Feldman 1971: xxv–xxvii; Jacobson 1996, etc. In the following, the Latin text is taken from Harrington, et al. 1976.

[9] Although it should be noted that in *LAB* 56:1–2 is recounted the "fulfillment" of Moses' commandments concerning the king in Deut 17:15. The Decalogue, moreover, comes in the narrative retelling of Exodus (*LAB* 11:6–13), though with "theft" strangely omitted (Jacobson 196: 473–74 suggests a textual corruption of this section). The Decalogue also recurs in 44:6–7 in the order Theft-Murder-Adultery (cf. Jer 7:9 and Harrington 1985: 358 note *ad loc*).

the chapter is concerned with the last days of Moses. Specifically, Moses first testifies against Israel for their recalcitrance, foretelling their rebellion and punishment (19:1–5), God then adds a divinely sanctioned expansion and restatement of Moses's testimony (19:6), and Moses intercedes with God to have mercy on his people (19:8–9), to which God agrees (19:10–11). The chapter concludes with an account of Moses's death outside the promised land,[10] burial by the hand of God, and the angelic mourning which follows on his death (19:12–16). This, then, is chiefly based on the progression found in Deuteronomy 31–34, like the *Testament of Moses* (see § 4.7 below). While a number of texts have influenced Ps-Philo's composition in this section of his work,[11] Deuteronomy is the chief source.[12] Even though in the work as a whole the interest is in Moses *qua* Moses rather than in Deuteronomy *per se*, a strikingly integrative reading of Deuteronomy may be observed in *LAB* 19:4: Moses says, "I call to witness against you today heaven and earth" (*ego autem hodie testor vobis celum et terram*), a clear reminiscence of Deut 32:1. To establish the culpability of the Israelites, Ps-Philo cites Deut 5:27 indicating their acceptance of the covenant: "And you will remember, you wicked ones; for when I spoke to you, you answered, saying, 'All that God has said to us, we will do and hear (*Omnia que locutus est nobis Deus faciemus et audiemus*). But if we transgress or grow corrupt in our ways, you will recall this as a witness against us, and he will cut us off'." But perhaps more impressive than this reading of two different parts of Deuteronomy together in service of the whole is the way the movement of the chapter models itself after that found in Deuteronomy. Notably absent, however, from Ps-Philo's account is any retelling of Israel's repentance. As F. Murphy writes, "Restoration depends upon repentance in Deut. 30:1–2, but not in

---

[10] Ps-Philo offers the unique reason for Moses's death outside the promised land: "you will not enter it in this age lest you see the graven images with which this people will start to be deceived and led off the path" (19:7; translation from Harrington 1985), on which note Murphy 1993: 91; Jacobson 1996: 623. Fisk suggests that this may in fact be a result of Ps-Philo's exegesis of certain passages in Deuteronomy itself (i.e., 1:37; 3:26; 4:21; see Fisk 2001: 269–70).

[11] One striking difference from Deuteronomy is seen in that, in Deuteronomy, the curse is that the people will be dispersed from the land of Israel (e.g., Deut 4:27; 28:64–68; 30:1), in *LAB* 19:2 God is the one who leaves the land (*et irascetur Deus in vobis, et derelinquet vos, et discedet de terra vestra*), a change perhaps motivated by texts like Ezek 10:18–19.

[12] In addition to the following, note that *LAB* 19:2 mostly paraphrases Deut 31:16–18, but the threat of God sending enemies against them is from Deut 28:48–49; 19:3 recalls Deut 29:21 (EVV 29:22); 19:4 echoes Deut 30:19, 31:28, and 32:1; 19:5 compresses Deuteronomy 33 into a single line (*Et nunc ecce ego benedico tribus vestras, antequam finis meus veniat*); 19:6–7 depends on Deut 31:15–21 and 32:48–52; 19:10–16 retell and expand Deut 34 (cf. Jacobson 1996: 614–18; Fisk 2001: 264–81).

LAB 19" (1993: 90). Actually, however, this may not indicate a departure from Deuteronomy, but rather may show that Ps-Philo follows Deuteronomy 32, which does not mention human repentance but only divine action, rather than Deuteronomy 30. This would, moreover, be consistent with Ps-Philo's chief interest in Deut 31–34 in *LAB* 19. Though Israel is apparently doomed to sin, in the fullness of time (cf. *LAB* 19:14–15), God will act unilaterally to redeem his people in accordance with the covenant he has made with them, and not in response to human repentance.[13]

4.5. Tobit

The apocryphal Book of Tobit, most likely composed in the latter half of the 3rd c. BCE for Jews in the Eastern Diaspora (Otzen 2002: 57–59; Ego 2005; Bauckham 2008), displays a Deuteronomic influence in both its model of piety and its historical consciousness.[14] The book has been described as "an Israelite religious *novella*" that offers a parable about Israel's fate as a nation, from exile to restoration, by means of telling a story about a particular family in Diaspora (so esp. Bauckham 2008). The story takes place in an exilic setting, due to the apostasy of the northern tribes (1:3–5, 10), though the main protagonist, Tobit, is himself righteous (1:6–8). In fact, his obedience is specifically that commanded in Deuteronomy in reference to a number of distinct practices: bringing the first fruits (Deut 16:16; cf. Exod 23:14–17) to Jerusalem (Deut 12:10–14) to share with the priests (Deut 18:4), a second tithe to spend in Jerusalem (Deut 14:24–27) and a third to share with the poor, the orphans, the widows, and the sojourners (Deut 14:28–29).[15] Tobit falls into disfavor with the king when he is caught burying the bodies of executed Jews (1:17–20; 2:3–8; perhaps in line with Deut 21:22–23?). He also celebrates Pentecost and invites the poor to celebrate (cf. Deut 16:9–11, where the celebration is explicitly connected to sharing with the poor). Further, Tobit urges his son, "Do not keep over until the next day the wages of those who work for you, but pay them at once" (4:14; cf. Deut 24:14–15; Lev 19:13), a command that is later exemplified in the prompt payment of Azariah/Raphael (12:1–5). To-

---

[13] Ps-Philo's symbol for the covenant in *LAB* 19 is Moses's staff (see esp. 19:11). Why this symbol is chosen need not detain us, but for various suggestions see Murphy 1993: 94; Jacobson 1996: 638–39; Fisk 2001: 276–81.

[14] Many scholars have noted the role that Deuteronomy plays in Tobit; note esp. Di Lella 1979; Soll 1989: 219–31; Weitzman 1996; Moore 1996: 20; Fitzmyer 2003: 36, 47, 305; Hofmann 2003: 311–26; Bauckham 2008; Kiel 2008.

[15] It should be noted that the precise tithes are a matter of some debate (see Moore 1996: 108–115), though Josephus knows of three tithes in *Ant.* 4.240.

bit's exhortation to his son concludes with this: "So now, my child, remember these commandments, and do not let them be erased from your heart (καὶ νῦν, παιδίον, μνημόνευε τὰς ἐντολὰς ταύτας [G¹: τῶν ἐντολῶν μου], καὶ μὴ ἐξαλειφθήτωσαν ἐκ τῆς καρδίας σου)" (4:19), a charge that recalls the similar exhortations in Deut 6:6; 11:18.[16] Of course, Tobit is not solely indebted to Deuteronomy for its ethical vision, but it does seem that there has been a sapiential appropriation of Deuteronomic ideals (Collins 2005: 29), a fact more striking when brought into conjunction with the second Deuteronomic emphasis, that of its historical consciousness.

This Deuteronomic consciousness in fact lends the book its theological punch, esp. in chapters 13–14, without which it might remain a mere folkloristic tale of marriages and exorcisms. There are, however, earlier indications that Tobit addresses itself to the same plight as Deuteronomy. As noted above, the story is set in exile (Tob. 1:3–4), the paradigmatic punishment for disobedience to Deuteronomy's Torah. What is more, as Tobit himself experiences progressive hardships in this exilic setting, he complains to the Lord with a prayer that, like other penitential prayers (e.g., Dan 9; Ezra 9; Neh 9) has a Deuteronomic ring to it: "They sinned against you, and disobeyed your commandments. So you gave us over to plunder, exile, and death, to become the talk, the byword, and an object of reproach among all the nations among whom you have dispersed us (καὶ παρήκουσα τῶν ἐντολῶν σου, καὶ ἔδωκας ἡμᾶς εἰς ἁρπαγὴν καὶ αἰχμαλωσίαν καὶ θάνατον καὶ εἰς παραβολὴν καὶ λάλημα καὶ ὀνειδισμὸν ἐν πᾶσιν τοῖς ἔθνεσιν, ἐν οἷς ἡμᾶς διεσκόρπισας)" (3:3–4).[17] It is not, however, until chapters 13–14 that Tobit's individual plight and example explicitly become a type of Israel's exile and hoped-for restoration (cf. Soll 1989: 230).

Like Moses, Tobit receives a command to write down these things (12:20), after which he declares in "words of praise" a poetic song (cf.

---

[16] The textual history of Tobit is complicated. See, e.g., Fitzmyer 2003: 3–17; and note the two synopses by C. J. Wagner 2003 and Weeks, Gathercole, and Stuckenbruck 2004; a critical edition of the Greek recensions may be found in Hanhart 1983; the Qumran fragments, four Aramaic and one Hebrew (4Q196–200) in DJD 19 (Fitzmyer 1995): 1–76. The two main Greek recensions are the shorter, represented by Alexandrinus and Vaticanus and conventionally cited as G¹, and the longer version of Sinaiticus, cited as G¹¹. In general the Qumran manuscripts agree with the longer Greek recension preserved in Sinaiticus, the Vetus Latina, et al. Tobit was probably originally composed in Aramaic in the late 3rd or early 2nd c. BCE, but potentially translated into Hebrew quite early (see the discussion in Moore 1996; Fitzmyer 2003). For the passages here quoted the Hebrew or Aramaic is very fragmentary; thus, the Greek text is supplied, though this has been checked against the Hebrew and Aramaic where available.

[17] This is probably the better reading. The shorter Greek recension (G¹) reads παρήκουσαν γὰρ τῶν ἐντολῶν σου, καὶ ἔδωκας ἡμᾶς εἰς διαρπαγὴν καὶ αἰχμαλωσίαν καὶ θάνατον καὶ παραβολὴν ὀνειδισμοῦ πᾶσιν τοῖς ἔθνεσιν, ἐν οἷς ἐσκορπίσμεθα.

Deut 31:16–32:43; Weitzman 1996: 51–53). Though the song is ostensibly addressed as praise to God, it includes a striking rendition of the Deuteronomic pattern: "He will afflict you for your iniquities, but he will again show mercy on all of you. He will gather you from all the nations among whom you have been scattered. If you turn to him with all your heart and with all your soul, to do what is true before him, then he will turn to you and will no longer hide his face from you" (13:5–6; cf. Deut 30:1–10).[18] Tobit as a figure thus serves to rebuke Israel for her sin and to recall her to fidelity, in light of the impending judgment and restoration – a pattern that also carries over into chapter 14 (note, e.g., 14:5–6, and 14:8–9 in G[II]).[19] In this light, it seems that Tobit is intended, at least in its final redaction, to address an Israel in the situation toward which the latter chapters of Deuteronomy look, and to renew a hope for restoration achieved by divine fidelity in response to renewed obedience of the law.

4.6. Baruch

The apocryphal book of Baruch shares with Tobit a concern with exile and return. Probably composed sometime between the mid-2nd c. BCE and mid-1st c. CE, it is often assigned to as many as four different hands, though the final shape of the text is coherent and the evidence that Baruch is a composite work need not determine its interpretation.[20] In fact, even if the work is composite, it is "bound together by the common theme of exile

---

[18] 13:5–6 G[II]: μαστιγώσει ὑμᾶς ἐπὶ ταῖς ἀδικίαις ὑμων καὶ πάντας ὑμᾶς ἐλεήσει ἐκ πάντων τῶν ἐθνῶν, ὅπου ἂν διασκορπισῆτε ἐν αὐτοῖς. ὅταν ἐπιστρέψητε πρὸς αὐτὸν ἐν ὅλῃ τῇ καρδίᾳ ὑμῶν καὶ ἐν ὅλῃ τῇ ψυχῇ ὑμῶν ποιῆσαι ἐνώπιον αὐτοῦ ἀλήθειαν, τότε ἐπιστρέψει πρὸς ὑμᾶς καὶ οὐ μὴ κρύψῃ τὸ πρόσωπον αὐτοῦ ἀφ᾽ ὑμῶν οὐκέτι. 13:5–6 G[I]: καὶ μαστιγώσει ἡμᾶς ἐν ταῖς ἀδικίαις ἡμῶν καὶ πάλιν ἐλεήσει καὶ συνάξει ἡμᾶς ἐκ πάντων τῶν ἐθνῶν, οὗ ἐὰν σκορπισθῆτε ἐν αὐτοῖς. ἐὰν ἐπιστρέψητε πρὸς αὐτὸν ἐν ὅλῃ καρδίᾳ ὑμῶν καὶ ἐν ὅλῃ τῇ ψυχῇ ποιῆσαι ἐνώπιον αὐτοῦ ἀλήθειαν, τότε ἐπιστρέψει πρὸς ὑμᾶς καὶ οὐ μὴ κρύψῃ τὸ πρόσωπον αὐτοῦ ἀφ᾽ ὑμῶν.

[19] Di Lella 1979 sees nine major correspondences between Deuteronomy and Tob. 14:3–11 (here with only representative references): 1) Long life in the good land and prosperity dependent on fidelity (e.g., Deut 4:40; 30:6; 31:29; Tob 14:4). 2) The offer of mercy after sin and judgment (Deut 30:1–4; Tob 14:4–6); 3) Rest and security in the land (Deut 12:10–11; Tob 14:7). 4) The blessing of joy (Deut 12:12; Tob 14:7). 5) Fear and love of God (Deut 6:5, 13; 10:12–13; Tob 14:6–7, 9). 6) The command to bless and praise God (Deut 8:10; 32:3, 43; Tob 14:9). 7) Theology of remembering (Deut 5:15; 32:7; Tob 14:7, 9). 8) Centralization of cult (Deut 12:1–14; 16:6; Tob 1:4–6; 14:5, 7). 9) Final exhortation (Deut 30:15–20; Tob 14:9–11).

[20] For further discussion of possible sources and introductory issues, note Eissfeldt 1965: 592–94; Gunneweg 1975; Moore 1977: 255–316; Steck 1993; Watson 2004: 456–57 n. 71; Nickelsburg 2005: 94–97.

and return, which is often expressed in biblical idiom" (Nickelsburg 2005: 94). After a historical introduction that indicates the setting of the book in the Babylonian exile, i.e., in Deuteronomy's proverbial place of punishment (note esp. 1:1–9), there follows a long confession of sin (1:15–2:10; note also 1:13). This is intertwined with an acknowledgement that the punishments that have come upon the people are in accordance with the curses detailed by Moses (1:20: τὰ κακὰ καὶ ἡ ἀρά ἥν συνέταξε κύριος τῷ Μωυσῇ παιδὶ αὐτοῦ; 2:2–5: κατὰ τὰ γεγραμμένα ἐν τῷ νόμῳ Μωυσῆ).[21] The first major half of the book is completed by petition for mercy and restoration (2:11–3:8), together with an appeal to the promised end of exile (2:27–35). The Deuteronomic pattern is clear, though it is also refracted through the densely intertextual lens of Baruch's reading of Scripture – most notably, in this section, through the (also very Deuteronomic) prayer of Dan 9:4–19 (see Moore 1977: 291–93). It is striking that the curses that Moses details in Deut 28 become the historiographical lens to interpret Israel's history, even as the following promise of restoration shows the way forward together with the assurance that restoration has been decreed and made known in advance (esp. 2:27–35).

The second major half of Baruch, a poem on wisdom (3:9–5:9) is less explicitly bound to Deuteronomy but nevertheless exhibits the same basic structure as the first half, together with a few striking verbal reminiscences of Deuteronomy. The poem begins by asking the question, "Why is Israel in exile?" and answers that she has forsaken wisdom, i.e., the Torah (the two are explicitly identified in 4:1; cf. 3:9)[22] which is the way to life (3:9–4:4). The poem then appeals to the scheme of history in Deut 32 to explain the deliverance to a foreign nation (note the clear echo in 4:7 of Deut 32:16–17)[23] and suggests that restoration like that described in Second Isaiah is to follow (4:5–5:9).[24] Striking in both halves of Baruch is the role that the law plays in restoration. It is not, however, as is sometimes suggested, that obedience to the law brings blessing *tout simple*. Rather, in the prose prayer the law-abiding response of the people is achieved through a divine enablement, couched largely in terms drawn from Deut 30:1–10 (2:27–35). And in the poem of 3:9–5:9, while there are some suggestions

---

[21] Greek text from Ziegler 1957; note attempts at retroversion to the (hypothetical) Hebrew original in Tov 1975 (for 1:1–3:8) and Burke 1982 (for 3:9–5:9).

[22] Also striking is the application in 3:29–30 of Deut 30:12–13 to wisdom, an application that is both aided by and helps to accomplish the process of identifying wisdom as Torah, or perhaps better, Torah as wisdom. The text, of course, makes an interesting comparison with Paul's re-referentialization of Deut 30:12–14 in Rom 10:6–8 (cf. Suggs 1967; further see § 6.5.3 below).

[23] On which note Whitehouse 1913.

[24] The final section also bears a marked similarity to Ps Sol 11:3–8; see Whitehouse 1913: 572–73; Moore 1977: 314–16.

between obedience to the law and life (e.g., 4:1, 28), the dominant note is on the unilateral action of God to re-establish and restore his people in the land.[25] For the author of Baruch, Deuteronomy discloses both Israel's plight and the solution.

4.7. *Testament of Moses*

The *Testament of Moses*, also sometimes referred to as the *Assumption of Moses*, shares an interest in the final chapters of Deuteronomy.[26] Its narrative setting is in Transjordan, when Israel is on the cusp of entering the promised land and Moses calls Joshua to himself to exhort him to leadership.[27] This clearly recalls Deuteronomy 31–34, and the *Testament of Moses* is widely seen to be a rewriting of these chapters.[28] This is not, however, a straightforward retelling, but sets forth a proleptic overview of Israel's history as, for example, *Jubilees* 1 or *LAB* 19. In fact, in *T. Mos.* 1:5 the work is introduced as the book "of the prophecy, which was given by Moses according to the book of Deuteronomy" (*profetiae quae facta est*

---

[25] This reading of Baruch stands in some contrast to that offered by Watson 2004: 454–73.

[26] This text is extant in a single fifth or sixth century Latin palimpsest in Milan, discovered and published by A.-M. Ceriani in 1861, though there are various patristic references to an Assumption or Testament of Moses (for which see Denis 1970a: 63–67; 1970b: 128–41). For the problems of identifying the Testament and Assumption of Moses, note also Grierson 2008 (whose solution, however, is not the only possible one). For our purposes here, we concern ourselves with the extant text of the Latin manuscript, rather than its precise identification with other works (important though this may be for the study of, e.g., Jude 9). For the history of research, as well as the critical edition of the Latin text and translation used here, see Tromp 1993; note also Charles 1897; Laperrousaz 1970; Priest 1983; Hofmann 2000.

[27] Indeed, this lends to the account its "testamentary" nature (note 11:1); see Kolenkow 1973. Its time of composition has been a matter of debate. Some have suggested that it was written in the 1st c. BCE and updated in the 1st c. CE (so, influentially, Nickelsburg 1973) or composed entirely in the 1st c. CE (so, e.g., Tromp 1993; Atkinson 2004). One's position on the literary unity of the document has natural consequences for one's understanding of its date and, to some degree at least, its purpose. But it seems clear that, in its present form, it is written in opposition to Herodian policies, around 4 BCE – 6 CE, possibly in response to Varus' attack on Jerusalem in 4 BCE (for discussion, see Hofmann 2000: 21–32; Atkinson 2004). In this setting (or a similar setting of oppression), its author writes with the dual purpose of encouraging fidelity to the law and offering eschatologically-motivated hope in the midst of opposition. See n. 31 below.

[28] See, e.g., Nickelsburg 1973: 8–10; Harrington 1973; Hofmann 2000; 2003: 326–31; Atkinson 2006: 468–71. Klein 1973, however, suggests that it is almost impossible to identify the textual character of the references to Deuteronomy seen in the work.

a Moysen in libro Deuteronomio; cf. 3:11–12).[29] Moses, presumably because he was "prepared from the beginning of the world to be the mediator
of his covenant" (1:14) is able to divulge the history of Israel to Joshua in
advance as a means of providing encouragement until Israel is finally restored (cf. 1:18; 10:11–12:13). Israel's history is seen to pass through two
cycles of the Deuteronomic pattern.[30] In the first, Israel will begin to sin
(2:3–9), endure the punishment of defeat and exile (3:1–3), recall the prophetic warnings of Moses (3:4–14), and be restored by God to the land of
Israel in response to Daniel's intercession for them (4:1–9). In the second,
Israel again goes into decline under the Hasmoneans (5:1–6) and endures
punishment especially under Herod (6:1–9).[31] This is the point at which the
text passes from a *vaticinium ex eventu* to making actual predictions: the
eschatological suffering will intensify (7:1–8:5) until a righteous Levite
named Taxo chooses to die with his sons rather than to transgress the law
(9:1–7)[32] – thus performing a similar intercessory function as Daniel in
4:1–9 – and so forces God's hand to act to redeem his people and rout Israel's enemies (10:1–10). It is striking that "repentance" comes to be replaced by intercession (so Harrington 1973),[33] though admittedly repentance might be implicit in at least the first cycle (esp. 3:4–14). That the
text ends with an exhortation to obedience, however, should not go unno-

---

[29] Charles suggested that "In a book of Hebrew origin the phrase libro Deuteronomio
could not have been original" (1897: 55; so also Laperrousaz 1970), though a Semitic
original is no longer as foregone a conclusion as perhaps it once was (here, note esp.
Tromp 1993: 135–36). It is also, however, not at all impossible that if the original text
were Hebrew, this might contain a reference to משנה תורה (cf. *Sifre Deut.* § 160).

[30] Confirmation that the text's composer thinks in terms of a twofold scheme may be
seen in 9:2: "See, my sons, behold, a second (*altera*), cruel and unclean retribution is
made against the people, and a punishment without mercy, and it surpasses the first one."

[31] Herod is almost certainly the harsh king who rules "for thirty four years" (6:6) and
whose sons rule after him for shorter periods of time (6:7). This suggests that the *Testament of Moses* was composed or redacted shortly after Herod's death, while his sons
were still reigning. On the date and redaction of the *T.Mos*, see the discussion in the essays by John J. Collins and the response by Nickelsburg in Nickelsburg 1973: 15–43.
Nickelsburg's suggestion of an initial Antiochan composition with a final redaction
around 30 CE has been influential, but Tromp convincingly argues for a first c. CE dating
(1993: 116–17; cf. 120–23); so also Atkinson 2006.

[32] The similarities to 1 and 2 Maccabees (and esp. 2 Macc 7) are striking and may
reflect similar traditions, but that the *Testament of Moses* served as a source for the Maccabean literature is doubtful (*pace* Goldstein 1976: 39–40).

[33] Moses is the intercessor in 11:17; 12:6; cf. *LAB* 19:3: Moses prays for Israel's sin
(*qui in omni tempore oret pro peccatis nostris et exaudiatur pro iniquitatibus nostris*).
For discussion of the theme of Moses as mediator in these writings, see Hafemann 1990;
Horbury 2003.

ticed: "If they therefore do the commandments of God fully,[34] they will grow and prosper. But the sinners and those who neglect the commandments <must> miss the goods that have been foretold, and they will be punished by the nations with many torments" (12:10–11: *Facientes itaque et consummantes mandata Dei crescunt et bonam viam exigunt. Nam peccantibus et neglegentibus mandata <...> carere bona[m] quae praedicta sunt, et punientur a gentibus multis tormentis*).

The large scale setting in the time narrated by the final chapters of Deuteronomy in the transition from Moses to Joshua and the double instantiation of the Deuteronomic pattern are also complemented with a number of discrete textual engagements with the book of Deuteronomy itself.[35] Perhaps the key cluster is found in chapter three, in the midst of the realization of Israel in her punishment that these things have been foretold:

Then, on that day, they will remember me, each tribe saying to the other, and each man to his neighbour: 'Is it not this, the things which Moses formerly testified to us in his prophecies?' (*Nonne hoc est quod testabatur nobis tum Moyses in profetis*)....And having testified, he also called on heaven and earth to be witnesses, lest we should transgress his commandments, which he had mediated to us (*Testatus et invocabat nobis testes caelum et terram, ne praeteriremus mandata illius in quibus arbiter fuit nobis*). But since then, these things have come over us, in accordance with his words and his solemn confirmation (*quae advenerunt nobisde isto secus verba ipsius et secus adfirmationem ipsius*), which he testified to us in those days and which have come true up to our expulsion into the land of the East (3:10–13).

The reference to calling heaven and earth as witnesses suggests Deut 32:1 (cf. 30:19; 31:28), and thus positions the *Testament of Moses* as an actualization of the Song of Moses[36] – or, more accurately, a double actualization of the Song, once in a completed cycle and a second time now that Israel is on the cusp of a hoped-for redemption. Deuteronomy's openness to the future in curse or blessing is seized upon by the author of the *Testament of Moses* as a means of providing encouragement and a vehicle for promoting his own apocalyptic hopes for imminent restoration. As in some of the other voices surveyed in this chapter, the *Testament of Moses* finds in Deuteronomy a means of explaining the present and, what is more, of providing hope for a time of restoration beyond Israel's current troubles.

---

[34] Here I have modified Tromp's rendering "perfectly" to "fully" to avoid the danger of overtranslating *consummantes* (lit.: fulfilling).

[35] In addition to the following and other allusions that could be listed, note that the phrase "they will go whoring after strange gods" (*fornicabunt post deos alienos*) in 5:3 depends on Deut 31:16 (so Charles 1897: 17).

[36] So Hofmann 2003: "Die Geschichtsschau der AM erweist sich als eine Aktualisierung des Moseliedes, die zum rechten Verständnis der Tora in der konkreten geschichtlichen Situation des 1. Jh. n.Chr. anzuleiten vermag" (331; cf. 326–31).

4.8. Conclusion

These apocrypha and pseudepigrapha look to Deuteronomy for an unde-niably similar reason: to make sense of the present difficulty and to gain hope for a better future. That Deuteronomy's last chapters are seen to be the blueprint for the course of Israel's history suggests that it might not be too strong to speak of a Deuteronomic pattern in these texts. Such a pat-tern, however, should not be allowed to screen out the individual differ-ences among the works – at times grounded in differing interpretations of Deuteronomy itself. For example, the question of what effects the turning point toward restoration is answered in varying ways: does God respond to Israel's obedience to the law (so Tobit), act in response to the intercession of the righteous (Pseudo-Philo; *Testament of Moses*), or provide divine en-ablement to return to the law and obey it (Baruch; *Jubilees* 1)? At any rate, it is clear that the Deuteronomic pattern is not necessarily bound to a strict nomism, but that the emphasis can fall on either human initiative or divine deliverance, "vertically, from above." Perhaps it would be possible to claim that one can detect a different use of the Deuteronomic pattern: as diagnosis or as prognosis. The common element is a recognition of a fail-ure to walk in fidelity to the law (diagnosis), but the way forward ranges from renewed nomism (a Deuteronomic prognosis) to an apocalyptic the-ology of restoration (which can also claim a pedigree in Deut 32) – or some mixture of the two.

If we ask more specifically about the types of encounter with Deuteron-omy found in these texts, we notice that Deuteronomy is substantially re-written, especially in *Jubilees* 1, Pseudo-Philo and *Testament of Moses*. These works effectively inhabit the latter chapters of Deuteronomy in an act of imaginative appropriation, viewing history from the proleptic stand-point of Moses and his horizon of vision beyond the Jordan. For Baruch, 2 Maccabees and Tobit, on the other hand, Deuteronomy as the Law of Moses is an authoritative given, a normative interpretation of past history, sure ethical guide (esp. for Tobit) and also, on the basis of its past accu-racy, a faithful indicator of future restoration. From either horizon, how-ever, Deuteronomy is seen to both explain and address the current time of distress.[37]

---

[37] Nickelsburg stresses that these "were composed or have their fictional setting in times of distress.....Through biblical interpretation, historical fiction, prayers, and apoca-lypses, the authors employ or presume the Deuteronomic scheme in order to explain the present circumstances and promise a better future. This present distress is God's punish-ment for disobedience to the Torah, and repentance and obedience to the Torah will turn Israel's fortunes and restore the covenantal blessings" (2006: 232).

From these assorted works that vary in time, place and ideology, we turn our focus now to Alexandria, to a consideration of the last book of Moses in the philosophical exegesis of Philo the Jew.

Chapter 5

Deuteronomy in the Works of Philo of Alexandria

5.1. Introduction

Philo, an Alexandrian Jewish philosopher and statesman who flourished in the first half of the first century CE, wrote voluminously on the Pentateuch.[1] While it was once customary to dismiss Philo's work as that of a syncretistic "Hellenized" thinker who had lost any sense of fidelity to Israel's ancestral structures of belief and practice, scholarship over the past fifty years or so has increasingly stressed that Philo only makes sense as a Jew,[2] and, more specifically, as an *exegete* of Israel's Law.[3] Of course, like that of other ancient interpreters (or modern ones for that matter), Philo's exegesis can hardly be described as disinterested, and part of the fascination of his work lies in seeing the multiform and surprising ways in which the biblical text is made to serve his interpretative ends.

Philo's works show an overwhelming preference for the Pentateuch,[4] and that in Greek translation.[5] It is quite probable that this preference had

---

[1] For introductory surveys, see Goodenough 1962; Sandmel 1979; Borgen 1984a; 1984b; Schenck 2005.

[2] See Birnbaum 2006 for a broad overview of work on Philo's Jewishness.

[3] Peder Borgen, for example, can speak in 1997 of "a growing trend in Philonic scholarship" to consider Philo as an exegete of the Law of Moses (Borgen 1997: 9; cf. 1–13 and Borgen 1984b; Mack 1984; Amir 1988, etc.). The work of Nikiprowetzky (1977) was an important catalyst in such reconsideration of Philo as an exegete. He repeatedly stressed the importance of Scripture for Philo: "le texte de la Bible est le pole essentiel par rapport auquel s'orientent tous les développements philoniens" (1977: 5); "Philon doit être considéré avant tout comme un exégète qui n'exprime ses idées qu'en fonction du texte scripturaire" (1977: 181).

[4] For example, in the supplementary volume of the *Biblia Patristica* devoted to Philo's writings, there are 121 columns of references to the Pentateuch as opposed to roughly 6 for the other writings, most of which are less than explicit quotations; cf. also Amir 1988: 422–23. The status of the other writings for Philo has been a matter of dispute; in 1940, Knox suggested that Philo only knew them from pre-existing sources, but he was promptly refuted by Colson (1940). Recently, Naomi Cohen (2007) has suggested that Philo knew the prophets and the writings in a liturgical setting, though he did not hold them to be of the same importance as the Torah.

[5] Whether Philo knew any Hebrew has been a matter of debate, though most find no evidence that he did. Determining the precise nature of Philo's Greek biblical text has

its origin in the life of the synagogue (so Nikiprowetzky 1977: 174–80; Borgen 1997: 17–18), though admittedly this cannot be proven. It is clear, however, that Philo labored to understand and elucidate the biblical text not so much in strict line-by-line commentary (Hecht 1981: 148), as in a variety of literary forms and works. He is generally credited with having authored two or perhaps three large commentary projects and several smaller uncategorized works. The large works include the Exposition of the Laws of Moses, the Allegorical Commentary on Genesis, and perhaps also the Questions and Answers on Genesis and Exodus. A concern with Deuteronomy means that the first two of these are of greatest interest,[6] though occasionally we will reference his other works.

Any attempt to reduce the rich variation of Philo's philosophical exegesis to a single systematic explanation runs the risk of doing violence to his work and imposing an artificial unity on its manifold form. Nevertheless, we must hazard the attempt to discern the representative ways in which Philo engages Deuteronomy in his various projects, steering a course between the mirrored errors possible when faced with a prolific author like Philo: a discussion of generalities too vague to shed much analytical light on Philo's interpretive practice on the one hand, and an exhaustive catalogue of individual citations that threatens to lose its synthetic power on the other. In what follows, I first examine the ways in which Philo refers to Deuteronomy, seeking in his method of reference indications of how he thereby construes the book. Next, attention is turned to the roles Deuteronomy plays in the Exposition of the Laws of Moses before turning, finally, to examine some of the ways in which Deuteronomy functions in the Allegorical Commentary.

---

been complicated by a complex history of transmission by Christian hands. Ryle (1895) collected Philo's explicit quotations as a witness to the Septuagint, but did not take into account the processes of corruption and transmission (rightly Katz 1950: 132). Katz's study remains the most piercing investigation of the problem, though its results are of nominal relevance to our investigation. Cf. Howard 1973, who argued (unconvincingly in my opinion) against Katz's contention that Philo's text has been contaminated; in support of Katz, note Barthélemy 1978a: esp. 390–91; see also Passoni Dell'Acqua 2003; Kraft 2005. In addition, see Wasserstein and Wasserstein 2006: 35–45 on Philo's adaptation of the Aristeas legend, chiefly in heightening the idea of divine inspiration for the Septuagint.

[6] While Deuteronomy is occasionally referenced in the *Quaestiones*, it does not play the same sort of structural role as it does in the other major works; see the discussion of the subdued role of "secondary texts" in the *Quaestiones* in Runia 1991.

5.2. How Philo Refers to Deuteronomy

While ancient authors seldom identify their sources in a manner sufficiently precise for modern readers accustomed to the culture of the foot-
note, Philo does, from time to time, indicate not simply the author or
speaker, but also the work upon which he is drawing. In fact, Philo is our
first secure witness for all the names of the books of the Pentateuch in
Greek.[7] Philo refers to Deuteronomy as Δευτερονόμιον (cf. Deut 17:18
LXX) in *Leg.* 3.174 and *Deus* 50, and this title later becomes widespread
to refer to the book (cf. *Barn.* 10.2; Swete 1914: 198–214, etc.). He also,
however, apparently refers to Deuteronomy as 'Επινομίς (*Her.* 162, 250;
Spec. 4.160, 164), meaning something like an "appendix" or "an addition
to the law" and possibly modeled after a pseudo-Platonic treatise of that
name.[8] Naomi Cohen doubts whether this applies specifically to Deuteronomy, contending rather that this refers to a compendium of laws (1997b;
2007: 36–53). In light of the fact, however, that the title introduces a quotation from Deuteronomy in *Her.* 162 (Deut 25:13–16) and an allusion in
Her. 250 (Deut 28:28, 29), and especially given that it is used to refer to
the law the king must copy out in compliance with Deut 17:18–20 (*Spec.*
4.160, 164; cf. Josephus, *Ant.* 4.209–11; *Sifre Deut.* § 160), it seems difficult to avoid concluding that Deuteronomy is intended.[9] This title may indicate that Philo sensed the individuality of Deuteronomy in the way it re-

---

[7] See the presentation of the evidence in Cohen 1997b (also in Cohen 2007), though
some of the conclusions she draws from this are tenuous. More broadly, Ryle 1895 is still
useful, esp. xvi–xxxv (on Deut, xxiii–xxiv, 246–82). It is noted as a possibility that Aristobulus's reference to "the explanation of the entire law" (τῆς ὅλης νομοθεσίας
ἐπεξήγησις) refers to Deuteronomy in Dogniez and Harl 1992: 26, with reference to
Aristobulus, frag. 3 in Euseb. *Pr. Ev.* 13.12.1–2. Dogniez and Harl do not appear to support the idea, and Holladay is probably correct in saying that this refers more generally to
Leviticus, Numbers and Deuteronomy (Holladay 1995: 215 n. 75).

[8] So Colson: "As so applied it is not quoted from any other writer, and if the application is due to him it is a reasonable supposition that it is modeled on the pseudo-Platonic
treatise of that name" LCL 8:436; cf. LSJ, s.v. ἐπινομίς.

[9] Cohen's motivation seems to be to minimize any sense of distinction Philo had between the individual books of the Pentateuch. While her contention that some of the
words used to refer to the contents of Deuteronomy are taxonomical categories rather
than titles *per se* is well taken, her conclusion that "although Philo was familiar with the
separate names of the Pentateuchal books...it was *the Pentateuch as a whole and that
alone*, which served as his conceptual unit, as his point of reference" (1997b: 78 = 2007:
52, italics original) is impossible to maintain. Indeed, it is more difficult to make this
argument for Philo than for almost any other ancient writer. Much better is F. Siegert's
contention: "As in the *Epistle of Aristaeus* [*sic*], there are five sacred books and not just
one" (1996: 172), though he rightly goes on to note that "there is no doubt that Philo
views the Pentateuch as a unity, because it has one author" (1996: 173).

capitulates and re-presents the law from a charged rhetorical stance as Moses' last plea to Israel on the verge of entering the promised land.

This impression is confirmed by a number of descriptive generic terms Philo uses to introduce material drawn from Deuteronomy. For example, Philo sometimes introduces a quotation from Deuteronomy or string of allusions with the phrase, Moses "says in his exhortations" (ἐν τοῖς προτρεπτικοῖς φησιν; *Virt.* 47; cf. *Agr.* 78, 172; *Fug.* 142, 170 [though here with reference to Lev 25:11]; *Mut.* 42, 236).[10] It may be granted that this is something less than a full title for Deuteronomy, though it does indicate an important taxonomical judgment about the *content* of the book (Cohen 1997b: 70; 2007: 44). The same might be said for Philo's use of παραινέσεις: on two occasions it clearly introduces content from Deuteronomy, apparently construing it as Moses's collected charges (*Agr.* 84: ἐν ταῖς παραινέσεσιν; *Spec.* 4.131: ἐν ταῖς παραινέσεσι Μωυσῆς φησιν). Support for this interpretation may be sought in the transitional statement Philo supplies in his *De Specialibus Legibus* when he prepares to turn his attention to Deuteronomy: "These and similar injunctions to piety are given in the law in the form of direct commands and prohibitions. Others which have now to be described are of the nature of homilies giving admonitions and exhortations (κατὰ τὰς φιλοσόφους ὑποθήκας καὶ παραινέσεις)" (*Spec.* 1.299; note the same pairing at *Virt.* 70). In this way, even (or perhaps especially) if these terms do not denote alternative titles for Deuteronomy but rather taxonomical categories, they provide a window on Philo's construal of at least large sections of the book: Deuteronomy is a collection of Moses's exhortations or charges to Israel.[11]

Philo also differentiates specific portions of Deuteronomy and refers to these sections by terms that have a generic connotation. For example, he can speak of "the curses described in the Appendix" (*Her.* 250: ἐν ταῖς <ἐν> Ἐπινομίδι γραφείσαις ἀραῖς) and proceeds to paraphrase a portion of Deuteronomy 28. His fuller treatment of both blessings and curses (esp. in *De Praemiis et Poenis* to be considered in § 5.3.3 below) presupposes this prior generic judgment. Likewise, he speaks several times of "the great song" or "the greater song" (*Leg.* 3.105; *Post.* 121, 167; cf. *Virt.* 72–75) to refer to Deuteronomy 32 (apparently as distinct from the "other" song in Exodus 15). And the testamentary form of the Blessing of Moses

---

[10] Though Cohen raises *Leg.* 1.83 (τῶν προτρεπτικῶν λόγων) and *Det.* 11 (προτρεπτικὸς λόγος) against the identification with Deuteronomy, the form of those passages is not at all the same as the others, above all lacking the preposition ἐν and the dative plural common to the rest; the same may be said for Cohen's protestations against παραινέσεις.

[11] Cf. Dogniez and Harl: "Parfois [Philon] met l'accent sur le genre littéraire des discours de Moïse" (1992: 26); they then go on to speak of "exhortations" or protreptic discourse.

(or his "benedictions" or "prayers" as Philo refers to it: εὐχαὶ) in Deuteronomy 33 also receives Philo's special attention (*Mos.* 2.288; *Virt.* 76–79). All this suggests that for Philo Deuteronomy was not one undifferentiated whole, but that he was a sensitive reader of the law who recognized distinctions in genre and form and sought to interpret accordingly.[12] It is striking that especially the last chapters of Deuteronomy are singled out by Philo for such special attention, creating as they do a sort of multiform conclusion to the Pentateuch.

5.3. Deuteronomy in the Exposition of the Laws of Moses

The Exposition of the Laws of Moses is Philo's wide-ranging paraphrastic retelling of the Pentateuch.[13] F. Siegert has rightly claimed that in this work "Philo's intention is clearly to teach the Law in a framework of universal history from Creation to the *eschaton*. History – esp. the life of Moses and of the other Patriarchs – illustrates the Law, and the Law illustrates history" (1996: 180). Philo's treatise on the creation of the world (*De Opificio Mundi*) probably opened the series (see the explanation in *Mos.* 2.48; *Opif.* 1–3), followed by several treatises on the patriarchs, who are considered to be νόμοι ἀγράφοι ("unwritten laws"; *Decal.* 1; *Virt.* 194) or νόμοι ἔμψυχοι ("personified laws"; *Mos.* 1.162; 2.4);[14] to these latter belongs the *De Vita Mosis*.[15] Philo's treatise on the Decalogue then sets up a hermeneutical grid, more fully implemented in the *De Specialibus Legibus* whereby the specific commandments of the Torah are read as belonging to one of the "headings" (κεφάλαια) supplied by the ten commandments. The treatises "On the Virtues" (*De Virtutibus*) and "On Rewards and Punishments" (*De Praemiis et Poenis*) conclude the exposition. Philo probably wrote to strengthen Jewish self-understanding and identity

---

[12] See further Kamesar 1997, and note the broad threefold divisions of the Pentateuch that Philo provides in *Praem.* 1–3; *Mos.* 2.46–47. Kamesar points to the similar threefold division in Josephus, *Ant.* 1.18 (1997: 146).

[13] For Philo's activity in the Exposition classed as rewritten Bible, see Borgen 1997: 46–79.

[14] So *Abr.* 5, with reference to the patriarchs: οἱ γὰρ ἔμψυχοι καὶ λογικοὶ νόμοι ἄνδρες ἐκεῖνοι γεγόνασιν. Cf. *Abr.* 275–76.

[15] The place of this treatise in the Exposition of the Law is admittedly unsecure, though the argument made by Goodenough (1933) for its inclusion is generally followed. His further contention in that article, however, that the sections on the blessings and curses do not belong to *Praem.*, has been discredited. See, e.g., Colson's note in LCL 8: xix.

and to encourage Jewish sympathizers,[16] seeking to demonstrate the reasonableness of the Pentateuch and to convince his hearers of a coincidence of natural law, the unwritten law, and the Law of Moses (e.g., *Mos.* 2.14).[17] Deuteronomy functions in this complex whole in a number of different ways.

5.3.1. The Last Acts of Moses

Philo's retelling of Moses's story in his two-volume βίος is notable for its essentially non-Deuteronomic stance, especially when one considers the prevalence of the equation between Mosaic and Deuteronomic encountered in the Qumran materials. Philo views Moses, somewhat idealistically (Amir 1988: 425), through the lens of four roles suitable to the ideal ruler: king, high priest, legislator and prophet (cf. *Mos.* 2.1–12; 2.187, etc.), generally following the order of the Pentateuch in his retelling. In the last of these roles, that of prophet, one may perhaps detect the influence of Deuteronomy more readily (cf. Deut 18:15–22; 34:10–12). In some places Moses's prophetic role is added to the biblical material in Philo's retelling and so manifests itself earlier in Philo's version than in the original (e.g., *Mos.* 1.57), though more often Philo simply interprets material in Exodus, Leviticus and Numbers as evidence of Moses's prophetic authority. Deuteronomy appears as the base text for his paraphrase only when it is strictly necessary: in the retelling of Moses's death (*Mos.* 2.288–91).[18] The account in Philo's hands is remarkably brief and turned as a further proof of Moses's ability to prophesy, in that he prophesies blessings for the tribes of Israel (2.288) and foretells his own death, burial place, and Israel's mourning for him (2.291; cf. Nikiprowetzky 1977: 196). Perhaps most striking is Philo's insistence that, of Moses's prophecies for the tribes (i.e., Deuteronomy 33), "some of these have already taken place, others are still looked for, since confidence in the future is assured by fulfillment in the

---

[16] So Borgen 1997: "he probably primarily has in mind his fellow Jews and the non-Jewish sympathizers, as exemplified by the group of people who took part in the annual Septuagint festival" (143–44; cf. *Mos.* 2.25–40). Cf. also Nikiprowetzky 1977: 202; Borgen 1984b: 118; contra, e.g., Goodenough 1933, who argues that Gentiles were the primary audience.

[17] So, essentially, Martens 1991 (cf. 2003: 159–64); Borgen 1997: 147; Najman 1999; 2003a; Bockmuehl 2000: 107–09.

[18] Neither here nor elsewhere does Philo indicate that Moses dies outside the promised land as recompense for his sin. Elsewhere, in *Migr.* 45, Philo says that Deut 34:4 ("I showed it to your eyes, but you shall not enter in") was not said, "as some unconsidering people suppose, to humiliate the all-wise leader; for indeed it is folly to imagine that the servants of God take precedence of his friends in receiving their portion in the land of virtue"; he then goes on to offer an allegorical explanation of Yahweh's statement to Moses.

past" (2.288). One might compare 4Q175's apparent presupposition that the Blessing of Moses discloses future events, or MMT's contention that only some of the blessings and curses have taken place (cf. § 3.2.3 and § 3.4 above).

In his treatise on the virtues (*De Virtutibus*), Philo revisits Moses's final actions, though without mentioning his death. The treatise is apparently intended to describe and commend the virtues Moses prescribes in the law, and deals in turn with courage, humanity, repentance, and nobility. Moses's last words and actions are brought in to serve as an example of the second virtue, humanity or benevolence (φιλανθρωπία), though, as Colson notes "evidently their main purpose is to give a supplement to the *Vita Mosis*"[19] (cf. *Virt.* 52–53). Thus, he begins with a re-telling of Moses's selection of Joshua as successor (55–71), of the Song of Moses (72–75), and of the Blessing of Moses (76–79), devoting the rest of his consideration of φιλανθρωπία to laws which specially illustrate that virtue. Philo construes the Song as Moses's final thanksgiving (*Virt.* 72: τελευταίαν...εὐχαριστίαν), and also as an exhortation to Israel to turn from their sins, with apparently an element of foretelling (*Virt.* 75):

Thus in his post amid the ethereal choristers the great revealer blended with the strains of thankfulness to God his own true feelings of affection to the nation, therein joining with his arraignment of them for past sins (ἔλεγχοι παλαιῶν ἁμαρτημάτων) his admonitions for the present occasion and calls to a sounder mind, and his exhortations for the future expressed in hopeful words of comfort which must necessarily be followed by their happy fulfillment (παραινέσεις αἱ πρὸς τὰ μέλλοντα διὰ χρηστῶν ἐλπίδων, αἷς ἐπακολουθεῖν ἀναγκαῖον αἴσια τέλη).

Whether or not thanksgiving is really as constitutive an aspect of the original Song as Philo would suggest (though note, similarly, Tobit [§ 4.5 above] and Josephus [§ 7.2.3 below]), he certainly recognizes its hortatory character and also clearly reads it as expressing a judgment about the future. As in *De Vita Mosis*, the Blessing of Moses in Deuteronomy 33 is similarly seen as referring to a reality not yet present: "That these benedictions will be fulfilled we must believe (τελεσφορηθήσονται πιστευτέον), for he who gave them was beloved of God the lover of men (φιλάνθρωπος) and they for whom he asked were of noble lineage and held the highest rank in the army led by the Maker and Father of all" (*Virt.* 77). Thus, the final chapters of Deuteronomy offer both a characterization of Moses and a prophetic foretelling of Israel's history.

---

[19] LCL 8: xiv–xv.

5.3.2. Re-ordering and Commending the Law

Philo's fullest treatment of the Law according to its literal sense is found in his treatises *De Decalogo* and *De Specialibus Legibus*. Perhaps the most striking aspect of these works is that Philo has introduced an ordering principle to the apparently random manner in which the laws in the Pentateuch are presented. The Decalogue, according to Philo, due to its special status as having been spoken directly by God himself, serves as a series of headings under which the particular laws may be classed.[20] *De Decalogo* provides a brief outline of the sorts of commandments each heading covers, while *De Specialibus Legibus* provides much more detail, even if Philo's explanations of the relationship between the particular command and the heading that purportedly subsumes it are sometimes strained. Of course, the Decalogue is found in both Exodus 20 and Deuteronomy 5, and while Philo certainly evinces the harmonization of the two so prevalent in antiquity, the order of his sixth, seventh, and eighth commands (adultery, murder, theft) suggests that Philo has followed the order found in Greek Deuteronomy.[21] An interesting comparison between the method of Philo and the Temple Scroll might be drawn: the Temple Scroll harmonizes by re-casting all the particular laws as direct divine speech, while Philo obtains hermeneutical leverage from the fact that certain commands are cast in divine speech while others are not, though ultimately both seek to provide holistic and somewhat actualizing interpretations of the laws of the Pentateuch with reference to a higher unity. One might also suggest that Paul's contention that the love command (Lev 19:18) epitomizes not only the law but also the Decalogue (Rom 13:8–10) is in some ways the opposite move to express a similar basic point (on which see further § 6.3.1): whether the particular laws are an expansion of the originally succinct Decalogue or whether the Decalogue or the love command summarizes the deepest concerns of the particular laws, both directions of movement are involved in making judgments about the priorities of the Law.

---

[20] Cf. *Decal.* 154: οἱ δέκα λόγοι κεφάλαια νόμων εἰσι; see further *Decal.* 18, 154–75; *Spec.* 2.189; 4.132; *Praem.* 1–3; *Mos.* 2.188f; *Her.* 173; cf. also Dogniez and Harl 1992: 82–83; Borgen 1997: 60. Philo's suggestion may be echoed, even if only partially, in the suggestion of Braulik 1985, who argues that Deut 12–26 takes the Decalogue as its ordering principle (1985: 271 [1988: 254]: "Die Einzelgesetze erscheinen dadurch als Konkretisierung des Dekalogs").

[21] Cf. *Decal.* 168–71; *Spec.* 3.7–4.40; *Her.* 173. For similar order, note also Rom 13:9–10; Luke 18:19–20; perhaps James 2:11; and the Nash Papyrus. Note the discussion in Freund 1989; Kellermann 2001, esp. 161–70. Himbaza's argument that Philo follows Exodus rather than Deuteronomy based on the fact that motifs from Exodus appear in the surrounding context (2002: 421–24) fails to consider that Philo often conflates his sources on microcompositional levels. To ask Philo to choose between Exodus and Deuteronomy does not do justice to the complexities of his approach.

Philo conceives of the two tables of the ten commandments as setting forth divine and human obligations respectively, with the command to honor one's parents functioning in a mediating capacity between the two (cf. *Decal.* 50–51). Above (§ 5.2) I noted Philo's special construal of Deuteronomy as hortatory discourse in the transitional statement at *Spec.* 1.299, under the general heading of the second commandment, the prohibition of idolatry. It is notable that Philo enlarges on this hortatory dimension with an expansive re-presentation of Deut 10:12–22, supplemented by Deut 30:11–14, the latter a text of no small importance to Paul (see § 6.5.3 below). But whereas Paul re-writes the text to excise any notion of "doing," Philo's use of the text is in greater continuity with its original sense of commending obedience to the law as an obtainable task: "Only must the soul give its assent and everything is there ready to your hand" (*Spec.* 1.302), though he follows this with Deuteronomy's admission that "some are uncircumcised in heart" (1.304).

Much of *De Specialibus Legibus* is concerned with a relatively straightforward retelling of Israel's laws. So, over the course of his retelling, Philo adduces, *inter alia*, the injunction against false prophets (Deut 13:1–18 with 23:17–18; *Spec.* 1.315–23), the cancellation of debts in the seventh year (Deut 15:1–3; *Spec.* 2.71–73), the release of Jewish slaves in the seventh year (Deut 15:12–18; *Spec.* 2.79–85); the offering of firstfruits (Deut 26:1–11; *Spec.* 2.215–22); the case of the rebellious son (Deut 21:18–21; *Spec.* 2.231–32); laws about sexual immorality (Deut 22:13–21; *Spec.* 3.79–83); the punishment for a woman who grasps the genitals of a male in a fight (Deut 25:11–12; *Spec.* 3.175–77); and the law of witnesses (Deut 17:6 and 19:15; *Spec.* 4.53–54).[22] Elsewhere in the treatise Philo evinces a more actualizing interpretation: for example, the injunction in Deut 19:14 not to move the boundary stone is referred to "the safeguarding of ancient customs" (*Spec.* 4.149; cf. 149–50; *Post.* 89–90). Similarly, Deut 17:15 ("you will set over yourself a ruler") is taken as a reference to electing a ruler (*Spec.* 4.157; note also the elaboration of the law of the king in 157–69). In a slightly different vein, Philo discusses the virtue of justice by means of a running paraphrase on Deuteronomy 6 (*Spec.* 4.136–42). Such examples could be multiplied.

Much of this material is significant for the way in which Philo commends a relatively straightforward obedience to Deuteronomy's injunctions, perhaps in conjunction with the restricted pedagogical aim of his Exposition. While he may be allegorically-inclined in much of his corpus, the allegorical interpretation of the law does not negate or evacuate obser-

---

[22] Some of this material is repeated in *De Virtutibus*.

vance of its concrete precepts.[23] Philo is even in places more literal than Paul, as in his discussion of the regulations concerning the treatment of animals: Moses, Philo writes, "did not set up consideration and gentleness as fundamental to the relations of men to their fellows only, but poured it out richly with a lavish hand on animals of irrational nature and the various kinds of cultivated trees" (*Virt.* 81). Philo then goes on to call attention to Deut 25:4 ("Do not muzzle the ox while it is treading out the grain") as a law that he "admires", apparently read in a literal sense (*Virt.* 145; contrast 1 Cor 9:9–10).[24] Deuteronomy, for Philo, serves as a source of ethical and religious authority, together with the other books of the Pentateuch. Though in a different form than the Temple Scroll or the Damascus Document, Philo similarly feels the need to update Deuteronomy to speak to his day, to re-present it in order to respond to the hortatory impulse of its words.[25]

5.3.3. Blessing, Curse, and the Hope of Restoration

Philo comments not only on the particular laws in the Pentateuch, but also on the sanctions for those laws in blessing and curse (esp. Lev 26 and Deut 27–28).[26] This material is chiefly found in his treatise on rewards and pun-

---

[23] Philo does say, however, parenthetically that "we must not neglect the opportunity where possible of using the same point to bring out more than one moral" (*Spec.* 4.204). The *locus classicus* proving that Philo's allegorical renderings do not eviscerate or obviate a literal observance is his discussion of circumcision in *Migr.* 92 (see further § 5.4 below).

[24] See the different understanding in *Arist.* 144: "Do not take the contemptible view that Moses enacted this legislation because of an excessive preoccupation with mice and weasels or suchlike creatures"; and 169: "In the matter of meats, the unclean reptiles, the beasts, the whole underlying rationale is directed toward righteousness and righteous human relationships."

[25] Another instance of this hortatory concern is found in Philo's expansion of Deut 8:11–20, itself sermonic in tone, into his own exhortation against pride (*Virt.* 163–74).

[26] See Borgen 1997: 47–48; 269 n. 8. Mendelson (1997) argues that Deuteronomy 28 is important for Philo, but that Philo embraces some aspects of it and qualifies others. He argues that in the "Cain trilogy" (*Sacr., Det., Post.*) "Philo appears to question the formulations on reward and punishment found in Deuteronomy" (105). His contention, however, that Philo's raising "the hypothetical case of a wicked person who had the temerity to think that he had successfully eluded punishment" is a significant indication that "Philo was prepared to consider the complexities of the problem" beyond that found in Deuteronomy fails to do justice to the fact that this is in fact an exegetical interpretation of Leviticus 26 at this point (*Praem.* 149; contra Mendelson 1997: 108–09). It is more difficult to find Philo consciously striving to free himself from Deuteronomy in either *Virt.* or *Praem.*, though *Praem.* 119 is admittedly a partial qualification. Also, it is not clear that one can draw a linear or chronological progression from *Virt.* and *Praem.* to the Cain Trilogy. In the end, Mendelson does acknowledge the problem: "Instead of adopting a model of dynamic change over the course of Philo's lifetime, we can think in terms of

ishments, *De Praemiis et Poenis*. The structure Philo intended for the treatise (cf. *Praem.* 7) is only partially fulfilled, whether due to Philo's change of plans or the transmission of the manuscript tradition. But after an apparent lacuna at *Praem.* 78,[27] he goes on: "A clear testimony is recorded in the Holy Scriptures. We will cite first the invocations which he is accustomed to call benedictions (τὰς εὐχὰς...ἃς εὐλογίας εἴωθεν ὀνομάζειν)" i.e., the blessings of Deut 28 (*Praem.* 79). He then states that victory in war is the first blessing for obedience, supporting his contention with a paraphrase of Deut 30:11–14, once more as an indication that obedience to the commands is attainable (*Praem.* 80–81). Philo reads the Septuagintal form of Deut 30:14, with its threefold reference to the word being "in your hand and in your heart and in your hands" (ἐν τῷ στόματί σου καὶ ἐν τῇ καρδίᾳ σου καὶ ἐν ταῖς χερσίν σου),[28] and specifies this to refer to speech, thought, and action respectively and in combination denoting the whole person (so also *Post.* 84–88). He thus emphasizes the need for holistic obedience:

> Now while the commandments of the laws are only on our lips our acceptance of them is little or none, but when we add thereto deeds which follow in their company, deeds shown in the whole conduct of our lives, the commandments will be as it were brought up out of the deep darkness into the light and surrounded with the brightness of good fame and good report (*Praem.* 82).[29]

Philo then proceeds to detail and expand upon some of the blessings (79–126), including, for example, the monetary blessing of prosperity (so *Praem.* 98–107 relying on, e.g., Deut 7:13; 15:6; 28:3, 4, 8). Philo concludes his discussion of the blessings by reiterating the importance of obeying the law: "These are the blessings invoked upon good men, men who fulfill the laws by their deeds, which blessings will be accomplished by the gift of the bounteous God, who glorifies and rewards moral excellence because of its likeness to Himself" (*Praem.* 126).

Next follows Philo's discussion of the curses (*Praem.* 127–61). Among others, Philo mentions the destruction of crops (*Praem.* 127–33; cf. Deut 28:38–42); cannibalism (*Praem.* 134–36; cf. Deut 28:53–57); slavery (*Praem.* 137–40; cf. Deut 28:48); and bodily maladies (*Praem.* 143–46; cf. Deut 28:22, 27, 35). He emphasizes that the curses come upon those who

---

the coexistence of opposing forces in Philo's mind" (125; cf. 124–25), though this weakens the force of his overall argument.

[27] See Colson's note in LCL 8: 455.

[28] The phrase "and in your hands" is absent in the MT, and also in Paul's citation of this text in Rom 10:8 (see further § 6.5.3 below).

[29] Cf. *Virt.* 183–86 where Deut 30:11–14 is adduced as an exhortation to repentance with the same point about the threefold reference of the text; see in discussion Bekken 1995; 2007.

disregard the holy laws of justice and piety, who have been seduced by the polytheistic creeds which finally lead to atheism and have forgotten the teaching of their race and of their fathers, in which they were trained from their earliest years to acknowledge the One in substance, the supreme God, to whom alone all must belong who follow truth unfeigned instead of mythical figments (*Praem.* 162).

It is clear that Philo's conception of disobedience to the law has been enlarged to encompass the type of apostasy he sees as a current threat (instance the apostasy of Philo's nephew, Alexander). The hortatory function of the promise of blessing and the threat of curse, in other words, is directed to the present.[30] This once more demonstrates the importance that obedience to the Torah's concrete commands has for Philo, as well as the ongoing validity of the Torah's covenant stipulations in blessing and curse, found chiefly in Deuteronomy.

In light of the way in which the last chapters of Deuteronomy provide a review of Israel's history in texts like 4QMMT (§ 3.2.3 above), one might ask whether Philo has obscured any sense of national destiny in favor of an individualizing exhortation. At one point, Philo renders the Diaspora in allegorical, personal terms: individuals "should not despair of changing for the better or of a restoration to the land of wisdom and virtue from the spiritual dispersion which vice has wrought" (*Praem.* 115; cf. Deut 30:4). But this is not Philo's only stance. While eschewing the violent apocalyptic visions of destruction for Israel's enemies, Philo does hope for an apparently non-violent re-gathering of dispersed Jews when they repent: "For even though they dwell in the uttermost parts of the earth, in slavery to those who led them away captive, one signal, as it were, one day will bring liberty to all. This conversion in a body to virtue will strike awe into their masters, who will set them free, ashamed to rule over men better than themselves" (*Praem.* 164). Then they will be gathered together as a people out of their dispersion (165). At this point God will intervene to turn the curses on Israel's enemies (cf. Deut 30:7): "Everything will suddenly be reversed, God will turn the curses against the enemies of these penitents the enemies who rejoiced in the misfortunes of the nation and mocked and railed at them" (*Praem.* 169). Indeed, even in Philo's figural appropriation of the Diaspora imagery, God's ability to re-gather exiles functions as a given (cf. *Praem.* 117). This is not a major theme in Philo's writings, nor does he develop an elaborate description of eschatological events, but he is

---

[30] Note the allusion to Deut 28:67 in *Flacc.* 167, an instance of what Borgen terms "applied exegesis" that serves as a "theological interpretation of historical events" (1997: 285): "Then when the night had quite closed in he would go indoors, praying in his endless and boundless sorrow that the evening might be morning, so much did he dread the darkness and the weird visions which it gave him, if he chanced to fall asleep. So in the morning again he prayed for evening, for to the gloom that surrounded him everything bright was repugnant."

aware of Deuteronomy's exile-and-return schema and does not merely spiritualize it. Similarly, elsewhere Philo expresses the hope that, "though our nation has not prospered for many a year" it may be that if Israel renews its obedience, "each nation would abandon its peculiar ways, and, throwing overboard their ancestral customs, turn to honoring our laws alone" (*Mos.* 2.43–44).[31] Philo's hope that Gentiles will join Israel in observing the Law stands, clearly, in contrast to Paul's hopes for the Gentiles on the issue of Law, but evinces an arguably similar desire to see Gentiles join the assembly of Israel.

5.4. Deuteronomy in the Allegorical Commentary on Genesis

Perhaps one of the most widely recognized aspects of Philo's exegesis is its figural or allegorical character, and this characterization is drawn above all from his sprawling Allegorical Commentary. This work consists of individual treatises, some lost, that cover the chief parts of Genesis 2–41. While this work is ostensibly concerned with Genesis, in fact Philo often brings in subordinate texts, drawn mainly from the Pentateuch, to illumine his discursive exegetical and philosophical forays. To discuss every place where Deuteronomy appears would be tiresome, and so, after articulating a sketch of Philo's allegorical practice, some representative engagements with Deuteronomy are here described.

The phenomenon of Philonic allegory has not always been kindly received in biblical scholarship, but Philo's practice is often more sophisticated than certain dismissive comments might lead one to expect. Often, though not always (Mack 1984: 261–62), a figurative reading of a text is "triggered" by a difficulty in the literal sense (Dawson 1992: 103). For example, in commenting on Gen 4:16 ("And Cain went out from the face of God"), Philo notes the absurdity of claiming that God has a face and that one might escape from the presence of God, and says:

Let us here raise the question whether in the books in which Moses acts as God's interpreter we ought to take his statements figuratively (τροπικώτερον), since the impression made by the words in their literal sense is greatly at variance with truth....the only thing left for us to do is to make up our minds that none of the propositions put forward is literally intended and to take the path of figurative interpretation (δι' ἀλληγορίας ὁδὸν) so dear to philosophical souls (*Post.* 1, 7).[32]

---

[31] On these texts, note Borgen 1997: 261–81.

[32] Cf. *Post.* 51: "It would seem, then, since all this is at variance with reality, that it is better to take the words figuratively (ἀλληγοροῦντας)..."

Elsewhere, however, Philo sees no competition between the literal and the figurative senses,[33] though he complains about those who insist on either one to the detriment of the other.[34] Philo famously protests against those who use the figurative meaning of circumcision as a reason for neglecting its concrete practice (*Migr.* 88–92; cf. *QG* 3.48) and further expresses concern for the liturgical praxis of the physical Temple in Jerusalem (cf. *Spec.* 1.67–68; *Legat.* 156; Borgen 1997: 18–19). Thus, Dawson's summation is apt: "the difference between moving through the letter to the spirit and replacing the letter by the spirit remains fundamental" (1992: 119; cf. 73–126).[35] Philo considers the biblical text to be capable of multiple reference, and seeks to render its various meanings with the thickest possible description (cf. *Contempl.* 78).[36]

How does Deuteronomy resource this operation in practice? Two examples, both drawn from Deuteronomy 21, must here suffice to illustrate different ways in which Deuteronomy functions in his figural interpretation. The first occurs in Philo's treatise on drunkenness, *De Ebrietate*. The treatise is nominally concerned with Gen 9:20–29, and especially v. 29: "And he [i.e., Noah] drank the wine and became drunk." Philo discusses Moses's use of wine as a symbol for different things, and the first of these, "folly" or "foolish talking" (ληρεῖν καὶ παραπαίειν), is said to be caused by "lack of discipline or education" (ἀπαιδευσία). He then goes on to enlarge upon this using Deut 21:18–21, the law about the parents' right to denounce a rebellious son (*Ebr.* 13–95). First, the accusations against the son are ex-

---

[33] In the *Quaestiones*, Philo sometimes offers first a discussion of the literal sense (τὸ ῥητόν), then a discussion of the figurative, deeper sense (τὸ πρὸς διάνοιαν); though much of the Greek original of this work is lost, numerous fragments survive which suggest that the Armenian original has been a relatively faithful transmission of its Greek parent-text (in Greek, note here *QE* 2.21; 2.38).

[34] "Philo as interpreter of the Bible is fighting, as it were, on two fronts: against the extreme allegorists who abolish the literal meaning of Mikra, and against the literalists, who do not want to go beyond the literal sense" (Amir 1988: 445). Cf. Shroyer 1936; Hay 1991.

[35] In contrast to, e.g., the estimation of Amir 1988: 426: "The act of allegorization, which purports to bring out the meaning really intended by Moses, consists of divesting the thing named by the word of its concreteness, leaving an intrinsic meaning which is conceptual, abstracted from all spatial-temporal being, absolutely valid, eternal."

[36] What is more, allegory provided Philo with a way of responding to the Hellenistic culture which both fascinated and repelled him. In his endeavor to transform this culture, Philo subsumes the philosophical resources of his day to the priority of Mosaic revelation, ultimately reinterpreting and subverting the former to serve the latter (though this process is not without its reciprocal effect). In this light, Borgen aptly characterizes Philo as "a conqueror, on the verge of being conquered" (1984b: 150–54). But a conqueror still he is, and Dawson's claim is equally correct: "Philo's allegorical reading of scripture revises Greek culture by subordinating it to Jewish cultural and religious identity; his interpretation is not a synthesis but a usurpation" (1992: 113).

pounded and filled with expansive content (15–29), using, e.g., etymology to determine a broader range of meaning (cf. 23). But then Philo suggests that the parents are not simply biological parents, but that the father should be construed as right reason or philosophy, while the mother is lower learning or custom (33–34). Asking the question how one responds to each parent then provides Philo with a method of describing the errors of folly and the benefit of honoring one's "parents," with occasional references back to the rebellious son of Deuteronomy 21 (*Ebr.* 33–92). In this way, then, Philo undertakes a sort of *Sachkritik*, or perhaps better, a reading in light of a moral and philosophical *discrimen* whereby he engages the deepest concerns of the text (as he sees it), within the loose framework provided by the Mosaic injunction in Deut 21:18–21. Elsewhere, it should be noted, this does not prevent Philo from providing an apparently straightforward literal reading of the same verses of Deuteronomy (*Spec.* 2.232).

Second, it is instructive to note how Philo treats Deut 21:22–23, a text also of interest to Paul (see § 6.5.1 below). To return to Philo's treatise on Cain's exile, he suggests that the country into which Cain goes is called "Tossing" (σάλος).[37] From Philo's point of view, only God has real stability, while all else is inevitably subject to movement, especially as one becomes alienated from the divine.[38] This explains the curses in Deut 28:65, 66: "He will not give you rest, nor will there be a standing (στάσις) for the sole of your foot...your life will be hanging (κρεμαμένη) before your eyes" (*Post.* 24). This applies above all to the foolish person who is always shifting his or her views, a point that is then buttressed by the citation of Deut 21:23: "This is why the lawgiver says in another place that 'he that hangs on a tree (τὸν κρεμάμενον ἐπὶ ξύλου) is cursed by God,' for, whereas it behooves us to hang upon God, the man of whom we are thinking suspended himself from his body, which for us a wooden barb."[39] "Hanging

---

[37] This is based on a Hebrew etymology, to a collection of which Philo evidently had access, to judge from the prevalence of such comments in his work.

[38] Cf. *Post.* 23: "Proximity to a stable object produces a desire to be like it and a longing for quiescence. Now that which is unwaveringly stable is God, and that which is subject to movement is creation. He therefore that draws nigh to God longs for stability, but he that forsakes Him, inasmuch as he approaches the unresting creation is, as we might expect, carried about." See further Siegert 1996: 170, with reference to *Mut.* 54, 57, 87; *Somn.* 1.246; 2.226, etc.

[39] The precise meaning of Philo's phrase ἐν ἡμῖν ξύλινος ὄγκος, translated by Colson and Whitaker as "a log-like mass in us" is somewhat obscure, though clearly Philo is describing the body in terms of the ξύλος of Deut 21:23. It is possible, as above, to take the word ὄγκος as a double entendre: to refer to a "mass" but also to a "barb" (cf. LSJ s.v.), admittedly a somewhat rarer use but one in which Philo's point may preserve something of the original sense of being suspended on a tree. The standard German and French translations are similar to Colson and Whitaker: "der den hölzernen Stoff in uns darstellt" (Heinemann); "qui est en nous un fardeau matériel comme le bois" (Arnaldez).

on a tree" is then further re-defined as succumbing to bodily desire (ἐπιθυμία) instead of clinging to hope (ἐλπὶς). In this way, Philo weaves a thick tapestry of metaphorical identifications in order to express in vividly scriptural language his conviction that the foolish person, by indulging bodily craving, is destined to be cast on his or her own fragile resources rather than being supported by the unshakeable God. Like the apostle Paul, he forges a connection between the curses set forth in Deuteronomy 27–28 and the cursed one on the tree in Deut 21:22–23, though their respective ways of reaching that point could hardly be more different, nor could the implications they draw from it. It is important to recognize that, whereas Philo has definite philosophical starting points that influence how he comes to interpret the scroll of Deuteronomy (here: that only the divine has stability), the concrete details of the text also give shape to the conclusions to which Philo comes.[40] Philo's exegesis is more dialogical and less unilateral in its philosophical interpretation than is sometimes alleged, though its essentially *ad hoc* nature should not be underestimated.

5.5. Conclusion: Deuteronomy in the Works of Philo

Deuteronomy, then, functions in a number of ways in the Philonic corpus. Philo is well aware of its discrete existence, senses that the last book of the Pentateuch takes a different rhetorical stance from the others, and often refers to its hortatory dimension. The fact that he refers to Deuteronomy by name reinforces a sense of its discrete physical existence, most likely in scroll form – and thus as a book and not simply an intertext. He recognizes as discrete subunits the blessings and curses (Deut 27–30), the Song of Moses (32), and the Blessing of Moses (33), assuming simultaneously their relevance to his day and their predictive dimension which reserves full prosperity for a future time of obedience and grace. Philo especially highlights these aspects of Moses's last actions, though elsewhere in retelling Moses's story he tends to follow parallel accounts in Exodus-Numbers rather than Deuteronomy. Indeed, in contrast to the language employed at Qumran, Philo's "dialect" often sounds more Middle Platonic than Deuteronomic *per se*.

What is more, Deuteronomy remains for Philo, together with the other books of Mosaic Law, an inexhaustible source of theological and ethical authority. The Decalogue, Philo suggests, is given in God's own first-

---

[40] As in the first example, Philo also elsewhere treats this text literally, saying that Deut 21:22–23 is a concession born of humanitarian concerns (*Spec.* 3.152), and going on to reject the propriety of someone suffering in another's place (e.g., a father for a son, etc.: *Spec.* 3.153–57).

person discourse and orders the particular laws under ten headings; by this means Philo attempts to provide an organic explanation for the importance of what might at first appear to be marginal or arbitrary precepts. These particular laws are often given in updated form to preserve the immediacy of Deuteronomy's demand and its applicability to Philo's situation. Obedience to the laws in their literal and not simply their figurative sense is crucial for Philo, and forms the precondition for personal blessing and ultimately for the re-gathering of the dispersed Jews and the attraction of Gentile converts. Presumably both Philo's stress on law observance and his preoccupation with the Pentateuch stem directly from his exposure to the reading of Torah in the common life of the synagogue.

By their very nature Philo's figural reading strategies are difficult to reduce to a strict typology. But both of the examples adduced above represent in different ways the interpretative moves Philo tends to make in his allegorical works. Sometimes Deuteronomy lends a structural shape to a longer discussion (so *Ebr.*), while other times Deuteronomy is brought in to make a certain point in the argument before receding from view once more (so *Post.*). Often Philo simply adduces Deuteronomy to provide authoritative theological or ethical maxims (e.g., *Post.* 12, 69, etc.; cf. Paul's use of theological axioms drawn from Deuteronomy in § 6.4.2).

In the end, Philo has an overwhelming conviction that the biblical text speaks to his present concerns, and so he performs sometimes elaborate acts of correlation in order to bring that relevance to bear in specific situations. Philo's flexibility in appealing to Deuteronomy stems from a dual conviction about the authority and excess of divine communication in the Law,[41] though this does not preclude him from engaging in sometimes surprisingly sensitive acts of contextual interpretation. For Philo, Deuteronomy is above all a *useful* book of exhortation, of law, of theological reflection, and he employs it accordingly to all these ends.

Continuing the chronological march through the Second Temple period, we turn now to consider a radical Jew of a different stripe and his equally formative encounter with Deuteronomy.

---

[41] Note his conviction about the inspiration of Moses in *QE* 2.29: "For when the prophetic mind becomes divinely inspired and filled with God, it becomes like the monad, not being at all mixed with any of those things associated with duality. But he who is resolved into the nature of unity, is said to come near God in a kind of family relation, for having given up and left behind all mortal kinds, he is changed into the divine, so that such men become kin to God and truly divine."

Chapter 6

Deuteronomy in Paul's Letters

6.1. Introduction

After long years of reciting, praying, memorizing, debating, teaching, and ordering his life in conformity with its precepts, Paul the Pharisee had an unexpected hermeneutical irruption in his understanding of Deuteronomy. In a vision of the resurrected Jesus, whom he then recognized as Lord and Christ, Paul was confronted with a revelatory commission that initiated an apostleship he would repeatedly characterize as slave-like. Under the lordship of this Jesus, the last book of Torah did not cease to be for the apostle an authoritative word from God, but deepened in its significance as he learned to recite, pray, memorize, debate, teach and order his life according to the scroll of Deuteronomy and according to Jesus the Messiah. That the old and the new would come into some tension was perhaps unavoidable, but Paul was convinced that in holding to both Deuteronomy and to Jesus, he was serving not two masters but one. The letters he wrote in the course of his missionary endeavors show some record of this multi-faceted encounter, and in this chapter I take up and examine this evidence to see how Paul's reading of Deuteronomy might be characterized. Naturally in the scope of a single chapter one cannot hope to be exhaustive in discussing such a wide variety of texts. In the following presentation, I will strive for economy of expression in the hope that, even if certain details must be passed over in silence, what is lacking in detail may be gained in synthesis.

6.2. How Paul Refers to Deuteronomy

Paul marks his quotations of Deuteronomy by several different introductory phrases. The most common of these use the perfect form γέγραπται and so emphasize the authority and ongoing relevance of Deuteronomy's voice. Most often these quotations function to ground other assertions in Paul's line of argument (so Deut 27:26 in Gal 3:10; Deut 21:23 in Gal 3:13; Deut 25:4 in 1 Cor 9:9; Deut 29:3 in Rom 11:8; Deut 32:35 in Rom

12:19).[1] Almost as numerous in Paul's introductions are verbs of speaking, with Moses (Deut 32:21 in Rom 10:19), the law (Deut 5:21 in Rom 7:7) or even Righteousness-from-Faith (Deut 9:4, 30:12–14 in Rom 10:6–8) as speaker (note also the undefined speaker of Deut 32:43 in Rom 15:10).[2] Deuteronomy's character as law is emphasized at least three times (Deut 25:4 in 1 Cor 9:9; Deut 5:21 in Rom 7:7; and Deut 5:17–19, 21 in Rom 13:9).[3] Already with this brief examination of the way Paul introduces his Deuteronomy citations we can see something of the apostle's stance toward the book: Deuteronomy is a written authority with a voice whose relevance to the present situation is granted. It is νόμος, and as such is capable of speaking itself or being spoken by Moses or even by the personified Righteousness-from-Faith to address Paul's contemporary situation.

In all of these instances, the quotation character of the passages is indicated for the reader or hearer by introductory formulae, interpretative comments, or both. In two places, however, Paul adduces substantially verbatim passages from Deuteronomy without any indication to the audience of his intention to quote: Deut 17:7 par in 1 Cor 5:13 and Deut 19:15 in 2 Cor 13:1.[4] This is naturally a more difficult problem for those who take an audience-oriented stance toward defining Paul's quotations than

---

[1] Note Deut 21:23 in Gal 3:13 "For it is written" (ὅτι γέγραπται); Deut 32:35 in Rom 12:19: "For it is written" (γέγραπται γάρ); Deut 27:26 in Gal 3:10: "For it is written that" (γέγραπται γὰρ ὅτι); Deut 25:4 in 1 Cor 9:9: "For it is written in the law of Moses" (ἐν γὰρ τῷ Μωϋσέως νόμῳ γέγραπται); Deut 29:3 in Rom 11:8: "Just as it is written" (καθὼς γέγραπται).

[2] Note Deut 32:21 in Rom 10:19: "First Moses says" (πρῶτος Μωϋσῆς λέγει); Deut 32:43 in Rom 15:10: "And again he [or 'it'] says" (καὶ πάλιν λέγει); Deut 5:21 in Rom 7:7: "Unless the law had said" (εἰ μὴ ὁ νόμος ἔλεγεν); Deut 9:4, 30:12–14 in Rom 10:6–8: "But the righteousness from faith speaks this way" (ἡ δὲ ἐκ πίστεως δικαιοσύνη οὕτως λέγει).

[3] Note Deut 25:4 in 1 Cor 9:9: "For it is written in the law of Moses" (ἐν γὰρ τῷ Μωϋσέως νόμῳ γέγραπται); Deut 5:17–19, 21a in Rom 13:9 (simply with τὸ γὰρ and a comment afterwards that places them among the commands: καὶ εἴ τις ἑτέρα ἐντολή, though FG b add γέγραπται); Deut 5:21 in Rom 7:7: "Unless the law had said" (εἰ μὴ ὁ νόμος ἔλεγεν).

[4] In fact, Paul has probably introduced minor variations in the wording of both texts. In the first, the singular person of the original verb (ἐξαρεῖς) has been adapted to its new context by being changed to plural form (ἐξάρατε). In the second, he has apparently abridged his quotation by omitting the repetitive ἐπὶ στόματος and μαρτύρων from the second clause. While identifying intentional omissions is certainly complicated by the fluid text of the LXX in the first century CE, the manuscript tradition is stable enough to suggest that in both of these instances the changes should be credited to Paul and not to a divergent *Vorlage*. On the problem, see esp. Koch 1986; Stanley 1992. Koch considers that 1 Cor 5:13 and 2 Cor 13:1 can only be considered citations "with caution" (1986: 18).

for author-oriented investigations.[5] It also highlights the importance of not confining one's investigation of Paul's engagement with Deuteronomy to explicit quotations. Especially over the past twenty years, and with indebtedness to Richard Hays (1989), we have seen a renewed appreciation of Paul's less explicitly marked engagements with Scripture in methods that have been called by a bewildering array of terminology: allusions, echoes, intertextual engagements, implicit citations, textual reminiscences, verbal resonances, rewritten quotations, and so forth. What is more, the greater recognition of the importance of so-called rewritten Bible (cf. § 3.3 above), together with a broader sense of the role of biblical interpretation in the Second Temple period, has widened interest beyond explicit citations. Below, however, I will suggest that some echoes or allusions are of minimal relevance to the present type of investigation.

If we expand the list of explicit quotations of Deuteronomy to include also implicit citations and a few major allusions, we have the following (in order of their occurrence in Deuteronomy):

Deut 5:17–19, 21	Rom 13:9	Explicit quotation
Deut 5:21	Rom 7:7	Explicit quotation; cf. also Exod 20:17
Deut 6:4	1 Cor 8:4–6	Echo
Deut 8:17//9:4	Rom 10:6	Echo, mixed citation
Deut 10:17	Rom 2:11	Echo
Deut 17:7 par	1 Cor 5:13	Implicit citation
Deut 19:15	2 Cor 13:1	Implicit citation
Deut 21:23	Gal 3:13	Explicit quotation
Deut 25:4	1 Cor 9:9	Explicit quotation
Deut 27:26	Gal 3:10	Explicit quotation
Deut 29:3(4)	Rom 11:8	Explicit quotation; cf. also Isa 29:10
Deut 30:6	Rom 2:28–29	Echo; cf. also Deut 29:28(29)
Deut 30:11–14	Rom 10:6–8	Explicit quotation
Deut 32:17	1 Cor 10:20	Echo
Deut 32:21	1 Cor 10:22	Echo
Deut 32:21	Rom 10:19	Explicit quotation
Deut 32:35	Rom 12:19	Explicit quotation
Deut 32:43	Rom 15:10	Explicit quotation

Other echoes and allusions have, of course, been proposed (note the margins and indices to NA[27]), but, while the strength of echoes here adduced varies, I consider them to be among the most defensible.

The attentive reader will here notice that even some well-known allusions to Deuteronomy have thus been excluded from explicit consideration. It is worth briefly mentioning two such allusions, together with the

---

[5] The search for adequate criteria for identifying quotations has been a protracted one, with debates that are not altogether enlightening. See Koch 1986: 11–20; Stanley 1992: 33–37; Porter 1997, 2006. See further the discussion in § 1.3.5 above.

rationale for their exclusion: Deut 1:16 in 1 Cor 6:5b and Deut 32:5 in Phil 2:15. In both cases, reasonably strong grounds for the presence of an allusion to Deuteronomy have been advanced. In the former, we find the unique collocation of ἀνὰ μέσον and ἀδελφός only in Deut 1:16 and 1 Cor 6:5b. Further, the ἀνὰ μέσον is a Pauline *hapax* (cf. Matt 13:25; Mark 7:31; Rev 7:17), suggesting the presence of a "foreign object" in the text. What is more, both contexts concern the concept of judgment in the community.[6] In the latter case, Paul's γενεᾶς σκολιᾶς καὶ διεστραμμένης recalls uniquely Deuteronomy's Song of Moses, which indicts Israel as a γενεὰ σκολιὰ καὶ διεστραμμένη (32:5). Paul's interest in Deut 32 is well-documented (see further § 6.5.4 below), and it seems apparent that Phil 2:15 recalls Deut 32:5 (Waters 2006: 148–58). The presence of both these allusions can be further confirmed by reference to Hays's well-known tests for detecting the presence of an allusion (Hays 1989: 29–32). Most of Hays's tests, however, are designed to detect the mere *presence* of an allusion, not to suggest how one should determine its significance. Even after one has successfully argued for the presence of an allusion, the problem of "assertorial weight" presents itself (Hays 1989: 91). Does Paul intend to cast himself typologically as a new Moses appointing judges for a renewed Israel, or does he merely use the familiar language of Deuteronomy to express himself in a roughly analogous legal situation? Does Paul intend for the Philippians to grasp his allusion and consider the subtle reversal of fortunes implied, now conceiving of themselves as a renewed Israel but still in danger of the fleshly Israel's fate? Or does he merely speak with the language of the Song of Moses to present a contrast between believer and non-believer? The resolution of these questions will, in large part, depend upon global judgments made about Paul's use of Scripture elsewhere. Since this study is interested in ascertaining Paul's own global construals of Deuteronomy, to take such potentially ambiguous allusions into consideration, at least on a first reading, will correspondingly weaken our results and invite a charge of question-begging. Whether individual allusions or echoes and their import are clear enough to warrant inclusion in a study such as the present one will, of course, remain a matter of some debate.

To return to our list of Paul's more explicit engagements with Deuteronomy, a number of conclusions may be drawn. First, with the exception of the minor echo in Philippians just discussed, this distribution conforms to the well-known phenomenon to which Harnack drew attention over eighty years ago (1928): the engagement with Deuteronomy (as with other

---

[6] These points have been repeatedly urged by B. S. Rosner (1991; 1994; 2007: 125–26), though the NA[27] margin does not note the allusion.

OT material) is largely confined to the *Hauptbriefe*.[7] Second, these citations and allusions span all of the major portions of Deuteronomy, with the
possible exception of the prologue (chaps 1–4) and the blessing and death
of Moses (33–34).[8] In contrast to the impression one might receive from
reading the secondary literature, Paul did not simply read Deut 27–32 and
forget about the rest of the book. In fact, the reminiscences of chapters 5–
25 are almost as numerous as those of 27–32. This suggests a broad familiarity with the book – or rather, with the *scroll* of Deuteronomy, the
kind that one might expect from a first century Jew who had worshiped
and been trained in the synagogue.[9] This also may suggest that the various
versions of the *testimonia* hypothesis, i.e., the view that Paul's OT citations came to him chiefly from traditional usage and removed from their
original context, are insufficient to account for the nature and variation of
Paul's recourse to Deuteronomy (see further Lincicum 2008c and § 2.7
above). Third, however, although we can speak of a broad distribution of
interest across the scroll as a whole, it is also clear that certain favorite
passages present themselves. In fact, this observation can be strengthened
by placing Paul's letters alongside the sections of Deuteronomy that play a
role in contemporary liturgical consciousness (cf. § 2 above). The *tefillin*
and the *mezuzot*, along with the recitation of the *Shema'* and the excerpted
texts from Qumran, all demonstrate a sustained interest in Deut 5:1–6:9,
10:12–11:21, and 32:1–43.[10] As I suggested in the conclusion to § 2 above,
this selection of texts corresponds to a significant portion of Paul's quotations from Deuteronomy in a manner that is too striking to ignore (i.e.,

---

[7] This excludes, of course, the Pastorals, where one may note the repetition of two of
Paul's Deuteronomy texts now placed side by side (Deut 25:4 and 19:15 in 1 Tim 5:18
and 19 respectively), apparently due to Pauline tradition (so, e.g., Häfner 2007). The citation from the Decalogue in Eph 6:2 more nearly resembles the text of Exod 20:12 than
that of Deut 5:16.

[8] Allusions have been proposed for these chapters (e.g., Deut 1:16 in 1 Cor 6:5b [see
above], Deut 4:7–8 in Rom 3:1–2 and 33:12 in 2 Thess 2:13), but they are certainly less
than decisive.

[9] Recall the evidence adduced above (§ 2.3) for the public reading of the law in the
first century: Philo, *Hypoth.* 7.12–13 (in Eusebius, *Pr. Ev.* 8.7.12–13); Luke 4:16–20;
Acts 13:15; 15:21; Josephus, *Ant.* 16.43–45; *C. Ap.* 2.175–78; 1QS 6:6–8; 4Q251 1:5;
4Q266 5 ii:1–3 = 4Q267 5 iii:3–5; *T. Levi* 13:2; and the so-called Theodotus inscription
from Jerusalem. What is more, all of our early Greek manuscripts show evidence of being designed for public reading, and the importance of such an act of public reading is
strengthened when approached via the more sociological concerns with low literacy rates
and an interpenetration of the oral and the written on the one hand, and from the more
particularly archaeological and literary attestation to the synagogue and its activities on
the other. See further the discussion of Paul's education and participation in synagogue
in § 2.6 above.

[10] See the appendix for these texts.

Rom 7:7; 10:19; 12:19; 13:9; 15:10; 1 Cor 8:4–6; cf. in a more minor way, Rom 9:14; Gal 2:6; Phil 2:15, etc.). Even though we know very little of Paul's own liturgical praxis in the post-Damascus years, this suggests that whether Paul abandoned some of his prior liturgical commitments or decided to continue in them as far as possible (as Acts seems to suggest), he shared with the other Jewish authors examined in this study a penchant for reflection on the texts that were central to the life of the worshiping community. That these liturgically prominent texts have exercised an imprint on Paul's letters offers a promising account of this shared attestation.

Fourth, detailed textual comparisons of Paul's citations with the text of Deuteronomy show that Paul has apparently relied on a Greek *Vorlage*, some difficult textual issues notwithstanding. As I have suggested above (§ 2.6.2), although there are no compelling reasons to doubt Paul's knowledge of Hebrew and/or Aramaic, Paul has followed the Septuagint almost exclusively in his Old Testament citations, occasionally operating with a Greek text that has undergone correction to the Hebrew. In this we observe the implicit operation of Paul's halakhic conviction about the propriety of Greek as a language conveying Scripture and other liturgical actions (§ 2.6.2). Fifth, and finally, this list substantiates the relative importance of Deuteronomy to Paul, along with Isaiah, Psalms and Genesis. This same general distribution of importance attaching to specific books may also be found at Qumran (Brooke 1997), and in Second Temple Jewish literature more broadly. The widespread popularity of Deuteronomy to which this book bears witness is certainly reflected in Paul's letters as well. As the investigation of Paul's background, education, and experience of the synagogue above concluded, the "liturgical-anamnetic" encounter with Deuteronomy provides the most promising global model for thinking about how Paul came to know the scroll of Deuteronomy.

The discussion thus far has focused on the distribution of Paul's quotations from Deuteronomy and on the introductory formulae he uses, and made some suggestions about how Paul may be indebted to the synagogue for his knowledge of the scroll. But what does Paul actually *do* with Deuteronomy, and what does this tell us about his construal of the book as a whole? In what follows, I suggest that Paul operates with three interlocking construals of Deuteronomy. The first of these is as ethical authority.

6.3. Deuteronomy as Ethical Authority

Pauline scholars have long noted the plurality of Paul's sources of ethical authority in his letters. It is true that Paul's ethical engagements with the Old Testament are by no means as entirely straightforward as we might expect from a first-century Jew. As long ago as 1928, Adolf von Harnack, noting in an essay to which I have already alluded that the Old Testament seems to play little formative role in Paul's instruction outside of the *Hauptbriefe*, concluded,

From this it follows that from the beginning Paul did not give the Old Testament to the young churches as the book of Christian sources for edification. Rather, he based his mission and teaching wholly and completely on the gospel and expects edification to come exclusively from it and from the Spirit accompanying the gospel (Harnack 1995 [1928]: 44).

Harnack did not deny the importance of the Old Testament for the formation of Paul's own thought, but argued that Paul had recourse to Scripture in his letters only when he needed to extricate the gospel from judaizing influence, and did not intend to pass on his own estimation of his Scriptures to his young churches (Harnack 1995 [1928]: 27–28). Nowhere, perhaps, is this lack of substantiation and dependence upon Scripture more noticeable than in the ethics Paul prescribes – even within the *Hauptbriefe*. Until quite recently this position has been relatively unchallenged (note the impressive list of scholars who hold this position in Rosner 1994: 3–4; see also, e.g., Tuckett 2000).

By contrast, however, a number of recent substantive studies have sought to challenge this wide-spread view by demonstrating Paul's indebtedness to Scripture and to Jewish tradition based on Scripture for the formation of his ethics (Holtz 1981; Reinmuth 1985; Tomson 1990; Finsterbusch 1996; Hays 1996, 2005; more generally note Niebuhr 1987; Bockmuehl 2000; previously, see Michel 1929: 158–59, 212; Bonsirven 1939: 295–97). Such studies have shown that, while Paul's engagement with Old Testament ethical material is by no means entirely straightforward (Hays 1996), he remained firmly rooted within the Jewish milieu of his day. Without denying the importance of contemporary Greco-Roman philosophical ideas and dominical traditions for the behavior Paul promotes, Scripture and the interpretative tradition issuing from it are increasingly recognized as exerting pressure on the ethical direction Paul provides.[11]

6.3.1. The Decalogue

Perhaps the clearest use of Deuteronomy as an ethical authority in Paul also demonstrates something of the attendant indirection in ethical appeal: twice in Romans Paul quotes from the Decalogue, both times arguably to epitomize the Torah in paradigmatic function. In Rom 13:9a, Deut 5:17–

---

[11] Note the survey of these three "sources of Paul's ethical teaching" in Furnish 1968: 25–67.

19, 21a is quoted: οὐ μοιχεύσεις, οὐ φονεύσεις, οὐ κλέψεις, οὐκ ἐπιθυμήσεις: you shall not commit adultery, you shall not murder, you shall not steal, you shall not covet. This, then, omits Deut 5:20 (οὐ ψευδομαρτυρήσεις κατὰ τοῦ πλησίον σου μαρτυρίαν ψευδῆ) and shortens v. 21 to the imperative only, omitting the objects of prohibited desire (neighbor's wife, house, field, servants, etc.). Unlike Eph 6:2, which most closely follows the form of the Decalogue found in Exod 20:12 LXX (Moritz 1996: 154–55), here the order of the commandments (adultery, murder, theft) aligns with Deuteronomy LXX rather than Exodus (adultery, theft, murder).[12] This then makes it perhaps more likely that Rom 7:7 has Deut 5:21 rather than Exodus 20:17 in mind, if there are any grounds for discerning a specific textual tradition here.[13] The short snippet of text is in fact identical in both Deut and Exod (οὐκ ἐπιθυμήσεις).

Rom 7:7, with its singular introduction and Edenic overtones (note, *inter alia*, Lichtenberger 2004), suggests that the command not to covet epitomizes for Paul the law's confrontation with humanity apart from the Spirit, and so provides an opportunity for sin to produce covetousness. Paul engages in an apologetic defense of the law just here where one might expect a thoroughgoing proponent of a "law-free gospel" to condemn it (7:7–13). The commandment is not faulty in and of itself, but it is powerless. For Paul, the νόμος, even before the Spirit, provides a crucial epistemological function in defining sin: "Therefore the law is holy, and the commandment is holy and just and good" (7:12). The difficulty is, of course, that the νόμος has been hijacked by ἁμαρτία.

But why should the tenth commandment be employed here? If Paul intends, as a wide-spread interpretation holds, to evoke the Adamic history with the use of a retrospective ἐγώ,[14] why not refer to the command in the

---

[12] Though it should be noted that the tradition is complicated by harmonization (the HT in both Exod and Deut has the order: murder, adultery, theft; some MSS of Exodus LXX have the Deuteronomy order, most likely by assimilation: see Wevers *ad loc*.). The order of Rom 13:9a is also found in Luke 18:20; Philo, *Decal*. 168–71; *Spec*. 3.7–4.40; *Her*. 173; perhaps James 2:11; Heb 13:4; and the Nash Papyrus. Note the discussion in Freund 1989; Albl 1999: 169 (though his contention that Paul's knowledge of this is due to its status as a pre-formed *testimonium* is unnecessary); Sänger 2001; Kellermann 2001, esp. 161–70.

[13] Stanley 1992: 103 says that Rom 7:7, while formally an instance of "limited selection" by leaving out the rest of the verse, is so common that "the foreshortening of the verse here is thus to be attributed to oral tradition, not to Paul's specific literary purpose" (103), following Koch 1986: 117.

[14] Naturally the long history of debate about how to interpret Rom 7 need not be rehearsed at this point. Certain links between Rom 7:7–13 and Gen 2–3, however, make an Adamic background likely: e.g., the sequence of a) being alive "apart from law" b) commandment given c) death, and the concept of the serpent (Gen 3:13) or sin (Rom 7:11) "deceiving" with the result of death.

garden, or to any other commandment for that matter? While Paul here joins Jewish contemporaries in emphasizing the importance of the command against ἐπιθυμία,[15] it is also crucial to note that his argument in Rom 7:7–25 only works with a command with a clear interior aspect.[16] It is also possible, however, as Jan Dochhorn (2009) has recently argued, that in this text we see the implicit results of an exegetical connection between the Hebrew texts of Deut 5:21 and Gen 3:6, via the unique collocation of the two catchwords חמד and אוה that occur in both places (though in the latter instance one is a verbal, the other a nominal form).[17] If Paul has been operating with this connection, presumably traditional in nature, then to offer the tenth commandment as the paradigmatic example of a commandment enables Paul to make a statement about a fundamental dynamic of how sin comes to power.[18] In this way, the last command of Deuteronomy's Decalogue comes to epitomize for Paul both the goodness of the law and its powerlessness, helpful and holy in identifying sin, but in that very identification providing a vehicle for sin to hijack in order to provoke humanity without the Spirit to deadly transgression – a picture of Israel's history *in nuce*. More specifically, this builds upon Paul's contention that his gospel is revealed χωρὶς νόμου, but μαρτυρουμένη ὑπὸ τοῦ νόμου (3:21), and anticipates his dual claims that though Israel possessed the law she failed to attain its goal (9:30–10:21)[19] and that it is those who believe that Jesus is Lord who truly fulfill the law by the Spirit (8:1–4). Paul does

---

[15] Note, e.g., *4 Macc.* 2:6; Philo, *Decal.* 142, 150, 173; *Spec.* 4.78; James 1:15; *Apoc. Mos.* 19:3 (on which, however, see n. 17 below). Cf. Black 1973: 102; Käsemann 1980: 194. That ἐπιθυμία does not have an exclusively sexual focus clearly militates against Gundry's attempt (2005) to render the chapter an autobiographical account of the pre-Christian Paul's struggle with sexual lust (so Ziesler 1988), though in his contention that Paul's ἐγὼ δὲ ἔζων χωρὶς νόμου ποτέ refers to childhood approximates a similar claim made already by Origen.

[16] As interpreters since at least Calvin have pointed out, but emphasized in more recent times clearly by Leenhardt 1957: 107; Ziesler 1988, 1989: 180, etc.

[17] He also suggests that a similar tradition may be found in *Apoc. Mos.* 19:3. In his edition of the textually related *Life of Adam and Eve*, however, Tromp 2005: 57, 109, 144, suggests that the phrase to which Dochhorn draws attention, τοῦτ᾽ ἐστιν τῆς ἐπιθυμίας. ἐπιθυμία γάρ ἐστιν πάσης ἁμαρτίας, may be a later gloss – presumably under the influence of Rom 7:7 and, possibly, 1 Tim 6:10 – and accordingly places it in brackets in his edition. On the relationship between *Apoc. Mos.* and *L.A.E.*, see Dochhorn 2009: 76 n. 31.

[18] Is there a similar reflection on the primacy of ἐπιθυμία in Col 3:5, where ἐπιθυμία is closely associated with πλεονεξία (perhaps a subspecies of ἐπιθυμία?) ἥτις ἐστιν εἰδωλολατρία?

[19] Compare Paul's statement that εὑρέθη μοι ἡ ἐντολὴ ἡ εἰς ζωήν, αὕτη εἰς θάνατον with his citation of Lev 18:5 in Rom 10:5.

not deny the moral force of the command, but uses precisely this force to understand – and to construct – the failure of Israel to attain life under law.

Likewise, in Rom 13:8–10, Paul simultaneously affirms and casts into fresh perspective the second table of the Decalogue:

Owe no one anything, except to love one another; for the one who loves another has fulfilled the law. The commandments, 'You shall not commit adultery, you shall not murder, you shall not steal, you shall not covet,' and any other commandment, are summed up in this word: 'Love your neighbor (πλησίον) as yourself.' Love does no wrong to a neighbor; therefore, love is the fulfilling of the law.[20]

Looking for an ordering principle or an epitome of the law is, of course, not something unique to Paul. As noted above (§ 5.3.2), in his treatises *On the Decalogue* and *On the Special Laws*, Philo treats the individual commandments of the Decalogue as "headings" (κεφάλαια) under which the various other commandments of the Pentateuch can be arranged. Paul may be restricting the epitome of the law even further here, but perhaps not in a completely arbitrary way. Among the material omitted by Paul from his Deuteronomy citations (Deut 5:20, 21b)[21] are two occurrences of the word πλησίον (see Hübner 1997: 198), and it is arguably this "neighbor" who is the implied object of the actions prohibited by the second table of the Decalogue. Therefore, when Paul cites Lev 19:18 and says that in it the law is "brought to a head" (ἀνακεφαλαιοῦται),[22] he apparently sees Lev 19:18 as offering a pithy encapsulation or an inner logic of Deuteronomy's demand, and not as somehow negating or relativizing it.[23]

That Leviticus is seen as expressing the heart of Deuteronomy's command may seem surprising, especially in light of the fact that Paul twice appears to use Deuteronomy to correct Leviticus in its view of the law (Gal 3:10–14; Rom 10:5–8, on which see § 6.5.1 and § 6.5.3 respectively). Rather than occasioning surprise, however, this should caution us against

---

[20] The attempt of some exegetes to see the theme of the chapter as "law in general," i.e., both civil and religious law, is thoroughly unconvincing. See, e.g., Leenhardt 1957: 190 n. 1, contra whom, (and others like him), see, e.g., Käsemann 1980: 361.

[21] In fact, א (P) 048. 81. 104, et al. supply the omitted ninth commandment, οὐ ψευδομαρτυρήσεις, though its omission is much more likely to be original. So also Murray 1968: 2.161; Stanley 1992: 174–76; Metzger 1994: 467.

[22] Cf. Gal 5:14, where Paul also cites Lev 19:18 and says similarly, though not identically, that ὁ πᾶς νόμος ἐν ἑνὶ λόγῳ πεπλήρωται. The text was a favorite in early Christian circles. Note Matt 5:43; 19:19 (intriguingly, in connection with the Decalogue); 22:39; Mark 12:31, 33; Luke 10:27. On Lev 19:18 in Jewish literature, see Stuhlmacher 1994: 209.

[23] Käsemann shows the difficulty of his own position when he says, "The real problem of the text [13:8–10] is that there is no polemicizing against the *nomos*, let alone against another law" (1980: 361), and goes on to suggest that Paul is merely following tradition here.

urging a monolithic construal of either book for Paul, such that Deuteronomy always trumps Leviticus or vice versa.[24] Though it seems clear that Paul often favors Deuteronomy over Leviticus in the sense that the former figures much more prominently in his letters than the latter, Leviticus is certainly not entirely absent in his writing. In addition to the explicit citations of Lev 18:5 and 19:18 (cf. also 2 Cor 6:16 with Lev 26:11–12, though its Pauline character is disputed), Paul uses cultic examples drawn from Leviticus at 1 Cor 10:18 (cf. Lev 7:6–15), Rom 3:25 and 8:3 (note the widespread use in Leviticus of ἱλαστήριον and περὶ ἁμαρτίας respectively). Even more intriguing, Paul may bring Leviticus and Deuteronomy together in Rom 12:19 as well (on which see § 6.3.5 below).

Paul does not, like Philo and Josephus, draw attention to the first person speech of God in the Decalogue (in fact, his argument in Romans 7 requires him to refer to the "law" speaking), but the fact that both times he employs the Decalogue in Romans it has a paradigmatic or epitomizing tendency does demonstrate its unique role for him. It may be that the long liturgical preoccupation with the Decalogue invited the apostle to consider the inner logic of the commands and to see in the prohibition of coveting something expressing the fundamental dynamics of transgression. What is more, the prominence of the Decalogue and the sheer obviousness of one's obligation to obey its commands are the presupposition for Paul's distillation of these, together with "any other commandment," into the love imperative. Deuteronomy's Decalogue, especially its second table, expresses for Paul the basic moral commandments in a manner that is still unproblematically valid – even if he can assume this validity to argue to further conclusions.

6.3.2. Purge the Evil From Your Midst

The ethical authority of Deuteronomy, however, also plays out more directly in Paul's letters. In 1 Corinthians 5, after seeking to persuade the Corinthians to abandon their factionalism and delight in rhetorical displays

---

[24] Watson's solution to this tension – a tension arguably heightened by his own reading – is a consistent, but unsatisfying one (perhaps akin to the Pseudo-Clementine solution of looking for "false pericopes" in the law noted above, § 2.4 n. 90): "The solution to this problem is simply that Paul believes that he hears a plurality of voices within the Torah itself: the text that derives from the Sinai event is multiple and not singular in origin (cf. Gal. 3.19–20). From one angelic voice we learn that the person who does these things will live by them; from another we learn that all who are of works of law are under a curse; a third instructs us to love our neighbor as ourselves; a fourth is concerned with the observance of sacred times and seasons (cf. Gal. 4.9–10)" (2004: 520). Note the similar affirmation of a plurality of voices in the Torah, though in a different context, in Martyn 1997: 324–28 and *passim*.

of power in the alleged pursuit of wisdom (chs 1–4), Paul turns to address what he has heard orally reported to him about the Corinthian congregation (5:1a: ὅλως ἀκούεται).[25] There is πορνεία among the congregation: a certain man has "the wife of his father" (γυνή τοῦ πατρὸς), a *terminus technicus* for one's step-mother (see esp. Lev 18:8; 20:11; Deut 23:1; 27:20; cf. Gen 37:2; Lev 18:11). Paul initially rebukes them for condoning, indeed being "puffed up" about, a sexual offense that would not be tolerated among the unbelieving Gentiles (5:1).[26] He then proceeds to urge the Corinthians to expel the offender from the congregation for the destruction of his flesh and ultimate salvation,[27] pressing his point by a series of mixed metaphors whose referents are difficult to keep entirely clear, but whose point is not obscure:[28] the commandment to put the man outside of the community is repeated four times (vv. 2,[29] 4–5, 7, 13). In 1 Cor 5:13, Paul's admonitions come to a head with the unmarked quotation[30] of a refrain drawn from Deuteronomy: ἐξάρατε τὸν πονηρὸν ἐξ ὑμῶν αὐτῶν ("Drive out the evil one from among you").[31] The phrase in fact occurs in Deut 17:7; 19:19; 21:21; 22:21, 24; 24:7 (καὶ ἐξαρεῖς τὸν πονηρὸν ἐξ ὑμῶν αὐτῶν) and with "from Israel" in 17:12; 22:22 (καὶ ἐξαρεῖς τὸν

---

[25] Some MSS (P[68] ℵ[2] Ψ 1881, etc.) have ὀνομάζεται here, presumably under influence from Eph 5:3, where πορνεία is also at issue.

[26] See Conzelmann 1975: 96 n. 29 for Roman law prohibiting such a relationship; for Jewish rulings, note Tomson 1990: 97–103. In light of the entire chapter, however, the judgment of Lindemann 2000 seems precisely backwards: "Paulus trifft seine Entscheidung offensichtlich nicht aufgrund der Tora....Das von ihm genannte Kriterium ist vielmehr die Tatsache, daß derartiges nicht einmal ἐν τοῖς ἔθνεσιν vorkomme" (132).

[27] "For the destruction of his flesh" is a notoriously murky phrase to understand. In general terms, however, Käsemann's analysis stands: "The judgment which is exercised through the charismatic proclamation still stands in the service of grace, is one pole of the offer of grace and, precisely by announcing God's justice on earth, is directed towards the conversion and salvation of the guilty and the preservation of the community" (1969: 68).

[28] The metaphors themselves are drawn largely from the feast of Passover (Exod 12:8–21; Deut 16:2–16; cf. Héring 1959: 41). Compare the referentially slippery "veil" in 2 Cor 3.

[29] The use of the phrase ἀρθῇ ἐκ μέσου ὑμῶν in 5:2 may already anticipate Paul's citation in 1 Cor 5:13; at least some MSS add the prefix ἐξ to the verb to conform to 5:13 (Ψ Maj Did).

[30] Stanley omits the quotation from his discussion because it is not signaled as a quotation to the reader (1992: 33–37, 195 n. 44); note, however, Heil 2005: 90–91.

[31] Though the form of the verb has a varied textual history, the Pauline form is almost unique (see Wevers *ad loc.*), and so should probably be attributed to the apostle's use of the plural form to exhort the congregation as a whole (see n. 4 above).

πονηρὸν ἐξ Ἰσραήλ); for the concept, note also 13:5(6); 19:13; 21:9.[32] Almost all of these places refer to capital punishment for various crimes, including false prophecy and idolatry, refusing to obey the priest, bearing false witness, rebelling against parents, a woman's having pre-marital sex or a man sleeping with another man's wife or fiancée, and kidnapping. Several of these themes (notably idolatry, authority, and sex), find their way into 1 Corinthians, widely seen to be Paul's most 'halakhic' letter – or at least the letter in which he treats themes in a manner which resembles halakhic reasoning.[33] Paul uses the final citation in an emphatic manner to punctuate his exhortation with urgency (compare the final citations in 1 Cor 1:26–31; 2 Cor 5:16–6:2; note Koch 1986: 277–78).

Though the offence against which Paul is reacting is often seen against the background of Lev 18:7–8, it is also striking to note an interesting set of collocations in Deut 22:21–23:10. Here the phrase that Paul cites occurs twice to regulate sexual relationships, followed closely afterward with a prohibition of the very act that Paul is here condemning (Deut 23:1 LXX: οὐ λήμψεται ἄνθρωπος τὴν γυναῖκα τοῦ πατρὸς αὐτοῦ). This in turn is immediately followed by a discussion of who may enter εἰς ἐκκλησίαν κυρίου (23:2, 3, 4, 9). As William Horbury (1985 [1998]) has suggested, Deut 23 served as a *locus classicus* for discussions of the regulations for exclusion from the community – coinciding with a broader contemporary shift in punishment from death to excommunication as penalty.[34] This seems to be reflected in Paul's citation of Deuteronomy's standard ruling

---

[32] The fact that the phrase recurs throughout Deut renders unlikely McDonough 2005's suggestion that Paul bases the structure of 1 Cor 5–6 on the broader context of Deut 17.

[33] So, e.g., Richardson 1980; Tomson 1990, etc. The expulsion refrain also echoes through the Temple Scroll's halakhic discussions: 11Q19 54.17–18; 56.10; 61.10; 64.6; 66.3–4. Paul also, like the Temple Scroll, gives direction for appointing judges (1 Cor 6:1–11; 11Q19 51.11–18) and offers halakhic reflection on marriage (1 Cor 7; 11Q19 65.7–66.17) – and in both cases subtle connections to Deuteronomy may be discerned (see, e.g., Rosner 2007: 127–28 for indications of Deut behind 1 Cor 7 on marriage, esp. Deut 24:1–4 in 1 Cor 7:39–40). For a broader comparison of Paul and the Temple Scroll with reference to Deuteronomy, see Lincicum 2009.

Rosner's interesting contention that we should see in the vice list of 1 Cor 5:11 a correspondence with Deuteronomy's major infractions probably outruns the evidence, and involves some stretching of concepts to align with their alleged co-referents (1994: 68–70; 2007: 121–25); in critique, note Tuckett 2000, though the latter's contention that Christology and not Scripture is Paul's ethical norm in this passage poses what for Paul would surely be a false dichotomy.

[34] Horbury thus offers a more convincing tradition history concerning expulsion from the community than the magical parallels adduced by Collins 1980. Note also Horbury's illuminating discussion of Septuagintal influence on New Testament conceptions of the church (1997), an influence clearly reflected here.

for capital punishment, where it is manifestly taken to refer to expulsion rather than execution (cf. 5:5).[35]

What is equally striking, however, is Paul's assumption that this injunction is addressed directly to the Corinthian situation. A concern for the ritual purity of Israel is transposed to a concern for the ethical purity of the largely Gentile Corinthian congregation. Without over-reading the significance of Paul's use of the Deuteronomic expulsion formula here, it is worth noting that Paul addresses the Corinthians as the ἐκκλησία τοῦ θεοῦ (1:2) who should conceive of themselves as the temple of God (3:16–17), and so maintain the purity proper to Israel. Whether all of Paul's audience would have discerned in Paul's exhortation the words of Deuteronomy is doubtful (so rightly Stanley 2004), but the phrase joins a whole network of judgments Paul makes to identify the Corinthians as part of the covenant people of God (cf. also § 6.5.4 below on 1 Cor 10). In this way, Deuteronomy addresses the Corinthians with the ethical demand to preserve moral purity in an address whose immediacy conceals prior theological judgments.

6.3.3. Muzzling the Ox

This sense of immediacy is perhaps even more notable in Paul's citation of Deut 25:4 just a few chapters later. In the midst of his discussion of food sacrificed to idols (1 Cor 8:1–11:1),[36] Paul offers himself as an example for the Corinthians to imitate in renouncing the exercise of their freedom for the sake of love. In a subsection variously defined as consisting of 9:1– 14 (Garland 2003); 9:1–18 (so Soards 1999; Lindemann 2000); or 9:1–27 (Barrett 1968; Fee 1987; Horsley 1998), Paul delineates in detail the authority which he in turn refuses to insist upon – including the "right to eat and drink" at the community's expense (v. 4), and the "right not to work" (v. 6), but to be supported by the community (9:7). Margaret Mitchell rightly stresses that Paul "draws richly upon a variety of exempla: the behavior of the other apostles (9:4–6), common human wisdom (9:7), Scriptural proofs (9:8–11), common practice once more (9:12c), cultic norms (9:13), and finally a word of the Lord (9:14)" (1991: 247).[37] It is in

---

[35] Cf. also Deut 27:20, where the man who sleeps with the wife of his father is "cursed" (ἐπικατάρατος). Might this further illuminate 5:5?

[36] For discussions of the sociological elements of 1 Cor 8:1–11:1, note the influential statement of Theissen 1982: 121–43; cf. Horrell 1996: 105–09, 142–50. The underlying sociological analysis of Theissen was challenged by Meggitt (1999, 2001) who sought to show that the Pauline communities operated at the subsistence level of absolute poverty, but see the important responses by Martin (2001) and Theissen (2001).

[37] My analysis in this section presupposes that Paul's ἀπολογία (v. 3) should not be seen as primarily addressed to his detractors, but serves as the opportunity for him to

the midst of this exemplary argument that Paul claims not to be speaking solely κατὰ ἄνθρωπον, and introduces support from Scripture in a manner that has puzzled his readers ever since. Paul here adduces what is "written in the law of Moses" as an authority: οὐ κημώσεις βοῦν ἀλοῶντα ("You shall not muzzle an ox while it is treading out the grain").[38] Paul has already been trading on agricultural metaphors in the near context (cf. 1 Cor 9:7 with Deut 20:6),[39] but what is surprising is his statement that follows the quotation: "Is it for oxen that God is concerned? Or does he not speak entirely/surely (πάντως)[40] for our sake? It was indeed written for our sake..." While Deut 25:4 was subject to a range of interpretations among Paul's rough contemporaries, none quite approximates the apostle's.[41]

---

present himself as an example of not exercising one's freedom (so, rightly, Mitchell 1991: 130–38, 243–50; Martin 1995: 82–83; cf. also Willis 1985). The role of 1 Cor 9 as an *exemplum* was already noted by the humanist scholar John Colet, *ad loc*. This stands in contrast to those who point to the chapter as an interpolation on apostolic authority that interrupted the flow of Paul's argument concerning food sacrificed to idols, now less common than it once was. The exemplary aspect of the chapter, however, should not be pressed so absolutely that no aspect of defense remains, contra esp. Mitchell 1991, who argues that one cannot take a view of 1 Cor 9 as both an *apologia* and an *exemplum* because the two are at rhetorically crossed purposes (see esp. 1991: 244–45 and n. 330). Might Paul's subsidiary purpose of defending himself against τοῖς ἐμὲ ἀνακρίνουσίν in fact go some way toward explaining why Paul's prose is so tortuous in this passage? What is more, Mitchell's insistence that the accusation against Paul that he did not take the Corinthians' money while he took others' is "scarcely possible" (246) encounters its own difficulties. Does not Paul protest too much, even granting the exemplary character of his rhetorical self-presentation? These considerations are even more weighty in considering the fallout of 1 Corinthians that we find in 2 Corinthians (however the unity of the latter epistle is judged). In critique of Mitchell's broader argument about the purpose of 1 Corinthians as the establishment of unity, note Ciampa and Rosner 2006 (who may, however, commit the inverse error of Mitchell by privileging chs. 5–14 over 1–4).

[38] Deut 25:4: οὐ φιμώσεις βοῦν ἀλοῶντα. The variation between the verbs is difficult, with some strong variation within the tradition of 1 Corinthians itself (φιμώσεις P[46] ℵ A B[2] C D[1] Ψ 33. 1881; Or Epiph; κημώσεις B* D* [which also has this reading at 1 Tim 5:18] F G 1739). Cf. 1 Tim 5:18: βοῦν ἀλοῶντα οὐ φιμώσεις. See Stanley 1992: 195–96, who notes that the external evidence for φιμώσεις is actually stronger than for κημώσεις, but that the argument is from the *lectio difficilior*. He ultimately suggests that it is impossible to decide (196). Metzger 1994: 492 gives the same reasoning.

[39] Already noted by Gough 1855: 80.

[40] Both senses of the adverb are attested (cf. LSJ s.v.), and one's broader sense of the import of the passage determines which aspect one sees here. But the precise nuance need not be decisive.

[41] The Temple Scroll seems to have reflected on the curious placement of the law not to muzzle the ox while it is treading out the grain in Deut 25:4: it relocates the law to a discussion of other laws about animals (11Q19 52.12–13). Philo calls attention to Deut 25:4 as a law that he "admires," apparently read in a literal sense (*Virt.* 145). At times Josephus supplies explanatory reasons for commands that are stated apodictically in the original, and he does this in his re-telling of Deut 25:4: "Do not muzzle the mouths of

Commentators have generally espoused one of three opinions on the text: that here Paul employs a (proto-)Rabbinic method, in continuity with the literal sense of the original text;[42] that he uses a purely "allegorical" hermeneutic;[43] or that his interpretation should be described as an "eschatologically determined" reading of the text.[44] In contrast to the parallels from Philo and the *Letter of Aristeas* that are sometimes adduced to claim 1 Cor 9:9 as an instance of a strictly allegorical interpretation, Paul seems to be motivated by a sense of immediate address borne by the eschatological situation at hand. This is made clear by comparing his statement in 1 Cor 9:10 ("It was indeed written for our sake") with his statement in the next chapter that "These things happened to them to serve as an example, and they were written down for our instruction, on whom the ends of the ages have come" (1 Cor 10:11). Moreover, it should not be denied that the placement of Deut 25:4 in the context of Deuteronomy 25 and its concern to regulate interpersonal relationships may have served as a stimulus to the apostle's reflections. Likewise, the explanatory comment in 9:10 lends itself to understanding Paul's statement in 9:9 as a statement with axiomatic import.[45] But Paul is clearly not concerned with the original sense so much as the present import of the text (especially if his δι᾽ ἡμᾶς is taken in a restrictive sense as referring to apostles). In this sense, we may

---

oxen when they thresh the ears of corn on the threshing-floor, for it is not right to bar from the fruit those who have joined in the work and who have exerted themselves with regard to its production" (*Ant.* 4.233; cf. *C. Ap.* 2.213). If his paraphrase is more generalizing than the original precept, it stops short of Paul's primary application of the text to apostles. Note also the legal extension of Deut 25:4 in the *Sifre to Deuteronomy* (§ 287), in contrast to Paul's quite different extension in 1 Cor 9:9. Compare also *Arist.* 144: "Do not take the contemptible view that Moses enacted this legislation because of an excessive preoccupation with mice and weasels or suchlike creatures"; and 169: "In the matter of meats, the unclean reptiles, the beasts, the whole underlying rationale is directed toward righteousness and righteous human relationships."

[42] So Allo 1934: 217; Orr and Walther 1976: 241; Kaiser 1978; Instone Brewer 1992; Horsley 1998: 126; Garland 2003: 410; Verbruggen 2006; Rosner 2007: 128–30.

[43] So Lietzmann 1949: 41; cf. also Lohse 1997; Gräßer 2006.

[44] So Barrett 1968: 205–06; Fee 1987: 407–08; Lang 1994: 116; Witherington 1995: 207–08; Lindemann 2000: 204–05; (Hanson 1974: 161–66 straddles these options). See also the excursus reviewing various opinions in Lindemann 2000: 204–05.

[45] Since J. Weiss, some have taken 9:10b as a quotation: NA[27] refers to Sir 6:19; others refer to a lost apocryphal work or to Isa 28:24, 28. So, e.g., Conzelmann 1975: 155 (somewhat equivocally: cf. 155 n. 41); Koch 1986: 41–42; Stanley 1992: 196–97; Soards 1999: 185; Lindemann 2000: 205; Heil 2005: 126–30. However, taking the ὅτι as causal and so explicative (cf. BDF § 456; Wallace 1996: 460–61), makes good sense of the sentence as an explanation of Paul's understanding of the preceding quotation of Deut 25:4 using the terms of the latter to make his point. Those who do not see a quotation here include, *inter alia*, UBS[4]; Allo 1934: 218; Barrett 1968: 206; Fee 1987 409 n. 68; Lang 1994: 116; Garland 2003: 411.

see here a sort of eschatologically-determined halakhic reasoning, that is, the formulation of ethical decisions based on the conviction that the text must address the present age and should be interpreted so to do. Once more, the ethical power of Deuteronomy to address the Corinthians is thus mediated by the eschatological irruption which now constitutes those Gentile Corinthians as members of the people of God – the irruption of the cross and resurrection which discloses Jesus Christ as the one Lord and re-referentializes the law accordingly. It should not be missed, however, that the present text is "a clear example of Paul using the Torah as a guide for Christian conduct" (Rosner 2007: 130) – even if, in his state of "apostolic exceptionalism," Paul in turn refuses to insist upon the privilege which he goes to such lengths to substantiate.

6.3.4. The Testimony of Two or Three Witnesses

Although in 2 Corinthians Deuteronomy plays a more subdued role than in 1 Corinthians,[46] the single Deuteronomy citation that does appear is employed to motivate the Corinthians by threatening them with judicial action. In 2 Cor 13:1 Paul adduces, in an unmarked citation, Deuteronomy's "law of witnesses" from Deut 19:15: ἐπὶ στόματος δύο μαρτύρων καὶ τριῶν σταθήσεται πᾶν ῥῆμα.[47] Nearing the end of the defense of his apostolic authority that occupies 2 Cor 10–13 (Strecker 1992),[48] Paul's threat

---

[46] Although it should be noted that the explicit use of Scripture is not as intensive in this letter as in the other *Hauptbriefe*. NA[27] notes the following: Exod 32–34 in 2 Cor 3; Ps 115:1 (LXX) in 4:13; Isa 49:8 in 6:2; the disputed catena of mixed citations in 6:16–18; Exod 16:18 in 8:15; Prov 22:8 in 9:7 Ps 111:9 (LXX) in 9:9; Isa 55:10 in 9:10; Jer 9:23 in 10:17; Deut 19:15 in 13:1.

[47] It appears that Paul has abridged Deut 19:15: ἐπὶ στόματος δύο μαρτύρων καὶ ἐπὶ στόματος τριῶν μαρτύρων σταθήσεται πᾶν ῥῆμα (see Hübner 1997: 394–95) and that 1 Tim 5:19 may be a further abridgement of Paul: ἐπὶ δύο ἢ τριῶν μαρτύρων. Note also Deut 17:6: ἐπὶ δυσὶν μάρτυσιν ἢ ἐπὶ τρισὶν μάρτυσιν ἀποθανεῖται ὁ ἀποθνήσκων. Koch (1986: 117–18) considers it likely (*wahrscheinlich*) that the abbreviated text in 2 Cor 13:1 reflects a pre-Pauline, oral formulation, especially in light of Matt 18:16 and the similar omission made there (ἐπὶ στόματος δύο μαρτύρων ἢ τριῶν σταθῇ πᾶν ῥῆμα); this is possible in principle, but it is not clear how one would acquire proof of this assertion. Stanley 1992 does not consider this in his audience-oriented study.

[48] While the heyday of partition hypotheses for the Pauline letters is probably past, 2 Corinthians has enjoyed the most persuasive and persistent arguments for a composite nature. Specifically, most of the discussion centers on the question of the identification of the "letter of tears" (cf. 2 Cor 2:4–9; 7:8–12), and whether this should be identified with 1 Corinthians, 2 Cor 10–13, or another letter now lost. Note the balanced discussion in Horrell 1996: 296–312, who ultimately suggests that 2 Cor 10–13 should be identified with the "letter of tears" and comprises a separate (and probably earlier) letter from 2 Cor 1–9; cf. Welborn 1995. Arguing for the original unity of 2 Corinthians are Bieringer 1994; Hall 2003: 86–106; cf. also Matera 2003: 24–32 and many other recent commenta-

to come against the Corinthians in punishment is couched in the legal requirements for convicting criminals (already anticipated in 12:14). The
implication seems to be that the Corinthians' failure to recognize Paul's
authority shows their complicity in transgression before God. What is
more, Paul turns the tables on the Corinthians, for while they have put Paul
on trial, he now reverses the charges to show that their evaluation of his
apostolic credentials will actually turn out to be an act of vindication or
condemnation for *themselves*. But who are the other witnesses? It appears
that, as Lietzmann (1949: 160) complained, the three witnesses (τρεῖς
μάρτυρες) have been reduced to three statements (τρεῖς μαρτυρίαι) by the
same witness.[49]

At this point it is helpful to recall one stream of interpretation concerning the law of witnesses in Second Temple Judaism, discussed briefly
above (§ 3.2.2). In particular, the Damascus Document states:

Any matter in which a man sins against the law, and his fellow sees him and he is alone:
if it is a capital matter, he shall report it in his presence, with reproach, to the Inspector;
and the Inspector shall personally record it, until he does it again in the presence of
someone, and he too reports it to the Inspector; and if he is caught again in the presence
of someone, his judgment is complete (CD-A 9.16–20; trans. García Martínez and Tigchelaar 1997).

What is crucial to note here is that this passage is concerned with the
"combination of witnesses." That is, in contrast to later rabbinic rulings
(see Neusner 1973; Schiffman 1975; 1983: 73–88), this text suggests that
an infraction need not be seen by two witnesses simultaneously in order
for the offending party to be liable for his offense; rather, individual witnesses are recorded and have a cumulative effect. Now compare this with
Paul. He writes: "This is the third time I am coming to you: 'let every matter be established on the report of two and three witnesses.' I warned those
who sinned before and all the others, and I warn them now while absent, as
I did when present on my second visit, that if I come again I will not spare
them" (13:1–2). It seems that Paul is operating under the same assumption
as the Damascus Document: individual witnesses can be combined to have
a cumulative effect. But Paul goes even further, because the individual

tors. I simply note the discussion here, though one's view on the original unity of 2 Corinthians does not determine how one takes the citation in 13:1.

[49] The interpretation of Paul's successive visits as witnesses goes back at least to
Chrysostom, *Hom. in 2 Cor.* 29 (PG 61 col. 596): Οὕτω δὴ καὶ ἐνταῦθα ποιεῖ, ἀντὶ
μαρτυριῶν τὰς παρουσίας αὐτοῦ τιθεὶς καὶ τὰς παραγγελίας. Note also Calvin *ad loc.*;
Héring 1958: 101, and many others. Contrast Strachan 1935: 38; Allo 1937: 335; Hughes
1962: 474–75, who think the view would be either overly subtle or unworthy of Paul because of its disregard for the original intention of the law. It is also worth noting Paul's
tendency to muster two or three Scriptural witnesses elsewhere (e.g., Rom 10:19–21;
15:9–13, etc.). See also the survey of material related to witness laws in van Vliet 1958.

witnesses are not separate individuals but his own successive visits (Thrall 2000: 2.872–76), or possibly two visits and one letter (so Furnish 1984: 575). Either way, this understanding of Paul's text as indebted to a notion of the combination of witnesses is surely not a "farfetched" and "allegorical interpretation" (contra Barnett 1997: 598 n. 23). There may be some innovative apostolic halakhah behind his warning here, but Paul is still operating within a tradition of interpretation concerning the law of witnesses.

6.3.5. Vengeance Is Mine

Finally, in Romans 12:19 Paul appeals to Deut 32:35 as a ground to exhort the Romans not to take vengeance themselves: ἐμοὶ ἐκδίκησις, ἐγὼ ἀνταποδώσω, λέγει κύριος ("Vengeance is mine, I will repay, says the Lord").[50] The standard LXX texts here read ἐν ἡμέρᾳ ἐκδικήσεως ἀνταποδώσω. This instance probably reflects Paul's reliance on a Greek text of Deuteronomy that has been revised toward the Hebrew. A marginal reading in a Syriac MS published by W. Baars (1968: 148; cf. Fernández Marcos 2000: 138), provides a reading from Symmachus that approximates the text seen in Rom 12:19 (and Heb 10:30, etc.).[51] In this way, it appears likely that in Romans we see an instance of a "proto-Symmachian" reading – that is, an instance of a Symmachian reading employed before the historical Symmachus lived and worked. N. Fernández Marcos retroverts the reading into Greek as ἐμοὶ ἐκδικήσεις καὶ ἀνταποδώσω (2000: 138).[52] Although ἐκδίκησις is plural instead of singular and ἐγὼ is missing, it appears that we see in these texts a witness to a Greek text that has been corrected toward a variantly pointed Hebrew original.[53] The quotation is also interesting for its addition of λέγει κύριος, but this is probably to be as-

---

[50] Cf. similarly Heb 10:30, which may be dependent on Paul; see Rothschild 2009: 96–97, 104–05, *pace* Koch 1986: 77 n. 96. The same conclusion was already reached by Döpke 1829: 267.

[51] Also seen in *Tg. Onq.* and *Frag. Tg.*, as well as in the Latin tradition. For the latter, note Tertullian (*Adv. Marc.* 2.18) who cites Deut 32:35 in this form: *mihi defensam et ego defendam* (cf. Lagrange 1950b: 308). Cf. also the Vulgate at Deut 32:35: *mea est ultio et ego retribuam*, though at Rom 12:19 the Vulgate has *mihi vindictam ego retribuam dicit Dominus* (note the different renderings of the Vetus Latina at Heb 10:30, though all displaying a similar structure).

[52] Cf. Wevers 2006 *ad loc.*, who offers the Latin rendering *mihi ultio et retribuam*.

[53] So Stanley 1992: "Now the Pauline wording can be understood as a literal reproduction of a Greek text that had been revised to bring it into line with a Hebrew text that contained the same first person singular form of שׁלם that appears in Symmachus and the Targumim" (172; cf. 171–73). *Pace* Koch 1986: 77–78, who ascribes the change not to a Hebraizing revision but to oral usage.

I am grateful to Marketta Liljeström of the University of Helsinki for sharing her expertise in the Syrohexaplaric evidence with me.

cribed to Paul's parenetic concern rather than, as some have suggested, a background in early Christian prophecy.[54]

But perhaps more striking than the form of the citation is its content. In words that may recall the first half of Lev 19:18 (οὐκ ἐκδικᾶταί σου ἡ χείρ), Paul urges the Romans not to avenge themselves (μὴ ἑαυτοὺς ἐκδικοῦντες). Rather, they are to "give place to wrath"[55] – a wrath that the subsequent citation shows to be divine in nature. At this point Paul cites Deuteronomy as a ground (γέγραπται γάρ) for his exhortation: in light of the "nearness" of salvation (cf. 13:11), the Romans need not exercise vengeance on their own behalf. This is not because Paul believes, as Dodd so modernly put it, "the moral order will look after itself" (1932: 200), but because Paul believes a day of justification is coming when God will render to each one a due reward according to their works – and for the unrighteous, this will be a ἡμέρα ὀργῆς (cf. 2:5–6).[56] What is more, Paul's citation comes from Deuteronomy's Song of Moses, which, as we shall see, he reads as a prophetic foretelling of the rebellion of Israel, the inclusion of the Gentiles, and the ultimate reconciliation of both in worship before God (§ 6.5.4). This statement is drawn from near the end of the Song, and it is just possible that Paul conceives of the repayment of vengeance described here as the prelude to that apocalyptic reconstitution with which the Song climaxes – though such an interpretation should not be pressed. What is more immediately available to us is the fact that Deuteronomy's statement is held to be unproblematically valid as a norm by which to form ethical paraenesis.[57] Further, by here bringing Lev 19:18 and Deuteronomy together – Leviticus to express the negative prohibition and Deuteronomy to supply the motivating ground – Paul may anticipate his collocation of Leviticus and Deuteronomy in 13:8–10 (see § 6.3.1 above).

---

[54] Ellis (1957: 107–12; 1978: 182–87) suggested that all of the λέγει κύριος quotations in the New Testament owe their origin to Christian prophecy (so also, tentatively, Stanley 1992: 173–74). Persuasive critiques have been leveled against this by Aune 1983: 342–46. What is more, the textual variation which Ellis ascribed to the paraphrase of the prophets is now better explained by reference to a Greek text corrected toward the Hebrew. It may be that Paul simply adds the phrase for parenetic emphasis, to call attention to the fact that it is the κύριος who speaks (*pace* Ellis 1978: 184, the introductory formula in this case [γέγραπται γάρ] does not fulfill that role, and in the previous three chapters [i.e., 9–11], Paul often identifies the speaker of OT citations; e.g., 9:27, 29; 10:19–21, etc.).

[55] On the idiom διδόναι τόπον as "to give an opportunity," see BDAG s.v. τόπος. Cf. also Eph 4:27; note further Heb 12:17: μετανοίας γὰρ τόπον οὐχ εὗρεν.

[56] Cf. Stendahl 1962: "The non-retaliation is undoubtedly based and motivated by the deference to God's impending vengeance" (354).

[57] Compare CD 9.1–8 citing Lev 19:18 (!) and Nah 1:2 to a similar purpose, though apparently the restriction against seeking vengeance is toward those within the community ("against his fellow": על רעהו).

6.3.6. Conclusion: Deuteronomy as Ethical Authority

In this way, then, the apostle has variously appealed to the last book of the law to offer guidance to the fledgling communities he founded or encountered on his missionary journeys. While we do not see Deuteronomy function in a straightforward capacity as legal authority in the same way we find in, say, the *Sifre*, it must be kept in mind that these are letters to largely Gentile, or at best mixed Jewish and Gentile, churches. Nevertheless, Deuteronomy does serve as an ethically authoritative resource for the apostle more than perhaps has been realized – and a critical study of various allusions to Deuteronomy would further substantiate this claim (for which see Rosner 1994). One also sees a sense of immediacy brought about by the eschatological situation, a sense that the Gentiles are now included among those for whose sake Deuteronomy was written. Nevertheless, the scroll of Deuteronomy certainly does *not* fulfill the role of guarding the entrance to the covenant that we find in some of the Dead Sea Scrolls (e.g., 1QS 2). Deuteronomy is thus, we might say, construed by Paul as a legal authority with an ad-hoc character and an immediacy imparted to it by the eschatological situation at hand. More specifically, we see Paul employ it as a bearer of preceptual commands to be obeyed in the service of love (Deut 5:17–19, 21a), as an epitome of the law in confrontation with humanity according to the flesh (Deut 5:21a), as an authority enforcing its own standards of moral purity for the assembly of God (Deut 17:7 par), as a word directed to the present question of apostolic remuneration (Deut 25:4), as supplying the judicial framework for the Corinthians' self-incrimination (Deut 19:15), and as a normative motivating ground for non-retaliation (Deut 32:35). The Decalogue looms large in these ethical reflections, perhaps the result of a long-standing liturgical preoccupation leading to a sense that in it is expressed the basic will of God for right living. It is equally clear, however, that Paul's ethical appropriation of Deuteronomy goes well beyond the Decalogue. The variety of these appeals renders it unlikely that Paul intends to relativize Deuteronomy as an ethical authority in any thoroughgoing way. This also makes it clear, however, that any understanding of Paul's construal of Deuteronomy as ethical authority can only function as a heuristic guide in light of the way his paraenesis is indissolubly theological.

6.4. Deuteronomy as Theological Authority

The theological character of Paul's appeals to Deuteronomy already come to evidence in considering his ethical use of the book. In this light, it is worth briefly considering how some of Deuteronomy's language about the one God resources the apostle's pastoral direction to his churches under the broad rubric of theological authority. In the nature of the case, some of these suggestions must be more tentative, as specific literary dependence is difficult to prove for cases involving crucial and broadly circulating theological concepts such as monotheism. Nevertheless, there are a few places where Deuteronomy's influence in particular may be detected.

6.4.1. The Shema'

The liturgical setting that drove home the ethical importance of Deuteronomy may have exercised an equally profound influence on theology proper. In one instance in particular, Paul describes Jesus Christ in the language of Israel's great national confession (Deut 6:4), or, conversely, interprets the confession itself christologically. In 1 Cor 8:1–6, Paul turns to address the Corinthian disagreement over proper conduct with respect to meat sacrificed to idols.[58] In so doing, he begins by establishing common ground with the group commonly referred to as the "strong" in Corinth, yet seeks to subtly transform their orientation toward the weak to exhibit the forbearance and love proper to those who have Christ as their master.[59] As part of Paul's expression of his agreement with the Corinthian "strong" position that monotheistic belief excludes belief in the reality of idols (a provisional position that is given further nuance in 1 Cor 10),[60] he affirms that "an idol is nothing in the world and there is no God but one" (8:4: οὐδεὶς θεὸς εἰ μὴ εἷς).[61] He then goes on, after conceding the phenomenological existence of many gods and many lords (i.e., many objects of wor-

---

[58] See nn. 36–37 above.

[59] The precise identity of the weak is difficult to ascertain, but it is difficult to frame the schism along purely Jewish and Gentile lines. As Theissen writes, "it is quite possible that there were two different types of weak Corinthians: a gentile Christian type who always used to eat such consecrated meat but developed a guilty conscience after conversion to Christianity, and a Jewish Christian type who had always avoided such ritually slaughtered meat and who, after conversion, could exercise his unaccustomed freedom from restrictive ritual rules only with a bad conscience" (1982: 124).

[60] The very fact that disagreements abound on whether Paul is citing a Corinthian slogan and if so, how far that slogan extends shows that Paul has tightly integrated his argument in this passage, framing the question already in terms of his desired answer.

[61] Waaler 2008 suggests this may be an echo of the first commandment (and note his appendix for similar texts that deny the existence of other gods besides the one God: 450–52). This is possible, though faint – though it should be noted that some MSS add ἕτερος after θεὸς in this verse in apparent assimilation to the first commandment (א² Maj sy; cf. Lindemann 2000: 191). Admittedly, however, the content of the first commandment in its prohibition of idolatry underlies all of 1 Cor 8:1–11:1.

ship), to counter this with what appears to be a Christological expansion of the *Shema'*.[62] He writes in 8:6:

ἀλλ' ἡμῖν εἷς θεὸς πατὴρ
ἐξ οὗ τὰ πάντα καὶ ἡμεῖς εἰς αὐτόν,
καὶ εἷς κύριος Ἰησοῦς Χριστὸς
δι' οὗ τὰ πάντα καὶ ἡμεις δι' αὐτοῦ.

But for us there is one God, the Father,
From whom are all things and we for him,
And one Lord, Jesus Christ
Through whom are all things and we through him.

Paul has thus combined a doxological assertion about God as creator with Israel's confession of the *Shema'*. As Richard Bauckham writes, "Paul has in fact reproduced all the words of the statement about YHWH in the *Shema'* (Deut. 6:4: 'The LORD our God, the LORD, is one'), but Paul has rearranged the words in such a way as to produce an affirmation of both one God, the Father, and one Lord, Jesus Christ" (1998: 38; cf. 36–40).[63] Of course, as noted above (§ 2.4–5), Deut 6:4–9 played an important role in Jewish life and liturgy during the Second Temple period, and was probably recited, together with Deut 11:14–21 and Num 15:37–41, twice each day, as well as being among the passages included in the *tefillin* and *mezuzot*.[64] One aspect of its importance is its function as a great monotheistic confession of Israel. This, then, makes all the more striking, though perhaps also all the more necessary, Paul's transformation of this text in 1 Cor 8:4–6.

It is crucial to grasp, however, that Paul does not present this as a *correction* or an *addition* to the *Shema'*, but as an interpretation of it that discloses its true referent.[65] Recognizing 1 Cor 8:6 as an expansion of the *Shema'* suggests that any attempt to see Paul affirming Jesus Christ as standing in contrast not only to "so called gods and lords" (8:5) but simul-

---

[62] Recent arguments for seeing 8:6 as an interpretation of the Shema' have been made by, *inter alia*, Rainbow 1987 (though he does not stress the connection with Deuteronomy); Wright 1992: 120–36; Bauckham 1998; Hofius 2002a; 2002b; Rosner 2007: 126–27; and esp. Waaler 2008, who has made the most extensive case to date. Inexplicably, some commentators (e.g., Fee 1987) make no mention of Deuteronomy here.

[63] As Rainbow suggests (1987: 30), "The essential content of this confession [i.e., the *Shema'*] could be summarized in abbreviated formulae such as εἷς θεός or μόνος θεός." Further, Waaler makes the crucial observation that the more foundational a text is, the easier it is to detect reference to it without explicit or extensive quotation.

[64] Cf., e.g., 4Q130; 8Q3; XQPhyl 2; Mur 4; *m. Tam.* 4:3–5:1; *b. Men.* 34b–35a *bar*; *b. Men.* 28a. More fully, see §§ 2.4–5 above and Waaler 2008.

[65] Hofius 2002a calls this "eine christliche Exegese von Dtn 6,4 LXX" (177) and goes on to say that 1 Cor 8:6 is not "eine Erweiterung und Ergänzung des Sch°ma'", sondern seine Auslegung und Entfaltung" (180).

taneously in contrast to the one God will be thoroughly unconvincing. For Paul's argument to work, Jesus as the one Lord must be in the closest possible sense associated with the one God – closely enough to be considered on the creator side of the creator-creation divide (δι' οὗ τὰ πάντα).[66] This is, then, an actualizing interpretation of the *Shema'* which seeks to contemporize it by re-presenting it in a way that reflects new (or newly disclosed) Christological realities. From Paul's perspective, he is presenting the true intent of Israel's confession of the *Shema'* by including Jesus within the divine identity and so making him also the object of the correlative human fidelity there confessed.[67] Paul has engaged in an act of *correlation* between God's word in Deuteronomy and God's action in the present. It is this striking fact that constitutes 1 Cor 8:1–6 as "one of the theologically most important texts in the Corpus Paulinum" (Lindemann 2000: 188). Although in this context we can do no more than point to the existence of the phenomenon, it is clear that this implicitly acknowledges the importance of Deuteronomy, but also the difficulty of any straightforward apprehension or application of Deuteronomy without some degree of actualization or "presentifying" interpretation.

6.4.2. Theological Axioms

More briefly, it may also be the case that some of Paul's theological axioms have their roots in Deuteronomic soil. In this context we come up against the limits of a purely literary investigation. Is it likely that Paul consciously thinks of his theological assertions as stemming from the interpretation of a text? Especially here it is useful to recall the discussion of the liturgical and educational reception of Deuteronomy mentioned above

---

[66] It may be that Paul's language of "many gods and many lords" versus the one God and the one Lord is indebted to Deut 10:17: ὁ γὰρ κύριος ὁ θεὸς ὑμῶν, οὗτος θεὸς τῶν θεῶν καὶ κύριος τῶν κυρίων. For Paul's further allusions to this verse, see § 6.4.2 below.

[67] So, e.g., Hurtado can speak with reference to this text of the "binitarian shape" of early Christian devotion (1988: 2, 97–98). Wright argues that "Paul has placed Jesus *within* an explicit statement, drawn from the Old Testament's quarry of emphatically monotheistic texts, of the doctrine that Israel's God is the one and only God, the creator of the world" (1992: 129, going on to speak of a "christological monotheism" 129 and an "unprecedented bifurcation within monotheism" 130). Bauckham suggests similarly that "Paul is including the Lord Jesus Christ in the unique divine identity. He is redefining monotheism as Christological monotheism" (1998: 38). And Hofius argues that "Das zweigliedrige Bekenntnis sagt mithin *nicht*: Es gibt den *einen* und *einzigen* Gott, von dem das Sch^ema' spricht; und neben und unter ihm gibt es noch eine Art δεύτερος θεός, nämlich den κύριος Ἰησοῦς Χριστός. Vielmehr gilt: Der „Vater" Jesu Christi und der „Sohn" dieses Vaters *sind* der εἷς θεός, neben dem es keinen anderen Gott gibt" (2002a: 179, emphasis original; cf. 2002b: 186–87).

(§ 2), in which fundamental theological assertions are not simply analyzed or interpreted, but meditated upon and internalized – to the point that it is probably better to picture Paul thinking *with* Deuteronomy about the one God rather than thinking *of* Deuteronomy itself.[68] In this context, then, three distinct theological *topoi* may find their derivation from Deuteronomy.

First, Paul repeatedly claims that "God is faithful" – πιστὸς ὁ θεός (1 Cor 1:9; 10:13; 2 Cor 1:18). This seems to respond to the statement found twice in Deuteronomy (and Deuteronomy alone) to the same effect (see Deut 7:9 and 32:4, though phrased attributively instead of predicatively: θεὸς πιστός).[69] Second, Paul's assertion that "God shows no partiality" (Gal 2:6: πρόσωπον ὁ θεὸς ἀνθρώπου οὐ λαμβάνει; cf. Rom 2:11: οὐ γάρ ἐστιν προσωπολημψία παρὰ τῷ θεῷ) may be ultimately derivative of Deuteronomy's, "For the Lord your God, he is God of gods and Lord of lords, the great and strong and terrible God, who does not regard a person nor will he by any means take a bribe" (ὅστις οὐ θαυμάζει πρόσωπον οὐδ᾽ οὐ μὴ λάβῃ δῶρον) (10:17).[70] Though the verbal link is not strong, the connection of the one-ness of God with his impartiality may suggest that Paul's thinking on ethnic universalism is at least to some degree indebted to his reflection on Deuteronomy's monotheism.[71] This is further strengthened, third, by Paul's use of "one God" language in contexts discussing justification, perhaps ultimately indebted to the confession of the *Shema‘*.[72] In Rom 3:29–30, Paul makes the connection most explicit: ἢ

---

[68] Note the perceptive comments of Hans Hübner: "Nun wäre es zu kurz gedacht, wollten wir das bewußte und sicherlich weithin auch unbewußte Aufgreifen von alttestamentlichen Aussagen durch die neutestamentlichen Autoren und ihr Sich-Bewegen in alttestamentlicher Idiomatik lediglich als eine Rezeption von *Texten* interpretieren. Denn das Beheimatetsein im Alten Testament ist ja weit mehr als das bloße Vertrautsein mit einem Buch. Es ist eben nicht ein rein literarischer Vorgang, den die Literaten des Neuen Testamentes praktizierten! Indem sie nämlich mit den Schriften des Alten Testaments vertraut sind, sind sie zugleich mit der *Wirklichkeit* vertraut, aus der diese Schriften erwachsen sind und wovon sie Ausdruck geben" (1993: 19).

[69] But note πιστός with κύριος in Ps 144:13; Wis. Sol. 14:1; 17:10 (cf. 2 Thess 3:3), and in Isa 49:7: πιστός ἐστιν ὁ ἅγιος Ἰσραηλ.

[70] So already Döpke 1829: 198–99. See esp. Bassler 1982: 7–44 for documentation of the emergence of a divine impartiality tradition. In some ways the statement in Rom 2:11 is the conclusion toward which Rom 1:18–3:20 as a whole presses.

[71] Another possible theological axiom may be found in Deut 32:4 (θεὸς πιστός καὶ οὐκ ἔστιν ἀδικία), obliquely reflected in Rom 9:14 (μὴ ἀδικία παρὰ τῷ θεῷ; μὴ γένοιτο).

[72] On "one God" language in Paul, see esp. Rainbow 1987; Waaler 2008. Guerra 1995: 74–101 offers a discussion of the "one God" *topos* in Romans and elsewhere in Jewish apologetic literature, although his argument that the one God language is *not* indebted to the Shema is somewhat curious. He is technically correct that Deut 6:4 does not

'Ιουδαίων ὁ θεὸς μόνον; οὐχὶ καὶ ἐθνῶν; ναὶ καὶ ἐθνῶν, εἴπερ εἷς ὁ θεὸς ὅς δικαιώσει περιτομὴν ἐκ πίστεως καὶ ἀκροβυστίαν διὰ τῆς πίστεως ("Or is he the God of Jews only? Is he not also of Gentiles? Yes, also of Gentiles, since God is one – who will justify the circumcised by faith and the uncircumcised through faith").[73] It is notable that all of these maxims function as basic theological assertions assumed to be authoritatively valid statements from which further inferences can be drawn.

6.4.3. Conclusion: Deuteronomy as Theological Authority

Thus, Deuteronomy's voice is still construed as an important and on-going theological authority, a voice that properly speaks God – and yet, for all this, still subject to further interpretation or refinement in light of the new events in Jesus Christ. This interpretation or refinement is not, according to Paul, the invention of a *novum*, but rather a deepened grasp of the *res* to which the text itself testifies. It is striking, though perhaps not entirely surprising, to see the central confession of Israel, recited by Paul and other Jews twice each day, brought into transformative interaction with Jesus Christ. Deuteronomy's witness, however, still retains its full theological force, and it is just as true to say that the very forcefulness of this witness exercises a constraint on Paul as it is to say that Paul's Christology exercises an imprint on Deuteronomy. The two, for Paul, are mutually interpretative realities.

6.5. Deuteronomy as the Lens of Israel's History

We turn, now, to a third construal of Deuteronomy in Paul's letters: as a lens by which to interpret Israel's history – and in particular the history of Israel as now seen from Paul's perspective as an apostle of Christ to the nations.

6.5.1. Blessing and Curse

Paul's two citations of Deuteronomy in Galatians 3:10 and 13, perhaps the earliest explicit engagements with Deuteronomy we have from Paul's pen, arguably evince a broad conception of Israel's history – and specifically, of Israel's plight. Within the complex argument of Galatians 3, Paul plays on the blessing and curse polarity that marks the Pentateuch to further his argument that those who believe are the true heirs of Abraham. In Gal 3:6–

---

speak of εἷς θεὸς but εἷς κύριος, but as he concedes, there is a close relationship between them in context (88).

[73] Cf. Gal 3:20: ὁ θεὸς εἷς ἐστιν.

14, as part of his larger argument that Gentiles are children of Abraham through faith in Christ rather than by Torah observance (3:1–29), Paul seeks to ground in Scripture his assertion that the Galatian Gentile believers received the Spirit through the hearing of faith and not by law observance (3:2). In 3:6–9 Paul argues from the example of Abraham that "those who are from faith will be blessed together with Abraham, the man of faith" (οἱ ἐκ πίστεως εὐλογοῦνται σὺν τῷ πιστῷ Ἀβραάμ).

Paul's evocation of the blessing promised to Abraham in Gen 12:3 (cf. 18:18) and associated with faith (Gen 15:6) calls forth its structural opposite: curse associated with works of the law (the dichotomy has been operating since Gal 2:16). The structure of blessing and curse is one that marks the Pentateuch as a whole, but by associating faith with the former and law observance with the latter, Paul makes a wide-ranging judgment about Israel's history. In support (γάρ) of his claim that blessing and faith go together, Paul cites Deut 27:26 to prove the connection between curse and works of law: "those who are from the works of the law are under a curse" (ὅσοι ἐξ ἔργων νόμου εἰσίν ὑπὸ κατάραν).[74] In precisely which sense Deut 27:26 is meant to prove this assertion is hotly debated,[75] for on a surface reading of the text Paul's citation appears to prove precisely the opposite assertion (so, e.g., Lagrange 1950a: 69; Betz 1979: 145). While many have assumed that Paul must be operating with the unspoken premise that it is impossible to fulfill the law,[76] that solution has been justly and repeatedly criticized in recent years. Apart from the fact that Paul nowhere advances such a statement when it might have readily served his ends, whether the law can be fulfilled perfectly or not is strictly irrelevant to the question Paul is seeking to answer (see esp. 3:21b).[77] Others have made the suggestion that Paul merely intends to associate law with curse (Sanders

---

[74] The phrase "from works of the law" has been disputed over the past thirty years or so, largely in response to Dunn's contention that boundary markers are primarily in view; much depends on how one parses that "primarily" and how one understands the parallel phrase in 4QMMT. See Dunn 2008a, 2008b, 2008c for his statement and references to other literature in the debate.

[75] My engagement with the vast secondary literature at this juncture will necessarily be circumscribed; for fuller surveys of other approaches and critical responses, see, in addition to the commentaries, Scott 1993a; Wakefield 2003: 65–94; Silva 2007; Moyise 2008b: 63–77.

[76] So Calvin (*ad loc.*): "Either Paul reasons badly or it is impossible for men to fulfill the law." Note also, e.g., Lietzmann 1971: 19 ("dieser notwendige Gedanke ist hier als selbstverständlich nicht ausgesprochen"); Ridderbos 1953; Schreiner 1984; Longenecker 1990: 118; Waters 2006: 99, etc.

[77] In reality, many of these approaches operate with a second implied premise, that perfect law observance would merit eternal life. This, however, should not be seen as the meaning of Lev 18:5 in this context and further comes into direct conflict with Paul's statement in 3:21b. In critique, see, e.g., Wright 1992: 144–46; Wakefield 2003, etc.

1983), though this is notoriously unsatisfactory. While not without its weaknesses, I suggest that the more promising interpretation is that which sees Paul operating here under the model of covenant theology, with his citation of Deut 27 tapping into the broader context of Deut 27–30.[78]

Paul first cites from Deut 27:26 (ἐπικατάρατος πᾶς ὅς οὐκ ἐμμένει πᾶσιν τοῖς γεγραμμένοις ἐν τῷ βιβλίῳ τοῦ νόμου τοῦ ποιῆσαι αὐτά).[79] Deut 27:26 functions within Deuteronomy 27 as the final curse that sums up and represents the preceding curses that are more specific in nature (27:15–25).[80] But Paul has extended this representative nature by altering the quotation to speak, not of "in all the words of this law" (as in Deut 27:26 LXX), but of "all the things written in the book of the law."[81] While this may appear to be a minor change, the inserted phrase is found throughout Deut 28–30 more widely (see esp. 28:58 and 30:10), and so emphasizes the representative nature even further. The "curse of the law," then, is the curse the law threatens for those who disobey it.[82] As a number of commentators have argued, the curse may have national as well as individualistic overtones, and Paul here stands in the line of those who survey Israel's history retrospectively and find it lacking – and this in a double sense. First, in the Deuteronomic, *a posteriori* sense. That Israel has experienced the curse in her history has proven that the law does not in fact lead to blessing but to curse: "the likeliest explanation as to why Paul considers Israel to be 'under' a curse (ὑπὸ κατάραν) is that the Deuteronomic

---

[78] This general approach is shared, with important differences, by Thielman 1989; Wright 1992: 137–56; Scott 1993a, 1993b, 1993c; Watson 2004; Ciampa 2007. One of the reasons this line of argument has been attacked is an undue stress on the association of curse with exile. For Deut 27–30, the exile is the covenant punishment *par excellence*, but it is not co-extensive with the curse, which is for Paul's argument the really important matter and the explicit point of identification he labors to establish in this passage – not the exile. P. Esler's critique of Wright, however, seems to miss the mark at this point. He writes, "[Paul's] overall strategy is to launch an onslaught on the central aspect of that part of Israelite scripture relied upon by his opponents, the covenant at Sinai, by stigmatising it as solely productive of a curse from which Christ liberated us, while pointing out that an older part of sacred history, recounted in Genesis 15, had foretold the blessings which would come to the gentiles" (1998: 191), though in fact Gen 15 is also central to Wright's account of Paul. For a brief response to the critique by Wisdom 2001 and Waters 2006, note Lincicum 2008a.

[79] In the LXX, Deut 27:26 reads: ἐπικατάρατος πᾶς ἄνθρωπος, ὅστις οὐκ ἐμμενεῖ ἐν πᾶσιν τοῖς λόγοις τοῦ νόμου τούτου ποιῆσαι αὐτούς. On the changes, which likely come from Paul's hand, see esp. Stanley 1992: 238–43.

[80] It is possible that these passages, together with Lev 18:5 and some other key texts, were being cited by Paul's opponents (so Longenecker 1990: 116), but we surely cannot know as much about the Galatian 'Teachers' and their theology as Martyn 1997 suggests.

[81] Note Stanley 1992: 238–43; Ciampa 2007 *inter alia*.

[82] *Pace* esp. Betz 1979: 149.

'curse' to which Dan 9:11 refers came 'upon' the people (ἐφ᾽ ἡμᾶς)" (Scott 1993b: 657).[83] Therefore, for the Galatian agitators to invite Gentile converts to join the observance of the law is confronted by a historical *reductio ad absurdum* – so Paul argues. But the fact that Israel's history was open to competing interpretations suggests that a negative interpretation of the ability of the law to bring blessing may also be understood in a second, *a priori* sense: because Christ died and righteousness comes to Jew and Gentile by faith, the law must necessarily have failed to – or not have been designed to – achieve justification (cf. Gal 2:21). In this sense Paul's argument is probably impossible to characterize as a one way direction from either plight to solution or from solution to plight: once again, Scripture and gospel are mutually interpretive.

If Paul in 3:10 can be seen to be activating this Deuteronomic framework, then 3:11–12 introduces the tension that will lead to Paul's further explanations in 3:15–25 about the nature and purpose of the law. In these verses Paul deliberately sets Hab 2:4 against Lev 18:5 in order to cast into sharp relief the difference between the faith which has always been answered by justification in Israel's history (cf. 3:6–9) and the demand for obedience that never actually eventuated in the life promised (cf. 3:10).[84] This is clearly a radical interpretation of the Torah, and one can imagine the controversy that Paul's statement ὁ νόμος οὐκ ἔστιν ἐκ πίστεως might have caused. But this is clearly the νόμος under a particular aspect, which Paul argues at greater length in 3:15–25 (so also Wakefield 2003; Silva 2007). By thus suggesting that οἱ ἐξ ἔργων νόμου have fallen under the curse of the covenant, and so implying that observance to the law is powerless to remove such a curse, Paul prepares for the Christological punchline of 3:13: "Christ redeemed us from the curse of the law by having become a curse on our behalf." If the covenantal reading of Deut 27:26 is

---

[83] Scott further suggests that Paul here expresses "the negative side of the traditional hope – already articulated in Deuteronomy 27–32 – which looks forward to the inclusion of the Gentiles in the restoration of Israel (cf. Deut. 32:43, cited in Rom 15:10)" (1993c: 802; identically in 1993b: 659; more fully, 1993a: 213–17).

[84] The practice of exploiting Scriptural contradictions is well-established in Jewish sources; see Dahl 1971; Vos 1992; cf. also Martyn 1997: 328–34, though, *pace* Martyn, there is no sense in which Paul suggests that the inconsistencies remove the Torah from its divine origin. Note his comment: "The voice of God and the voice of the Law are by no means the same. It was the Law, not God, that pronounced a curse on the crucified one" (1997: 321). Further, Thielman 1989 raises the possibility that Paul's reading of Lev 18:5 may already be determined by the covenant curses in Lev 26 itself – an intriguing hypothesis, though difficult to confirm.

correct, then Paul has in mind specifically Jewish Christians as the referent of his ἡμᾶς here – that is, those who labored under the law's curse.[85]

This striking statement of exchange (Vouga 1998: 75; cf. 2 Cor 5:21) is then grounded by the citation of Deut 21:23, in which Paul found a unique connection between curse and crucifixion.[86] He puts this to theological use in Gal 3:13 to suggest that only by enduring the curse himself was Christ then able to nullify its power and release the blessing that is the curse's structural opposite.[87] The redemption of Israel from the curse of the law has the intended purpose (note the dual ἵνα constructions of 3:14) of ensuring that the Gentiles enjoy the blessing of Abraham (i.e., the justification described in 3:6–9) and that the promised Spirit might come to all by faith (recalling 3:2). It is surely significant that in describing the removal of the covenant curse, Paul suggests that the intention of the covenant with Abraham can then be fulfilled (Williams 1988). Here it is important to note that if Paul shares with some of his contemporaries a Deuteronomic diagnosis of Israel's situation, his prognosis is specifically bound up with the crucifixion (and implicitly the resurrection) of the Son of God, and so

---

[85] If the curse is something from which Paul can say that "we" needed to be redeemed, then it is unlikely that Paul restricts the curse solely to his opponents (contra Wisdom 2001; Silva 2007: 799). Those who see a reference to Jewish Christians here include Duncan 1934: 99; Lagrange 1950a: 71; Lietzmann 1971: 19; Betz 1979: 148; Wright 1992: 143, etc. As Betz suggests, the Galatian Gentile Christians were not under the curse of the law, but ὑπὸ τὰ στοιχεῖα τοῦ κόσμου (cf. 4:8–11), though Paul does forge a vague association between the two concepts. Those who see both Jew and Gentile in view include Bruce 1982; Fung 1988: 148–49; Martyn 1997: 317; Waters 2006: 113. A weakness in the suggestion of Stanley 1990 that "under the curse" means merely "under the threat of the curse" is that Christ ends up redeeming from a merely possible curse.

[86] The association of Deut 21:22–23 with crucifixion rather than post-mortem impalement may also be seen in 11Q19 64.6–13; cf. 4Q524 frag. 14; 4QpNah 3+4 1.6–8 (see § 3.1.2 above). Cf. two later Jewish traditions: the Targum MS V (Vatican Ebr. 440), at Deut 21:22 reads: "and you shall crucify him on a wood[en gallows]" (Klein 1980: 2:175). *Sifre* considers but rejects crucifixion as the referent of Deut 21:22 (§ 221). For allusions to the text elsewhere in early Christianity, note esp. Wilcox 1977. Some have suggested that this text played an important role in persecution of Christians – perhaps even in Paul's own persecution of Christians (e.g., Bruce 1982: 166; Fung 1988: 151). While this is possible, substantial criticism has been leveled at the suggestion; see Tuckett 1986; O'Brien 2006.

[87] Gal 3:13 reads: ἐπικατάρατος πᾶς ὁ κρεμάμενος ἐπὶ ξύλου, while Deut 21:23 LXX reads: ὅτι κεκατηραμένος ὑπὸ θεοῦ πᾶς κρεμάμενος ἐπὶ ξύλου. The change from κεκατηραμένος ὑπὸ θεοῦ to ἐπικατάρατος has been explained in a number of ways. Some have suggested that this avoids associated Christ with being cursed directly by God, and this may play some role. The substitution, however, ties this citation more closely with the preceding citation from Deut 27, and so forms a tighter thematic link between them; so also, e.g., Moyise 2008b: 65 and n. 2.

naturally rejects the nomistic exhortations that characterize some other Jewish contemporaries. In this compactly argued section, Deuteronomy thus has a dual function: it both announces the curse to which Israel in her disobedience is subject, but also hints at the means by which that curse has been overcome, resulting in blessing to the nations.

6.5.2. True Circumcision and the Covenant

In Romans, Paul puts Deuteronomy 29–32 to use in some striking ways in order to address questions of human agency, Gentile inclusion in the people of God, and the fate of Israel. In Romans 2, Paul displays hints of the Deuteronomic framework we suggested was present in Galatians 3, culminating in 2:25–29, in which Paul's contention that circumcision of the heart is by the Spirit and not by the letter answers the idea found in both Deuteronomy and the prophets that "circumcision of the heart" is a divine initiative. This, in turn, corresponds to an understanding of the rebuke speech of Deut 29 of which we find fuller evidence in Romans 11. It should not be overlooked that the words of Deut 29 are spoken in rebuke to Israel as Moses institutes the Moab covenant in the context of Deuteronomy – and before the divinely initiated circumcision of the heart in 30:1–10, the Christologically powerful statement of the nearness of the word in 30:12–14 and the apocalyptic intervention that Paul finds narrated by the Song of Moses in 32:1–43. In this section I will examine Paul's reading of Deut 29:1–30:10 insofar as it can be determined. In the next two sections, I will turn to Paul's Christological transformation of Deut 30:12–14 and his reading of the Song of Moses.

It is convenient to begin with the citation of Deuteronomy 29 in Romans 11. In arguing that the failure of a majority of his fellow Jews to believe the gospel does not imply the faithlessness of God, Paul appeals to the concept of the "remnant," of which he provides himself as the first, though not the only, example (11:1–6). Paul deduces (τί οὖν;) from this that "what Israel was seeking, it did not attain; the elect obtained it, but the rest were hardened (ἐπωρώθησαν)" (11:7). Paul finds this state of hardening to be in accordance with what Scripture has already announced (καθὼς γέγραπται). Here Paul introduces his mixed citation of Deut 29:3 (HT 29:4) and Isa 29:10. Paul has extracted the phrase "a spirit of stupor" from Isa 29:10 and inserted it into Deut 29:3 as follows:

Rom 11:8: ἔδωκεν αὐτοῖς ὁ θεὸς πνεῦμα κατανύξεως, *ὀφθαλμοὺς* τοῦ μὴ βλέπειν καὶ ὦτα τοῦ μὴ ἀκούειν, ἕως τῆς σήμερον ἡμέρας.

Deut 29:3 LXX: καὶ οὐκ ἔδωκεν κύριος ὁ θεὸς ὑμῖν καρδίαν εἰδέναι καὶ *ὀφθαλμοὺς* βλέπειν καὶ ὦτα ἀκούειν ἕως τῆς ἡμέρας ταύτης.

Isa 29:10: ὅτι πεπότικεν ὑμᾶς κύριος <u>πνεύματι κατανύξεως</u> καὶ καμμύσει τοὺς ὀφθαλμοὺς αὐτῶν καὶ τῶν προφητῶν αὐτῶν καὶ τῶν ἀρχόντων αὐτῶν.

One can see that Paul has made his customary adjustments to the citation for its new epistolary position, but the conflated quotation also brings the voices of Moses and Isaiah together. As Ross Wagner expresses it, "the reading strategy commended by Paul's rhetoric in Romans 10:19–21 – that Moses and Isaiah are to be heard testifying in concert against Israel – now comes into play as Paul conflates the words of these two witnesses into a single scriptural voice" (2002: 242).[88] What is more, by further defining Israel's "hardening" in terms of Isaiah's πνεῦμα κατανύξεως ("a spirit of stupor"), not only does Paul ascribe the present state of Israel's unbelief to God's purposive action, but he may also be portraying Israel's state as one from which some recovery can be made (so also Stanley 1992: 161; Shum 2002: 234). "Stupor," even if divinely induced, is a state from which one can awake – especially if the same divine power is directed toward the awakening (note the argument Paul is about to embark upon in 11:11–26).

But the main thrust of Paul's citation is to establish divine intention in Israel's unbelief. Here it is crucial to recall the context of Deuteronomy 29. The chapter is a resumé and re-establishment of the covenant, together with a sure prediction of Israel's failure to keep it. The curses have just been enunciated in Deuteronomy 27–28, and are assumed to be on the brink of a terrible realization in Israel's history. The εὐλογία is not mentioned at all in Deuteronomy 29; it has simply faded from view, not to be reintroduced until 30:1. Deut 29:3 LXX thus functions as a guarantee that Israel's failure (experienced by Deuteronomy's audience as actual) is not beyond God's providential outworking. In this way, perhaps paradoxically, the ground is prepared for the restoration which is detailed in 30:1–10, a restoration that is arguably divinely initiated. Thus, Moses's words are a stiff warning, re-appropriated by Paul for the Israel of his own day, but they are not God's last word. Even if Paul knows that the blinding and deafness lasts ἕως τῆς σήμερον ἡμέρας, he also knows that Deuteronomy 30 comes after Deuteronomy 29.

---

[88] This conflation was enough, however, to force Origen to admit his ignorance as to the source of the citation (*Comm. Rom.* 8.8.3). Wagner (2002: 240–57) further suggests that Isa 6:9–10 may be a subtext by means of which Paul has linked these two texts together. For further elaboration of the changes in the form of the citation, see Koch 1986: 170–71; Stanley 1992: 158–63. The relocation of the negative particle now requires the articular infinitive (cf. BDF § 400), perhaps under influence from the following citation (so Stanley 1992: 162). The addition of σήμερον may be an unconscious harmonization to Deut's cadences (so Wagner 2002), could reflect harmonization already within the text of Deut LXX itself (so Koch 1986) or perhaps simply "evokes the contemporizing thrust of the citation" (Jewett 2007: 663).

We must go all the way back to Romans 2 to see the next stage in Paul's reading of Deuteronomy 29–30. In Romans 2, Paul turns his attention from Gentile to Jewish sin, arguing that non-Christ-believing Jews are also ἀναπολόγητος ("without excuse"). Paul uses some standard methods of inner-Jewish polemic and prophetic critique to formulate his argument,[89] but finally arrives at a position that goes beyond other polemical positions in a process of radical redefinition with far-reaching consequences. Along the way, Paul uses two phrases in his language describing the fate of the hypocrite that hearken back to repeated refrains from Deuteronomy's covenant curses: in 2:8 ὀργὴ καὶ θυμός recalls Deut 29:22, 23, 27; and in 2:9 θλῖψις καὶ στενοχωρία recalls Deut 28:53, 55, 57.[90] Paul's use of these stock phrases drawn from Deuteronomy to describe the fate of the disobedient may subtly hint that he is already operating as a prosecutor appealing to the terms of the covenant.[91] It is also worth recalling that Paul's use of the divine impartiality statement is found in 2:11. Whether we identify the Gentiles in 2:14–16 who do what the law requires as Christian or not,[92] it is clear by the time Paul reaches 2:25–29 that he has Gentile Christians firmly in view. There he redraws the boundaries concerning the question of "keeping the law's requirements" (δικαιώματα φυλάσσειν) – an especially Deuteronomic formulation that occurs only here in Paul (Rom 2:26, though note φυλάσσω in a similar context in Gal 6:13).[93] Paul draws attention to the nature of circumcision, essentially divorcing its physical observance from the demand of the law in order to claim that true circumcision is an eschatological state determined by the Spirit that enables one to fulfill the law – regardless of whether one is physically circumcised.

Two connections to Deuteronomy are striking in this context, one less often noticed than the other. The connection that is conceptually most im-

---

[89] *Pace* Sanders 1983: 123–35, there is no evidence that Paul has simply taken over a pre-formulated synagogue homily.

[90] Scott 1993b: 660 n. 64; Ito 1995.

[91] This may be another place where we see Paul thinking *with* Deuteronomy (cf. § 6.4.2); that is, the problems he is seeking to understand and explain are problems most naturally resolved (for a Jewish writer of his day) by recourse to Deuteronomy. Whether he wants to communicate these literary underpinnings to the Roman congregations is, of course, difficult to ascertain, and one should certainly allow that such an act of communication is at the very least removed from his intentional priorities as we can discern them.

[92] The passage has, of course, been long debated. Gathercole 2002 offers some indication of previous research, together with a persuasive argument that 2:14–16 refers to Christian Gentiles, not righteous non-Christian Gentiles (taking φύσει to modify μὴ νόμον ἔχοντα rather than τὰ τοῦ νόμου ποιῶσιν), though the position is still not without its difficulties (esp. 2:15b).

[93] Deut 4:40; 6:2; 7:11, 12; 8:11; 10:13; 11:1; 26:16, 17; 28:45; 30:10, 16.

portant is also the most readily recognizable: in effecting the reversal of circumcision and uncircumcision, Paul appeals to the concept of a "circumcision of the heart" (περιτομὴ καρδίας) in 2:28–29. The physical circumcision of Genesis 17 has already been reinterpreted within the Old Testament itself, though generally in the direction of polemicizing against those who are not circumcised in heart in addition to the flesh rather than holding out circumcision of the heart as an *alternative* to physical circumcision.[94] The concept appears twice in Deuteronomy (10:16; 30:6; cf. also similarly Jer 4:4), and most commentators suggest that Deut 30:6 looms large in the conceptual background[95] – perhaps here augmented with traditions that associate God giving his Spirit (Ezek 36:26–27) or writing the law on the heart (Jer 38:33–34 LXX).[96] Paul's innovation is to radically prioritize circumcision of the heart over physical circumcision, at the same time effectively accusing non-Christ-believing Jews of an "ethical epispasm" that has rendered their physical circumcision null and void.

To argue this, Paul sets up a series of contrasts: circumcision vs. uncircumcision, manifest vs. hidden, flesh vs. heart, letter vs. Spirit. It is in one of these sets that we see the second, lesser recognized connection to Deuteronomy. Rather than see these oppositions as a species of Middle-Platonic dualist hermeneutics,[97] it is possible to see them at least partially arising from a reading of Scripture itself. While this has been seen to be the case for the pairs circumcision and uncircumcision, flesh and heart, letter and Spirit, it has passed with less notice that the same can be said for manifest and hidden. This may have been less noticed because it is most often understood as a simple "inward/outward" duality. The inward/outward reading is facilitated, naturally, by Paul's mention of the "circumcision of the heart," implicitly understood as opposing a circumcision of the outward flesh (i.e., the penis). This is not strictly incorrect, but the almost universal tendency in English translations to translate ἐν τῷ

---

[94] So Ezek 44:6–9 polemicizes against those "uncircumcised in heart and flesh" (ἀπερίτμητος καρδίᾳ καὶ ἀπερίτμητος σαρκί). Note further Jer 4:4; 9:24–25 LXX (the latter is particularly striking, v. 25: πάντα τὰ ἔθνη ἀπερίτμητα σαρκί, καὶ πᾶς οἶκος Ἰσραηλ ἀπερίτμητοι καρδίας αὐτῶν.).

[95] The LXX, however, does not translate the Hebrew מול with περιτέμνω here (which only appears in Deut 10:16), but with περικαθαριεῖ. Aquila, however, renders the verb as περιτεμεῖται. Whether Paul here relied on a Greek text revised toward the Hebrew, knew the interpretative traditions stemming from the Hebrew, or thought solely of Deut 10:16 is impossible to ascertain entirely, though we have seen above (§ 6.3.1) that Paul is at least occasionally aware of Hebrew traditions (cf. also § 6.5.4 below on the "Rock" in 1 Cor 10:4).

[96] Note also *Jub* 1:23, where both spirit and circumcision of heart are mentioned together. For a broad survey, see Berkley 2000.

[97] As esp. Boyarin suggests (1994: 78–81, 93–97). In critique of Boyarin on the specific issue of circumcision, see Barclay 1998; for a broader response to Boyarin's brilliant if misguided presentation of Paul, note Dawson 2001: 19–46.

φανερῷ and ἐν τῷ κρυπτῷ by "outwardly" and "inwardly" respectively[98] obscures the apocalyptic background of these terms and their ultimate roots in Deut 29:28 (EVV 29:29): τὰ κρυπτὰ κυρίῳ τῷ θεῷ ἡμῶν, τὰ δὲ φανερὰ ἡμῖν καὶ τοῖς τέκνοις ἡμῶν εἰς τὸν αἰῶνα ποιεῖν πάντα τὰ ῥήματα τοῦ νόμου τούτου. Paul has a vocabulary to speak of "inwardness" (note ἔσω ἄνθρωπος in Rom 7:22 [cf. Eph 3:16] and esp. 2 Cor 4:16, where ὁ ἔξω ἡμῶν is contrasted with ὁ ἔσω ἡμῶν), but "hiddenness" is something conceptually distinct. Occasionally commentators do note that the opposition should not be reduced to an inward/outward duality,[99] but only rarely is it further noted that the pairing is uniquely attested in Deut 29:28.[100]

The significance of this only becomes clear once it is realized that Deut 29:28 served an important hermeneutical function in a range of Jewish thinking. The Hebrew terms from Deut 29:28, נסתרות and נגלות, are especially important in the self-understanding of the Qumran community and their conception of Torah as including both things that are manifest to all Israel and hidden things that have only been shown to the covenanters who, in turn, have searched them out. So we read in 1QS that the "men of injustice," i.e., non-sectarian Jews, are "not included in his covenant since they have neither sought nor examined his decrees in order to know the hidden matters (הנסתרות) in which they err by their own fault and because they treated revealed matters with disrespect (והנגלות עשו ביד רמה) [lit: "they do the revealed things with a high hand" cf. Num 15:30]; this is why wrath will rise up for judgment in order to effect revenge by the curses of the covenant..." (1QS 5.11–12).[101] In other Jewish documents the hidden and the revealed are specified in different ways, but the fact

---

[98] Note the following translations: "inwardly" (RSV; NIV; NEB; NRSV; NASB; ESV; AV; JB; Moffatt); "outwardly" (RSV; NIV; NRSV; NASB; ESV; AV; Moffatt) "in externals" (NEB). Perhaps other languages have fared better; cf. the Vulgate: *non enim qui in manifesto Iudaeus est neque quae in manifesto in carne circumcisio sed qui in abscondito Iudaeus et circumcisio cordis in spiritu non littera cuius laus non ex hominibus sed ex Deo est.* Luther: "auswendig" and "der's inwendig verborgen ist." Note also the interesting translation of Tyndale: "For he that is in open is not a Jew, neither it is circumcision that is openly in the flesh. But he that is a Jew is hidden, and the circumcision of heart, in spirit, not by the letter whose praising is not of men, but of God."

[99] E.g., Dunn 1988: 123; Barclay 1998: 554.

[100] Berkley (2000: 99–100, 157) does, unlike most, notice the link, though does not appear to be aware of the broader reception of Deut 29:28 and its possible implications for the passage at hand.

[101] Note the following additional uses: נסתרות: CD 3.14; 1QS 5.11; 11.6 (sg.); 1QH^a 4.9 (though the context is fragmentary); 1QH^a 26.15; 4Q268 1.7; 4Q401 frag. 14 2.7 and 17.4 (only partially preserved); 4Q427 frag. 7 1.19; 4Q463 1.4; 4Q508 2.4. נגלות: CD 15.13; 1QS 1.9; 5.9, 12; 8.1, 15; 9.13, 19; 1QH^a 4.2 (fragmentary context); 8.4; 4Q259 3.8 (sg.); 3.18 (sg.); 4Q266 frag. 8 1.4 (sg.); 4Q508 2.4.

remains that the language of Deut 29:28 comes to shape how certain streams of Jewish authors think about the nature of revelation.[102]

If I am correct in seeing a use of these terms to elucidate the discussion of circumcision, then at least two further points of insight are gained from this. First, it should be noted that Deut 29:28 occurs only six verses before 30:6, the statement about circumcision of the heart that many commentators see lying behind this passage. Not only does this strengthen the likelihood of the presence of the allusion, it also suggests a second corollary: the novelty that is so evident in Paul's argument (i.e., circumcision of the heart obviates the need for circumcision of the flesh) may be portrayed as an aspect of the "hidden" that has only come to light since God's action in Christ. That is, Paul describes the interior reality of circumcision as an instantiation of that category of eschatologically "hidden" mysteries that belong to God's good pleasure to reveal in his time. Paul's argument in Romans suggests that the time of that revelation has begun (note esp. the use of ἀποκαλύπτεται in Rom 1:17, 18 and Paul's μυστήριον concept), though full revelation must await the end (Rom 8:18).[103] It is clear that the conclusion toward which Paul presses in Rom 2:28–29 is that the uncircumcised can be the true Jew (so Fridrichsen 1994 [1922]; Schweizer 1974), and the language of eschatological revelation joins the equally eschatological concepts of the gift of the Spirit and the law written on the heart to effect the radical reversal Paul believes has been inaugurated in Christ (Käsemann 1980: 74–75).

Thus, we can see that Paul's reading of Deut 29:1–30:10 has a definite progression. In chapter 29, Israel is rebuked for the disobedience which has led to the realization of the curse, even as it is simultaneously main-

---

[102] Shemesh and Werman 1998: point to traditions in both the Qumran documents and rabbinic literature that evince a discourse generated by Deut 29:29(28) concerning the hidden and revealed things, and specifically what their referent might be. This is generally taken either to be revealed laws known to all Israel and hidden laws revealed to the sect (CD 3.12–17), revealed laws and those hidden laws to be revealed at some point to all of Israel (*Sifre Num.* 69; *Midr. Prov.* 26), or to sins that are either hidden or revealed (*b. Sanh.* 43b; *Mek.* 5). In addition, *4 Ezra* 14:6 may also rely on Deut 29:28(29) (so Stone 1990: 419); note further Wis 7:17–21. Cf. also Bockmuehl 1990: 13–15, 42–45; Fraade 1998: 65; 77: "Whereas the earlier revelation was נגלה, revealed to *all* of Israel, the more recent revelation was נסתר, hidden from unworthy Israel as a whole and made known to the covenantal returnees *alone.*"

[103] This, then, may lend greater plausibility and depth to the passing comment of Berkley 2000: "The possibility of gentile inclusion in the people of God was always 'hidden' with God" (100). Cf. also Oepke 1965; and Bultmann and Lührmann 1974. The latter suggest that "the primary reference [of φανερός] is to what is visible to sensory perception" (2), but they also mention the eschatological connotations associated with the word in contexts of coming to perception (3, citing Mark 4:22 par; 3:12 par; Luke 8:17a; Mark 6:14; Acts 7:13; 1 Cor 11:19; 14:25; Phil 1:13; 1 Cor 3:13).

tained that God himself intervened to make it so. This last statement is a strengthening of Deut 29:3 with Isa 29:10 to clarify the potentially ambiguous statement of Deuteronomy that God simply did not intervene to make it otherwise. For Paul, the disobedience can be ascribed to the purpose of God, which means that the undoing of that disobedience can also be ascribed to his purpose. Paul therefore fuses Deuteronomy's "circumcision of the heart" with other prophetic visions of the eschatological enablement of God's people (the Spirit and the law written on the heart), and interprets this to have come about now for uncircumcised Gentiles as well as for Jews – a new state of affairs that was previously hidden but has now come about through the revelatory action of God in Christ. But it is possible to read Deut 30:1–14 as simply a repetition of the call to obedience to the law, and even to see the restoration there promised as a *response* to previous human repentance. Does Deuteronomy 30 simply repeat the injunction to obedience in a louder voice? Paul turns to Deut 30:12–14 as a means by which to guarantee the unilateral nature of that restoration.

6.5.3. The Nearness of the Word

In Rom 10:6–8 Paul performs another striking act of rewriting Deuteronomy with profound Christological consequences. The investigation of this text yields results that are especially striking when seen alongside the transformation of Deuteronomy in 1 Cor 8:4–6.

In the course of his attempt in Rom 9–11 to address theologically the problem of Jewish unbelief in the gospel and the concomitant Gentile Christian boasting,[104] Paul first heightens the stakes by juxtaposing the various blessings Israel has enjoyed with his own sorrow at their unbelief (9:1–5). Immediately, however, he affirms that "it is not as though the word of God has fallen" (9:6a) – the thesis that he labors to establish in the ensuing chapters. He first argues that "not all from Israel are Israel," and seeks to demonstrate that God's "purpose according to election" has always been at work in Israel's history, choosing some and rejecting others (9:6b–29). Indeed, the Lord's creative calling has even constituted his

---

[104] Most commentators now agree that Paul probably wrote Romans for a handful of interlocking purposes (though these are variously assessed by different authors): Paul wants there to be (1) unity among Jewish and Gentile believers in the Roman congregations in order (2) to have the church in Rome support his appeal and collection for Jerusalem and (3) support him in his Spanish mission. Note the discussion in Wedderburn 1988; the essays in Donfried 1991; Jewett 2007: 80–91, etc. Since the study of Gamble 1977 demonstrating that Rom 16 is an integral part of the letter, statements to the effect that Paul's epistle is not directed specifically to issues in Rome itself (e.g., that of Manson in Donfried 1991) have tended to fall out of favor.

people "not from the Jews only but also from the Gentiles" (9:24).[105] The inclusion of Gentiles in the righteousness of the covenant community is closely (and paradoxically) bound up with the failure of most Jews to recognize the τέλος of the law in the Messiah (9:30–10:4). The "righteousness" that Israel unsuccessfully sought and the Gentiles unintentionally found is available to all indiscriminately on the basis of faith in the Messiah (10:5–13).[106]

One of the most noticeable facets of Paul's argument in Rom 9–11 is his desire to establish a continuity of God's action in Christ with Israel's history – a concern that admittedly runs throughout Romans (cf. Rom 4), but is especially focused in these chapters on the question of the people of God. In Rom 10:5–8, Paul adduces in support (γὰρ) of his contention that the law finds its τέλος in Jesus Christ a discussion of two types of righteousness (anticipated already in 9:30–31): the righteousness from the law (τὴν δικιαοσύνην τὴν ἐκ [τοῦ] νόμου) and the righteousness from faith (ἡ ἐκ πίστεως δικαιοσύνη), each with its own witness in the law. Moses writes about the former, while the latter is itself personified and speaks the words of Deuteronomy.[107] In accordance with the oppositions he has been constructing throughout Romans, Paul places Lev 18:5 as a witness to righteousness from the law.[108] In light of his use of Lev 18:5 in Gal 3:12,

---

[105] At this juncture Paul quotes Hosea 2:25 LXX and 2:1 LXX – texts that anticipate Paul's application of the negative epithets of Deut 32:21 to Gentiles in Rom 10:19. See § 6.5.4 below.

[106] Notice the extensive use of πάς in this section. On the flow of the text, see Barrett 1982 (though some of his statements would be phrased differently had they been written 'post-Sanders').

[107] Käsemann 1980: 284 probably overstates the significance of the difference between "writing" and "speaking" here, but the difference does at least hint that, in the present context, what is in writing belongs with the γράμμα. While Paul often introduces his citations by γέγραπται, this is often a means to affirm the present relevance of Scripture without specifying a speaking subject. The present tense verbs he uses are almost always verbs of speaking, and this instance is unique for Paul; thus, *pace* many commentators (e.g., Eckstein 1988: 207; Schreiner 1998: 554), there may in fact be significance to the distinction here – though this recognition stops well short of a full-blown theological construct based upon a fundamental "letter vs. spirit" separation.

[108] The text of Lev 18:5 in Rom 10:5 is difficult, with several variations. The two main options are a) with γράφει τὴν δικαιοσύνην τὴν ἐκ [τοῦ] νόμου ὅτι and αὐτὰ and αὐτοῖς in the citation of Leviticus; so P⁴⁶ D² F G Maj sy⁽ᵖ⁾ NA²⁷ Dunn 1988: 599; Moo 1996: 643 n. 1 and many commentators; b) γράφει ὅτι τὴν δικαιοσύνην τὴν ἐκ [τοῦ] νόμου with some witnesses omitting αὐτὰ and attesting αὐτῇ instead of αὐτοῖς; so ℵ* A D* 33* 81. 1739, NA²⁵ and see Moo 1996: 643 n. 1 for commentators who hold this view. c) A third reading, that of B, is notable in combining readings a) and b) by having the syntactical structure of the former but with attesting both αὐτὰ and the αὐτῇ of the latter. It is possible that the reading of B, if original, could account for the other two in terms of assimilation to Lev 18:5 as quoted in Gal 3:12 on the one hand, and smoothing

the oppositional structure of Paul's rhetoric in Romans, and especially in light of the transformation of Deuteronomy which follows, it is likely that Paul intends to set up a contrast between Leviticus and Deuteronomy here.[109] Lev 18:5 speaks of "the one who does them," i.e., the one who does the commandments, while Paul has, as we shall see, extensively re-written Deuteronomy to expunge any notion of doing. Arguably Paul invokes Leviticus not as a witness to any sort of merit theology whereby one might 'earn' one's way to heaven, but rather as an example of the conditional logic of the covenant: human behavior in accordance with the terms of the covenant will meet with life, the promised end of that covenant. In contrast to this scenario of human obedience that leads to life, Paul opposes his interpretation of Deuteronomy. That this contrast is a Pauline construct should not be ignored (so rightly Watson 2004).

In setting Deuteronomy against Leviticus, Paul has made three substantial interpretative judgments that are expressed in his presentation of the text. First, Paul introduces the text with words drawn from Deut 8:17 or 9:4 (where they occur identically in similar contexts):[110] μὴ εἴπῃς ἐν τῇ καρδίᾳ σου ("Do not say in your heart..."). In both Deut 8 and 9, Israel is warned not to grow proud after they have entered the land of promise and say in their hearts, "My strength and the might of my hand have made for me this great power" (8:17), or "It is because of my righteousness (Διὰ τὴν δικαιοσύνην μου) that the Lord brought me in to inherit this good land" (9:4). In this sense, "To 'speak in the heart,' then, is to forget that the success is *entirely* God's doing from start to finish" (Dunn 1988: 2.602; cf. Eckstein 1988: 208–9). Paul invokes the stress against self-reliance as the lens through which his reading of Deut 30:12–14 is to be seen.

Second, as I have already hinted, Paul excises any notion of "doing" the commandment from the original.[111] This presentation of the text shows what Paul has omitted in underline:

Deut 30:12–14: [ἡ ἐντολὴ] οὐκ ἐν τῷ οὐρανῷ ἐστιν λέγων Τίς ἀναβήσεται ἡμῖν εἰς τὸν οὐρανὸν καὶ λήμψεται ἡμῖν αὐτήν; <u>καὶ ἀκούσαντες αὐτὴν ποιήσομεν.</u> οὐδὲ πέραν τῆς θαλάσσης ἐστὶν λέγων Τίς διαπεράσει ἡμῖν εἰς τὸ πέραν τῆς θαλάσσης

---

out syntactical roughness on the other. Hübner 1997: 168–69 prefers this reading, but it must be admitted that the external evidence is not strong in its favor. For general discussion, see Jewett 2007: 621–22; Sprinkle 2008: 166–67 n. 2. Ultimately the sense of the passage is not greatly affected by one's choice, though perhaps more emphasis on the instrumental function of human righteousness would be found in the b) and c) readings.

[109] More fully, see Sprinkle 2008, who also supplies a helpful survey of the range of interpretation of Lev 18:5 in Second Temple sources.

[110] Although the mention of δικαιοσύνη in the latter leads many commentators to favor 9:4 over 8:17.

[111] See Lagrange 1950b: 256; Koch 1986: 129–32; Stanley 1992: 128–33; Watson 2004: 436–39.

καὶ λήμψεται ἡμῖν αὐτήν; <u>καὶ ἀκουστὴν ἡμῖν ποιήσει αὐτήν, καὶ ποιήσομεν.</u> ἐγγὺς σοῦ ἐστιν τὸ ῥῆμα σφόδρα ἐν τῷ στόματί σου καὶ ἐν τῇ καρδίᾳ σου <u>καὶ ἐν ταῖς χερσίν σου αὐτὸ ποιεῖν.</u>

Deut 30:12–14: [The command] is not in heaven that one should say, "Who will ascend for us into heaven and take it for us? <u>And once we have heard, we will do it.</u>" Nor is it on the other side of the sea that one should say, 'Who will cross over to the other side of the sea for us and take it for us? <u>And when he has caused us to hear it, we will do it.</u>" The word is very near you, in your mouth and in your heart <u>and in your hands, in order for you to do it.</u>

This, in turn, prepares the way for Paul's third change, an interpretative re-referentialization of the text.[112] Paul engages in what we might call trans-formative deixis by interspersing comments in his citation of the text that specify Christ as the object of the actions (as opposed to "the command-ment"): "Do not say in your heart, 'Who will ascend into heaven?' – that is, to bring Christ down, or 'Who will descend into the abyss?'[113] – that is, to bring Christ up from the dead. But what does it say? 'The word is near you, in your mouth and in your heart' – that is, the word of faith that we proclaim."[114] Here can also be observed the characteristically Pauline 'slippage' as Deuteronomy's commandment is replaced with Christ who, in turn, is metonymically elided into the message about him, the "word of faith" (ῥῆμα τῆς πίστεως).[115] This word of faith, however, itself carries the force of a commandment to be met with ἡ ὑποκοὴ πίστεως (1:6; 16:26).[116]

---

[112] Of course, this is an etic description; from Paul's own perspective, one might speak of a clarification of Deuteronomy's true referent.

[113] Reference to the "abyss" (ἄβυσσος) as opposed to the "sea" (θάλασσα) of Deut 30:13 may be explained with reference to Ps 107:26 (106:26 LXX: ἀναβαίνουσιν ἕως τῶν οὐρανῶν καὶ καταβαίνουσιν ἕως τῶν ἀβύσσων), or possibly with reference to an alternative text of Deuteronomy, which may be reflected in *Tg. Neof.* here as well. Stuhlmacher 1994 suggests that "Together with the Jewish exegesis of his time, Paul sees in the sea, concerning which in Deut. 30:13 it is said, 'Who will go over the sea for us?' the depth of chaos of the underworld and therefore reads Deut. 30:13 and Ps. 107:26 with and into one another" (156; so also Käsemann 1980: 288; cf. Jeremias 1964). It may also be, however, that Paul has introduced the innovation to correspond more closely to the places one might search for Christ.

[114] Rom 10:6–8: μὴ εἴπῃς ἐν τῇ καρδίᾳ σου· τίς ἀναβήσεται εἰς τὸν οὐρανόν; τοῦτ' ἔστιν Χριστὸν καταγαγεῖν· ἤ· τίς καταβήσεται εἰς τὴν ἄβυσσον; τοῦτ' ἔστιν Χριστὸν ἐκ νεκρῶν ἀναγαγεῖν. ἀλλὰ τί λέγει; ἐγγύς σου τὸ ῥῆμα ἐστιν ἐν τῷ στόματί σου καὶ ἐν τῇ καρδίᾳ σου, τοῦτ' ἔστιν τὸ ῥῆμα τῆς πίστεως ὃ κηρύσσομεν.

[115] Many commentators fail to notice the Christological identification here implied, if still holding to a broadly Christological understanding of the text as a whole.

[116] One insight among many which I owe to Markus Bockmuehl in private conversa-tion.

Paul's formal method can be paralleled in part from both the Qumran *pesharim* and from Philo's writings, and progress in understanding the nature of biblical interpretation in Second Temple Judaism over the past fifty years or so have put an end to at least some of the scandal Paul's use of Deuteronomy in these verses once caused.[117] It is also clear, however, that such formal parallels cannot *materially* explain Paul's interpretation here. Paul normally operates with a certain Christological reticence in his reading of Scripture (though see 1 Cor 8:4–6 in § 6.4.1 above); what prompts him to the transformation of the text we see here? Part of the answer may in fact lie in a global construal of Deuteronomy. If one asks, "What is Deuteronomy fundamentally about?" one could do worse than to answer: the Torah. But already within the horizon of Deuteronomy itself we find a certain identification of God with Torah (e.g., Deut 4:7–8; McConville 2000). What is more, the whole thrust of Deuteronomy tells against a legalistic interpretation of the law (so rightly, e.g., Leenhardt 1957: 152; Murray 1968: 2.52; Via 1974; Hays 1989: 77–82; Wagner 2002: 165–68). So for Paul to identify the "word" of Deuteronomy with Christ simply extends (and to a certain extent radicalizes) a trajectory already begun within Deuteronomy itself.

It may be possible, however, to press beyond this general understanding if we consider some of the other appeals Paul makes to the final chapters of Deuteronomy. I will return to this question in the conclusion to this section (§ 6.5.5). For the moment it is sufficient to note that Paul infuses Deut 30:12–14 with a Christological *pro nobis*. Within Deut 30, these verses function as an exhortation to the obedience requisite to restoration, but Paul suggests that God has fulfilled the condition for restoration in Christ.

---

[117] So, e.g., Dodd 1932: "As an interpretation of Scripture this is purely fanciful" (166). Schmidt 1972: 176–77 registers some of the embarrassment of commentators at Paul's OT usage here. Lim (1997) has suggested that Paul nowhere engages in what might strictly be called pesher exegesis, but certain features of his interpretative activity can be described as "pesheresque." Curiously, Lim only mentions Rom 10:6–8 in passing, though his unpublished D.Phil. thesis does devote a few pages to it (1991: 158–60; cf. also 102–06). Philo paraphrases Deut 30:11–14 a number of times. In *Mut.* 236–38, he uses Deut 30:14 to speak of three ways of repentance – in thoughts and words and deeds (διανοίᾳ, λόγοις, πράξεσιν), corresponding to the LXX's heart, mouth and hands; similarly in *Praem.* 79–84; *Virt.* 183–84; *Prob.* 66–70; *Somn.* 2.179–80; *Post.* 84–86 (though here Philo suggests that the correspondence is to words, plans and actions [ἐν λόγοις, ἐν βουλαῖς, ἐν πράξεσι]). Bekken (1995; 2007) has offered some illuminating parallels between Philo's technique and Paul's in formal terms, but, Bekken's protests notwithstanding, Paul's eschatological perspective remains distinct from Philo's more philosophical approach (rightly Käsemann 1980: 287). Also often mentioned in this connection is Bar 3:29–30, in which Torah and Wisdom are linked via Deut 30:11–14 (cf. Suggs 1967 and § 4.6 above). That Paul is indebted to the mediation of wisdom traditions in the present context, however, remains without convincing proof.

What is left is simply to receive this – via the "mouth" and "heart" that spill over from Paul's citation into his message to the Roman church (10:9–10).

6.5.4. Sin, Restoration, and the Gentiles

In the previous chapter I suggested that Philo views the Song of Moses as generically unique and prophetic in nature (§ 5.3.1), and the next chapter will suggest a similar conception in Josephus (§ 7.2.3). While Paul gives us fewer direct statements about his approach to the Song, it similarly appears to be a significant text for Paul, and its dynamics nicely pre-figure (and perhaps give rise to) those in Paul's letter to the Romans. In addition to the citation of Deut 32:35 in Rom 12:19 which has already been discussed (§ 6.3.5), Paul also cites Deut 32:21 in Rom 10:19 and Deut 32:43 in Rom 15:10.

Following on from the Christological rewriting of Deut 30:12–14, Paul works backward, in a series of rhetorically loaded questions, from the necessity of "calling on the name of the Lord," established by his quotation of Joel 2:32 [3:5 MT] in 10:13, through four successive steps to arrive at the necessity of preachers being sent (10:15). This allows Paul to affirm that preachers have in fact been sent while simultaneously identifying the proclamation of such preachers (including, presumably, his own) with that of the heralds of Israel's restoration foretold by Isaiah (52:7).[118] Again as Isaiah foretold, "not all obeyed the gospel." At this point (10:17), Paul makes an axiomatic inference that summarizes 10:14–16 and provides a transition into the discussion of 10:18–21.[119] The statement of 10:17 calls forth two questions in response from Paul. Is Israel perhaps unable to fulfill the conditions of 10:13–15 because they have not heard?[120] Rather, Paul asserts, they have heard, for in the words of the psalmist, "Their voice has gone out into all the earth, and their words to the ends of the world" (Ps 18:5 LXX). As God revealed himself through his creation (Ps 18:1–6 LXX) and his Torah (18:7–11 LXX), so has he revealed himself through the gospel proclaimed throughout all the world. Perhaps, then, Israel has heard but not known? In response to this question, Paul invokes the witness of Moses, then of Isaiah.

---

[118] On which see Wagner 2002: 170–178.

[119] Note the verbal links, unfortunately lost in English translation: ὑπακούω (10:16); ἀκοή (10:16); ἀκοή (10:17); ἀκούω (10:18). See Dunn 1988: 2.620.

[120] The questions of 10:18–19 are both somewhat awkward because of the double negative. However, "In cases like Ro 10:18f; 1 Cor 9:4f μή is an interrog[ative] word and ου negatives [sic] the verb. The double negative causes one to expect an affirmative answer" (BDAG: 646; so also BDF § 427 (2)).

Paul draws the witness of Moses from the Song of Moses (Deut 32). The Song itself, together with the "Blessing of Moses" of chapter 33, functions as Moses' last will and testament to the people of Israel. As such, the Song holds a key place in Deuteronomy and the Pentateuch as a whole, as its widespread influence also suggests. The framework of the Song in 31:9–30 and 32:44–47 closely identifies the Torah with the Song (e.g., cf. 31:9–13 with 31:19–22), suggesting that the Song contains the Torah *in nuce*.[121] Though the precise poetic structure of the Song is difficult to determine exactly,[122] its dramatic progression is quite clear.[123] After an introduction and call of heaven and earth to witness (32:1–3), Moses lays forth the theme of the Song: God has been faithful, but Israel has repeatedly turned aside in flagrant disobedience (32:4–6). Yahweh's primeval election and redemption of Israel are recounted, and his parental care for Israel is extolled (32:7–14). In 32:7–14 Yahweh is the subject of the verbs, but this changes dramatically in 32:15–18 as Israel is portrayed as apostate and self-satisfied, turning away from the God who made him and sacrificing to other deities. Yahweh is again portrayed as the subject as he reacts to Israel's infidelity (32:19–25), the punishment detailed in 32:23–25 reminiscent of the covenant curses of chapter 28.[124] Finally, the Lord relents because of concern for his name among the nations, and in view of Israel's weakness after punishment. In the end, the Lord will vindicate both himself and his people, resulting in praise to God (26–43). In this way, the Song more or less recapitulates the storyline of Deut 27–30 though lacking, importantly, any notion of repentance as the condition for restoration.

Paul's first citation comes from 32:21b. Deut 32:21 itself is an answer to Israel's idolatry in 32:16: "They provoked him[125] to jealousy with strange gods; with abominations they provoked him to anger." In response, the Lord "spurned them" because of the "provocation of his sons and his daughters" (32:19). In a striking twist of retributive irony, the Lord answers Israel according to their sin:[126] "They have provoked me to jealousy

---

[121] See Wagner 2002: 199–200.

[122] See, *inter alia*, attempts by Christensen 2002: nine sections; Wright 1962: seven sections; Skehan 1993: three sections.

[123] See Olson 1994: 147–50 for an analysis of the dramatic structure and movement of the poem.

[124] See: Sword/War – 32:23, 25 = 28:25, 49–57; Famine – 32:24a = 28:38–42, 47, 51, 52–57; Plague/Pestilence – 32:24bc = 28:21–22, 27–28, 58–61; Wild Beasts – 32:24d = 28:26; For people of all ages – 32:25 = 28:54–57. So also Wagner 2002: 195 n. 224.

[125] The LXX has rendered this as God's speech: "They provoked *me* to jealousy..."

[126] As Knight 1995: 75 writes, "this is a theological interpretation of the striking pronouncement in the Mosaic legislation, 'an eye for an eye' (Exod. 21:24)."

with a not-god; they have provoked me to anger with their vanities.[127] So I will provoke them to jealousy with a not-people; I will provoke them to anger with a foolish nation." Israel was to love the Lord their God with all their being (Deut 6:4–9), but forsook their covenant Lord for other gods who, in reality, are "not-gods". Therefore, in an "emphatically just" punishment (Tigay 1996: 307), Yahweh will turn his favor away from his covenant people to a "not-people," perhaps by granting them military victory over Israel and so provoking Israel to jealous anger (22–25). Though various attempts to identify the original referent of the "not-people" and "foolish nation" of v. 21 have been made, it is likely that the identity of the nation is "deliberately obscured" to enhance the perennial application of the Song.[128] Further, the phrase "not-people" deliberately plays on Israel's status as the covenant people: "The phrase has the added effect of designating this agent of judgment as a people that did not enjoy the chosen status of Israel, yet one that, even so, would now overcome Israel in this rejection of the chosen."[129]

To this point in the Song, the picture for Israel is bleak. Using images of harlotry and filial rebellion, Moses describes them as "no longer his children" (5), "a crooked and twisted generation" (5), a "foolish and senseless people" (6) who "forsook God who made him and scoffed at the Rock of his salvation" (15), "children in whom is no faithfulness" (20).[130] Has Yahweh perhaps "spurned" his people forever (cf. 32:19)? A partial reprieve comes in 32:26–27, where Yahweh relents because of his own reputation among the aggressors. But Israel is not yet vindicated, and there may be deliberate ambiguity in the subjects of vv. 28–30, suggesting the blurring of lines between Israel and the nations in their corporate foolishness.[131] The decisive turn, however, comes in the strong declaration of 32:36 that "Yahweh will vindicate his people and have compassion on his servants, when he sees that their power is gone and there is none remain-

---

[127] Clearly, the reference to הבל has idols in view, as both the context and the lexical range of the word make clear. Tigay 1996: 308 translates it as "futilities," literally "puffs of breath," "vapor," "one of the Bible's pejorative terms for idols." Though the term occurs 86 times in the Hebrew Bible, this is one of only three instances where it is translated by εἴδωλον (elsewhere only at Jer 14:22; 16:19). *Tg. Neof.* and *Tg. Ps.-J.* are both explicit about "idols" in the context of 32:16–21.

[128] Nelson 2002: 373; so also Christensen 2002: 807.

[129] McConville 2002: 457; cf. Craigie 1976: 383–384.

[130] Did Deut 32:20 LXX suggest itself to Paul (children in whom no 'faith' is)? So Hays 1989: 83. Dunn 1988: 2.625, points out this is the only occurrence of πίστις in the Torah.

[131] So McConville 2002: 462. Of course, this may also be one feature of the Song that facilitated Paul's reading of it as a positive statement about Gentile inclusion in the covenant community.

ing, bond or free." This vindication of his people will be, in turn, the Lord's own vindication (cf. 32:39 with 32:26–27). In other words, the salvation of Israel after judgment is a part of God's vindication as the faithful covenant Lord.

Is there any indication in the Song of Moses that Gentiles will participate in the ultimate prosperity of Israel? After all, the Song does speak in rather bloody terms of Yahweh's vengeance on his enemies (32:39–42), which seems to imply that all does not end well for the "not-people" of 32:21. Three factors, however, may have facilitated a positive understanding of Gentiles in the Song. First, the language of vengeance is applied to "adversaries," "those who hate me," and "the enemy," but never to Gentiles *per se*.[132] Thus, such language need not necessarily entail Gentiles *qua* Gentiles. Second, much of one's view of this problem will be bound up with the thorny textual issue at 32:43,[133] where the MT *may* be read as making a positive statement linking Yahweh's people with the nations,[134] but the LXX is fully explicit in this regard.[135] Finally, the Song is about what is to take place "in the end of days" (31:29: ἔσχατον τῶν ἡμερῶν; note also the ἐπ᾽ ἐσχάτων of 32:20). Some of the Song's unusual features (e.g., no mention of patriarchs, the exodus, or the covenants that form the major part of Deuteronomy), may be explained by its eschatological focus. McConville suggests that

Deuteronomic themes have been deliberately eschatologized, with the playing down of Egypt, desert, exile and return, and the adoption of certain concepts familiar in prophetic visions of the future. This includes a future action of Yahweh stored up for the right time (34; cf. Mal. 3:16; Dan. 12:9), a day of vengeance and the requital of Yahweh's enemies (35; cf. Is. 2:12; 34:8; 61:2), atonement for the land of Israel (43; cf. Zech. 13:1–2; Joel 3:21[4:21]).[136]

---

[132] So also Wagner 2002: 317 n. 38.

[133] See Skehan 1993: 168; cf. Skehan 1954 for text-critical notes on the Qumran and LXX text-types over against the MT. For a different reconstruction of the evidence, see Rofé 2002. Of course, the other thorny textual issue in the Song is at 32:8, which is not unconnected to the judgment one makes about 32:43; see Tov 1992: 269; van der Kooij 1994.

[134] Interestingly, the Jewish commentator Tigay 1996: 314, says that v. 43 "implies that God's salvation of Israel has importance for the world at large...this is implicitly an invitation to the nations to revere the Lord as Israel does and a promise that if they do so, He will treat them as He does Israel (when it is meritorious)" (following the medieval Jewish commentator Rashbam).

[135] On which see the further discussion later in this section. The evidence from Qumran (e.g., 4Q44) may not be as patient of a Gentile-inclusive reading, though it does not exclude them. See generally Wagner 2002: 316 n. 36.

[136] McConville 2002: 461–62, following Luyten 1985: 344–45.

This survey of the Song has already begun to make clear why the storyline Paul found in it served his argument in Romans so well.

Paul summons Moses as his first prophetic witness against Israel:[137] "First Moses says,[138] 'I myself will provoke you to jealousy by a not-nation; by a nation without understanding I will provoke you to anger.'"[139] In Deut 32, this verse stood mid-way through the cycle of Israel's history: they were guilty of idolatry and so Moses prophetically declared that Israel would be punished by means of God's transferring his favor to a Gentile nation in preference to them. Paul now claims that this has taken effect in the unbelief of the Jews and the salvation of the Gentiles in his own day. Moses was the prophet *par excellence* (Deut 34:10), and the pairing of him with Isaiah may suggest that Moses is here functioning in a prophetic office (Quesnel 2003: 333–34) – a fact more striking in light of the Song's explicitly eschatological focus. Paul, living in the generation of those "on whom the ends of the ages has come" (1 Cor 10:11b) sees the Song of Moses as a pre-announced plan according to which the Gentiles would be included in response to Israel's disobedience. What is more, the Song is repeatedly said to be a "witness" against Israel, so it follows that "since Moses' day, Israel has known the plot their national story would follow. Clearly, Paul stands on solid narrative ground when he quotes from Moses'

---

[137] For Moses as a prophet here, see Quesnel 2003: 333–34., esp. 333–34. His tentative suggestion that Moses in Romans 9–11 be seen as representative of Israel's stages in salvation history (334–35), however, should probably be rejected as outrunning the evidence.

[138] On the introductory formula, note "David says" (Rom 4:6–8; 11:9–10) and "Isaiah says" (10:16, 20, 21; 15:12). Note also the parallels that Ellis 1957: 48–49 adduces to such introductions to scripture in other Jewish literature.

[139] πρῶτος Μωϋσῆς λέγει· ἐγὼ παραζηλώσω ὑμᾶς ἐπ' οὐκ ἔθνει, ἐπ' ἔθνει ἀσυνέτῳ παροργιῶ ὑμᾶς. Paul drops the introductory καὶ and changes the pronoun to ὑμᾶς (*bis*). The latter change, though not vastly important, has evoked some discussion. It is certainly not the case that Paul has made the change to address Gentile Christians in vv. 19–20, and then Jewish non-believers in v. 21 (contra Reinbold 1995). Rather, as Paul's usage of the παραζηλόω motif in Romans 11 makes clear, unbelieving Israel should be construed as the antecedent of 'you' (so also Schreiner 1998: 573 n. 23). This, further, makes better sense of Paul's question in 10:19a (again, contra Reinbold 1995). Neither is it simply "to make it clear that the object has changed and that he is now referring to Israel" in light of the third person plurals in the quotation of Ps 18:5 LXX (as Bell 1994: 96, and Koch 1986: 110, assert). Rather, as Stanley points out, the opening words of v. 19 make such a transition clear (1992: 143). Therefore, the change probably serves to heighten the rhetorical impact of the quotation upon the hearers, and to stress that God is even now saying these things to unbelieving Israel of Paul's own day. So, generally, Stanley 1992: 144; Dunn 1988: 2.625; Wagner 2002: 190. Hübner 1984: 97, writes, "Paulus ändert das Zitat so, dass dieses Ich Gottes sich an das Du Israel richtet."

Song to defend his claim that Israel 'has known.'"[140] Paul's selection of this text that speaks of the Gentiles as a "not-nation" concurs with his tendency to read negative epithets as referring to Gentiles: "not my people" (9:25–26; cf. Hos 2:23/1:10); those "not pursuing righteousness" (9:30); "a no-nation" (10:19; cf. Deut 32:21); "those not seeking me" (10:20; cf. Isa 65:1); "those to whom it was not announced concerning him...those who have not heard" (15:21; cf. Isa 52:15).[141] The first movement of the Song is accusation.

In fact, Paul also makes some strong allusions to this first movement of the Song in his letter to the Corinthian church concerning food sacrificed to idols. He uses the example of "our fathers" (10:1: οἱ πατέρες ἡμῶν) in the wilderness as an exhortation for the Corinthians to shun idolatry and anything that might lead to it (cf. 10:14), in this context especially eating food that has been sacrificed to idols in cultic contexts. While there are a number of points in his discussion that could be described as Deuteronomic,[142] for our present concerns it is worth noting two allusions to the

---

[140] Wagner 2002: 193. This explanation of the answer to the question is to be preferred to that of Cranfield, who suggests, "The point of the quotation here is that, if Gentiles who, in relation to the knowledge of God, are, compared with Israel, but no-peoples, foolish nations, have come to know, then it certainly cannot be supposed that Israel has not known" (1979: 2.539). It is possible that this should be seen as a subtext, but the context of Deut 32 should control the main assertion.

[141] See Wagner 2002: 83, 188. Cf. Hübner 1984: 97.

[142] Note the influential article by Meeks (1982) for midrashic connections, though whether this is a fully formed midrash on one specific text is questionable. For a reading that sees this as standing squarely within the Deuteronomic tradition, note Oropeza 1998, who concludes: "Both the Song of Moses and Paul's message in 1 Corinthians 8–10 serve to remind God's people about the implications of breaking their covenant with the one true God to serve idols. In other words, a warning against apostasy may be considered as a leitmotiv in Deuteronomy 32, and 1 Corinthians 8–10, and this aspect is almost categorically overlooked or not properly appreciated by scholars when interpreting Paul's message" (1998: 61).

In addition to the evidence adduced by Meeks and Oropeza, it is also worth pondering whether the single explicit citation from Paul, drawn from Exod 32:6 in 1 Cor 10:7 ("The people sat down to eat and drink and rose up to play") is not to be understood in a Deuteronomic sense. Note, e.g., Deut 31:20: "For when I have brought them into the land flowing with milk and honey, which I promised on oath to their ancestors, and they have eaten their fill and grown fat, they will turn to other gods and serve them, despising me and breaking my covenant" (cf. also Deut 32:15 and the theme we noted above from Deut 8–9 warning against rebellion after satiation [§ 6.5.3]; further, *Jub* 1:8; *1 Clem.* 3:1). In fact, one finds the connection with this Exodus citation and Deuteronomy in the later *Sifre to Deuteronomy*: "A person rebels against the Omnipresent only in prosperity" (§ 43; cf. § 318), followed soon after with a quotation from Exod 32:6. Further, in light of the allusions to Deut 32 to be considered here, it may be that Paul's identification of Christ with the "Rock" of 10:4 owes something to Deut 32's repeated epithet for God as

Song of Moses in 10:20 and 10:22.[143] Without conceding that an "idol is anything" (10:19), Paul writes that for idolaters, "what they sacrifice, they sacrifice to demons and not to God" or possibly, "they sacrifice to demons and to what is not God" (10:22: ἃ θύουσιν, δαιμονίοις καὶ οὐ θεῷ [θύουσιν]). This repeats, with only a slight change in verb tense, a phrase from the first movement of the Song, in which Israel's idolatry is announced: ἔθυσαν δαιμονίοις καὶ οὐ θεῷ (Deut 32:17). Paul goes on to say that eating food sacrificed to idols and participating in the Eucharistic celebration are incompatible. He punctuates this with two questions, the first of which is drawn from the same text that Paul cites in Rom 10:19: "Shall we provoke the Lord to jealousy?" (παραζηλοῦμεν τὸν κύριον; cf. Deut 32:21a: αὐτοὶ παρεζήλωσάν με ἐπ᾽ οὐ θεῷ). Paul appears to see the Israelites' negative example in the desert as a paradigmatic instance of idolatry and warns the Corinthians lest they too become a rebellious people of God.[144]

Returning to Paul's argument in Romans 9–11, we see the next stage of Paul's reading of the Song. The theme of "provocation to jealousy" which he introduced in 10:19 is a provocation, in the first instance, to the jealousy of anger. As Paul's argument proceeds, however, and especially in 11:11–14, Paul develops the theme of jealousy in a positive sense. If, in fact, we see the provocation to jealousy theme in Rom 11:11–14 as rooted not only in Deut 32:21, but also in the entire context of the Song of Moses, this positive turn becomes more readily understandable. In this sense, then, while being "provoked to jealousy" in Rom 10:19 may appear to be a mostly negative reaction on the part of the Jews (i.e., "provoked to jealous anger"), 11:11–14 suggests that Paul hopes to win some of his kinsmen by their jealousy of the Gentiles who are being saved (i.e., "provoked to jeal-

---

"the Rock" (32:4, 15, 18, 30, 31; cf. 32:37); though the LXX consistently renders the Hebrew צוּר as θεός, this may be an instance where Paul knows the Hebrew tradition.

[143] Noting the allusion of 1 Cor 10:20 to Deut 32:16–17 are, *inter alia*, Craigie 1976: 382; Bell 1994: 251–255; Barrett 1968: 236; while 10:22's allusion to 32:21, is noticed by Fee 1987: 473–74. More fully, see Hays 1989: 91–94; Wagner 2002: 203–05; Rosner 2007: 130–31. Further, Rosner suggests that the 1 Cor 10:22b ("Are we stronger than him?") also alludes to Deut 32 (see esp. Rosner 1994: 195–203).

[144] Later Christian use of Deut 32:21 in large measure follows Paul, though now the resonances sound supersessionist rather than prophetic: Justin Martyr, *Dial.* 119, cites Deut 32:16–23, concluding that God promised to Abraham "a nation of similar faith, God-fearing, righteous, and delighting the Father; but it is not you, 'in whom is no faith'" (cf. 32:20b). Clement, *Strom.* 2.9 adds the explanatory note: "And I will anger you by a foolish nation, *that is, by one that has become disposed to obedience.*" Origen takes a strong supersessionist reading (combining with 1 Cor 1:27) in *Cels.* 3.73; *Princ.* 4.4; cf. *Cels.* 2.79.

ous emulation").[145] Of course, one does not need the Song of Moses to see this, but the Song adds depth by suggesting that such provocation will actually achieve its goal. Given that the Song tells of Israel's election, unfaithfulness, punishment, and vindication, might it be that Paul draws on the Song precisely because it is so close to the scheme he advocates in Rom 9–11?[146] Or better, that Paul has even derived his insights from meditation on the Song? Might this also account for how Paul arrives at the "mystery" of the final salvation of Israel in Rom 11:25–27?[147] If Paul read the Song of Moses as a prophesied narrative in which he found himself living, he would be aware that one phase remained. In fact, we see evidence of Paul's awareness of this in Romans 15.

The final movement of the Song remained: the Lord still needed to vindicate his people Israel and unite Jew and Gentile in worship to him (Deut 32:26–43). In fact, it is here that the Greek translation of the Song may have proved beneficial to Paul's Gentile mission. In contrast to, e.g., the Temple Scroll or the *Sifre*, which take a consistently negative stance toward Gentiles, Paul has read the Song of Moses looking *for* the inclusion of the Gentiles. In fact, throughout Deuteronomy the LXX tends to translate *ad sensum* when referring to a "people" or a "nation," using λαός for Israel and ἔθνος for Gentiles[148] (within Deut 32 see λαός in 32:6, 9, 36, 43 and ἔθνος in 32:8 [2x], 21 [2x], 28, 43; though HT has גוי in 32:8, 21, 28, 43 and עם in 32:6, 8, 9, 21, 36, 43). Therefore, when the LXX has in 32:43c εὐφράνθητε ἔθνη μετὰ τοῦ λαοῦ αὐτοῦ it is clear that this is a summons for Gentiles to worship *with* Israel. The LXX translator may even have played on the double possibility of עם to mean either "with" or "people," and so produced the double translation we have before us.[149] But whether this was a Septuagintal innovation or whether this translation reflects a non-extant Hebrew *Vorlage*, the text of the Song of Moses that

---

[145] Bell 1994: 156–157. Cf. Quesnel 2003: 332: "Paul donne au motif de la jalousie une signification nouvelle: les juifs non chrétiens deviendront jaloux des disciples de Christ issus du paganisme, et cette jalousie aura sur eux un effet positif, celui de leur faire regretter leur endurcissement pour les faire entrer à leur tour dans l'aire du salut (reprise du verbe παραζηλοῦν en Rm 11.11, 14)." So also Watson 2004: 449: jealousy is "a necessary moment of dawning insight."

[146] Wagner 2002: 194, writes, "By tapping into the Song of Moses through his quotation of 32:21, Paul sets up a suggestive intertextual relationship between this well-known poetic depiction of Israel's election, unfaithfulness, and redemption and his own account in Romans of Israel's stumbling and ultimate salvation."

[147] As suggested by Bell 1994: 273; note also Stuhlmacher 1994: 161; Watson 2004: 449. My reading of the jealousy motif, while it shares some similarities with Wright 1992: 231–57, ultimately differs on Rom 11:25–27.

[148] See Harl 1993: 188–89.

[149] So Wevers 1995: 534.

Paul read clearly ended with Jew and Gentile beside each other in worship. And it is this text that Paul quotes in Rom 15:10, thus functioning as a key answer to the problem posed by his earlier citation of Deut 32:21 in Rom 10:19, i.e., the inclusion of the Gentiles is to provoke the Jews to jealousy for their ultimate salvation together. In these two citations of Deuteronomy's Song of Moses some key dynamics of Romans are nicely epitomized. Therefore, in a meaningful way the Song of Moses can be said to be foundational for Romans as a whole.[150]

6.5.5. Conclusion: Deuteronomy as the Lens of Israel's History

The sheer number of textual engagements with Deut 27–32 in Paul is enough to suggest that section's significance for the apostle. Paul nowhere offers a straightforward sequential interpretation of these chapters because, of course, such a presentation does not suit the purpose of his letters. Those interested in the coherence or otherwise of the apostle's reading of any part of Scripture will have to reconstruct it from the various textual engagements found in letters written to different communities over ten or more years. The task is daunting, but with Deut 27–32 we may be in a position to reconstruct such a reading, in broad strokes, at a level that is impossible elsewhere. I suggest we can best see the contours of the apostle's interpretation if we approach these chapters backwards, beginning with the Song of Moses. In that Song Paul finds history told in advance – ranging from Israel's election to their disobedience, the Lord's plan to provoke them to jealous anger and then jealous emulation through the Gentiles, and the ultimate restoration of Israel with Jew and Gentile beside one another in worship. That restoration is nowhere dependent upon a prior human act. Rather, the Song describes such restoration in terms of unilateral divine action on behalf of Israel. This apocalyptic interventionist reading of Deut 32, understood in light of God's action in Christ, controls the reading of Deut 27–30,[151] where Christ now fulfills the condition of the covenant (30:11–14), thus grounding the obedience brought about by the newly re-

---

[150] Hays 1989: 164 famously suggests that "Deuteronomy 32 contains Romans *in nuce.*" The Song also has an influence in other early Christian literature, being alluded to in Matt 17:17; Mark 8:37; 10:45; Luke 9:41; Acts 2:40; Heb 1:6 (the possibility that this text is dependent upon a *Vorlage* preserved in Ode 2 appears to me unlikely; *pace* Steyn 2000); Rev 6:10, 15:3–4, 19:2. On the use of the Song of Moses elsewhere in the NT, and in post-biblical Judaism more generally, in addition to §§ 3–8 of the present work, see especially Bell 1994: 217–85.

[151] Thus, there is some truth in Waters' contention that "there are patterns of reading that are peculiar to Deut 27–30, and patterns of reading that are peculiar to Deut 32" (2006: 237; see also 237–241), though his reading is generally more atomistic than necessary.

vealed circumcision of the heart (29:29, 30:6), and providing the answer to Israel's divinely overseen failure to obey (29:4). The fact that such intervention happened is further proof that the curse threatened by Deuteronomy had been actualized (Deut 27:26), though also overcome through the mechanism hinted at by Deuteronomy as well (Deut 21:22–23).

6.6. Conclusion: The Shape of Paul's Deuteronomy

At the end of this examination of Paul's engagement with Deuteronomy, limited though it must remain, how might we answer the question with which we began? Can we offer some characterization of the shape of Paul's Deuteronomy, or must we conclude that we can only observe fragments of an inevitably contradictory encounter?[152] I take it that each of the basic construals which have been described is in some sense irreducible, that is, that one should not be silenced or simply negated by reference to another. Arguably the best way to hold together the disparate evidence we have here examined is to extend the suggestion that Paul reads Deuteronomy backwards, in at least two senses. First, and perhaps most clearly, Paul reads Deuteronomy retrospectively from the standpoint of an apostle of Christ to the nations. The apocalyptic[153] elements in Paul's thought and experience have disrupted a straightforward nomistic appeal to Deuteronomy, at least as far as Gentile inclusion in the people of God is concerned and the attendant problem of Deuteronomy's curse. So while Paul can share a Deuteronomic diagnosis of Israel's history (even while in fact further redefining this notion), he does not show evidence of the Deuteronomic prognosis of so many contemporaries because in Christ the solution to the plight has already been disclosed. In this sense, to ask whether Paul argues from plight to solution or from solution to plight is something of a false dichotomy: plight and solution clarify one another; Scripture and gospel are mutually interpretive. What is more, because faith in the one Lord constitutes the people of God, Deuteronomy cannot have its entrance-

---

[152] So Watson, who otherwise offers the most synthetic account of Paul's appeals to Deuteronomy: "There is a striking discrepancy between this parenetic use of texts from Deuteronomy and the motif of 'the curse of the law', which likewise appeals to Deuteronomy. How can it be that laws which continue to guide individual and communal conduct are at the same time the bearers of a curse? This is one of the more obvious examples of a real 'contradiction' within Paul's understanding of the law" (2004: 425).

[153] The term "apocalyptic" is admittedly problematic (see the long critique by Matlock 1996; though note the recent defense in Childs 2008: 194–218). Though a full defense would be out of place here, in the present context, it is used with reference to the sudden revaluation of the existing order in light of the death and resurrection of Christ in the middle of history.

keeping function any longer. The re-referentialization of Deuteronomy's word of Torah now discloses Christ as the law's goal.

But there is a second sense in which Paul reads Deuteronomy backwards: he presents the scroll to his fledgling churches through the lens of its final chapters first, and only then does he come to its ethical chapters. This is less a statement of epistolary presentation than it is of conceptual presentation. Because Paul is convinced that Deuteronomy ultimately speaks to the people of God composed of Jew and Gentile who are welcomed by the one God on the basis of faith in Jesus Christ, he believes that the circumcision of their hearts by the Spirit now enables them to fulfill the law – not as an entrance requirement but as an epistemological guide to what is holy, just and good, though filtered through the apocalyptic disclosure and irruption of the cross and resurrection of Christ. In this sense, the ethical reading of Deuteronomy is grounded in the Christological and pneumatological reading.

It is further notable that Paul does in fact operate with a Christological hermeneutic in his reading of Deuteronomy, but of a particular kind. While Richard Hays has justly restored focus to Paul's "ecclesiolocentric" or "ecclesiotelic" hermeneutic, this may be more suited to Paul's interpretation of prophetic books – most notably, Isaiah. Paul's is not a crass Christological hermeneutic that seeks to find Jesus hidden behind every verse of Deuteronomy, but he does make some striking statements about the identity of Christ through rewriting Deuteronomy – including him in Israel's confession of the *Shema'* (1 Cor 8:4–6), identifying him with and by the gracious word of Torah (Rom 10:6–8), interpreting his death by means of Deuteronomy's curse (Gal 3:10–14). Of course, the ecclesiocentric hermeneutic is not absent in Paul's reading of Deuteronomy. One thinks especially of his reading of the Song of Moses as prefiguring Gentile inclusion in the people of God, as well as Paul's ethical instruction that implicitly considers the Gentiles as those for whose sake Deuteronomy was written. For Paul, the Christological and the ecclesiological foci of Deuteronomy are both to be found in the text – and both are characterized by an eschatological awareness of living in Deuteronomy's "end of days."

It will be recalled that the plan of the present study eschews the traditional bi-partite presentation of "Jewish background" and then "Paul" (§ 1.4). Rather, Paul is here set in a chronological chain of Jewish encounters with the end of the Pentateuch. We therefore next consider how Deuteronomy functions for Paul's younger contemporary, Flavius Josephus.

Chapter 7

Deuteronomy in the Works of Josephus

7.1. Introduction

The Jewish historian Joseph son of Matthias, better known by his Roman name, Flavius Josephus, penned an account of the Jewish revolution against Rome (*Bellum judaicum*), wrote a sprawling retelling of Israel's history and customs (*Antiquitates judaicae*) to which he appended a self-defensive report of his own actions in the revolution (*Vita*), and concluded his literary output with an apologetic tract for the Jewish nation (*Contra Apionem*). Josephus was born of priestly descent around the time of the call/conversion of the apostle Paul (ca. 37–38 CE; cf. *Vita* 5), and fought in the war against Rome before being taken captive and brought to Rome by Vespasian and Titus. There he sought to render intelligible the history and fortunes of the Jewish nation to pagan and Jew alike, enjoying the literary patronage of the Flavian house to support him in his efforts.[1] His explanatory labors, especially in the *Antiquitates*, necessarily entail an engagement with Israel's holy books, and Deuteronomy figures distinctively among them in his treatment.

7.2. Deuteronomy as Constitution, Law, and Biography

Josephus claims that in his *Antiquitates*, he has "translated from the sacred writings (ἐκ τῶν ἱερῶν γραμμάτων μεθηρμήνευκα)" (*C. Ap.* 1.54).[2] The statement is striking because, first, the portion of his work that paraphrases the biblical text only comprises roughly half of the final product (Books 1–11), and secondly, because even in these books, his method appears to be

---

[1] On these introductory matters, see esp. the treatments in Attridge 1984; Bilde 1988; Rajak 2002.

[2] Translations of Josephus used here are as follows, unless otherwise indicated: for *Bellum*, the LCL edition by H. St. J. Thackeray (sometimes modified); for *Antiquitates* 1–4, Feldman 2000 (I have modified Feldman's "Moyses" to "Moses" for consistency); for *Vita*, Mason 2001; for *Contra Apionem*, Barclay 2007. Greek text is from the LCL edition.

more periphrastic than translational.[3] Nevertheless, Josephus, like the author of the Temple Scroll, is prepared to insist that he has offered a full and precise rendering of the biblical text: "This narrative will, therefore, in due course, set forth the precise details of what is in the Scriptures according to its proper order (κατὰ τὴν οἰκείαν τάξιν). For I promised that I would do this throughout the treatise, neither adding nor omitting anything (οὐδὲν προσθεὶς οὐδ' αὖ παραλιπών)" (*Ant.* 1.17; cf. also, e.g., 4.196–97; 10.218; *C. Ap.* 1.42). In fact, Josephus makes numerous omissions (notable among which are the episode of the golden calf in Exod 32 and any indication of the sin of Moses), substantially rearranges his material, and makes a range of additions from the odd detail to entire narratives.[4] Of Josephus's promises not to omit or add to the material, Per Bilde has rightly commented that "readers of *Ant.* are astonished by these statements" (1988: 92). Such statements, however, form something of a *topos* in ancient literature;[5] while the precise connotations are debated, the phrase most likely indicates Josephus's intention to assure his readers of the substantial reliability of his account (so van Unnik 1949: 138). What is more, and again comparable to the Temple Scroll, the phrase indicates compliance with Deuteronomy's injunction not to add to or detract from the divine command (4:2; 13:1 [12:32 EVV]), though perhaps somewhat creatively conceived. Crucial to note here is that Josephus explicitly presents his work as a rendering of the biblical account.

The precise nature of the biblical text that Josephus seeks to render, however, has been a matter of some debate. In the prologue to *Ant.*, he says that the content of his work has been "translated from the Hebrew accounts (ἐκ τῶν Ἑβραϊκῶν μεθηρμηνευμένην γραμμάτων)" (*Ant.* 1.5). Indeed, almost all scholars recognize that a Hebrew *Vorlage* most likely functioned as one of Josephus's chief sources, but greater uncertainty has attached to the question of whether he was served in subsidiary capacity by Greek and Aramaic versions.[6] The satisfactory resolution of such problems

---

[3] "Josephus means by μεθερμηνεύειν (and the various synonymns for it which he uses on occasion), not a word-for-word translation such as we find in Aquila's work, but an exegetical translation, including an interpretation, which proceeds from the resolution of linguistic idioms to the clarification of local peculiarities" (Pelletier 1989: 103).

[4] See esp. Feldman 2000: 7 n. 22 for a list of these; note also Bilde 1988: 92–98; Feldman 1998: 37–46.

[5] E.g., 11Q19 54.5–7; *Arist.* 310–11; Philo, *Spec.* 4.143–44; *Didache* 4.13, etc. Note the broad survey of Jewish, Christian and pagan usage, before the discovery of the Dead Sea Scrolls, in van Unnik 1949 (on which, however, see Goldenberg 1980: 180 n. 4); Inowlocki 2005; for Rabbinic literature, see Basser 1987: 24 n. 23 and 25 n. 24; cf. also Feldman 2000: 7 n. 22.

[6] Feldman 1998: 23–36 (cf. Feldman 1988: 455–66) marshals evidence for Josephus's dependence on a Hebrew text, Greek text, and possibly Aramaic Targum (though the last

is complicated by Josephus's thoroughly periphrastic method of rewriting his sources and our partial knowledge of the diverse traditions of the biblical text in the late first century CE. That Josephus knows of the Septuagint is clear from his re-telling of the Aristeas legend (see *Ant.* 12.11–118; cf. *Ant.* 1.10–11; *C. Ap.* 2.45–47),[7] and it is possible that he made occasional supplementary use of it.[8] An instructive caution is rendered by consideration of the text of Samuel that Josephus had before him; while it was once customary to assign his *Vorlage* to the Septuagint without reservation, the Qumran discoveries have demonstrated that the Septuagint's Hebrew *Vorlage* may be responsible for differences from the (later) standard MT. While there may be some variation in how closely Josephus follows his biblical text, with more freedom in the Pentateuch than in the historical books (perhaps because he knows the Pentateuch more thoroughly? so Cohen 1963–1964), it is clear that his retelling of Deuteronomy is at least lexically independent of the LXX translation (so esp. Harl 1995).

Indeed, as noted in § 2.3, Josephus also supplies us with some information about his method of encountering the biblical text. He links his knowledge of the Scriptures with both his education in Jerusalem (*Vita* 8–9)[9] and his priestly descent (*C. Ap.* 1.54; cf. *Bell.* 3.352; *Ant.* 20.262–63; Bilde 1988: 61). When Josephus presses the connection between the ideals of Jewish education and the knowledge and practice of Torah (e.g., *Ant.* 4.209–13; *C. Ap.* 1.60; 2.175–78), we may be justified in reading such

---

of these is especially difficult). He also notes, however, that "In any case, that Josephus was not following the Septuagint (or at least our Septuagint) blindly is clear from the fact that he definitely disagrees with the Septuagint's version of Deut. 22:1, which rules a domesticated animal found wandering on the road to be a lost object, whereas Josephus and the Mishnah assert that it is not (*Ant.* 4.274; *Baba Mezia* 2:9)" (Feldman 1998: 31). Nodet 1996 concludes that Josephus used a Hebrew text "qui vient probablement des archives du Temple de Jérusalem [cf. *Vita* 418], a de fortes parentés avec la source de la Septante ... bien plus qu'avec le texte hébreu traditionnel... Cependant, bien que Josèphe connaisse l'existence de [la LXX], au moins par la *Lettre d'Aristée* qu'il cite, il ne l'a jamais réellement vue" (6); cf. esp. 29–33; Nodet 1995: xi–xiii. In a review of Nodet 1996, however, N. Fernández Marcos writes in disagreement, "Josephus as well as the translators of the Old Latin had at their disposal a Septuagint already revised and much more plural than the Septuagint transmitted by the known manuscripts" (1998: 112). But he then concedes: "Probably he is right but, since we are dealing with nuances, I would like to emphasize again the difficulty of drawing textual conclusions from Josephus' narrative due mainly to Josephus' habit of paraphrasing and to the scarce knowledge we have of the prehexaplaric Septuagint" (1998: 112).

[7] On which see esp. Pelletier 1962b: 251–76; Pelletier 1989; Wasserstein and Wasserstein 2006: 45–50.

[8] So Pelletier 1989: in Books 1–5 "he seems to have taken as his primary source the Hebrew, occasionally utilizing the Septuagint and certain Jewish traditions found in rabbinical literature, to which he added some rhetorical amplifications of his own" (99).

[9] See Mason 2001 *ad loc*; Rajak 2002: 27.

statements as at least implicitly autobiographical. His knowledge of Deuteronomy, then, is not a strictly theoretical one, but finds its roots in an education in the context of praxis and liturgy. What is more, that Josephus received from Titus scrolls taken from the fallen Temple (*Vita* 418) probably implies that the windfall to Josephus's personal library supplied him with the opportunity to further deepen his acquaintance with, among others, the scroll of Deuteronomy.

Josephus's treatment of Deuteronomy in the *Ant.* is concentrated in 4.176–331, though he occasionally references Deuteronomy beyond those parameters. Here we shall consider his engagement with the last book of the Pentateuch[10] under three aspects: as the constitution of Israel, as law, and as a biographical chronicle of the last deeds and words of Moses.

7.2.1. The πολιτεία of Israel

In his introduction to the *Ant.*, Louis Feldman suggests that its most basic themes are the antiquity of the Jewish people and their institutions, the superiority of both their constitution and their philosophy, and the moralizing tone of the story (2000: xxii–xxxiv). Clearly these are intertwined, but Josephus reads Deuteronomy especially in the service of the first two of these themes, as the constitution of Israel notable for its justice and antiquity. To make such a claim in the late first century involves one in political counter-claims. After the "year of the four emperors" and Domitian's anti-republicanism, the issue of political constitution was a live one: "Whether they dared to speak of it openly or not, every educated person in Rome must have been thinking about issues of political constitution" (Feldman 2000: xxvi; cf. xxxiv). In fact, Josephus characterizes the interest his work will have for "all the Greeks" by drawing attention to its focus on "our entire ancient history and constitution of the state" (*Ant.* 1.5). And at the end of his *Contra Apionem*, he says retrospectively, "I have given an exact account of our laws and constitution in my previous work on our *Antiquities*" (2.287).[11]

While a constitutional interest runs throughout Josephus's work, he arguably especially reads the self-referential Torah/*nomos* and covenant language of Deuteronomy (e.g., Deut 1:5; 4:8, 44; 29:20, 21, 27; 30:10, etc.)

---

[10] It is perhaps worth noting parenthetically that Josephus recognizes five distinct scrolls of Moses (*C. Ap.* 1.39).

[11] Indeed, πολιτεία occurs only three times in *Bell.*; twice in *Vita*. It occurs most often in *Ant.* (61 occurrences [with another occurrence at 19.284 in MS E]) and *C. Ap.* (17 occurrences): in this context, note esp. *Ant.* 4.184, 191, 193, 194, 195, 196, 198, 223, 230, 292, 302, 310, 312; πολίτευμα also occurs four times in *Ant.* and six times in *C. Ap.*

in terms of constitutional polity.[12] For example, near the beginning of his paraphrase of Deuteronomy, Josephus claims to present "the arrangement of our laws that are relevant to the constitution" (4.198). Again, in the retrospective statement Josephus makes near the end of his re-telling of Deuteronomy, he writes: "Such, therefore, is the constitution that Moses left behind. Moreover, he transmitted laws that had been written in the fortieth year earlier, about which we shall speak in another work" (*Ant.* 4.302).[13] This statement appears to be a paraphrase of Deuteronomy's own self-referential statement in 28:69 [EVV 29:1]: "These are the words of the covenant that the LORD commanded Moses to make with the people of Israel in the land of Moab, besides the covenant that he had made with them at Horeb" (so also Nodet 1995: 104* n. 8). Deuteronomy provides an authoritative indication of the type of polity God himself intends.[14]

Indeed, to see Deuteronomy as a foundational political document responds to some of Deuteronomy's own basic impulses, and at least one contemporary Old Testament scholar has claimed that Josephus's interpretation is fundamentally correct (McBride 1987; also Fraade 2006a). To call Deuteronomy the constitution of Israel involves one in a holistic construal of the book, an imaginative judgment about the shape and chief concerns of the work as a totality that still leaves room for its subsidiary parts to function in relation to the complex whole. The political construal of the book also allows Josephus to emphasize the hortatory tone of Deuteronomy in a way relatively consonant with the sensibilities of his Greco-

---

[12] Compare *Ant.* 4.194: "Having said this, he gave them in a book the laws and the arrangement of the constitution that had been recorded." Might this singular reference to a book be especially concerned with Deuteronomy (cf. Deut 31:9, etc.)?

[13] The "other work" is probably the treatise that Josephus mentions several times, "On Customs and Causes," either lost or never completed. For further references to this work, note *Ant.* 1.25; 3.94; 4.198, etc. (see the full list of references in Feldman 2000: 10 n. 34). Altshuler 1979 argued that the work was incorporated into a revised version of *Ant.*, though his theory cannot be proven.

[14] This society is essentially a priestly aristocracy, according to Josephus, although in *C. Ap.*, he also coins the term "theocracy": "[S]ome have entrusted the power of government to monarchies, others to the rule of the few, others again to the masses. But our legislator took no notice of any of these, but instituted the government as what one might call – to force an expression –a 'theocracy' (θεοκρατίαν), ascribing to God the rule and power" (2.164–65). In *C. Ap.* 2.145–286, Josephus offers a brief discussion "about the whole structure of our constitution and about its individual parts (καὶ περὶ τῆς ὅλης ἡμῶν καταστάσεως τοῦ πολιτεύματος καὶ περὶ τῶν κατὰ μέρος)" (2.145). *Contra Apionem*, however, rather than being a biblical paraphrase like the *Antiquities*, has been called "probably the earliest Jewish theological synthesis" (Vermes 1982: 301), and likely shares a genealogical relationship with Philo's *Hypothetica* (so Kamlah 1974: Vermes 1982: 301–02 n. 50; Feldman 1998: 52–53 and n. 63). Whether one should see, with Amir 1994, in the progression from the "aristocracy" of *Ant.* to the "theocracy" of *C. Ap.* a conceptual rather than simply terminological development, is questionable.

Roman contemporaries.[15] The direct, first-person speech of Moses, retained from the biblical precursor, occupies *Ant.* 4.177–93. As Feldman
notes, it "departs widely from that in Deuteronomy" (2001: 393 n. 530),
but captures something of the original tone, especially in its loose paraphrase of the Deuteronomic framework. For example, in a passage especially recalling Deut 8:11–20, but with reminiscences also of Deut 4:26–28
and 28:64, Josephus has Moses exhort the Israelites, "For if you are led
forth by [wealth] into contempt and belittling of virtue, you will lose also
the good will of God. Having made Him your enemy, and having been
conquered in arms, you will be deprived of the land that you will acquire,
with the greatest censures, by those yet to come. Scattered throughout the
inhabited world, you will fill both every land and sea with your slavery"
(*Ant.* 4.190). Here the language of "virtue" (ἀρετή) comes to re-describe,
in more publicly accessible terms, the obedience which Deuteronomy
commends. Similar accommodations are made throughout Josephus's retelling of the individual statutes of Israel's constitution.

7.2.2. The Laws

Another basic construal of Deuteronomy for Josephus, and clearly related
to the first, is as binding legal authority. Like both Philo and the author of
the Temple Scroll, Josephus rearranges Deuteronomy's laws.[16] Josephus
appears to be somewhat embarrassed by the apparent lack of order in the
biblical laws and, near the beginning of his paraphrase of Deuteronomy, he
forthrightly informs his audience of his intention to reorder them: "The
arrangement of each topic according to its class (τὸ κατὰ γένος ἕκαστα
τάξαι) has been innovated by us. For the writings were left by him in scattered condition (σποράδην), just as he ascertained each item from God. I
considered it necessary to mention this beforehand, so that some blame
may not be assigned to us for having erred by my fellow countrymen who
encounter this text" (*Ant.* 4.197).[17] While Josephus's own principle of ar-

---

[15] So Feldman (1998: 66), following Brooke 1994, speaks of "exhortatory historical
exegesis, the chief hallmark of which is the recollection of the past either in order to encourage or admonish readers to emulate their forebears or to dissuade them from copying
them."

[16] Feldman (1998: 68), following Yadin, suggests there may be parallels between the
Temple Scroll's classification of laws and Josephus's, though Altshuler (1982) rightly
cautions that such parallels pale in comparison to the more striking differences between
the two approaches to classifying the laws. He writes, "Whereas TS seeks to emphasize
the particularity of Israel, a cult and nation set apart from the abominations of foreigners,
AJ tones down biblical themes of exclusivity and heightens instead laws that are universalistic and ethical in nature" (1982: 11).

[17] On Josephus's reordering of the laws, see esp. Altshuler 1982; Bilde 1988: 81;
Nodet 1995: 48 n. 5. His statement that Moses left the writings in a scattered condition

rangement is not always entirely clear, the following clusters of laws may be roughly discerned: the holy city, temple, law (Deut 6, 7, 11, 12, 14, 16, 21–23, 31; *Ant.* 4.199–213); judicial and administrative laws (Deut 16, 17, 19, 21; *Ant.* 4.214–24); laws of agriculture (Deut 14, 19, 22–27; *Ant.* 4.225–43); family and marriage laws (Deut 21, 22, 24, 25; *Ant.* 4.244–65); laws of restitution and other communal laws (Deut 15, 22–24; 27; *Ant.* 4.266–91); laws of wartime (Deut 20, 22, 24; *Ant.* 4.292–301); and the last words and death of Moses (Deut 13, 23, 24, 27–29, 31–34; *Ant.* 4.302–31).[18] While Deuteronomy's influence may be occasionally observed before Josephus's focused paraphrase in Book 4,[19] it is striking to note a change in tone once Josephus re-tells the individual commandments of Deuteronomy. David Altshuler's observation can hardly be improved upon:

Without exception, Josephus narrates the laws of Exodus 25–40, Leviticus and Numbers in indicative verbs, but he phrases the laws of Exodus 20–23 and Deuteronomy in imperatives. While neither collection is in strictly biblical form, the laws in Book 3 read like customs the Jews once practiced or now happen to observe (cf. Lev. 1:1, 4:1!), but those in Book 4 sound very much like the commands of God through Moses as described in Deuteronomy (1982: 4).

This may be related to Josephus's intention to present Deuteronomy as the constitution of Israel, and possibly also reflects a preference for Deuteronomy's formulations of specific ethical demands.

In his account, Josephus retells the commands with a certain actualizing tendency. For example, Josephus appears to have rewritten Deuteronomy in several places to exclude a Samaritan interpretation of the proper place of worship.[20] Elsewhere he rewrites commands to reflect more Hellenized

---

jars with his earlier assertion that "Moses ascertained carefully from God the arrangement of the laws (τὴν διάταξιν τῶν νόμων), when he encamped the army beneath Mount Sinai, and he transmitted it in written form to the Hebrews" (*Ant.* 3.286).

[18] This largely follows Altshuler 1982: 3–4, with some slight modifications. There is only partial overlap with this order of laws and that found in *C. Ap.* 2.190–219. Thus, that list begins with the oneness of God and the first commandment, linked to the single temple: "One temple of the one God – for like is always attracted to like – common to all people as belonging to the common God of all" (*C. Ap.* 2.193); then goes on to include marriage laws (2.199–203), education of children (2.204), burial practices (2.205), honoring one's parents and other community laws (2.206–208), and laws about aliens and kindness to others (2.209–14).

[19] For example, there are, unsurprisingly, several small harmonizations in the retelling of the promulgation of the ten commandments (e.g., "observe" the seventh day rather than "keep" it; cf. Feldman 2000: 253 n. 195), an event which Josephus places within the framework of Exodus rather than Deuteronomy (*Ant.* 3.90–92). Note also, e.g., *Ant.* 4.86, etc.

[20] Note that his rewriting of Deut 12 and 16 specifically mentions a "city" and so precludes Gerizim (*Ant.* 4.200, 203) and that Moses commands the altar to be set up *between*

sentiments. For example, in expanding Deut 20:10, "When you approach a town to attack it, you shall offer it terms of peace," Josephus reformulates it in Roman garb ("send an embassy and heralds": *Ant.* 4.296; cf. Feldman 1998: 415).[21] Some of his modifications, on the other hand, appear to reflect contemporary halakhic judgment (see Goldenberg 1976–1977), though the extent to which Josephus reflects the halakhah of his day is disputed. It is clear, however, that Josephus is not unrestrained in his actualization,[22] nor is he, like Philo, concerned with offering allegorical interpretations of the laws. Josephus does grant that there are allegorical aspects of the Torah,[23] but he limits these to the symbolism of the tabernacle (*Ant.* 3.123, 146, 180–87) and Temple (*Bell.* 5.212–18). At times Josephus supplies explanatory reasons for commands that are stated apodictically in the original, as in his restatement of Deut 25:4: "Do not muzzle the mouths of oxen when they thresh the ears of corn on the threshing-floor, for it is not right to bar from the fruit those who have joined in the work and who have exerted themselves with regard to its production" (*Ant.* 4.233; cf. *C. Ap.* 2.213). If his paraphrase is more generalizing than the original precept, it stops short of Paul's primary application of the text to apostles (see § 6.3.3). Also noticeable is a certain tendency to supply harsher punishments for transgression, perhaps in an effort to convince his audience of the moral superiority of the Jewish law.[24]

---

the two mountains (*Ant.* 4.305–08), not on Gerizim as in the biblical account (and in its sequel in *Ant.* 5.68–70). See esp. Thornton 1996; Feldman 1998: 38.

[21] In *C. Ap.*, however, Josephus is explicitly concerned with the refutation of pagan charges against Jews. There he quotes Lysimachus as describing Moses instructing the Israelites "to show goodwill to no-one, nor to give the best but the worst advice, and to reduce to ruins whatever sanctuaries or altars of the Gods they encountered" (1.309). Josephus presents his refutation of the charge as Mosaic in origin (i.e., he makes an addition to the biblical account): "He prescribed other measures, of which a sample is necessary: to give fire, water, and food to all who request them; to point the way; not to ignore an unburied corpse [cf. Tobit]; and that the decisions made even towards enemies should be kind" (*C. Ap.* 2.211; cf. also *Ant.* 4.276, contra also Juvenal, *Sat.* 14.103–4: *non monstrare vias eadem nisi sacra colenti, quaesitum ad fontem solos deducere verpos*; note Stern 1980: no. 301).

[22] For example, Sarah Pearce has argued that the high court of *Ant.* 4.218 does not refer to the Sanhedrin, as one might expect if a thorough actualizing tendency were at work; see Pearce 1995a; 1995b: 273–99.

[23] "Some things the lawgiver cleverly denotes symbolically; other things he formulates allegorically with solemnity; but whatever things it was advantageous to set forth with simplicity these things he revealed with utter plainness" (*Ant.* 1.24). Feldman (1998: 53) points to some parallels with Philo's allegorical interpretation.

[24] For example, in a summary statement, he says: "Thus let those who in any way whatever have been condemned by the laws be put to death" (*Ant.* 4.265). This tendency to increase the punishment of transgression to the death penalty is especially pronounced

7.2.3. Last Acts and Words of Moses

Another primary function of Deuteronomy is to offer a biographical rendering of the character of the lawgiver, Moses himself, thus guaranteeing the supremacy of the constitution and its laws. In a statement that sheds light on the method of *Ant.*, Josephus says, against the self-promotion of Apion, that "As for our own men, who were worthy of no less praise, they are familiar to those who read our *Antiquities*" (*C. Ap.* 2.136). This throws into relief the way in which the Pentateuch is viewed as the story of its individual characters, chief among whom is Moses, the famous man, with the giving of the law as one of his most noble deeds (one might compare the "praises of famous men" in Sir 44). It is perhaps unsurprising to note that his description of Moses has been Hellenized in several ways (see esp. Feldman 1998: 374–442). In short, as Feldman writes,

Because the *Antiquities* is an apologetic work directed primarily to non-Jews,[25] Josephus portrays Moses as embodying the qualities of the great heroes of the Greeks and Romans, notably the external qualities of good birth and handsome stature, precociousness in his youth, and the four cardinal virtues of wisdom, courage, temperance, and justice, supplemented by what was, in effect, a fifth cardinal virtue, piety (1998: 441).

Of course, much of this biographical rendering has been supplied by Exodus, Leviticus and Numbers, but Deuteronomy plays the key role of recounting Moses's last actions, words and final end.

We may detect four primary loci of interest in the final acts of Moses, corresponding roughly to Deut 27–30, 31–32, 33, and 34 respectively. Josephus's account of Deut 27–30 focuses chiefly on the covenant ratification ceremony, with only cursory description of the blessings and curses: "On the following days, for he held an assembly continuously, he gave them blessings, together with curses for those who would not live in accordance with the laws but would transgress what had been enacted in them" (*Ant.* 4.302). He then goes on to describe the covenant ceremony that the Israelites should enact when they have entered the land (*Ant.* 4.305–08; cf. also *Ant.* 5.70), though again without detailed description of the curses (cf. Feldman 2000: 395 n. 557). Josephus then juxtaposes the covenant renewal of Deut 29 as happening on the next day, when Moses "made them swear to keep the laws and, showing themselves accurate estimators of the intention of God, not at all to transgress them – either

---

in *C. Ap.* 2.207, 215–17. It is perhaps notable that Philo prescribes the death penalty where the biblical text does not (e.g., *Spec.* 2.252, 255), as does Tob 6:13.

[25] This statement needs to be tempered with the awareness that apologetic literature always has a confirmatory function for "insiders," and Jews anxious about the status of their nation in the face of Roman counter-claims might have been among the most enthusiastic members of *Ant.*'s first audiences.

showing favor to relatives or yielding to fear or [believing] that any other reason would be more cogent than the keeping of the laws" (*Ant.* 4.309; cf. Deut 29:10–21). Here we then find some indication of the biblical curses, though these are significantly transformed into predictions:[26] Moses "predicted, as the Divinity revealed to him, that if they transgressed the worship of Him, they would experience sufferings: their land would be filled with the weapons of their enemies; their cities would be razed to the ground; their Temple would be burnt down; they would be sold into slavery to men who would show no pity for their misfortunes; and, suffering these things, they would repent to no avail" (4.312–13). Especially notable is the addition of the destruction of the Temple and the note of finality, i.e., that repentance becomes ineffective (contrast Deut 30:1–10). One other major difference, perhaps understandable from Josephus's viewpoint after the war of 66–70 CE, is that Josephus casts this prediction as cyclical in nature: "Although the God who created you will give back to your citizens both your cities and your Temple, the loss of these will occur not once but often" (*Ant.* 4.314). What is more, Josephus omits the hope of return to the land (cf. Deut 30:1–10), an illustration of his ambiguous stance toward the Diaspora, which occurs in Josephus as both punishment (e.g., *Ant.* 4.189–91, 312–14) and as blessing (*Ant.* 4.115–16; *C. Ap.* 2.282; *Bell.* 2.399).[27]

Josephus also retells the giving of the Song of Moses, apparently on the same day as the delivery of blessings and curses (and so between Deut 27–28 and Deut 29–30):[28] "Then he read to them a poem in hexameters, which he has left behind in a book in the Temple, containing a prediction of what will be, in accordance with which everything has happened and is happening, since he has not at all deviated from the truth" (*Ant.* 4.303).[29] Several aspects of this compact description are striking. First, Josephus adds the Hellenistic touch that the poem is in hexameters, the same meter as the Homeric epics (see Feldman 1998: 401), an addition he also makes in recounting the Song of the Sea (i.e., Exod 15; *Ant.* 2.346). What is more, there appears to be a certain "individualization" of the Song, that is, a

---

[26] Amaru (1980–1981) notes that Josephus systematically omits reference to the land covenant and transforms promises of inheriting the land into predictive statements.

[27] See esp. Amaru 1980–1981: 223–26. She also suggests that Josephus "deleted the theology of covenanted land because he did not want the land to be a focal point, as it was for Davidic messianism, with all its revolutionary implications in Josephus' day" (229).

[28] This relocation may suggest that these chapters were closely associated for Josephus (contra Waters 2006: 64–66).

[29] Contra Feldman 2000: n. 1043 *ad loc*, this almost certainly refers to Deut 32, not Deut 33.

sense that it exists on its own "in a book in the Temple."[30] In part this may respond to the Deuteronomic frame of the Song (esp. 31:9, 24–26), but may also indicate an awareness of its liturgical importance.[31] The fact that the recounting of the Song appears here in Josephus's narrative, however, should caution against pressing this individualization too strongly. In terms of the content of the Song, Josephus refrains from any attempt to re-present the poetry,[32] but summarizes its essence as a prediction of remarkable accuracy. Whether this prediction includes any sort of transcendent eschatological perspective or simply functions in terms of immanent human history, it is clear that Josephus considers the events of his own day to be encompassed in its range.[33] Here it is worth mentioning that Josephus's view of the Blessing of Moses (Deut 33), though only briefly expressed, evinces the same predictive perspective: "After Moses had said these things at the end of his life, and with a blessing had prophesied to each of the tribes the things that in fact were to be..." (*Ant.* 4.320). This predictive function for the Blessing of Moses is shared with Qumran and Philo.

One other aspect of Josephus's stance toward the Song of Moses is worth recounting. In *C. Ap.*, in stressing the importance of law observance for Jews, Josephus writes, "each individual, having the internal witness of the conscience, has come to believe – as the legislator prophesied (νομοθέτου προφητεύσαντος) and as God provided firm assurance – that to those who keep the laws and, should it be necessary to die for them, meet death eagerly, God has granted renewed existence and receipt of a better life at the turn [of the ages]" (2.218). Especially the Maccabean literature, with which Josephus was familiar (e.g., in his *Bellum*), turns to Deut 32 (esp. 32:36, 39) to express the hope of resurrection for martyrdom (§ 4.3). In light of Josephus's emphasis on the predictive element of the Song in *Ant.*, it does not stretch the imagination to think of Deut 32 as the antecedent of the "lawgiver's prophecy" here, especially as this is immediately followed by the admission that "I would have hesitated to write this now, were it not evident to all from the facts that, to date, many of our people on many occasions have nobly undertaken to suffer anything rather than utter even a single word in contravention of the law" (*C. Ap.* 2.219), a rather clear allusion to the Maccabean martyrs.

---

[30] Cf. *Ant.* 3.38: "A writing lying in the temple reveals that God foretold to Moses that water would thus issue forth from the rock."

[31] So esp. Nodet 1995: 105 n. 3.

[32] A consistent technique for Josephus (see Basser 1987).

[33] The Song of Moses is also seen as predictive in Philo (see § 5.3 above); in Paul (see § 6.5.4 above); for the Song as predictive in rabbinic literature, see § 8.2–8.3 below; cf. Feldman 1998: 423 n. 87. Josephus also shares with Philo the view that the Song has a strong element of thanksgiving (*Ant.* 4.318).

Finally, Josephus's biographical interest in Deuteronomy concludes with the end of its protagonist: "While he was bidding farewell to Eleazaros and Iesous, and was still conversing with them, a cloud suddenly stood over him and he disappeared in a certain ravine. But he has written of himself in the sacred books that he died because he was afraid that they might dare to say that because of the abundance of the virtue surrounding him he had gone up to the Divinity" (*Ant.* 4.326). That Josephus intended by this description to foreclose on certain lines of interpretation of Moses's disappearance has not precluded a variety of interpretations from arising. Is Josephus claiming that Moses really died in opposition to the Samaritan deification of Moses (so Feldman 1998: 375–76; 397 n. 47) or other groups who thought of Moses as apotheosized (so Haacker and Schäfer 1974: 147–51; Tabor 1989; Nodet 1995: 112–13 nn. 5–7; Feldman 2002: 250–53)? Or is he claiming that Moses really was taken up alive, although he wrote of himself that he died in order to forestall inordinate preoccupation with his ascension (so Rappaport 1930: 39; Begg 1990)? Either way, Josephus intends to emphasize the piety and virtue of Moses, and the idea that Moses dies outside of the promised land for his own sin is not to be countenanced. Rather, because of his great stature as lawgiver, Moses "shall be remembered as long as the universe shall endure not only among Hebrew men but also among foreigners" (*Ant.* 2.216).

7.3. A Deuteronomic View of History

Finally, we may note a further aspect of Deuteronomy's influence on Josephus, perhaps less tangible than the previous examples but no less powerful. One of Josephus's chief differences from contemporary Greco-Roman historians is the theological perspective he adopts, closer to the biblical authors than to, say, Herodotus (so, rightly, Rajak 2002: 9). To be more precise, his perspective has a Deuteronomic angle to it, i.e., he operates from the stance that God is faithful to reward obedience and to punish transgression. For example, in his statement of the theme of *Ant.*, Josephus writes as follows:

On the whole, one who would wish to read through it would especially learn from this history that those who comply with the will of God and do not venture to transgress laws that have been well enacted succeed in all things beyond belief and that happiness lies before them as a reward from God. But to the extent that they dissociate themselves from the scrupulous observance of these laws the practicable things become impracticable, and whatever seemingly good thing they pursue with zeal turns into irremediable misfortunes (*Ant.* 1.14; cf. also 1.20, 23, 72; 6.307; 7.93; 17.60; 19.16).

Clearly this theme is found beyond the scroll of Deuteronomy itself, chiefly in the so-called Deuteronomistic history, but the importance of Deuteronomy as a fountainhead of this view should not be overlooked. In a certain sense, Deuteronomy thus supplies the optic through which both Scripture and history are to be interpreted; alternatively, the implementation of Deuteronomy's interpretation of history in the biblical story provides a model for those, like Josephus, seeking to interpret Israel's more recent history. Indeed, as Harold Attridge has argued, "The most explicit statement explaining the notion of divine providence in terms of God's rewarding virtue and punishing vice occurs in the last speech of Moses which introduces the final summary of the laws (IV. 176–95)" (1976: 90; cf. 71–107), a section which is, of course, a sustained paraphrase of Deuteronomy. This perspective animates not just Josephus's evaluation of individual lives, but the national fate of Israel in its war against the Romans: "Most profoundly, Josephus sees the War from a theological i.e. 'prophetic' or 'Deuteronomic' point of view, because he interprets the arrival of the Romans, the fall of Jerusalem, the burning of the Temple and all of the disasters of the War suffered by the Jewish people as God's punishment for the sins of the people (*Bell.* 2.455; 5.19)" (Bilde 1988: 75; cf. 55, 184–85; note also *Bell.* 5.391–93, 95). The theme that God rewards the righteous and punishes the wicked is so widespread in Josephus that to document it exhaustively would be both tedious and unnecessary.[34] What is crucial here to note is that Josephus has internalized and adopted a Deuteronomic perspective on history, exhibiting a depth of influence that goes beyond the simple quotation of a string of words. The lack of sustained focus on blessings and curses in his explicit paraphrase of Deuteronomy may thus be explained by the fact that he implicitly adopts their action-and-consequence scheme more broadly in his historical method.

7.4. Conclusion: Deuteronomy in the Works of Josephus

To return to our set of guiding questions, then, how might we characterize the shape of Josephus's reading of Deuteronomy? His method is thoroughly paraphrastic, perhaps in part because of the translation he professes to make from the Hebrew writings. He is concerned with accuracy, though this concern does not eventuate in a slavish literalism that keeps him from incorporating his own additions of perspective into his re-telling of the biblical account. The specific interest which he devotes to Deuteronomy is

---

[34] See esp. Attridge 1976; Altshuler 1982:6; Basser 1987: 25; Feldman 2000: xxviii–xxxii; and in addition to the passages from *Bell.* and *Ant.* cited above, *Vita* 83; *C. Ap.* 2.143–44, etc.

relatively evenly distributed across its major sections: he treats, in turn, the opening exhortation of Moses, the individual statutes that make up its legal code, the covenant renewal ceremony together with a brief indication of blessings and curses, the Song and Blessing of Moses, and the death (or at least ascension) of Moses. Not all of the legal material, however, has been of equal interest to Josephus. He himself notes that he will focus on the constitution, and a downplaying of the cult is discernible in his presentation. Further, his slight focus on blessings and curses may be partially explicable by reference to the theological perspective from which he narrates his history.

In his re-presentation of Deuteronomy's legal material, Josephus makes numerous actualizing changes to reflect his understanding of the commandments, discredit competing interpretations, and appeal to his Greco-Roman audience, although his updating is not unrestrained. His interest in Deuteronomy's final chapters is intriguing: he reads especially the Song and Blessing of Moses as predictive, even dictating the outcome of events in his own day, but he also reads the Song as cyclical instead of linear in nature. Josephus appears to read Deuteronomy 32 as the historiographical statement of someone in his own image, a historian in advance of the event, disclosing the fundamental dynamics of the movement of Israel's history. This type of reading, while future-oriented in one sense, probably falls short of witnessing to a full-fledged transcendently eschatological perspective.

Finally, if we ask about the context of Josephus's encounter with Deuteronomy, we are led directly to the liturgical and educational milieu of the first century. It should be recalled that much of our knowledge of Torah instruction within the context of synagogue and school is drawn from Josephus (cf. *Bell.* 3.352; *Ant.* 20.262–63; *Vita* 8–9 [and see Mason 2001 *ad loc*]; *C. Ap.* 1.60; 2.175, 178; Bilde 1988: 61; Rajak 2002: 27). Perhaps most poignantly for Deuteronomy, we encounter in quick succession the reading of the law, the teaching of the law to children, the recitation of the *Shema'* twice a day, and the practice of the *mezuzah* and *tefillin* (*Ant.* 4.209–13). Clearly this responds to sections of Deut 5–11, but also provides a significant indication of the pressure and trajectory of the text. Josephus's re-telling of Deuteronomy is thus not simply a promulgation but also a result of a thorough grounding in Deuteronomy, sprung from the life-animating wells of praxis.

In chronological terms, Josephus' life straddles the end of the Second Temple period and the beginning of the post-destruction era. In the next chapter, we turn to examine some trajectories of Jewish interpretation that are firmly rooted in the post-Second Temple era and so provide useful soundings of continuities and ruptures in the Jewish encounter with Deuteronomy.

Chapter 8

Later Trajectories of Interpretation: *Sifre* and Targums

8.1. Introduction

Although our concern is chiefly with the shape, presence and force of Deuteronomy in the Second Temple period, to examine briefly the interpretative developments in some post-Second Temple Jewish works serves to highlight both continuities and ruptures in traditional understandings of Deuteronomy. Naturally, the diverse and diffuse traditions of post-Second Temple interpretation of Deuteronomy defy easy generalization, but here we focus on the two most significant interpretative endeavors of Deuteronomy's Jewish reception in Tannaitic and Amoraic times, namely, the midrashic work *Sifre to Deuteronomy* and the Aramaic Targums. We deliberately bypass other forms of engagement with Deuteronomy in the post-Second Temple period, specifically those stemming from Christian circles[1] and the interpretations implicit in the early versions.[2] The early reception of Deuteronomy in Christian proto-orthodox and demiurgical circles is an intriguing field, but lies beyond our present concern because of the seismic hermeneutical shifts of interpretation in the Christian tradition during and after the first century – and because of the practical need to

---

[1] For Deuteronomy in later pagan (i.e., polemical) authors, see § 2.3.3 n. 61 above; also note the sub-literary reception of Deuteronomy in magical texts and in inscriptions surveyed in Lincicum 2008b and 2008d respectively.

[2] Especially the Syriac Peshitta, the Old Latin, and "the three," i.e., Symmachus, Aquila and Theodotion. While there are undoubtedly examples of interpretative renderings in each of these versions, the Old Latin is probably Christian in origin (so Kedar 1988), while the Peshitta's early history is difficult to discern (Dirksen 1988), though it shares some interpretative traditions with the Targums (Maori 1998). Discerning interpretative elements in the early Greek revisions is problematized by the fact that they are generally Hebraizing in tendency (cf. Fernández Marcos 2000: 109–54). For some attempt, however, to isolate interpretative elements of Deuteronomy in one of these versions, that by Symmachus, note Salvesen 1991: 142–76, 186–87, 191. She suggests that one finds "an avoidance of any expression which would impugn the sovereignty or dignity of the One God of Israel" (e.g., Sym. at Deut 4:12) and a lack of acknowledgement, common also to the Targums, of the reality of other gods (pointing to Sym.'s rendering of Deut 4:19; 29:25; 31:20). Symmachus was probably a Jewish, not an Ebionite Christian, translator (cf. 283–97).

circumscribe the area of this investigation: *ars longa, vita brevis*. Although Jewish readings of Deuteronomy naturally underwent hermeneutical development (as this chapter indicates), such shifts are not as total as those encountered in, e.g., Marcion (cf. Irenaeus, *Adv. Haer.* 1.27.1) or Ptolemy's "Letter to Flora" (in Epiphanius, *Pan.* 33.3.1–7.10), or even in proto-orthodox writers.[3] Among the Apostolic Fathers, *1 Clement* refers Deuteronomy to the Corinthians, perhaps extending Paul's strategy in 1 Cor 10 (*1 Clem.* 3.1; 29.1–3; cf. 53.1–5) and the *Epistle of Barnabas* has a certain Deuteronomic tendency (cf. 9.5; 10.2; 15.1, etc.), but Deuteronomy is somewhat eclipsed by Genesis, Psalms and Isaiah as a major resource in the early Church as a whole. It is hermeneutically telling that the earliest extant Christian commentarial concern with Deuteronomy (i.e., a holistic attempt to render the text explicable in a sequential manner) are the *quaestiones* in the 5th c. by Augustine (CCSL 33: 276–311, 445–53) and Theodoret (PG 80: 401–56). The homilies on Deuteronomy traditionally ascribed to Origen are probably spurious (but cf. PG 12: 805–18; 17: 23–36), though note should also be made of Cyril of Alexandria, *Glaphyrorum in Deuteronomium Liber* (PG 69: 643–78).[4] As Balás and Bingham conclude from their survey of patristic interpretation, "The book of Deuteronomy did not exercise the attention of the early Church Fathers, at least when the references to Deuteronomy were juxtaposed to another book of the Pentateuch such as Genesis. Yet this is not to say that Deuteronomy was entirely neglected...Certain texts from Deuteronomy did find their way into Christological discussions" (2004: 285). No doubt study of these fields would yield interesting perspectives on Deuteronomy, but the complicating factors, whether hermeneutical (in the case of self-consciously Christian readings) or practical (e.g., problems identifying the ideological provenance of early versions and their relatively meager interpretative yield), suggest that such areas are better left for another investigation.

8.2. Mishnaizing Scripture: *Sifre to Deuteronomy*

The *Sifre* is a midrash,[5] probably dating in its final redaction to the mid- to late third century CE (Fraade 1991: 185–86 n. 56; Stemberger 1996: 273),

---

[3] For Deuteronomy in other New Testament authors, see esp. Moyise and Menken 2007.

[4] For some indication of patristic interpretation of Deuteronomy, see Lienhard 2001.

[5] We leave aside the Mishnah itself to concentrate on more extended engagement with Deuteronomy, but for a masterful recent account of the Mishnah's interpretative strategies (or "resources" as he terms them), see Samely 2002. In addition to the *Sifre*, there were perhaps two other Tannaitic midrashim to Deuteronomy, of which only fragmentary

on significant sections of Deuteronomy (esp. Deut 1:1–30; 3:23–4:1; 6:4–9; 11:10–26:15; 31:14–34:11). As such it is the first extant attempt at a commentarial exposition of the book of Deuteronomy. Of course, the genre of "commentary" in antiquity does not entail a mere dispassionate repetition and explication of a text's contents, but involves making sense of the text for the present, actualizing and appropriating its guiding vision. In *Sifre*'s case, this means that the compilers of the work seek in Deuteronomy a guide in matters halakhic and theological. In Jacob Neusner's words, "Out of that book's [i.e., Deuteronomy's] singleton cases and ad hoc rules, the Rabbinic sages seek generalizations and governing principles. These concern Israel's social order. But the same process extends to the laws of history…To state matters simply, this authorship 'mishnaizes' Scripture" (2004: 102). One senses this expansive tendency clearly in the question that runs throughout *Sifre* as an introductory prompt: "How on the basis of Scripture do we know that…?" (...שׁ אומר אתה מנין):[6] Deuteronomy is beckoned to absorb the world. Thus, *Sifre* brings legal reasoning to ask about the precise entailments and extensions of biblical commandments, and seeks to answer the questions with precision (for a good example, note the rulings about the forgotten sheaf from Deut 24:19 in §§ 282–83).[7]

At an exegetical level, *Sifre* engages Deuteronomy in both part and whole (see esp. Fraade 1991; 2005). Its comments often focus on one phrase, sometimes removed from its original context and often susceptible to multiple interpretations and joined with other biblical texts. For example, Deut 32:1 receives no less than thirteen different, at times competing, interpretations (§ 306; see Fraade 1991: 128–49).[8] On the other hand, the composition is bound to the structure of Deuteronomy and moves sequentially through the book (n.b., including both the narrative frame and the legal code). It also makes some rather large-scale interpretative judgments about the overall shape of the book through both the repetition of key themes and through some intriguing reading strategies. Among the former, one is struck by the repeated references to the conditionality inherent in possession of the land and in blessing more broadly (cf. §§ 38, 40, 114, 118, 306, etc.). As *Sifre* succinctly summarizes: "The Torah has said, 'The

---

quotations in later works have survived, on which see Stemberger 1996: 273–75; Kahana 2002. The later *Deuteronomy Rabbah* (450–800 CE?) preserves some similar traditions to *Sifre* (e.g., at *Deut. R.* 1.2), but is much less bound to Deuteronomy itself, perhaps being a collection of homilies (Stemberger 1996: 306–08).

[6] English translations follow Neusner 1987; the Hebrew text is taken from Finkelstein 1939.

[7] Note also the extension of Deut 25:4 (§ 287), in contrast to Paul's quite different extension in 1 Cor 9:9.

[8] Elsewhere Fraade speaks of a high "degree of ungraded heterogeneity of multiple interpretations" in *Sifre* (1991: 123).

blessing and the curse.' 'The blessing:' if you obey, 'the curse:' if you do not obey" (§ 54).[9] Indeed, which commandments are valid inside and which outside the land of Israel is a prominent concern of *Sifre* (e.g., §§ 39, 40, 44, 59; cf. § 43, etc.), reflecting not only contemporary concerns about the dispersion but also geographical disputes about the boundaries of the land of Israel and so the applicability of laws regulating agriculture and tithing (note the discussion in Bockmuehl 2000: 61–70). One might also point to a concern with the complex of sages, learning and suffering (e.g., §§ 14, 32, 34, 35; cf. Basser 1984: 6–10) and a negative stance toward "the nations" (§§ 311, 320, 329, 333, 343; cf. Fraade 1991: 67, 228 n. 229).

In terms of reading strategies, we have already drawn attention to the dynamic of whole and part that characterizes *Sifre*'s sequential journey through Deuteronomy. It is also worth noting, however, that *Sifre* is aware of its own progression, aware of how the parts of Deuteronomy relate to one another. The sequence of the blessing of Deut 33 following the harsh words of Deut 32 is seen to be significant (§ 342) – it is right that words of blessing should follow words of rebuke.[10] *Sifre* (§ 1) also shares with the Targums the "rebuke tradition" of reading Deut 1:1 (on which see § 8.3 below). One might also suggest that, while *Sifre* may be said to unfold within an eschatological horizon that occasionally comes to light (e.g., §§ 8, 34, 41, 47, 130, 310 on the Messiah, etc.), one finds a less intensely eschatological reading of the final chapters of Deuteronomy than in some previous interpreters. The blessing of Moses, for example, is generally read retrospectively, as indicating the course of the biblical story rather than strictly speaking eschatologically (cf., e.g., § 355). And while the midrash on the Song of Moses ends with, "how great is this song! For it contains lessons for the present, for the past, and for the future, for this world and for the world to come" (§ 333), the horizon of eschatological expectation seems to have receded. What is more, biographical details about Moses are less prominent than anecdotal stories about the sages. No doubt such differences reflect the changed ideological landscape of third century Rabbinic circles, but also show that Deuteronomy is susceptible to a range of political and eschatological appropriations. In this way one be-

---

[9] Conversely one can see in *Sifre* an interesting connection between the Deuteronomic warning not to rebel once settled in the land (e.g., Deut 8:11–20) and the Golden Calf incident: "A person rebels against the Omnipresent only in prosperity" (§ 43; cf. § 318), followed soon after with a quotation from Exod 32:6; see § 6.5.4 above for Paul's use of the same citation.

[10] Compare *Pesiq. Rab Kah.* supplement 1.5: "Inasmuch as at the beginning of Deuteronomy, Moses rebukes Israel – *These are the [sharp] words which Moses spoke unto all Israel* (Deut. 1:1) – therefore at the conclusion of the Book, Moses turns around and blesses them – *And this is the blessing*" (trans. from Braude and Kapstein 1975; cf. Clarke 1998: 6 n. 2).

gins to see that the interpretations on offer in the Second Temple period, in the years before *Sifre*, are not somehow historically inevitable, but that the similarities in interpretation do in fact reflect shared traditions.

8.3. Deuteronomy as Rebuke and Prophetic Poetry: Targums

Like the *Sifre*, the Targums to Deuteronomy by their very nature preserve a complete, if not always holistic, rendering of the book. While the phenomenon of targumizing can be traced to the Second Temple period, as evinced by the Targums of Leviticus and Job from Qumran, as well perhaps as the Genesis Apocryphon (cf. Alexander 1988a: 247), the extant Targums to Deuteronomy stem from centuries later. Like much Rabbinic literature, the Targums are difficult to date with any precision because of their slow growth over time, incorporating diverse traditions from various time periods (York 1974; Kaufman 1985, etc.), though the earliest final redactions probably stem from the third century CE. While one sometimes encounters a tendency to treat all targumic activity as purely liturgical in origin, in addition to serving as the Aramaic translation of the Hebrew text in synagogue worship the Targums probably also found their place in school and sometimes private settings (note the influential statement by York 1979; cf. Alexander 1988a: 238). The synagogue, however, is the most characteristic setting for the Targum, and in this light the Targums may have been the chief interpretative mediation of the biblical text to the common people, conveying the meaning and not simply the wording of the text to the assembled hearers (so esp. Flesher 2002).[11]

Perhaps the most restrained of the Targums is that of *Onqelos*. For the most part the additions and modifications to the text are minor: the addition of "Memra," "Shekinah," the Temple, the updating of geographical place names (e.g., in chapter 3), the explicit mention of *tefillin* and *mezuzot* in 6:8–9 and 11:18–20, "idols of the nations" instead of "other gods," and so on   (Grossfield 1988a: 12–14, 19–30). Many of these changes would be consistent with a process of reverential re-delivery of the text so as to heighten and preserve the majesty of God (cf. also at 21:23). Two more substantial changes, however, may indicate some of the characteristic features of Deuteronomy for *Onqelos*, as indeed for the other Targums as well. First, like several other Targums, *Onqelos* construes Deut 1:1 as a

---

[11] The relationships between the various Targums are a matter of some contention; for our purposes, we are more concerned with the traditions they preserve than the question of their sources and inter-relationships, though it is generally clear that *Neofiti* and *Ps-Jonathan* are later and more expansive than the Palestinian Fragment Targums and *Onqelos*.

rebuke. Although it is not as expansive as some other Targums at this point, to take the initial introduction of Deuteronomy as a rebuke of Israel arguably reflects an understanding of the hortatory context of the entire book – or at least the narrative frame (Deut 1–11, 27–34).[12] Second, both Deuteronomy 32 and 33 are subject to an uncharacteristically free and expansive rendering. In fact, however, while such expansion is rare for *Onqelos*, these chapters are expanded in all of the Targums, as in *Sifre*, noted in § 8.2 above.[13] While perhaps the multivalency of the Hebrew poetry in Deut 32 and 33 has contributed to the more interpretative renderings,[14] it may also be that such chapters were the focus of special concern because of their perceived importance as the last words of Moses (note that Moses is called a "prophet" in *Tg. Onq.* Deut 32:1). If *Onqelos* reads Deut 32 as less positive toward Israel than some of its targumic peers,[15] it also includes in its rewriting of Deut 33 the foretelling of defeat for Israel's enemies and the redemption of the land of Israel by divine intervention (esp. *Tg. Onq.* Deut 33:26–29).

Such an expansive tendency in Deut 32 and 33 is also in evidence in the fragmentary Palestinian Targum(s).[16] What is striking about such texts is the prominence of Deut 32–34 in the preserved remains. For much of Deuteronomy the selection criteria for what receives comment remains obscure, but these chapters appear to receive the most sustained attention. As in *Neofiti*, Moses appears at the beginning of Deuteronomy 32 alongside

---

[12] On the "rebuke tradition," note Stegner 1992, although his proposal for the connection to the NT is not entirely convincing.

[13] For connections between *Tg. Onq.* Deut 32 to *Sifre*, note Drazin 1982: 8–10; Grossfield 1988a: 15–18.

[14] So Klein: "But poetic passages always receive fuller targumic treatment than do narratives or legal sections" (1986: 1: xxvi).

[15] So Bernstein 2002: "The Song, for Onqelos, is not primarily a description of Israel's history, but of their backsliding away from God. The focus in Onqelos, as in the Hebrew text, is on God alone, God who punishes Israel and then avenges Himself upon the nations who do not recognize His hand in all this" (37).

[16] This is essentially a group of stemmatically related Targums preserved in various manuscripts, of which *Neofiti 1* appears to be a late rendering. For the text and translation, see Klein 1980; 1986. For Deuteronomy, note the following: MS D preserves Deuteronomy alternating between "stretches of literal translation and passages of expansive midrashic interpretation" (Klein 1986: 1: xxiii). MS F_2 attests Deut 34:5–12 in a "festival-liturgical collection" (cf. Klein 1986: 1: xxiii–xxiv). MS AA contains Deut 26:2–3; 26:8–27:8, possibly a reading for Shavu'ot. MS Br preserves Deut 1:1–5:9 and MS DD contains 61 verses or partial verses from Deut 23–33, with Deut 32 and 33 translated in full. MS P (Paris Bibliothèque nationale Hébr. 110) preserves parts of Deut 1, 3, 6, 7, 8, 11, 12, 14, 16, 17, 19–22, 24–34; MS V (Vatican Ebr. 440) preserves parts of Deut 1–9, 11–34; MS British Museum Or. 10794, folio 8 preserves part of Deut 1–5; with other MSS in Klein's apparatus.

Isaiah as a prophet who testifies against a recalcitrant Israel, and is then referred to as a prophet throughout Deut 32[17] and 33.[18] At at least one of the major manuscripts explicitly historicizes Deut 32 with its rendering of 32:24: "I will incite against them the teeth of the four kingdoms" (MS V; cf. *Frg. Tg.* Gen 15:12 and Klein 1980: 2:185). This simply makes more explicit the fact that Deut 32 is read as a template for Israel's history, a re-told history which, according to these Palestinian Targums, does not de-nude Israel of its righteous entirely, but separates the righteous within Is-rael from the wicked who receive God's punishment (Bernstein 2002: 51).

Tg. Neofiti, which appears to be a late and somewhat eclectic edition of the Palestinian Targum (so, e.g., Kaufman 1985; McNamara 1997),[19] in addition to some of the characteristic targumic changes reflecting a certain "transcendentalization" of God, also preserves both the rebuke tradition of Deut 1:1 and the expansive tendency in Deut 32 and 33. Indeed, Deut 32 is highly expanded in *Neofiti*, with clear links to other midrashic expansions, though, as McNamara points out, "the history of the composition of the Pal. Tg. midrash on Deuteronomy 32 remains to be written" (1997: 146 n. 1). What is more, Israel's history is re-told in a fuller fashion (e.g., Deut 32:11) and the keeping of the law is explicitly inserted into Deut 32 (see vv. 14, 29–30), which accords with a certain tendency to insert the law at other places in Deuteronomy (e.g., 6:5; 13:4–5; 19:9; 30:2, 6, 20).[20] Two other rhetorical features of *Neofiti* may be noted. First, the Targum intro-duces numerous additions of the phrase, "said Moses" to disambiguate the "me" of Deuteronomy's first-person address (e.g., at 2:1, 2, 9, etc.). This change, however, while subtle, has the jarring effect of distancing the im-mediacy of the text's address as Moses's speech, and perhaps reflects a heightened sense of the passing of time between Moses's day and the tar-gumist's. Second, in the blessings of Deut 28, one finds the repeated intro-duction, "My people, children of Israel, blessed shall you be...," though there is no corresponding addition to the curses. This seems to reflect a contemporary liturgical setting and the ongoing force of Deuteronomy's blessings for *Neofiti*'s community.

---

[17] In the Paris MS (P).

[18] נבייא דיר: note MS T-S AS 72.75,76,77, folio 2v l.7 = Klein 1986: 1: 358–59, Klein's MS DD.

[19] See further the valuable list of parallels from Rabbinic literature assembled by Levine 1978.

[20] Note also *Tg. Neof.* Deut 27:8: the law should be "written, engraven and very dis-tinct; and to be read and translated into seventy languages," i.e., presumably to be avail-able for the Gentiles (trans. from McNamara 1997).

Tg. Ps.-Jonathan, whose origins are shrouded in mystery,[21] preserves various haggadic (e.g., *Tg. Ps.-J.* Deut 21:8; 25:18) and halakhic (e.g., *Tg. Ps.-J.* Deut 22:22; 24:6) expansions. It also preserves the "rebuke tradition" of Deut 1:1: "These are the words of reproof that Moses spoke with all of Israel" (אילין פיתגמי אוכחותא די מליל משה עם כל ישראל).[22] The holistic implications of this phrase are further stressed in *Ps.-Jonathan*, as the same phrase introduces the curses at Deut 28:15, where, however, the covenant with the patriarchs also guarantees God's ongoing commitment to Israel. Deuteronomy is understood as a word of rebuke, of exhortation, but also of promise. In addition to expansions at Deut 32–34,[23] there is also a considerable expansion of the Ten Commandments, esp. 5:16–33 (cf. also *Tg. Neof.*). For example, the commandment against murder becomes, "My people, Israelites, do not be murderers, neither companions nor partners with murderers, nor shall there be seen in the congregation of Israel (those who have a part) with murderers; lest your sons who arise after you also learn to be with murderers; for it is because of murderers that the sword emerges upon the world" (*Ps.-J.* Deut 5:17), an expansion which is paralleled in *Ps.-J.* at Exod 20:12–26 (see Clarke 1998 *ad loc*). What is more, *Tg. Ps.-Jonathan* also radicalizes the Deuteronomic principle:

So you shall know that the Lord your God is a judge, strong and faithful, who keeps the covenant and benevolence, to a thousand generations, to his friends, the righteous, and to those who keep his commandments; who pays, in this world, to those who hate him, the reward of their good works in order to destroy them in the world to come and who does not delay (the retribution) of those who hate him but while they are living pays them, in this world, their recompense (*Ps.-J.* Deut 7:9–10; similarly, though less extensively, in *Tg. Onq.* and in *Tg. Neof.*).[24]

This radicalization of the Deuteronomic principle may be connected with *Ps.-Jonathan*'s repeated exhortations to his contemporaries to achieve

---

[21] As its translator says, "The question of when, where, and by whom the targum was composed is unanswerable" (Clarke 1998: 3).

[22] Translations from Clarke 1998; Aramaic text from Clarke 1984. *Tg. Ps.-J.* to 1:1 significantly expands the reasons for Israel's rebuke; note Maher 1994: 266–69, who suggests that *Sifre* may well have been *Ps.-J.*'s source.

[23] Bernstein 2002 characterizes *Ps.-Jonathan*'s reading of Deut 32 as historiographical, a fact that would cohere well with the overview of Israel's history given to Moses by the Memra of the Lord in *Tg. Ps.-J.* Deut 34:1–4.

[24] Cf. *Tg. Ps.-J.* Deut 30:19–20: "Choose then the way of life, which is the Law, so that you may live in the life of the world to come, you and your children, by loving the Lord your God, by heeding his Memra, and by drawing near to his Fear. For the Law with which you are occupying (yourselves) is your life in this world and the prolongation of your days in the world to come. And you will be gathered at the end of the exile and you shall live upon the land that the Lord promised to your fathers, Abraham, Isaac, and Jacob to give to them." Note also *Tg. Ps.-J.* Deut 30:15.

greater obedience (e.g., at Deut 15:11 [contrast *Tg. Neof.*], 29:4 [29:3 HT], 30:1–6, etc.).

8.4. Conclusion: Later Trajectories of Interpretation

Both *Sifre* and the Targums reflect a later period of composition than the other literature surveyed in this investigation, and it is only natural to see certain sociological changes reflected in them. We find in both a tension: the final chapters of Deuteronomy, especially 32–34, are broadly expanded, but there is conversely something of a constriction of the eschatological horizon – perhaps in light of the failed Bar Kochba revolt and its charged political eschatology. Nevertheless, both *Sifre* and the Targums offer a fascinating glimpse into Deuteronomy's reception in the synagogue and school. Various traces of a liturgical origin can be found, especially in the Targums, and this may also account for certain actualizing tendencies as well. In *Sifre*, we see the result of questions posed to Deuteronomy: how far does Deuteronomy provide guidance for a life of fidelity to God and his law? What is more, for *Sifre* it is not so much a case of legal actualization of Deuteronomy as much as legal application, the extension of fundamental principles to cover like cases. Perhaps the very nature of a lemmatized commentary discourages the same sort of strong actualization and rewriting prevalent in earlier authors – though *Sifre* could certainly not be described as disinterested. Finally, it is worth noting that in both *Sifre* and the Targums we see evidence of large scale construals of Deuteronomy. The structural sequence of blessing following curse is seen as significant in *Sifre*, and the Targums make much of their rendering of Deut 1:1 as words of rebuke. Deuteronomy is, for these authors, a book that opens in rebuke, but ends in blessing.

It now remains for us to draw the results of this investigation together and to take note of what gains we have achieved in specifying the shape of Deuteronomy in the Second Temple period.

Chapter 9

Conclusion: Paul's Deuteronomy

This study began by expressing the hope that consideration of a wide range of engagements with Deuteronomy would help to establish a field of reception in which Paul might be critically viewed as one instantiation of the Jewish encounter with the end of the Pentateuch. To draw the results of this investigation together now provides some account of this encounter and Paul's stance in relation to his fellow-interpreters.

9.1. Paul's Deuteronomy and Others'

The habituating impulse of liturgical recitation ensured that Deuteronomy would have a widespread influence. If Paul and the other authors here surveyed produced their literary output in their mature adult years, by this time they would have heard Deuteronomy in its entirety perhaps dozens of times. This, together with the sheer physical presence of the scroll of Deuteronomy itself, suggests that for these authors Deuteronomy is not a hypertext, an intertext, a fragment – rather it is a book that in its very physicality suggests a certain wholeness.

In this light, it is worth pausing to consider the sheer amount of material to take into account. This in itself goes some way toward indicating the prevalence and popularity that Deuteronomy enjoyed. Of course, not every text written by a Jewish author from the third century BCE to the second century CE concerns itself with Deuteronomy, and no doubt reasons could be marshaled to explain its relative lack of attestation among, for example, sapiential sources (though note Tobit and Baruch above). But it is just as clear that Deuteronomy is a 'catholic' text whose influence spans time and place, lending definition to the sectarians of the Judean desert as much as to the urbane Philo, resourcing Josephus in Rome and the targumists in the East. The sheer prevalence of Deuteronomy constitutes it as something of a hermeneutical force, a foundational document with which to be reckoned. This singular hermeneutical force left in its wake a variety of responses, as §§ 3–8 so amply demonstrate. The very givenness of Deuteronomy as divine word necessitated interpretation and re-interpretation as

Jewish authors sought to understand and express their fidelity to Deuteronomy's vision in a world of changing circumstances and pressures.

In terms of the specific questions posed in the introduction to Part II, the preceding pages have shown the variety of answers put to them by various texts. Deuteronomy is widely re-written, whether in snippets, as in the Damascus Document, 4QMMT, Baruch, and Paul in 1 Cor 8 and Rom 10, or in a more systematic fashion, as in the Temple Scroll, *Testament of Moses*, Philo, Josephus, and the Targums. It is also quoted formally as an authoritative source, usually on the lips of Moses but also as Law or Song, as in Paul and 2 Maccabees, or much more fully in the lemmatized commentarial venture of the *Sifre*. With the possible exception of the Temple Scroll, the authority of Deuteronomy does not seem to be reflected differently in a quotation as opposed to an echo or a rewriting, though of course the assertorial weight might change due to varying rhetorical functions. The Temple Scroll itself also attests to the importance of Deuteronomy, even if it is seen as attempting to surpass it (though I have suggested above [§ 3.2.2] that this is not the most compelling interpretation of the Scroll).

Interest in Deuteronomy is well-attested across its span, but a number of texts concentrate especially on its closing chapters. This may simply be due to our relative lack of legal texts from the period, as some of the most substantial interest in Deuteronomy's legal section stems from manuscripts recovered from the Qumran finds – the motivation to copy and preserve Second Temple legal texts is absent in later Christianity and Rabbinic Judaism for different reasons, but with the same result. It may also be that Deuteronomy is more difficult to distinguish from its parallel content in Exodus, Leviticus and Numbers in certain instances. Nevertheless, in addition to the halakhic employment of Deuteronomy in the Temple Scroll, Damascus Document, 4QMMT, and the later *Sifre*, both Philo and Josephus spend proportionately at least as long expounding the legal sections of Deuteronomy as the narrative frame. In this light, § 6.3 has drawn attention to several instances in which Paul offers ethical instruction based on the last book of the Pentateuch, and so participates in this broad ethical interest of the Second Temple period. If the volume of his ethical recourse to Deuteronomy does not match that of all his Jewish peers, the particularity of the problems to which he addresses himself in his pastoral letters may provide some explanation. Strikingly, several texts rearrange Deuteronomy's precepts: the Temple Scroll rearranges and rewrites them from a first-person divine perspective, Philo gathers them under the ten headings supplied by the Decalogue, Paul further crystallizes the Decalogue by means of the love command, and Josephus arranges them in rough topicality to illustrate the constitution of Israel. Apparently the order and structure of Deuteronomy's laws was less than clear, and there was some attempt to search for or impose an order on the scattered precepts. It is also worth noting that wherever legal exegesis occurs, except in the later *Sifre*, it demonstrates an actualizing tendency.

In reference to the closing chapters of Deuteronomy, at least two different stances toward the material may be discerned. First, these chapters supply biographical material for the last words and actions of Moses, a unique contribution of Deuteronomy to the canonical portrait of Israel's leader. A biographical interest may be discerned especially in Pseudo-Philo (*LAB* 19), Philo's *de Vita Mosis*, and Josephus's *Antiquitates*. Such biographical interest usually serves a larger interpretative goal of the author (e.g., Philo showing that Moses is a prophet, Josephus demonstrating the fame and virtue of the lawgiver, etc.). Paul, at least in his surviving letters, shows no interest in such biographical representations of Moses. Perhaps the single exception is drawn from Exodus rather than Deuteronomy: the story of the Golden Calf (Exod 32–34), which Paul interprets theologically at length in 2 Cor 3. Second, interest in the final chapters of Deuteronomy stems from those seeking to understand Israel's plight. These can be divided into two perspectives. The first employs a fictionalization to stand with Moses on the other side of the Jordan and consider Israel's history in advance. This perspective highlights divine justice and also suggests that, since the predictions have been correct about the judgment, they must be correct about the restoration as well. In fact, similar conclusions can be drawn from those who stand at the current horizon and look back toward Moses's words as retrospectively vindicated in light of Israel's apostasy. Among the former, proleptic perspective, we might place the *Testament of Moses*, *Jubilees* 1, *LAB* 19, and the *Apocryphon of Jeremiah* C fragments from Qumran (4Q385a, 4Q387a, 4Q388a, 4Q389, 4Q390);[1] among the latter, retrospective perspective belong 4QMMT, Baruch, 2 Maccabees, Tobit, Philo and Josephus. What is more striking than any difference in perspective, however, is the widespread recourse to the final chapters of Deuteronomy to understand the past as well as to comprehend the future, individual differences in interpretation notwithstanding. This stands in contrast, for example, to *Sifre*'s reading of the Blessings of Moses that identifies them as already having been realized within biblical history, rather than partially realized and partially remaining. It is with this second group of authors, who consider that the final chapters of Deuteronomy shed light on Israel's history in retrospect, that Paul may be fruitfully compared.

What is more, the evidence for the distinctiveness of Deuteronomy varies from author to author. Perhaps Philo offers the strongest evidence of

---

[1] In fact, however, the *Apocryphon of Jeremiah* C fragments apparently attest both proleptic and retrospective perspectives.

this, with his Greek title for the book and sensitive literary reading of the different genres and impulses of the book itself. But Josephus also renders the book in a distinctive way, as the hortatory constitution of Israel, a reading that arguably does some justice to Deuteronomy itself. There is some scattered indication, however, that other authors were also aware of distinctively Deuteronomic elements, as in the name of the Song of Moses supplied by the author of 2 Maccabees, or the curses referred to by Baruch, 4QMMT or Philo in *Praem.* Of course the distinctiveness of Deuteronomy is more or less assumed by the holistic renderings of *Sifre* and the Targums. While Paul does not employ the Greek title of the book, this is not unusual for the apostle, and his ascriptions of Deuteronomy to Moses, the law, or even the "Righteousness-from-Faith" suggest that he is not unaware of the original context from which he draws his quotations.

Finally, when we encounter statements about how these authors come to know Deuteronomy, we are led directly to the liturgical and educational context of the synagogue and the public reading of the law. This is most explicitly so with Josephus, but the same may be confidently claimed of the Qumran sectarians, Philo, Paul, and the Targums – and probably, though less certainly, of the other authors whose works we have had occasion to examine. While such evidence is not entirely forthcoming (and why should it be?), it should be noted that the widespread interest in Deuteronomy, broadly spread across its chapters, presupposes some type of holistic encounter with the text that would be most readily gained in synagogue and school.

Of course, such a comparative exercise inevitably brings to light numerous differences and idiosyncrasies among interpreters. While a covenantal understanding of Deuteronomy appears to be widespread, 1QS is unique in its prescribed emulation of the covenant ceremony of Deut 27–29. The Temple Scroll stands as the lone exemplar of its radical program of rewriting Deuteronomy, even if other examples of so-called Rewritten Bible can be adduced as comparisons of a less extreme variety. Among the examination of Israel's history found in the Apocrypha and Pseudepigrapha, § 4.8 above noted that the question of what effects the turning point toward restoration is answered in varying ways: does God respond to Israel's obedience to the law (so Tobit), act in response to the intercession of the righteous (Pseudo-Philo; *Testament of Moses*), or provide divine enablement to return to the law and obey it (Baruch; *Jubilees* 1)? While Philo's role as an exegete of Deuteronomy has sometimes been underestimated, his Middle Platonic presuppositions do lead him to approach the last book of the Pentateuch with a particular agenda and particular questions in mind. Paul's interventionist reading of the Song of Moses suggests an understanding of Deut 27–30 as emphasizing that the conditions for restoration have been met in Christ; this is naturally without parallel from his Jewish contemporaries. Likewise, Josephus' envisioning of Deuteronomy as the Mosaic constitution of Israel provides him with a fitting answer to Roman imperial politics, but stands unique among other construals of Deuteronomy. The same might be said for the legal reasoning of the *Sifre* or the rebuke tradition of the Targums. Clearly there is no single Jewish response to Deuteronomy, and the fidelity of a Jewish response cannot simply be judged by appeal to a parallel strategy elsewhere. If we can speak of a family resemblance, clearly we are not examining sets of identical twins.

This investigation, then, has provided at least a rough map of the field of reception which Deuteronomy has created, a ground survey of the impact crater caused by end of the Pentateuch. Deuteronomy is a book that binds the future to itself by its constant appeals to remember the message that it mediates (so Assmann 2007: 212–28). From the extent and character of these Jewish responses to Deuteronomy, the power of that appeal can be measured. In these encounters we see the *Nachleben* of the scroll of Deuteronomy, passed from hand to hand. And in tracing this *Nachleben*, we see in operation the conviction that the expression of obedience to a text like Deuteronomy must be more than simple repetition, for, as Jacob Neusner once wrote, "Sameness, five hundred years later, is the greatest difference."[2]

9.2. Paul's Deuteronomy and Deuteronomy's Paul

As much as this study has emphasized the transformation of Deuteronomy at the hands of various authors, there is a reciprocal point to be made: Deuteronomy itself exercises a transforming influence on those whom it encounters. One can speak not simply of Paul's Deuteronomy, but also of Deuteronomy's Paul. Clearly, Paul is not a foundationalist who feels the need to construct his discourse with Scripture from the ground up, citing chapter and verse to substantiate every statement, but he certainly is concerned with a dialogical engagement and subjection to Scripture as the *viva vox dei*. He is accountable to Deuteronomy's address, including himself among the generations Moses proleptically exhorts. The problem that Harnack noticed long ago, namely that Paul's scriptural quotations are by and large confined to the *Hauptbriefe*, is certainly striking; but the inference one draws from this fact can be reversed: if it is a problem that Paul quotes so little Scripture in some places, it is equally problematic that he quotes

---

[2] As quoted in Stemberger 1996: 129.

so *much* Scripture elsewhere (and especially problematic for Harnack's contention that Marcion was Paul's true heir).

This pressure exercised by Deuteronomy, mediated through liturgy, has been received by Paul with a threefold construal of the book as ethical authority, theological authority, and a lens for the interpretation of Israel's history. The constraint of being bound to Deuteronomy is matched by the potential for new vision such boundedness supplies. If Paul knows by revelation that the crucified Jesus has been raised as Lord and Christ, he instinctively understands the import of such an intervention through the lens of Deuteronomy's prophetic judgment on Israel's history. If Paul's commission as a Jewish apostle to the nations comes to him wholly from without, he turns to Deuteronomy 29–32 (and, e.g., Isaiah 40–55) to make sense of the role of the Gentiles in the people of God. If Paul can acknowledge the radical newness of the revelation of God in Christ, he is emphatic that this God is none other than the one God confessed twice daily in the *Shema'* – a confession Paul had been binding to his very body for many years. If the redemption from the law's curse brought about a reconsideration of the law under a particular aspect, Paul remained convinced of the sheer propriety of God's demand for right living, for Jew as well as Gentile, as expressed in Deuteronomy. It is an interesting thought experiment to ponder how different Pauline theology would be had Paul chosen the route of Marcion and simply cut himself free from his ancestral heritage.

This reading of Paul's encounter with Deuteronomy thus stands alternately in contrast and continuity with some of those recently offered by other interpreters – though I have been instructed by all of them. With Hays, Wagner, Watson, and much recent scholarship, in this book I see Paul as a creative and thoughtful reader of Scripture.[3] Unlike Hays, however, I seek to chart in Paul's recourse to Deuteronomy a conversation about some of Israel's *loci communes*. This concern for a shared conversation is common also to Watson's presentation, but the survey of voices included is here broader, with the intention of allowing the full range of a polyphonic encounter to be heard. With this goes the recognition that the image of Paul we produce will be influenced by the authors with which we set the apostle in dialogue. Like Rosner, I seek in Paul's ethical vision a real engagement with Deuteronomy, but also try to relate his ethical appropriations of Deuteronomy to his equally numerous citations from elsewhere in the same scroll. With Scott, Bell, Watson, and Waters, *inter alia*, this reading takes seriously Paul's special concern for the closing chapters of Deuteronomy. Unlike Waters, I suggest that Paul has an integrative

---

[3] Note should also be taken of the complementary presentation of many of the same texts that are reviewed here under a different perspective in Lierman 2004, which focuses on Moses *qua* Moses rather than, e.g., Deuteronomy as text.

reading of Deut 27–32 in which Paul makes a series of interpretative judgments to read the questions of restoration after the curse of the covenant and of Gentile inclusion in the people of God in light of God's intervention in Israel's history in the death and resurrection of the Christ. Unlike Watson, I suggest that Paul does not read Deuteronomy with a single question in mind, but has an approach to the book that might be deemed "aspectual." In the same way that Paul is capable of viewing the human subject under different "aspects" (as flesh, as body, as soul, etc.),[4] so Paul does not simply consider Deuteronomy as posing or answering the question about Israel's ability to perform the law *tout simple*. While Paul does participate in the discourse of Jewish authors about the plight and restoration of Israel and does so with specific reference to the closing chapters of Deuteronomy, he also participates in the moral and theological discourses that similarly lead him to the heart of Deuteronomy – not as a book prescribing the terms of the covenant, but as the offer of a moral and theological word from the God and Father of the Lord Jesus Christ. At the very least, Paul has transformed this covenantal imperative to include belief in Jesus as Lord and Christ as the *sine qua non* of membership in the people of God (Rom 10:5–21). Such a transformation, however, does not destroy for the apostle Deuteronomy's force as Torah under every aspect.[5]

It is tempting to speculate further about what Paul omits to mention from Deuteronomy. Naturally we see a lack of emphasis on law-keeping as the essence of the covenant, perhaps understandable given Paul's theological commitments to the Gentile mission. But why does Paul not make use of the "prophet like Moses" *topos* seen in 4Q175 and in early Christianity? Does Paul consider the epithet of "prophet" to say too little? Perhaps because he conceives of his own apostolic commission in prophetic terms (so Sandnes 1991), even portraying himself as a new Moses (Bammel 1997), such language is thus unfit for Christ.[6] Again, why does Paul display such little emphasis on the biographical details of the end of Moses's life? Such questions are probably in part to be answered by noting that one would not necessarily expect such discussions in pastoral letters written to fledgling communities around the Mediterranean world. But beyond this, any suggestion can only be regarded as an argument from silence.

It is in the particular dialectic of fidelity and radicalism – even if only seminally – that Paul must be sought. Paul's reading of Deuteronomy in

---

[4] Compare the classic statement of Paul's anthropology in Bultmann 1980: 191–226.

[5] Traugott Holtz goes so far as to say, "the Law exists for the early church and for Paul only as an interpreted Law, but nevertheless as the Law" (1995: 67).

[6] Indeed, this prophetic self-consciousness may also go some way toward understanding the freedom which comprises one side of the apostle's dialogical engagement with Scripture.

some ways reflects certain well-known Jewish strategies of his day, but in other places he refuses these strategies, takes them as his point of departure and presses them to radical ends, or infuses them with Christological meaning. Of course, it should be kept in mind that there are no universally agreed upon "Jewish strategies" that all interpreters share and that could somehow serve as the essence of Jewish engagement with the book. Nevertheless, to see Paul's encounter with Deuteronomy as one particular instantiation of a broader Second Temple engagement with the end of the Pentateuch sheds interesting light on the apostle. The same experiment might be carried out with the other books in Paul's functional canon.[7]

9.3. Revisiting the Icon

I concluded the introductory chapter by suggesting that the present investigation could be conceived as offering a competing iconography to counter the types of images enshrined in the historiated initials of manuscripts of the *Bibles moralisées*. In those images, Paul stands over against the Jews as fundamentally other, repudiates the law, and joins in the church militant in her victory over a bound and blinded Lady Synagoga. Rather than these images as hermeneutical guides, I suggested that we might envisage Paul himself as wearing the pointed hat used to identify the Jews, one among many to lay claim to the guiding vision of Deuteronomy as entrusted to him by Lady Synagoga.

To forestall the risk of offering a purely iconoclastic presentation, however, one might also think of this investigation as involved in the retrieval and repristination of an earlier Pauline iconography, that found in the *traditio legis*. The *traditio legis* motif shows Christ delivering the law to his apostles, sometimes with the inscription written on the open scroll, *Dominus legem dat*.[8] While most often Peter receives or holds the scroll, examples found, e.g., on sarcophagi from Ravenna show Christ handing a scroll to Paul.[9] One could do worse, the argument of this book suggests, than to identify this as the scroll of Deuteronomy, given to the apostle to nourish

---

[7] For example, while much attention has been paid to Isaiah, it might still be interesting to see where the particular emphases of different authors lie (but note Shum 2002). Paul's Psalm citations also range over broad stretches of the Psalter (cf. Silva 2001).

[8] See esp. Hvalvik 2006 for examples and discussion of the motif, in which the scroll is most often handed to Peter (alternatively, Peter simply holds the end of an unrolled scroll for Christ to read aloud in promulgation). For the inscription on the scroll, see Hvalvik 2006: 417 and n. 53.

[9] See Klauser 1966: 83–84 and plate 35 (2); cf. Hvalvik 2006: 415.

the Gentile church and to make known the God of Israel's revelation in Jesus Christ: *Dominus Deuteronomium dat*.

Appendix

Biblical Passages in *Tefillin*, *Mezuzot* and Excerpted Texts

Tefillin are listed first, then *mezuzot*, then excerpted texts, with the Nash Papyrus and the rabbinic requirements for *tefillin* and *mezuzot* listed for comparative purposes. Where applicable, texts are primarily referenced by their publication in the DJD series. Biblical references are listed as given by the texts' respective editors. Biblical passages conforming to later Rabbinic requirements are placed in *italics*; those deviating from this later standard (in presence, since the criterion of absence is problematized by the fragmentary state of the mss.) in underline; where there is overlap, this is shown by the use of <u>*both conventions*</u>.

Name of Text[1]	Publication	Biblical Texts	Notes
1Q13 (1QPhyl)	D. Barthélemy, DJD I: 72–76 (pl. XIV)	*Exod 13:2–3; 13:7–9; 13:15–16(?)*; <u>Deut 5:1–21</u>; <u>5:23–27</u>; (probably ch. 6, though text is fragmentary); <u>10:17–18</u>; <u>10:21–11:1</u>; <u>11:8–11</u>; *11:12*.	Arm
4Q128 (4QPhyl A)	J. T. Milik in DJD VI: 48–51 (pls. VII–VIII)[2]	Recto: <u>Deut 5:1–14</u>; <u>5:27–6:3</u>; <u>*10:12–11:17*</u>; Verso: *Deut 11:18–21*; <u>*Exod 12:43–13:7*</u>.[3]	Arm; Written in the Qumran scribal practice (hereafter, QSP).[4]

---

[1] For *tefillin* and *mezuzot* in the DJD series, see esp. Tov 2002: 182–83. Also see the somewhat different, though very informative, presentation of the evidence in Tov 1997.

[2] One fragment of this was already published by Karl Georg Kuhn as 4Qphyl^c; see Kuhn 1957: 15–16.

[3] Recto and verso are only noted where applicable; later rabbinic practice forbade opistographic *tefillin* or *mezuzot* on analogy with biblical scrolls (see *b. Erub.* 98a; cf. *b. Men.* 33a).

[4] See esp. Tov 1992: 107–11; Brooke 2003: 57.

Name of Text	Publication	Biblical Texts	Notes
4Q129 (4QPhyl B)	J. T. Milik in DJD VI: 51–53 (pl. IX)[5]	Recto: *Deut 5:1–6:5*; Verso: *Exod 13:9–16.*	Arm; QSP
4Q130 (4QPhyl C)	J. T. Milik in DJD VI: 53–55 (pls. X–XI)	*Exod 13:1–10; 13:11– 16; Deut 6:4–9; 11:13–21.*	Arm
4Q131 (4QPhyl D)	J. T. Milik in DJD VI: 56 (pl. XII)	*Deut 11:13–21.*	Head; *Tefillin* D– F from the same case
4Q132 (4QPhyl E)	J. T. Milik in DJD VI: 56–57 (pl. XIII)	*Exod 13:1–10.*	Head; D–F from the same case
4Q133 (4QPhyl F)	J. T. Milik in DJD VI: 57 (pl. XIV)	*Exod 13:11–16.*	Head; D–F from the same case
4Q134 (4QPhyl G)	J. T. Milik in DJD VI: 58–60 (pl. XV)	Recto: Deut 5:1–21; Verso: *Exod 13:11– 12.*	Head; G–I from the same case; QSP?
4Q135 (4QPhyl H)	J. T. Milik in DJD VI: 60–62 (pl. XVI)[6]	Recto: *Deut 5:22–6:5*; Verso: *Exod 13:14b– 16.*	Head; G–I from the same case; QSP?
4Q136 (4QPhyl I)	J. T. Milik in DJD VI: 62–63 (pl. XVII)[7]	Recto: *Deut 11:13– 21*; *Exod 12:43– 13:10*; Verso: *Deut 6:6–7(?).*	Head; G–I from the same case; QSP?
4Q137 (4QPhyl J)	J. T. Milik in DJD VI: 64–67 (pls. XVIII– XIX)[8]	Recto: Deut 5:1–24a; Verso: 5:24b–32; 6:2– 3.	Head; J–K from the same case; QSP
4Q138 (4QPhyl K)	J. T. Milik in DJD VI: 67–69 (pl. XX)	Recto: Deut 10:12– 11:7; Verso: 11:7–12.	Head; J–K from the same case; QSP

---

[5] Kuhn's 4Qphyl[b] (1957: 11–15).
[6] Kuhn's 4Qphyl[d] (1957: 16–20).
[7] This had earlier appeared in Milik 1966: 105–06 (plate IIb).
[8] Kuhn's 4Q phyl [a] (1957: 5–11).

Name of Text	Publication	Biblical Texts	Notes
4Q139 (4QPhyl L)	J. T. Milik in DJD VI: 70 (pl. XXII)	Deut 5:7–24.	Head; L–N from the same case; QSP
4Q140 (4QPhyl M)	J. T. Milik in DJD VI: 71–72 (pl. XXI)	Recto: *Exod 12:44–13:10*; Verso: *Deut 5:33–6:5*.	Head; L–N from the same case; QSP
4Q141 (4QPhyl N)	J. T. Milik in DJD VI: 72–74 (pl. XXII)	Deut 32:14–20, 32–33.	Head; L–N from the same case. The two last verses were written in an open space perpendicular to the rest of the text. QSP
4Q142 (4QPhyl O)	J. T. Milik in DJD VI: 74–75 (pl. XXII)	Recto: Deut 5:1–16; Verso: *Deut 6:7–9.*	QSP
4Q143 (4QPhyl P)	J. T. Milik in DJD VI: 75–76 (pl. XXII)	Recto: Deut 10:22–11:3; Verso: *Deut 11:18–21.*	QSP
4Q144 (4QPhyl Q)	J. T. Milik in DJD VI: 76 (pl. XXIII)	Recto: *Deut 11:4–18*; Verso: *Exod 13:4–9*	QSP
4Q145 (4QPhyl R)	J. T. Milik in DJD VI: 77–78 (pl. XXIII)	Recto: *Exod 13:1–7*; Verso: *Exod 13:7–10*	
4Q146 (4QPhyl S)	J. T. Milik in DJD VI: 78 (pl. XXIII)	*Deut 11:19–21.*	May be from either a *tefillah* or a *mezuza.*
4Q147 (4QPhyl T)	J. T. Milik in DJD VI: 79 (pl. XXIV)	Undeciphered	
4Q148 (4QPhyl U)	J. T. Milik in DJD VI: 79 (pl. XXV)	Undeciphered	

Name of Text	Publication	Biblical Texts	Notes
5Q8 (5QPhyl)	J. T. Milik in DJD III: 178 (pl. XXXVIII)	Three compartments with very fragmentary, unreadable scrolls (left unrolled by Milik due to their poor condition).	Head?
8Q3 (8QPhyl)	M. Baillet in DJD III: 149–57 (pls. XXXII–XXXIII)	Group I: *Exod 13:1–10; Exod 13:11–16; Deut 11:13–21; Deut 6:4–9.* Group II: ??; <u>Deut 6:1–3</u>; <u>10:20–22</u>. Group III: <u>Deut 10:12–19</u>; <u>Exod 12:43–51</u>; <u>Deut 5:1–14</u>; <u>20:11</u> Group IV: ??; (poss: <u>Deut 10:13, 11:2, 5, 3</u>?); <u>11:1</u>; <u>11:6–12.</u>	Head
XQPhyl 1	Y. Yadin, *Tefillin from Qumran (XQPhyl 1–4)*[9]	<u>Exod 12:43–51</u>; *13:1–10*; <u>Deut 10:12–19</u>	Head
XQPhyl 2	Y. Yadin, *Tefillin from Qumran (XQPhyl 1–4)*	<u>Deut 5:22–33</u>; <u>6:1–3</u>; *6:4–9*	Head
XQPhyl 3	Y. Yadin, *Tefillin from Qumran (XQPhyl 1–4)*	<u>Deut 5:1–21</u>; *Exod 13:11–16*	Head

---

[9] This should be read with the substantial review by M. Baillet (1970).

Name of Text	Publication	Biblical Texts	Notes
XQPhyl 4	Y. Yadin, *Tefillin from Qumran (XQPhyl 1–4)*	Poss. *Exod 13:1–10*(?). Eight lines on recto, six lines on verso, but too fragmentary to be sure of the identification.	Head; Not originally part of the same *tefillah* as XQPhyl 1–3.[10]
Mur 4 (MurPhyl)	J. T. Milik in DJD II: 80–85 (pls. XXII–XXIV)	*Exod 13:1–10; 13:11–16; Deut 11:13–21; 6:4–9.*	Arm
XḤev/Se 5 (XḤev/SePhyl)	M. Morgenstern and M. Segal in DJD XXXVIII: 183–191 (pl. XXX)[11]	*Exod 13:1–16; Deut 6:4–9; Deut 11:13–21.*	Arm
34Se 1 (Phyl)	Aharoni 1961: 22–23 (pl. 11)	*Exod 13:2–10; 13:11–16.*	Two fragments may not belong to the same strip of parchment.
4Q149 (4QMez A)	J. T. Milik in DJD VI: 80–81 (pl. XXVI)	<u>Exod 20:7–12</u> (mixed with <u>Deut 5:11–16?</u>)	Mezuzah
4Q150 (4QMez B)	J. T. Milik in DJD VI: 81 (pl. XXVI)	*Deut 6:5–6;* <u>10:14–11:2</u>.	Mezuzah
4Q151 (4QMez C)	J. T. Milik in DJD VI: 82–83 (pl. XXVII)	<u>*Deut 5:27–6:9;*</u> <u>10:12–20</u>.	Mezuzah
4Q152 (4QMez D)	J. T. Milik in DJD VI: 83 (pl. XXVI)	*Deut 6:5–7.*	Mezuzah

---

[10] Yadin tentatively suggests that the original "Slip no. 4," now lost, might have contained Deut 10:20–22; 11:1–12; 11:13–21; see Yadin 1969: 33–34.

[11] Though not mentioned by the editors, this is apparently the same *tefillah* referred to by J. T. Milik 1957: 20.

Name of Text	Publication	Biblical Texts	Notes
4Q153 (4QMez E)	J. T. Milik in DJD VI: 83 (pl. XXVI)	*Deut 11:17–18.*	Mezuzah
4Q154 (4QMez F)	J. T. Milik in DJD VI: 83–84 (pl. XXVI)	Exod 13:1–4.[12]	Mezuzah
4Q155 (4QMez G)	J. T. Milik in DJD VI: 84–85 (pl. XXV)	Exod 13:11–16.	Mezuzah
8Q4 (8QMez)	M. Baillet in DJD III: 158–161 (pl. XXXIV)	*Deut 10:12–11:21*	Mezuzah
Mur 5 (MurMez)	J. T. Milik in DJD II: 85–86 (pl. XXIV)	27 lines, too fragmentary to tell from which text or whether this should be considered a *tefillah* or *mezuzah*.	Mezuzah?
4Q41 (4QDeut^n)	S. A. Crawford in DJD XIV: 117–28 (pls. XXVIII–XXIX)[13]	Deut 8:5–10; 5:1–6:1	Excerpted Text[14]
4Q15 (4QExod^d)	J. E. Sanderson in DJD XII: 127–28 (pl. XXI)	*Exod 13:15–16,* 15:1	Excerpted Text Exod 15:1 follows directly after 13:15–16

---

[12] This and the next *mezuzah* are shown in underline because the rabbinic judgment prescribed only the Deut passages for *mezuzot*.

[13] For the text's inclusion here, see further White 1990a; 1990b; Eshel 1991.

[14] I follow E. Tov's working categorization of excerpted texts as distinct from texts that include both quoted lemma and interpretation on the one hand, and rewritten biblical texts on the other (Tov 1995). Only excerpted texts that include Exodus and/or Deuteronomy are included here for comparative purposes (thus excluding 4QPs^b, 4QPs^{g,h}, 4QPs^n, 4QCant^a, 4QCant^b, 4QEzek^a, 5QPs, and various other MSS containing only certain psalms). Cf. further esp. Duncan 1997.

Name of Text	Publication	Biblical Texts	Notes
4Q16 (4QExod^c)	J. E. Sanderson in DJD XII: 129–31 (pl. XXI)	Exod 13:3–5	Excerpted Text
4Q37 (4QDeut^j)	J. A. Duncan in DJD XIV: 75–91 (pls. XX–XXIII)[15]	Deut 5:1–11, 13–15; 5:21–6:3; 8:5–10; 11:6–10, 12, 13; Exod 12:46–51; 13:1–5; Deut 32:7–8	Excerpted Text QSP
4Q38 (4QDeut^kl)	J. A. Duncan in DJD XIV: 93–98 (pl. XXIV)	Deut 5:28–32; 11:6–13; 32:17–18, 22–23, 25–27	Excerpted Text QSP
4Q44 (4QDeut^q)	P. W. Skehan and E. Ulrich in DJD XIV: 137–42 (pl. XXXI)[16]	Deut 32: 9–10(?); 32:37–43	Excerpted Text
5Q1 (5QDeut)	J. T. Milik in DJD III: 169–71	Deut 7:15–24; 8:5–9:2	Excerpted Text?[17]
4Q175 (4QTestimonia)	J. M. Allegro in DJD V: 57–60 (pl. XXI)[18]	Exod 20:21 (SamPent = Deut 5:28–29+18:18–19); Num 24:15–17; Deut 33:8–11; 4QapocrJosh(?) on Josh 6:26	Excerpted Text

[15] Cf. Duncan 1992.

[16] See originally Skehan 1954.

[17] Tov (1995), considers this as a possible excerpted text, but Duncan (1997) does not include this in her inventory. I include it here for the sake of completeness, though it does seem to lack some of the characteristics of other excerpted texts, not to mention providing the sole example of Deut 7 in an excerpted text.

[18] See Allegro 1956: 182–87; and esp. the important remarks and corrections of Strugnell 1970: 225–29.

Name of Text	Publication	Biblical Texts	Notes
Nash Papyrus	Cook 1903: 34–56 (pls. I–III).[19]	<u>Deut 5:6–21</u> (with substantial harmonizations and corrections toward Exod 20:2–17); *Deut 6:4–5*, prefaced by an introductory statement: "And these are the statutes and the judgments that Moses commanded the sons of Israel when they went forth from the land of Egypt" (Burkitt 1903: 407; cf. LXX Deut 6:4).	Excerpted Text Small sheet of papyrus which had apparently been folded several times.
Rabbinic *Tefillin*	E.g., *b. Men.* 34b–35a *bar.*	*Exod 13:1–10; 11–16; Deut 6:4–9; 11:13–21.* Or: *Exod 13:1–10; 11–16; Deut 11:13–21; 6:4–9.*	Arm/Head
Rabbinic *Mezuzot*	E.g., *b. Men.* 28a	*Deut 6:4–9; 11:13–21.*	Mezuzah

---

[19] Cf. also Burkitt 1903; Albright 1937.

Bibliography

1. Primary Sources

Aland, B., et al., eds. 1993a. *Novum Testamentum Graece.* 27th revised edition. Stuttgart: Deutsche Bibelgesellschaft.

—. et al., eds. 1993b. *The Greek New Testament.* 4th revised edition. New York: United Bible Societies.

Allegro, John M. 1968. *Qumrân Cave 4, 1 (4Q158–4Q186).* DJDJ 5. Oxford: Clarendon.

Aly, Zaki and Ludwig Koenen. 1980. *Three Rolls of the Early Septuagint: Genesis and Deuteronomy.* Papyrologische Texte und Abhandlungen 27. Bonn: Habelt.

Ameling, Walter. 2004. *Inscriptiones Judaicae Orientis. Band 2: Kleinasien.* TSAJ 101. Tübingen: Mohr Siebeck.

Arnaldez, R., C. Mondésert, J. Pouilloux, eds. 1961–1992. *Les Oeuvres de Philon d'Alexandrie.* 36 vols. SC. Paris: Cerf.

Baars, W. 1968. *New Syrohexaplaric Texts.* Leiden: Brill.

Barclay, J. M. G. 2007. *Against Apion. Translation and Commentary.* Flavius Josephus Translation and Commentary 10. Leiden and Boston: Brill.

Beentjes, Pancratius C. 1997. *The Book of Ben Sira in Hebrew: A Text Edition of All Extant Hebrew Manuscripts and a Synopsis of All Parallel Hebrew Ben Sira Texts.* VTSup 68. Leiden, New York, Köln: Brill.

Berger, K. 1981. *Das Buch der Jubiläen.* JSHRZ 2/3. Gütersloh: Gütersloher Verlagshaus.

Bilabel, Friedrich, ed. 1924. *Griechische Papyri (Urkunden, Briefe, Schreibtafeln, Ostraka etc.).* Veröffentlichungen aus den badischen Papyrus-Sammlungen Heft 4. Heidelberg: Im Selbstverlag des Verfassers.

Braude, William G. and Israel J. Kapstein. 1975. *Pesikta de-Rab Kahana.* Philadelphia: Jewish Publication Society of America.

Braude, William G., trans. 1959. *The Midrash on Psalms.* 2 vols. YJS 13. New Haven: Yale University Press.

Brownlee, William H. 1951. *The Dead Sea Manual of Discipline. Translation and Notes.* BASORSup 10–12. New Haven: American Schools of Oriental Research.

Ceylan, Ali and Thomas Corsten. 1995. "Inscriptions from Laodikeia in the Museum of Denizli." *Epigraphica Anatolica* 25: 89–92.

Charles, R. H. 1897. *The Assumption of Moses, Translated from the Latin Sixth Century MS., the Unemended Text of which is Published Herewith, together with the Text in Its Restored and Critically Emended Form.* London: Adam and Charles Black.

—. 1913. "The Book of Jubilees." *APOT* 2.1–82.

—. ed. 1913. *The Apocrypha and Pseudepigrapha of the Old Testament in English.* 2 vols. Oxford: Clarendon.

Charlesworth, J. H. 2008. "An Unknown Dead Sea Scrolls Fragment of Deuteronomy." http://www.ijco.org/?categoryID=28682. Accessed 3 June 2009.

—. ed. 1983–85. *The Old Testament Pseudepigrapha*. 2 vols. Garden City, NY: Doubleday.

Clarke, Ernest G. 1984. *Targum Pseudo-Jonathan of the Pentateuch: Text and Concordance*. Hoboken, NJ: Ktav.

—. with Sue Magder. 1998. *Targum Pseudo-Jonathan: Deuteronomy. Translated, with Notes*. The Aramaic Bible 5B. Edinburgh: T. & T. Clark.

Cohn, L., et al. 1909–64. *Die Werke Philos von Alexandria in deutscher Übersetzung*. 7 vols. Berlin: W. de Gruyter.

Colson, F. H., G. H. Whitaker and R. Marcus.. 1929–43. *Philo*. LCL. 10 volumes with 2 supplementary volumes. Cambridge, MA: Harvard University Press.

Cook, S. A. 1903. "A Pre-Massoretic Biblical Papyrus." *Proceedings of the Society of Biblical Archaeology* 25: 34–56.

Corsten, Thomas. 1997. *Die Inschriften von Laodikeia am Lykos, Teil I*. IGSK Band 49. Bonn: R. Habelt.

Cowley, A. 1923. *Aramaic Papyri of the Fifth Century B.C.* Oxford: Clarendon.

Cross, Frank Moore. 2002. "Testimonia (4Q175 = 4QTestimonia = 4QTestim)." Pages 308–28 in *The Dead Sea Scrolls: Hebrew, Aramaic, and Greek Texts with English Translations: Pesharim, Other Commentaries, and Related Documents*. Edited by James H. Charlesworth, et al. PTSDSSP 6B. Tübingen: Mohr Siebeck. Louisville: Westminster John Knox.

Dahmen, Ulrich. 2002. "Neu identifizierte Fragmente in den Deuteronomium-Handschriften vom Toten Meer." *RevQ* 20: 571–81

Danby, H., ed. and trans. 1933. *The Mishnah*. Oxford: Oxford University Press.

Denis, Albert-Marie. 1970a. *Fragmenta pseudepigraphorum qua supersunt graeca*. PVTG 3. Leiden: Brill.

Dimant, D. 2001. *Qumran Cave 4.XXI: Parabiblical Texts, Part 4: Pseudo-Prophetic Texts*. Partially based on earlier transcriptions by J. Strugnell. DJD XXX. Oxford: Clarendon.

Dogniez, C. and M. Harl. 1992. *La Bible d'Alexandrie 5: Le Deutéronome*. Paris: Cerf.

Drazin, Israel. 1982. *Targum Onkelos to Deuteronomy: An English Translation of the Text with Analysis and Commentary (Based on A. Sperber's Edition)*. New York: Ktav Publishing House.

Dunand, Françoise. 1966. *Papyrus Grecs Bibliques (Papyrus F. Inv. 266). Volumina de la Genèse et du Deutéronome. Introduction*. Recherches d'Archéologie, de Philologie et d'Histoire XXVII. Cairo: Imprimerie de l'Institut Français d'Archéologie Orientale.

—. 1971. *Papyrus Grecs Bibliques (Papyrus F. Inv. 266). Volumina de la Genèse et du Deutéronome (Texte et Planches)*. Extrait des Études de Papyrologie IX. Cairo: Imprimerie de l'Institut Français d'Archéologie Orientale.

Elliger, K., W. Rudolph, et al. eds. 1983. *Biblia Hebraica Stuttgartensia*. Stuttgart: Deutsche Bibelgesellschaft.

Epstein, I., ed. 1935–52. *The Babylonian Talmud*. 35 vols. London: Soncino.

Feldman, L. H. 2000. *Judean Antiquities 1–4: Translation and Commentary*. Flavius Josephus Translation and Commentary 3. Leiden, Boston, Köln: Brill.

Finkelstein, Louis. 1939. *Siphre ad Deuteronomium*. Breslau: M. & H. Marcus.

Fitzmyer, Joseph A. 1995. "Tobit." Pages 1–76 in idem, et al., *Qumran Cave 4, XIV: Parabiblical Texts, Part 2*. DJD XIX. Oxford: Clarendon.

Freedman, H. and M. Simon, eds. 1939. *Midrash Rabbah*. 10 vols. London: Soncino.

Gager, J. G. ed. 1992. *Curse Tablets and Binding Spells from the Ancient World.* Oxford and New York: Oxford University Press.

García Martínez, F. and E. Tigchelaar. 1997–1998. *The Dead Sea Scrolls Study Edition.* 2 vols. Leiden: Brill.

Grossfield, Bernard. 1988a. *The Targum Onqelos to Genesis: Translated, with a Critical Introduction, Apparatus, and Notes.* The Aramaic Bible 6. Edinburgh: T. & T. Clark.

—. 1988b. *The Targum Onqelos to Deuteronomy: Translated, with Apparatus, and Notes.* The Aramaic Bible 9. Edinburgh: T. & T. Clark.

Hanhart, Robert. 1976. *Maccabaeorum liber II.* 2nd ed. Septuaginta 9/2. Göttingen: Vandenhoeck & Ruprecht.

—. 1983. *Tobit.* Septuaginta 8/5. Göttingen: Vandenhoeck & Ruprecht.

Harrington, Daniel J. 1985. "Pseudo Philo." *OTP* 2.297–377.

—. Jacques Cazeaux, Charles Perrot and Pierre-Maurice Bogaert. 1976. *Pseudo-Philon, Les Antiquités Bibliques.* SC 229–30. Paris: Cerf.

Holladay, Carl R. 1995. *Fragments from Hellenistic Jewish Authors. Volume 3: Aristobulus.* SBLTT 39. Atlanta: Scholars.

Horbury, William and David Noy. 1992. *Jewish Inscriptions of Graeco-Roman Egypt.* Cambridge: Cambridge University Press.

Jacobson, Howard. 1996. *A Commentary on Pseudo-Philo's* Liber Antiquitatum Biblicarum, *with Latin Text and English Translation.* 2 vols. AGJU 31. Leiden: Brill.

Jastram, N. 1994. "4QNum[b]." Pages 205–67 in E. Ulrich and F. M. Cross, *Qumran Cave 4: VII.* DJD 12. Oxford: Clarendon.

Kee, H. C. 1983. "Testaments of the Twelve Patriarchs." *OTP* 1.775–828.

Kenyon, Frederic G. 1935. *The Chester Beatty Biblical Papyri: Descriptions and Texts of Twelve Manuscripts on Papyrus of the Greek Bible. Fasciculus V: Numbers and Deuteronomy.* London: Emery Walker.

Klein, Michael L. 1980. *The Fragment-Targums of the Pentateuch According to their Extant Sources.* 2 vols. Rome: Biblical Institute Press.

—. 1986. *Genizah Manuscripts of Palestinian Targum to the Pentateuch.* 2 vols. Cincinnati: Hebrew Union College Press.

Kotansky, Roy. 1994. *Greek Magical Amulets: The Inscribed Gold, Silver, Copper, and Bronze* Lamellae. *Part I: Published Texts of Known Provenance.* Papyrologica Coloniensia XXII/1. Opladen: Westdeutscher Verlag.

Kuhn, Karl Georg. 1957. *Phylakterien aus Höhle 4 von Qumran.* AHAW. Philosophisch-Historische Klasse 1. Heidelberg: C. Winter.

Laperrousaz, E.-M. 1970. *Le Testament de Moïse (Généralement appelé «Assomption de Moïse»).* Cahiers de Semitica 19. Paris: Libraire d'Amérique et d'Orient Adrien-Masonneuve.

Lienhard, Joseph T., ed. 2001. *Exodus, Leviticus, Numbers, Deuteronomy.* Ancient Christian Commentary on Scripture 3. Downers Grove, IL: InterVarsity.

Lüderitz, G. 1983. *Corpus jüdischer Zeugnisse aus der Cyrenaika.* Beiheft zum Tübinger Atlas des vorderen Orients Reihe B 53. Wiesbaden: L. Reichert.

Maier, Johann. 1985. *The Temple Scroll: An Introduction, Translation & Commentary.* Translated by R. T. White. JSOTSup 34. Sheffield: JSOT Press.

Mason, Steve. 2001. *Life of Josephus: Translation and Commentary.* Flavius Josephus Translation and Commentary 9. Leiden, Boston, Köln: Brill.

McNamara, Martin. 1997. *Targum Neofiti 1: Deuteronomy. Translated, with Apparatus and Notes.* The Aramaic Bible 5A. Edinburgh: T. & T. Clark.

Milik, J. T. 1966. "Fragment d'une source du Psautier (4Q Ps 89) et fragments des Jubilés, du Document de Damas, d'un Phylactère dans la grotte 4 de Qumrân." *RB* 73: 94–106.

—. 1977. "Tefillin, mezuzot et targums (4Q128–4Q157)." Pages 33–90 in R. de Vaux and J. T. Milik, *Qumrân Grotte 4. II.* DJD 6. Oxford: Clarendon.

Neusner, Jacob. 1987. *Sifre to Deuteronomy: An Analytical Translation.* 2 vols. BJS 98, 101. Atlanta: Scholars Press.

—. ed. 1982–93. *The Talmud of the Land of Israel.* 35 vols. Chicago: University of Chicago Press.

Nodet, Étienne. 1995. *Flavius Josèphe. Les Antiquités juives, Livres IV et V.* Paris: Cerf.

Noy, David. 1993–1995. *Jewish Inscriptions of Western Europe. Volume 1: Italy (Excluding the City of Rome), Spain and Gaul. Volume 2: The City of Rome.* Cambridge: Cambridge University Press.

Parry, Donald W. and Emanuel Tov, eds. 2005. *The Dead Sea Scrolls Reader, Part 3: Parabiblical Texts.* Leiden and Boston: Brill.

Pelletier, A. 1962a. *Lettre d'Aristée à Philocrate.* SC 89. Paris, Cerf.

Priest, J. 1985. "Testament of Moses." *OTP* 1.919–934.

Puech, Émile. 1997a. "Fragments du plus ancien exemplaire du Rouleau du Temple (4Q524)." Pages 19–64 in *Legal Texts and Legal Issues: Proceedings of the Second Meeting of the International Organization for Qumran Studies, Cambridge 1995.* Edited by M. Bernstein, F. García Martínez, and J. Kampen. STDJ 23. Leiden, New York, Köln: Brill.

—. 1998. *Qumrân Grotte 4. XVIII: Textes hébreux (4Q521–4Q528, 4Q576–4Q579).* DJD 25. Oxford: Clarendon.

Qimron, Elisha and John Strugnell. 1994. *Qumran Cave 4.V, Miqṣat Ma'ase ha-Torah.* DJD 10. Oxford: Clarendon.

Qimron, Elisha. 1996. *The Temple Scroll: A Critical Edition with Extensive Reconstructions.* Bibliography by F. García Martínez. Beer Sheva: Ben-Gurion University of the Negev Press. Jerusalem: Israel Exploration Society.

Qimron, Elisha, et al. 2006. "Some Works of the Torah." Pages 187–251 in *The Dead Sea Scrolls: Hebrew, Aramaic, and Greek Texts with English Translations: Damascus Document II, Some Works of the Torah, and Related Documents.* Edited by James H. Charlesworth and H. W. M. Rietz. PTSDSSP 3. Tübingen: Mohr Siebeck. Louisville: Westminster John Knox.

Rinaldi, Giancarlo. 1989. *Biblia Gentium.* Rome: Libreria Sacre Scritture.

Roberts, Colin H. 1936. *Two Biblical Papyri in the John Rylands Library, Manchester.* Manchester: Manchester University Press.

Scheck, Thomas P. 2002. *Origen: Commentary on the Epistle to the Romans, Books 6–10.* The Fathers of the Church. Washington, D. C.: The Catholic University of America Press.

Shutt, R. J. H. 1985. "Letter of Aristeas." *OTP* 2.7–34.

Skehan, P. W., E. Ulrich and J. E. Sanderson, eds. 1992. *Qumran Cave 4.IV: Palaeo-Hebrew and Greek Biblical Manuscripts.* DJD 9. Oxford: Clarendon.

Sperber, A., ed. 1956–68. *The Bible in Aramaic: Based on Old Manuscripts and Printed Texts.* 4 vols. Leiden: Brill.

Stegemann, H. 1967. "Weitere Stücke von 4QpPsalm 37, von 4Q Patriarchal Blessings und Hinweis auf eine unedierte Handschrift aus Höhle 4Q mit Exzerpten aus dem Deuteronomium." *RevQ* 6: 193–227.

Stern, Menahem. 1980. *Greek and Latin Authors on Jews and Judaism. Volume Two: From Tacitus to Simplicius.* Jerusalem: The Israel Academy of Sciences and Humanities.

Strecker, G. 1992. "Kerygmata Petrou." Pages 531–41 in W. Schneemelcher, ed., *New Testament Apocrypha, II: Writings Related to the Apostles, Apocalypses and Related Subjects.* Translation edited by R. McL. Wilson. Louisville, KY: Westminster John Knox.

Talmon, Shemaryahu. 1999. "Hebrew Fragments from Masada." Pages 1–149 in *Masada VI: Yigael Yadin Excavations 1963–1965 Final Reports.* Jerusalem: Israel Exploration Society and the Hebrew University of Jerusalem.

Thackeray, H. St. J., R. Marcus, A. Wikgren and L. H. Feldman. 1926–1965. *Josephus.* LCL. 10 volumes. Cambridge, MA: Harvard University Press.

Tov, E. 1975. *The Book of Baruch also Called I Baruch (Greek and Hebrew).* SBLTT 8. n.p., Scholars.

—. et al., eds. 1955–2008. *Discoveries in the Judaean Desert.* 40 vols. Oxford: Clarendon.

Tromp, J. 1993. *The Assumption of Moses: A Critical Edition with Commentary.* SVTP 10. Leiden, New York, Köln: Brill.

—. 2005. *The Life of Adam and Eve in Greek: A Critical Edition.* PVTG 6. Leiden and Boston: Brill.

VanderKam, J. and J. T. Milik. 1994. "216. 4QJubilees[a]." Pages 1–22 in H. Attridge, et al., *Qumran Cave 4, VII: Parabiblical Texts, Part 1.* DJD 13. Oxford: Clarendon.

Vermes, G., and M. D. Goodman, eds. 1989. *The Essenes According to the Classical Sources.* Sheffield: JSOT.

Wagner, Christian J. 2003. *Polyglotte Tobit-Synopse. Griechisch – Lateinisch – Syrisch – Hebräisch – Aramäisch.* Abhandlungen der Akademie der Wissenschaften in Göttingen, Philologisch-Historische Klasse, Dritte Folge, Band 258. MSU XXVIII. Göttingen: Vandenhoeck & Ruprecht.

Weber, R. et al. eds. 1994. *Biblia Sacra iuxta Vulgatam Versionem: Editio Minor.* Stuttgart: Deutsche Bibelgesellschaft.

Weeks, Stuart, Simon Gathercole, and Loren Stuckenbruck. 2004. *The Book of Tobit: Texts from the Principal Ancient and Medieval Traditions.* Fontes et Subsidia ad Bibliam pertinentes 3. Berlin and New York: de Gruyter.

Wevers, John William, ed. 2006. *Deuteronomium.* Septuaginta 3.2. 2nd ed. Göttingen: Vandenhoeck & Ruprecht.

Whitehouse, O. C. 1913. "The Book of Baruch or I Baruch." *APOT* 1.569–95.

Wintermute, O. S. 1985. "Jubilees." *OTP* 2.35–142.

Yadin, Y. 1969. *Tefillin from Qumran (XQPhyl 1–4).* Jerusalem: The Israel Exploration Society and the Shrine of the Book.

—. 1983. *The Temple Scroll.* 3 vols. in 4. Jerusalem: The Israel Exploration Society.

Ziegler, Joseph. 1957. *Ieremias, Baruch, Threni, Epistula Ieremiae.* Septuaginta 15. Göttingen: Vandenhoeck & Ruprecht.

2. Grammars, Concordances, Lexica and Reference Works

Abegg, Martin G., et al. 2003. *The Dead Sea Scrolls Concordance. Volume One: The Non-Biblical Texts from Qumran.* 2 parts. Leiden and Boston: Brill.

Allenbach, J., et al. 1982. *Biblia Patristica Supplément: Philon d'Alexandrie.* Paris: Centre National de la Recherche Scientifique.

Bauer, Walter. 2000. *A Greek-English Lexicon of the New Testament and other Early Christian Literature.* English editions by W.F. Arndt, F.W. Gingrich, and F.W. Danker. 3rd ed. Revised and Edited by Frederick William Danker (BDAG). Chicago: University of Chicago Press.

Blass, F. and A. Debrunner. 1961. *A Greek Grammar of the New Testament and Other Early Christian Literature.* Translated and revised by Robert W. Funk. Chicago: University of Chicago Press.

Borgen, Peder, Kåre Fuglseth, and Roald Skarsten, 2000. *The Philo Index: A Complete Greek Word Index to the Writings of Philo of Alexandria.* Grand Rapids and Cambridge: Eerdmans. Leiden, Boston, Köln: Brill.

Charlesworth, J. H. 1991. *Graphic Concordance to the Dead Sea Scrolls.* PTSDSSP. Tübingen: Mohr Siebeck. Louisville, KY: Westminster John Knox.

Denis, Albert-Marie. 1987. *Concordance grecque des Pseudépigraphes d'Ancien Testament.* Louvain-la-Neuve: Université Catholique de Louvain, Institut Orientaliste.

Freedman, D. N., ed. 1992. *Anchor Bible Dictionary.* 6 vols. New York: Doubleday.

Hübner, Hans. 1997. *Vetus Testamentum in Novo. Band 2: Corpus Paulinum.* Göttingen: Vandenhoeck & Ruprecht.

Kittel, G. and G. Friedrich, eds. 1964–76. *Theological Dictionary of the New Testament.* Translated and edited by G. W. Bromiley. 10 vols. Grand Rapids: Eerdmans.

Kuhn, Karl Georg. 1960. *Konkordanz zu den Qumrantexten.* Göttingen: Vandenhoeck & Ruprecht.

Lawrence H. Schiffman and James C. VanderKam, eds. 2000. *Encyclopedia of the Dead Sea Scrolls.* 2 vols. Oxford and New York: Oxford University Press.

Liddell, Henry George, Robert Scott and H. S. Jones with R. McKenzie. 1996. *A Greek-English Lexicon.* 9th ed. Oxford: Clarendon.

Martone, Corrado. 2001. *The Judaean Desert Bible: An Index.* Quaderni di Henoch 11. Turin: Silvio Zamorani.

Rahlfs, A. and D. Fraenkel. 2004. *Verzeichnis der griechischen Handschriften des Alten Testaments.* Septuaginta Supplementum I/1. Göttingen: Vandenhoeck & Ruprecht.

Rengstorf, Karl Heinrich. 1973–1983. *A Complete Concordance to Flavius Josephus.* 4 vols. Leiden: Brill.

Strack, H. and P. Billerbeck. 1926–28. *Kommentar zum Neuen Testament aus Talmud und Midrasch.* 6 vols. Munich: Beck.

van Haelst, Joseph. 1976. *Catalogue des papyrus littéraires juifs et chrétiens.* Paris: Publications de la Sorbonne.

Wallace, Daniel B. 1996. *Greek Grammar Beyond the Basics.* Grand Rapids: Zondervan.

3. Secondary Literature

Abasciano, Brian. 2007. "Diamonds in the Rough: A Reply to Christopher Stanley Concerning the Reader Competency of Paul's Original Audiences." *NovT* 49: 153–83.

Achtemeier, Paul J. 1990. "*Omne Verbum Sonat*: The New Testament and the Oral Environment of Late Western Antiquity." *JBL* 109: 3–27.

Aejmelaeus, A. 1987. "What Can We Know About the Hebrew *Vorlage* of the Septuagint?" *ZAW* 99: 58–89. Reprinted as pages 77–115 in A. Aejmelaeus, *On the Trail of the Septuagint Translators.* Kampen: Kok Pharos, 1993.

—. 1996. "Die Septuaginta des Deuteronomiums." Pages 1–22 in *Das Deuteronomium und seine Querbeziehungen.* Edited by T. Veijola. Schriften der Finnischen Exegetischen Gesellschaft 62. Göttingen: Vandenhoeck & Ruprecht.

Agua Pérez, A. del. 1983. "La Sinagoga: Origenes, ciclos de lectura y oración." *EstB* 41: 341–66.

Aharoni, Y. 1961. "Expedition B." *IEJ* 11: 11–24.

Albl, Martin C. 1999. *"And Scripture Cannot Be Broken": The Form and Function of the Early Christian* Testimonia *Collections.* NovTSup 96. Leiden, Boston, Köln: Brill.

Albright, W. F. 1937. "A Biblical Fragment from the Maccabaean Age: The Nash Papyrus." *JBL* 56: 145–76.

Alexander, Loveday. 1990. "The Living Voice: Scepticism Towards the Written Word in Early Christian and in Graeco-Roman Texts." Pages 221–47 in *The Bible in Three Dimensions: Essays in Celebration of Forty Years of Biblical Studies in the University of Sheffield.* Edited by D. J. A. Clines, S. E. Fowl and S. E. Porter. JSOTSup 87. Sheffield: Sheffield Academic Press.

Alexander, Philip S. 1988a. "Jewish Aramaic Translations." Pages 217–53 in Mulder 1988.

—. 1988b. "Retelling the Old Testament." Pages 99–121 in *It Is Written: Scripture Citing Scripture. Essays in Honour of Barnabas Lindars, SSF.* Edited by D. A. Carson and H. G. M. Williamson. Cambridge: Cambridge University Press.

—. 1996. "The Redaction-History of *Serekh ha-Yaḥad:* A Proposal." *RevQ* 17: 437–56.

—. 2003. "Literacy Among Jews in Second Temple Palestine: Reflections on the Evidence from Qumran." Pages 3–24 in *Hamlet on a Hill: Semitic and Greek Studies Presented to Professor T. Muraoka on the Occasion of his Sixty-Fifth Birthday.* Edited by M. F. J. Baasten and W. Th. Van Peursen. OLA 118. Leuven, Paris, Dudley, MA: Peeters.

Allegro, John M. 1956. "Further Messianic References in Qumran Literature." *JBL* 75: 174–87.

Allo, E.-B. 1934. *Première Épitre aux Corinthiens.* 2nd ed. Paris: Gabalda.

—. 1937. *Seconde Épître aux Corinthiens.* 2nd ed. Paris: Gabalda.

Altshuler, David. 1979. "The Treatise ΠΕΡΙ ΕΘΩΝ ΚΑΙ ΑΙΤΙΩΝ 'On Customs and Causes' by Flavius Josephus." *JQR* 69: 226–32.

—. 1982. "On the Classification of Judaic Laws in the *Antiquities* of Josephus and the Temple Scroll of Qumran." *Association for Jewish Studies Review* 7: 1–14.

Aly, Zaki. 1971. "Addenda." *EPap* 9: 227–28.

Amaru, B. A. 1980–81. "Land Theology in Josephus' *Jewish Antiquities.*" *JQR* 71: 201–29.

Amir, Y. 1988. "Authority and Interpretation of Scripture in the Writings of Philo." Pages 421–53 in Mulder 1988.

—. 1994. "Josephus on the Mosaic 'Constitution'." Pages 13–27 in *Politics and Theopolitics in the Bible and Postbiblical Literature.* Edited by H. G. Reventlow, Y. Hoffman and B. Uffenheimer. Sheffield: Sheffield Academic Press.

Anderson, Gary. 1998. "The Status of the Torah in the Pre-Sinaitic Period: St. Paul's Epistle to the Romans." Pages 1–23 in *Biblical Perspectives: Early Use and Interpretation of the Bible in Light of the Dead Sea Scrolls.* Edited by M. E. Stone and E. G. Chazon. STDJ 28. Leiden: Brill.

Assmann, Jan. 2007. *Das kulturelle Gedächtnis: Schrift, Erinnerung und politische Identität in frühen Hochkulturen*. 6th ed. Munich: C. H. Beck

Atkinson, K. 1997. "On Further Defining the First-Century CE Synagogue: Fact or Fiction?" *NTS* 43: 491–502.

—. 2004. "Herod the Great as Antiochus Redivivus: Reading the *Testament of Moses* as an Anti-Herodian Composition." Pages 134–49 in vol. 1 of *Of Scribes and Sages: Early Jewish Interpretation and Transmission of Scripture*. Edited by C. A. Evans. SSEJC 9. London and New York: T. & T. Clark.

—. 2006. "Taxo's Martyrdom and the Role of the *Nuntius* in the *Testament of Moses*: Implications for Understanding the Role of Other Intermediary Figures." *JBL* 125: 453–76.

Attridge, Harold W. 1976. *The Interpretation of Biblical History in the* Antiquitates Judaicae *of Flavius Josephus*. HDR 7. Missoula, MT: Scholars.

Aune, David E. 1983. *Prophecy in Early Christianity and the Ancient Mediterranean World*. Grand Rapids: Eerdmans.

Baillet, M. 1970. "Nouveaux phylactères de Qumrân (X Q Phyl 1–4). A propos d'une édition récente." *RevQ* 7: 403–15.

Balás, David L. and D. Jeffrey Bingham. 2004. "Patristic Exegesis of the Books of the Bible." Pages 271–373 in vol. 1 of *Handbook of Patristic Exegesis*. 2 vols. Edited by C. Kannengiesser. Leiden and Boston: Brill.

Balogh, Josef. 1927. "Voces Paginarum: Beiträge zur Geschichte des lauten Lesens und Schreibens." *Phil* n.s. 36: 84–109, 202–40.

Bammel, Ernst. 1997. "Paulus, der Moses des Neuen Bundes." Pages 205–14 in his *Judaica et Paulina. Kleine Schriften II*. WUNT 91. Tübingen: Mohr Siebeck.

Barclay, J. M. G. 1998. "Paul and Philo on Circumcision: Romans 2.25–29 in Social and Cultural Context." *NTS* 44: 536–56.

Bar-Ilan, Meir. 1988. "Writing in Ancient Israel and Early Judaism, Part Two: Scribes and Books in the Late Second Commonwealth and Rabbinic Period." Pages 21–38 in Mulder 1988.

Barnett, Paul. 1997. *The Second Epistle to the Corinthians*. NICNT. Grand Rapids: Eerdmans.

Barr, James. 1961. *The Semantics of Biblical Language*. Oxford: Oxford University Press.

—. 1979. *The Typology of Literalism in Ancient Biblical Translations*. MSU 15. Göttingen: Vandenhoeck & Ruprecht.

Barrett, C. K. 1957. *A Commentary on the Epistle to the Romans*. HNTC. New York: Harper & Row.

—. 1968. *A Commentary on the First Epistle to the Corinthians*. BNTC. London: Adam and Charles Black.

—. 1982. "Romans 9:30–10:21: Fall and Responsibility of Israel." Pages 132–53 in *Essays on Paul*. Philadelphia: Westminster.

Barthélemy, D. 1978a. "Est-ce Hoshaya Rabba qui censura le 'Comentaire allégorique'?" Pages 140–73, 390–91 in *Études d'histoire du texte de l'Ancien Testament*. OBO 21. Göttingen: Vandenhoeck & Ruprecht. Fribourg: Éditions Universitaires.

—. 1978b. "Pourquoi la Torah a-t-elle été traduite en grec?" Pages 322–40 in *Études d'histoire du texte de l'Ancien Testament*. OBO 21. Göttingen: Vandenhoeck & Ruprecht.

Basser, H. W. 1984. *Midrashic Interpretations of the Song of Moses.* American University Studies, Series VII: Theology and Religion, 2. New York, Frankfort on the Main, and Berne: Peter Lang.

—. 1987. "Josephus as Exegete." *JAOS* 107: 21–30.

Bassler, Jouette M. 1982. *Divine Impartiality: Paul and a Theological Axiom.* SBLDS 59. Chico: Scholars Press.

Bauckham, Richard. 1998. *God Crucified: Monotheism and Christology in the New Testament.* Grand Rapids: Eerdmans.

—. 2008. "Tobit as a Parable for the Exiles of Northern Israel." Pages 433–59 in his *The Jewish World Around the New Testament: Collected Essays I.* WUNT 233. Tübingen: Mohr Siebeck. Originally published as pages 140–64 in *Studies in the Book of Tobit: A Multidisciplinary Approach.* Edited by M. Bredin. LSTS55. London and New York: T. & T. Clark, 2006.

Baumgärtel, F. 1953. "Zur Liturgie in der 'Sektenrolle' vom Toten Meer." *ZAW* 65: 263–65.

Baumgarten, Joseph M. 1972. "Does *TLH* in the Temple Scroll Refer to Crucifixion?" *JBL* 91: 472–81.

Beall, Todd S. 1988. *Josephus' Description of the Essenes Illustrated by the Dead Sea Scrolls.* SNTSMS 58. Cambridge: Cambridge University Press.

Beard, Mary. 1991. "Writing and Religion: *Ancient Literacy* and the Function of the Written Word in Roman Religion." Pages 35–58 in *Literacy in the Roman World.* Edited by J. H. Humphrey. Journal of Roman Archaeology Supplementary Series 3. Ann Arbor, MI: University of Michigan.

Becker, Adam H. and Annette Yoshiko Reed, eds. 2003. *The Ways that Never Parted: Jews and Christians in Late Antiquity and the Early Middle Ages.* TSAJ 95. Tübingen: Mohr Siebeck.

Begg, Christopher. 1990. "Josephus's Portrayal of the Disappearances of Enoch, Elijah, and Moses: Some Observations." *JBL* 109: 691–93.

Bekken, Per Jarle. 1995. "Paul's Use of Deut 30.12–14 in Jewish Context." Pages 183–203 in *The New Testament and Hellenistic Judaism.* Edited by Peder Borgen and Søren Giversen. Oxford: Aarhus University Press.

—. 2007. *The Word is Near You: A Study of Deuteronomy 30:12–14 in Paul's Letter to the Romans in a Jewish Context.* BZNW 144. Berlin and New York: Walter de Gruyter.

Bell, Richard H. 1994. *Provoked to Jealousy: The Origin and Purpose of the Jealousy Motif in Romans 9–11.* WUNT 2/63. Tübingen: Mohr Siebeck.

Berkley, Timothy Wayne. 2000. *From a Broken Covenant to Circumcision of the Heart: Pauline Intertextual Exegesis in Romans 2:17–29.* SBLDS 175. Atlanta: Society of Biblical Literature.

Bernstein, Moshe J. 1994. "The Employment and Interpretation of Scripture in 4QMMT: Preliminary Observations." Pages 29–51 in *Reading 4QMMT: New Perspectives on Qumran Law and History.* Edited by John Kampen and M. J. Bernstein. SBLSymS 2. Atlanta: Scholars.

—. 2002. "The Aramaic Versions of Deuteronomy 32: A Study in Comparative Targumic Theology." Pages 29–52 in *Targum and Scripture: Studies in Aramaic Translations and Interpretation in Memory of Ernest G. Clarke.* Edited by Paul V. M. Flesher. Studies in the Aramaic Interpretation of Scripture 2. Leiden and Boston: Brill.

—. 2005. " 'Rewritten Bible': A Generic Category Which Has Outlived its Usefulness?" *Textus* 22: 169–96.

Berthelot, Katell. 2007. "Les titres des livres bibliques: Le témoignage de la bibliothèque de Qumrân." Pages 127–40 in *Flores Florentino: Dead Sea Scrolls and Other Early Jewish Studies in Honour of Florentino García Martínez*. Edited by Anthony Hilhorst, Émile Puech and Eibert Tigchelaar. JSJSup 122. Leiden and Boston: Brill.

Betz, Hans Dieter. 1979. *Galatians: A Commentary on Paul's Letter to the Churches in Galatia*. Hermeneia. Philadelphia: Fortress.

Bickerman, E. 1944. "The Colophon of the Greek Book of Esther." *JBL* 63: 339–62. Reprinted as pages 218–37 in vol. 1 of *Studies in Jewish and Christian History: A New Edition in English Including* The God of the Maccabees. Introduced by Martin Hengel. Edited by Amram Tropper. AJEC. AGAJU 68. Leiden and Boston: Brill, 2007.

Bieringer, R. 1994. "Plädoyer für die Einheitlichkeit des 2. Korintherbriefes: Literarkritische und inhaltliche Argumente." Pages 131–79 in *Studies on 2 Corinthians*. By R. Bieringer and J. Lambrecht. BETL 112. Leuven: Leuven University Press.

Bilde, Per. 1988. *Flavius Josephus between Jerusalem and Rome: His Life, His Works and their Importance*. JSPSup 2. Sheffield: JSOT Press.

Birnbaum, Ellen. 2006. "Two Millennia Later: General Resources and Particular Perspectives on Philo the Jew." *CBR* 4: 241–76.

Black, Matthew. 1973. *Romans*. NCB. London: Oliphants.

Blau, L. 1902. *Studien zum althebräischen Buchwesen I: Studien zum althebräischen Buchwesen und zur biblischen Literaturgeschichte*. Straßburg: Karl J. Trübner.

Bloedhorn, Hanswulf and Gil Hüttenmeister. 1999. "The Synagogue." Pages 267–97 in *The Early Roman Period*. Vol. 3 of *The Cambridge History of Judaism*. Edited by William Horbury, W. D. Davies and John Sturdy. Cambridge: Cambridge University Press.

Blumenkranz, Bernhard. 1966. *Le juif médiéval au miroir de l'art Chrétien*. Paris: Études Augustiniennes.

Boccaccini, Gabriele. 1991. *Middle Judaism: Jewish Thought, 300 B.CE to 200 C.E.* Minneapolis: Fortress.

—. 1998. *Beyond the Essene Hypothesis: The Parting of the Ways Between Qumran and Enochic Judaism*. Grand Rapids: Eerdmans.

—. ed. 2005. *Enoch and Qumran Origins: New Light on a Forgotten Connection*. Grand Rapids: Eerdmans.

Bockmuehl, Markus N. A. 1990. *Revelation and Mystery in Ancient Judaism and Pauline Christianity*. WUNT 2/36. Tübingen: Mohr Siebeck. Reprinted: Grand Rapids: Eerdmans, 1997.

—. 1995. "A Commentator's Approach to the 'Effective History' of Philippians." *JSNT* 60: 57–88.

—. 1998. "Redaction and Ideology in the *Rule of the Community* (*1QS/4QS*)." *RevQ* 72: 541–60.

—. 2000. *Jewish Law in Gentile Churches: Halakhah and the Beginning of Christian Public Ethics*. London: T. & T. Clark.

Bonsirven, J. 1939. *Exégèse rabbinique et exégèse paulinienne*. Paris: Beauchesne et ses Fils.

Boomershine, Thomas E. 1994. "Jesus of Nazareth and the Watershed of Ancient Orality and Literacy." *Semeia* 65: 7–36.

Borgen, Peder. 1984a. "Philo of Alexandria." Pages 233–82 in *Jewish Writings of the Second Temple Period*. Edited by Michael E. Stone. CRINT 2/2. Van Gorcum: Assen. Philadelphia: Fortress.

—. 1984b. "Philo of Alexandria: A Critical and Synthetical Survey of Research Since World War II." Pages 98–154 in *ANRW* 2.21.1. Berlin and New York: de Gruyter.

—. 1997. *Philo of Alexandria: An Exegete for His Time.* NovTSup 86. Leiden, New York, Köln: Brill.

Botha, P. J. J. 1992. "Greco-Roman Literacy as Setting for New Testament Writings." *Neot* 26: 195–215.

Bowman, Alan K. 1991. "Literacy in the Roman Empire: Mass and Mode." Pages 119–31 in *Literacy in the Roman World.* Edited by J. H. Humphrey. Journal of Roman Archaeology Supplementary Series 3. Ann Arbor, MI: University of Michigan Press.

—. and Greg Woolf. 1994. "Literacy and Power in the Ancient World." Pages 1–16 in *Literacy and Power in the Ancient World.* Edited by Alan K. Bowman and Greg Woolf. Cambridge: Cambridge University Press.

Bowman, J. 1959. "Phylacteries." Pages 523–38 in *Studia Evangelica.* Edited by K. Aland, F. L. Cross, J. Danielou, H. Riesenfeld and W. C. van Unnik. TU 73. Berlin: Akademie-Verlag.

Boyarin, Daniel. 1994. *A Radical Jew: Paul and the Politics of Identity.* Berkeley: University of California Press.

—. 2004. *Border Lines: The Partition of Judaeo-Christianity.* Divinations. Philadelphia: University of Pennsylvania Press.

Braulik, G. 1985. "Die Abfolge der Gesetze in Deuteronomium 12–26 und der Dekalog." Pages 252–72 in *Das Deuteronomium. Entstehung, Gestalt und Botschaft.* Edited by N. Lohfink. BETL 68. Leuven: Peeters. Reprinted as pages 231–55 in his *Studien zur Theologie des Deuteronomiums.* SBAB 2. Stuttgart: Verlag Katholisches Bibelwerk, 1988.

Brin, Gershon. 1987. "Concerning Some of the Uses of the Bible in the *Temple Scroll.*" *RevQ* 12: 519–28.

Brooke, George J. 1985. *Exegesis at Qumran: 4QFlorilegium in Its Jewish Context.* JSOTSup 29. Sheffield: JSOT.

—. ed. 1989. *Temple Scroll Studies: Papers Presented at the International Symposium on the Temple Scroll, Manchester, December, 1987.* Sheffield: JSOT Press.

—. 1993. "Torah in the Qumran Scrolls." Pages 97–120 in *Bibel in jüdischer und christlicher Tradition: Festschrift für Johann Maier zum 60. Geburtstag.* Edited by Helmut Merklein, Karlheinz Müller, and Günter Stemberger. BBB 88. Frankfurt a.M.: Hain.

—. 1994. "The Deuteronomic Character of 4Q252." Pages 121–35 in *Pursuing the Text: Studies in Honor of Ben Zion Wacholder on the Occasion of his Seventieth Birthday.* Edited by J. C. Reeves and J. Kampen. Sheffield: Sheffield Academic Press.

—. 1997a. "'The Canon within the Canon' at Qumran and in the New Testament." Pages 242–266 in *The Scrolls and the Scriptures: Qumran Fifty Years After.* Edited by Stanley E. Porter and Craig A. Evans. JSPSup 26. RILP 3. Sheffield: Sheffield Academic Press.

—. 1997b. "The Explicit Presentation of Scripture in 4QMMT." Pages 67–88 in *Legal Texts and Legal Issues: Second Meeting of the IOQS, Cambridge 1995. Published in Honor of Joseph M. Baumgarten.* Edited by M. J. Bernstein, F. García Martínez and J. Kampen. STDJ 23. Leiden: Brill.

—. 1997c. "Exegetical Strategies in *Jubilees* 1–2: New Light from 4QJubilees[a]." Pages 39–57 in *Studies in the Book of Jubilees.* Edited by Matthias Albani, Jörg Frey and Armin Lange. TSAJ 65. Tübingen: Mohr Siebeck.

—. 2000. "Rewritten Bible." *EDSS* 2:777–81.

—. 2003. "Deuteronomy 5–6 in the Phylacteries from Qumran Cave 4." Pages 57–70 in *Emanuel: Studies in Hebrew Bible, Septuagint, and Dead Sea Scrolls in Honor of Emanuel Tov*. Edited by S. M. Paul, et al. VTSup 94. Leiden and Boston: Brill.

—. 2005. "The *Temple Scroll* and the New Testament." Pages 97–114 in *idem, The Dead Sea Scrolls and the New Testament: Essays in Mutual Illumination*. London: SPCK. Originally pages 181–99 in Brooke 1989.

Bruce, F. F. 1982. *The Epistle to the Galatians: A Commentary on the Greek Text*. NIGTC. Grand Rapids: Eerdmans.

Büchler, A. 1892–94. "The Reading of the Law and Prophets in a Triennial Cycle." *JQR* 5: 420–68; *JQR* 6: 1–73.

Bultmann, Rudolph and Dieter Lührmann. 1974. "φαίνω, κτλ." *TDNT* 9: 1–10.

Bultmann, Rudolph. 1980. *Theologie des Neuen Testaments*. 8th ed. UTB 630. Tübingen: Mohr Siebeck.

Burke, David G. 1982. *The Poetry of Baruch: A Reconstruction and Analysis of the Original Hebrew Text of Baruch 3:9–5:9*. SBLSCS 10. Chico, CA: Scholars.

Burkitt, F. C. 1903. "The Hebrew Papyrus of the Ten Commandments." *JQR* o.s. 15: 392–408.

Burnyeat, M. F. 1997. "Postscript on Silent Reading." *CQ* 47: 74–76.

Byrskog, Samuel. 1994. *Jesus the Only Teacher: Didactic Authority and Transmission in Ancient Israel, Ancient Judaism and the Matthean Community*. ConBNTS 24. Stockholm: Almqvist & Wiksell International.

Callaway, Phillip R. 1989. "Extending Divine Revelation: Micro-Compositional Strategies in the Temple Scroll." Pages 149–62 in Brooke 1989.

Calvin, John. 1959–72. *Calvin's New Testament Commentaries*. 12 vols. Edited by David W. Torrance and T. F. Torrance. Edinburgh: Saint Andrew. Grand Rapids: Eerdmans.

Campbell, Douglas A. 2006. "An Evangelical Paul: A Response to Francis Watson's *Paul and the Hermeneutics of Faith*." *JSNT* 28: 337–51.

Campbell, Jonathan G. 1995. *The Use of Scripture in the Damascus Document 1–8, 19–20*. BZAW 228. Berlin: De Gruyter.

—. 2005. " 'Rewritten Bible' and 'Parabiblical Texts': A Terminological and Ideological Critique." Pages 43–68 in *New Directions in Qumran Studies: Proceedings of the Bristol Colloquium on the Dead Sea Scrolls, 8–10 September 2003*. Edited by Jonathan G. Campbell, William John Lyons and Lloyd K. Pietersen. London and New York: T. & T. Clark International.

Casson, Lionel. 2001. *Libraries in the Ancient World*. New Haven: Yale University Press.

Catto, Stephen K. 2007. *Reconstructing the First-Century Synagogue: A Critical Analysis of Current Research*. LNTS 363. London and New York: T. & T. Clark.

Chapman, David W. 2008. *Ancient Jewish and Christian Perceptions of Crucifixion*. WUNT 2/244. Tübingen: Mohr Siebeck.

Childs, Brevard S. 1979. *Introduction to the Old Testament as Scripture*. London: SCM.

—. 2008. *The Church's Guide for Reading Paul: The Canonical Shaping of the Pauline Corpus*. Grand Rapids: Eerdmans.

Chilton, Bruce. 2002. "Festivals and Lectionaries: Correspondence and Distinctions." Pages 12–28 in *The Gospels According to Michael Goulder: A North-American Response*. Edited by Chris Rollston. Harrisburg: Trinity Press International.

Christensen, D. 2002. *Deuteronomy 21:10–34:1*. WBC 6B. Nashville: Thomas Nelson.

Ciampa, Roy E. 2007. "Deuteronomy in Galatians and Romans." Pages 99–117 in Moyise and Menken 2007.

—. 2008. "Scriptural Language and Ideas." Pages 41–57 in *As It Is Written: Studying Paul's Use of Scripture*. Edited by Stanley E. Porter and Christopher D. Stanley. SBLSymS 50. Atlanta: Society of Biblical Literature.

—. and Brian S. Rosner. 2006. "The Structure and Argument of 1 Corinthians: A Biblical/Jewish Approach." *NTS* 52: 205–18.

Clark, W. P. 1931. "Ancient Reading." *CJ* 26: 698–700.

Cohen, Naomi G. 1963–64. "Josephus and Scripture: Is Josephus' Treatment of the Scriptural Narrative Similar Throughout the *Antiquities* I–XI?" *JQR* 54: 311–32.

—. 1986. "Philo's Tefillin." Pages 199–206 in *Proceedings of the 9ᵗʰ World Congress of Jewish Studies*. Division A. Jerusalem: World Union of Jewish Studies.

—. 1997a. "Earliest Evidence of the Haftarah Cycle for the Sabbaths between 17 *Tammuz* and *Sukkot* in Philo." *JJS* 48: 225–49.

—. 1997b. "The Names of the Separate Books of the Pentateuch in Philo's Writings." Pages 54–78 in *SPhilo* 9: *Wisdom and Logos: Studies in Jewish Thought in Honor of David Winston*. Edited by D. T. Runia and G. E. Sterling. BJS 312. Atlanta: Scholars Press. Reprinted in Cohen 2007: 25–53.

—. 2007. *Philo's Scriptures: Citations from the Prophets and Writings. Evidence for a Haftarah Cycle in Second Temple Judaism*. JSJSup 123. Leiden and Boston: Brill.

Cohen, Shaye J. D. 1999. "The Temple and the Synagogue." Pages 298–325 in *The Early Roman Period*. Vol. 3 of *The Cambridge History of Judaism*. Edited by William Horbury, W. D. Davies and John Sturdy. Cambridge: Cambridge University Press.

Cohn, Yehudah B. 2008. *Tangled up in Text: Tefillin and the Ancient World*. BJS 351. Providence, Rhode Island: Brown University.

Colet, John. 1985. *John Colet's Commentary on First Corinthians*. Edited and translated by Bernard O'Kelly and Catherine A. L. Jarrott. Medieval and Renaissance Texts and Studies 21. Binghamton, NY: Center for Medieval and Early Renaissance Studies.

Collins, A. Y. 1980. "The Function of 'Excommunication' in Paul." *HTR* 73: 251–63.

Collins, John J. 2005. "The Judaism of the Book of Tobit." Pages 23–40 in *The Book of Tobit: Text, Tradition, Theology*. Edited by Géza G. Xeravits and József Zsengellér. JSJSup 98. Leiden and Boston: Brill.

Collins, Nina L. 2000. *The Library in Alexandria and the Bible in Greek*. VTSup 82. Leiden: Brill.

Colorni, Vittore. 1964. *L'uso del Greco nella liturgia del Giudaismo Ellenistico e la Novella 146 di Giustiniano*. Extracted from *Annali di Storia del Diritto* 8. Milan: A. Giuffrè.

Colson, F. H. 1940. "Philo's Quotations from the Old Testament." *JTS* 41: 237–51.

Conzelmann, Hans. 1975. *1 Corinthians*. Hermeneia. Philadelphia: Fortress.

Cook, John Granger. 2004. *The Interpretation of the Old Testament in Greco-Roman Paganism*. STAC 23. Tübingen: Mohr Siebeck.

Cotton, H. M., W. E. H. Cockle and F. G. B. Millar. 1995. "The Papyrology of the Roman Near East: A Survey." *JRS* 85: 214–35.

Cox, Claude E. 1998. "The Reading of the Personal Letter as the Background for the Reading of the Scriptures in the Early Church." Pages 74–91 in *The Early Church in Its Context: Essays in Honor of Everett Ferguson*. Edited by A. J. Malherbe, F. W. Norris, and J. W. Thompson. NovTSup 90. Leiden: Brill.

Craigie, Peter C. 1976. *The Book of Deuteronomy*. NICOT. Grand Rapids: Eerdmans.

Cranfield, C. E. B. 1979. *A Critical and Exegetical Commentary on the Epistle to the Romans*. 2 vols. ICC. Edinburgh: T. & T. Clark.

Crawford, Sidnie White. 2000a. "The Rewritten Bible at Qumran." Pages 173–95 in *The Hebrew Bible and Qumran*. Edited by J. H. Charlesworth. The Bible and the Dead Sea Scrolls 1. N. Richland Hills, TX: BIBAL Press.

—. 2000b. *The Temple Scroll and Related Texts*. CQSS 2. Sheffield: Sheffield Academic Press.

—. 2005. "Reading Deuteronomy in the Second Temple Period." Pages 127–40 in *Reading the Present in the Qumran Library: The Perception of the Contemporary by Means of Scriptural Interpretations*. Edited by Kristin de Troyer and Armin Lange. SBLSymS 30. Atlanta: Society of Biblical Literature.

Cribiore, R. 1997. "Literary School Exercises." *ZPE* 116: 53–60 with corrigenda in *ZPE* 117: 162.

Crockett, L. 1966. "Luke 4:16–30 and the Jewish Lectionary Cycle: A Word of Caution." *JJS* 17: 13–46.

Culler, Jonathan. 1981. *The Pursuit of Signs: Semiotics, Literature, Deconstruction*. London and Henley: Routledge & Kegan Paul.

Cunningham, Valentine. 2002. *Reading After Theory*. Oxford: Blackwell.

Dahl, Nils A. 1971. "Widersprüche in der Bibel, ein altes hermeneutisches Problem." *ST* 25: 1–19.

Dahmen, U. 2003. "Das Deuteronomium in Qumran als umgeschriebene Bibel." Pages 269–309 in *Das Deuteronomium*. Edited by G. Braulik. ÖBS 23. Frankfurt am Main: Peter Lang.

Daniel, R. W. 1977. "Some ΦΥΛΑΚΤΗΡΙΑ." *ZPE* 25: 145–54.

Davies, W. D. and Dale C. Allison. 1988. *A Critical and Exegetical Commentary on the Gospel According to Saint Matthew*. Edinburgh: T. & T. Clark.

Dawson, David. 1992. *Allegorical Readers and Cultural Revision in Ancient Alexandria*. Berkeley and Los Angeles: University of California Press.

—. 2001. *Christian Figural Reading and the Fashioning of Identity*. Berkeley: University of California Press.

del Valle Rodríguez, Carlos. 2005. "Los primeros contactos de la Iglesia con el Talmud: El significado de la deuterosis." Pages 299–308 in Mauro Perani, ed., *"The Words of a Wise Man's Mouth Are Gracious" (Qoh 10,12): Festschrift for Günter Stemberger on the Occasion of His 65th Birthday*. SJ 32. Berlin and New York: Walter de Gruyter.

Denis, Albert-Marie. 1970b. *Introduction aux pseudépigraphes grecs d'Ancien Testament*. SVTP 1. Leiden: Brill.

Dewey, Arthur J. 1987. "A Re-Hearing of Romans 10:1–15." *Semeia* 39: 109–27.

Dewey, Joanna. 1987. "Textuality in an Oral Culture: A Survey of the Pauline Traditions." *Semeia* 39: 37–65.

Di Lella, Alexander. 1979. "The Deuteronomic Background of the Farewell Discourse in Tob 14:3–11." *CBQ* 41: 380–89.

Dimant, D. 1992. "New Light from Qumran on the Jewish Pseudepigrapha – 4Q390." Pages 405–448 in volume 2 of *The Madrid Qumran Congress: Proceedings of the International Congress on the Dead Sea Scrolls, Madrid 18–21 March 1991*. Edited by J. Trebolle Barrera and L. Vegas Montaner. STDJ 11. Leiden: Brill.

Dirksen, Peter B. 1988. "The Old Testament Peshitta." Pages 255–97 in Mulder 1988.

Dochhorn, Jan. 2009. "Röm 7,7 und das zehnte Gebot: ein Beitrag zur Schriftauslegung und zur jüdischen Vorgeschichte des Paulus." *ZNW* 100: 59–77.

Dodd, C. H. 1932. *The Epistle of Paul to the Romans*. MNTC. New York: Harper & Row.

—. 1952. *According to the Scriptures: The Sub-Structure of New Testament Theology.* London: Nisbet & Co.

Doering, Lutz. 2005. "Excerpted Texts in Second Temple Judaism. A Survey of the Evidence." Pages 1–38 in *Selecta colligere, II: Beiträge zur Technik des Sammelns und Kompilierens griechischer Texte von der Antike bis zum Humanismus.* Edited by Rosa Maria Piccione and Matthias Perkams. Alessandria: Edizioni dell-Orso.

Donfried, K. P., ed. 1991. *The Romans Debate.* 2nd ed. Peabody, MA: Hendrickson.

Döpke, Johann Christian Carl. 1829. *Hermeneutik der neutestamentlichen Schriftsteller.* Leipzig: Friedrich Christian Wilhelm Vogel.

du Toit, Andrie B. 2000. "A Tale of Two Cities: 'Tarsus or Jerusalem' Revisited." *NTS* 46: 375–402.

Duncan, George S. 1934. *The Epistle of Paul to the Galatians.* MNTC. New York and London: Harper and Brothers.

Duncan, Julie A. 1992. "Considerations of 4QDt^j in Light of the 'All Souls Deuteronomy' and Cave 4 Phylactery Texts." Pages 199–215 in vol. 1 of *The Madrid Qumran Congress. Proceedings of the International Congress on the Dead Sea Scrolls, Madrid 18–21 March 1991.* Edited by J. Trebolle Barrera and L. Vegas Montaner. 2 vols. STDJ 11. Leiden: Brill.

—. 1995. "New Readings for the 'Blessing of Moses' from Qumran." *JBL* 114: 273–90.

—. 1997. "Excerpted Texts of Deuteronomy at Qumran." *RevQ* 18: 43–62.

—. 2000. "Deuteronomy, Book of." *EDSS* 1:198–202.

Dunn, James D. G. 1988. *Romans.* 2 vols. WBC 38. Dallas: Word.

—. 2008a. [1985]. "Works of the Law and the Curse of the Law (Galatians 3.10–14)." Pages 121–40 in *The New Perspective on Paul.* Rev. ed. Grand Rapids: Eerdmans.

—. 2008b. [1997]. "4QMMT and Galatians." Pages 339–45 in *The New Perspective on Paul.* Rev. ed. Grand Rapids: Eerdmans.

—. 2008c. [2002]. "Noch einmal 'Works of the Law': The Dialogue Continues." Pages 413–28 in *The New Perspective on Paul.* Rev. ed. Grand Rapids: Eerdmans.

Eagleton, Terry. 2003. *After Theory.* New York: Basic.

Eastman, Susan. 2006. Review of F. Watson, *Paul and the Hermeneutics of Faith. JBL* 125: 610–14.

Eckstein, Hans Joachim. 1988. " 'Nahe ist dir das Wort'. Exegetische Erwägungen zu Röm 10,8." *ZNW* 79: 204–220.

Ego, Beate. 2005. "The Book of Tobit and the Diaspora." Pages 41–54 in *The Book of Tobit: Text, Tradition, Theology.* Edited by Géza G. Xeravits and József Zsengellér. JSJSup 98. Leiden and Boston: Brill.

Eissfeldt, Otto. 1965. *The Old Testament: An Introduction.* Translated by P. R. Ackroyd. New York and Evanston: Harper and Row.

Elbogen, Ismar. 1993. *Jewish Liturgy: A Comprehensive History.* Translated by Raymond P. Scheindlin. Based on the original 1913 German edition, and the 1972 Hebrew edition edited by Joseph Heinemann, et al. Philadelphia: The Jewish Publication Society.

Eleen, Luba. 1982. *The Illustration of the Pauline Epistles in French and English Bibles of the Twelfth and Thirteenth Centuries.* Oxford: Clarendon.

Elgvin, T. 2005. "The Yaḥad Is More Than Qumran." Pages 273–79 in Boccaccini 2005.

Ellis, E. Earle. 1957. *Paul's Use of the Old Testament.* London: Oliver and Boyd.

—. 1978. *Prophecy and Hermeneutic in Early Christianity.* WUNT 18. Tübingen: Mohr Siebeck.

Engberg-Pedersen, Troels. 2006. "Once More a Lutheran Paul?" *SJT* 59: 439–60.

Eshel, E. 1991. "4QDeut^n – a Text That Has Undergone Harmonistic Editing." *HUCA* 62: 117–154.

Eshel, H. 1992. "The Historical Background of the Pesher Interpreting Joshua's Curse on the Rebuilder of Jericho." *RevQ* 15: 409–20.

Esler, Philip F. 1998. *Galatians*. New Testament Readings. London and New York: Routledge.

Evans, Craig A. 2001. "Context, Family and Formation." Pages 11–24 in *The Cambridge Companion to Jesus*. Edited by Markus Bockmuehl. Cambridge: Cambridge University Press.

Fabry, Heinz-Josef. 1999. "Das Buch Levitikus in den Qumrantexten." Pages 309–43 in *Levitikus als Buch*. Edited by Heinz-Josef Fabry and Hans-Winfried Jüngling. BBB 119. Berlin and Bodenheim b. Manz: Philo.

—. 2000. "The Reception of the Book of Leviticus in Qumran." Pages 74–81 in *The Dead Sea Scrolls: Fifty Years After Their Discovery*. Edited by Lawrence H. Schiffman, Emanuel Tov and James C. VanderKam. Jerusalem: Israel Exploration Society.

Fagen, Ruth Satinover. 1992. "Phylacteries." *ABD* 5: 368–70.

Falk, Daniel K. 2007. *The Parabiblical Texts: Strategies for Extending the Scriptures Among the Dead Sea Scrolls*. LSTS 63. CQS 8. London: T. & T. Clark International.

Farrell, Thomas J. 1987. "Kelber's Breakthrough." *Semeia* 39: 27–45.

Fee, Gordon D. 1987. *The First Epistle to the Corinthians*. NICNT. Grand Rapids: Eerdmans.

Feldman, Louis H. 1971. "Prolegomenon." Pages ix–clxix in M. R. James, *The Biblical Antiquities of Philo*. New York: Ktav.

—. 1988. "Use, Authority and Exegesis of Mikra in the Writings of Josephus." Pages 445–518 in Mulder 1988.

—. 1998. *Josephus's Interpretation of the Bible*. Berkeley: University of California Press.

—. 2002. "The Death of Moses, according to Philo." *EstB* 60: 225–54.

Fernández Marcos, N. 1998. Review of É. Nodet, *Le Pentateuque de Flavius Josèphe*. *JSJ* 29: 110–13.

—. 2000. *The Septuagint in Context: Introduction to the Greek Versions of the Bible*. Translated by W. G. E. Watson. Leiden and Boston: Brill.

—. 2002. Review of Nina L. Collins, *The Library in Alexandria and the Bible in Greek*. *JSJ* 33: 97–101.

—. 2006. "Rewritten Bible or *Imitatio*? The Vestments of the High Priest." Pages 321–36 in *Studies in the Hebrew Bible, Qumran, and the Septuagint Presented to Eugene Ulrich*. Edited by Peter W. Flint, Emanuel Tov and James C. VanderKam. VTSup 101. Leiden and Boston: Brill.

Finsterbusch, K. 1996. *Die Thora als Lebensweisung für Heidenchristen: Studien zur Bedeutung der Thora für die paulinische Ethik*. SUNT, 20. Göttingen: Vandenhoeck & Ruprecht.

Fishbane, Michael. 1972. "Varia Deuteronomica." *ZAW* 84: 349–52.

—. 1985. *Biblical Interpretation in Ancient Israel*. Oxford: Clarendon.

Fisk, Bruce N. 2001. *Do You Not Remember?: Scripture, Story and Exegesis in the Rewritten Bible of Pseudo-Philo*. JSPSup 37. Sheffield: Sheffield Academic Press.

Fitzmyer, Joseph A. 1971. "'4QTestimonia' and the New Testament." Pages 59–89 in *Essays in the Semitic Background of the New Testament*. London G. Chapman. Originally published in *Theological Studies* 18 (1957): 513–37.

—. 1978. "Crucifixion in Ancient Palestine, Qumran Literature, and the New Testament." *CBQ* 40: 493–513.

—. 1979. "The Languages of Palestine in the First Century A.D." Pages 29–56 in *A Wandering Aramean: Collected Aramaic Essays*. SBLMS 25. Chico, CA: Scholars Press. Originally published in *CBQ* 32 (1970): 501–31.

—. 2000. "Qumran Messianism." Pages 73–100 in idem., *The Dead Sea Scrolls and Christian Origins*. Grand Rapids: Eerdmans.

—. 2003. *Tobit*. CEJL. Berlin and New York: de Gruyter.

Flesher, Paul V. M.. 2002. "Targum as Scripture." Pages 61–75 in *Targum and Scripture: Studies in Aramaic Translations and Interpretation in Memory of Ernest G. Clarke*. Edited by Paul V. M. Flesher. Studies in the Aramaic Interpretation of Scripture, 2. Leiden and Boston: Brill.

Ford, J. M. 1976. " 'Crucify Him, Crucify Him' and the Temple Scroll." *ExpTim* 87: 275–78.

Fox, G. G. 1942. "The Matthean Misrepresentation of *Tephillin*." *JNES* 1: 373–77.

Fraade, Steven D. 1991. *From Tradition to Commentary: Torah and Its Interpretation in the Midrash Sifre to Deuteronomy*. Albany: SUNY Press.

—. 1998. "Looking for Legal Midrash at Qumran." Pages 59–79 in *Biblical Perspectives: Early Use and Interpretation of the Bible in Light of the Dead Sea Scrolls*. Edited by Michael E. Stone and Esther G. Chazon. STDJ 28. Leiden: Brill.

—. 2005. "Deuteronomy in Sifre to Deuteronomy." Pages 54–59 in vol. 1 of *Encyclopedia of Biblical Midrash: Biblical Interpretation in Formative Judaism*. Edited by Jacob Neusner and Alan J. Avery-Peck. Leiden: Brill.

—. 2006a. "Deuteronomy and Polity in the Early History of Jewish Interpretation." *Cardozo Law Review* 28.1: 245–58.

—. 2006b. "Rewritten Bible and Rabbinic Midrash as Commentary." Pages 59–78 in *Current Trends in the Study of Midrash*. Edited by Carol Bakhos. JSJSup 106. Leiden and Boston: Brill.

—. 2007. "Rabbinic *Midrash* and Ancient Jewish Biblical Interpretation." Pages 99–120 in *The Cambridge Companion to the Talmud and Rabbinic Literature*. Edited by Charlotte Elisheva Fonrobert and Martin S. Jaffee. Cambridge: Cambridge University Press.

Freund, Richard A. 1989. "Murder, Adultery and Theft?" *SJOT* 2:72–80.

Fridrichsen, Anton. 1994. [1922]. "Der wahre Jude und sein Lob: Röm 2:28f." Pages 186–94 in *Exegetical Writings. A Selection*. Translated and edited by C. C. Cargounis and T. Fornberg. WUNT 76. Tübingen: Mohr Siebeck.

Fung, Ronald Y. K. 1988. *The Epistle to the Galatians*. NICNT. Grand Rapids: Eerdmans.

Furnish, V. P. 1968. *Theology and Ethics in Paul*. Nashville and New York: Abingdon.

—. 1984. *II Corinthians*. AB 32A. New York: Doubleday.

Gadamer, Hans-Georg. 1989. *Truth and Method*. 2nd ed. Revised translation by Joel Weinsheimer and Donald G. Marshall from the 5th German edition of *Wahrheit und Methode* in vol. 1 of Gadamer's *Gesammelte Werke*. New York and London: Continuum.

—. 2006. "Classical and Philosophical Hermeneutics." *Theory, Culture and Society*. 23: 29–56.

Gamble, Harry Y. 1977. *The Textual History of the Letter to the Romans: A Study in Textual and Literary Criticism*. SD 42. Grand Rapids: Eerdmans.

—. 1995. *Books and Readers in the Early Church: A History of Early Christian Texts.* New Haven and London: Yale University Press.

García Martínez, F. 1988. "Qumran Origins and Early History: A Groningen Hypothesis." *FO* 25: 113–36.

—. 1994. "Les manuscripts du desert de Juda et le Deutéronome." Pages 63–82 in *Studies in Deuteronomy.* Edited by F. García Martínez, et al. VTSup 53. Leiden: Brill.

—. 1995. "The Origins of the Essene Movement and of the Qumran Sect." Pages 77–96, 239–49 in *The People of the Dead Sea Scrolls: Their Writings, Beliefs and Practices.* By F. García Martínez and J. Trebolle Barrera. Translated by W. G. E. Watson. Leiden, New York, Cologne: Brill.

—. 2007. *Qumranica Minora I: Qumran Origins and Apocalypticism.* Edited by E. J. C. Tigchelaar. STDJ 63. Leiden and Boston: Brill.

—. and A. S. van der Woude. 1990. "A 'Groningen' Hypothesis of Qumran Origins and Early History." *RevQ* 14: 521–41.

Garland, David E. 2003. *1 Corinthians.* BECNT. Grand Rapids: Baker.

Gathercole, Simon J. 2002. "A Law unto Themselves: The Gentiles in Romans 2.14–15 Revisited." *JSNT* 85: 27–49.

Gavrilov, A. K. 1997. "Techniques of Reading in Classical Antiquity." *CQ* 47: 56–73.

Gerhardsson, Birger. 1996. *The Shema in the New Testament: Deut. 6:4–5 in Significant Passages.* Lund: Nova.

—. 1998. *Memory and Manuscript: Oral Tradition and Written Transmission in Rabbinic Judaism and Early Christianity* with *Tradition and Transmission in Early Christianity.* BRS. Grand Rapids: Eerdmans. Originally 1961 and 1964 respectively.

Gilliard, Frank D. 1993. "More Silent Reading in Antiquity: *Non Omne Verbum Sonabat.*" *JBL* 112: 689–94.

Gnilka, Joachim. 1998. "Zur Interpretation der Bibel: die Wirkungsgeschichte." Pages 1589–1601 in *The Interpretation of the Bible: The International Symposium in Slovenia.* JSOTSup 289. Sheffield: Sheffield Academic Press.

Goldenberg, D. 1976–77. "The Halakha in Josephus and in Tannaitic Literature: A Comparative Study." *JQR* 67: 30–43.

—. 1980. "Flavius Josephus or Josef ben Mattithiah." *JQR* 70: 178–82.

Goldstein, Jonathan A. 1976. *I Maccabees: A New Translation with Introduction and Commentary.* AB 41. Garden City, NY: Doubleday.

—. 1983. *II Maccabees: A New Translation with Introduction and Commentary.* AB 41A. Garden City, NY: Doubleday.

Goodacre, Mark S. 1996. *Goulder and the Gospels: An Examination of a New Paradigm.* JSNTSup 133. Sheffield: Sheffield Academic Press.

Goodenough, Erwin R. 1933. "Philo's Exposition of the Law and His De Vita Mosis." *HTR* 26: 109–25.

—. 1953–68. *Jewish Symbols in the Greco-Roman Period.* 13 vols. New York: Pantheon.

—. 1962. *An Introduction to Philo Judaeus.* 2nd ed. Oxford: Basil Blackwell.

Goodman, M. D. 1994. "Texts, Scribes and Power in Roman Judaea." Pages 99–108 in *Literacy and Power in the Ancient World.* Edited by Alan K. Bowman and Greg Woolf. Cambridge: Cambridge University Press.

Goody, Jack. 1986. *The Logic of Writing and the Organization of Society.* Cambridge: Cambridge University Press.

Gough, H. 1855. *The New Testament quotations, collated with the Scriptures of the Old Testament, in the original Hebrew and the version of the LXX; and with the other writ-*

ings, Apocryphal, Talmudic, and classical, cited or alleged so to be. London: Walton and Maberly.

Goulder, M. D. 1974. *Midrash and Lection in Matthew.* London: SPCK.

Grabbe, L. L. 1988. "Synagogues in pre-70 Palestine: A Re-Assessment." *JTS* 39: 401–10.

Graham, William A. 1987. *Beyond the Written Word: Oral Aspects of Scripture in the History of Religion.* Cambridge: Cambridge University Press.

Gräßer, Erich. 2006. "Noch einmal: 'Kümmert sich Gott etwa um die Ochsen?'." *ZNW* 97: 275–79.

Graves, Michael. 2007. "The Public Reading of Scripture in Early Judaism." *JETS* 50: 467–87.

Greenspoon, L. 1998. "The Dead Sea Scrolls and the Greek Bible." Pages 101–27 in vol. 1 of *The Dead Sea Scrolls after Fifty Years: A Comprehensive Assessment.* Edited by P. W. Flint and J. C. VanderKam. 2 vols. Leiden, Boston, Köln: Brill.

Greenstone, Julius H. 1905. "Phylacteries: Legal View." *JE* 10: 21–26.

Grierson, Fiona. 2008. "The Testament of Moses." *JSP* 17: 265–80.

Guerra, Anthony J. 1995. *Romans and the Apologetic Tradition: The Purpose, Genre and Audience of Paul's Letter.* SNTSMS 81. Cambridge: Cambridge University Press.

Guilding, Aileen. 1960. *The Fourth Gospel and Jewish Worship: A Study of the Relation of St. John's Gospel to the Ancient Jewish Lectionary System.* Oxford: Clarendon.

Gundry, Robert H. 2005. "The Moral Frustration of Paul before His Conversion: Sexual Lust in Romans 7:7–25." Pages 252–71 in *The Old is Better: New Testament Essays in Support of Traditional Interpretations.* WUNT 178. Tübingen: Mohr Siebeck.

Gunneweg, Antonius H. J. 1975. "Das Buch Baruch." Pages 165–81 in *JSHRZ* III/2. Gütersloh: Gütersloher Verlagshaus.

Haacker, K. 1997. *Paulus. Der Werdegang eines Apostels.* SBS 171. Stuttgart: Verlag Katholisches Bibelwerk.

—. and P. Schäfer, 1974. "Nachbiblische Traditionen vom Tod des Mose." Pages 147–74 in *Josephus-Studien. Untersuchungen zu Josephus, dem antiken Judentum und dem Neuen Testament. Otto Michel zum 70. Geburtstag gewidmet.* Edited by Otto Betz, Klaus Haacker and Martin Hengel. Göttingen: Vandenhoeck & Ruprecht.

Habicht, C. 1976. *2 Makkabäerbuch.* JSHRZ I/3. Gütersloh: Gütersloher Verlagshaus.

Hachlili, Rachel. 1976. "The Niche and Ark in Ancient Synagogues." *BASOR* 223: 43–53.

—. 1988. *Ancient Jewish Art and Archaeology in the Land of Israel.* HO VII: Kunst und Archäologie 1.2.B.4. Leiden: Brill.

Hafemann, S. J. 1990. "Moses in the Apocrypha and the Pseudepigrapha." *JSP* 7: 79–104.

Häfner, Gerd. 2007. "Deuteronomy in the Pastoral Epistles." Pages 136–51 in Moyise and Menken 2007.

Hall, David R. 2003. *The Unity of the Corinthian Correspondence.* JSNTSup 251. London and New York: T. & T. Clark.

Halverson, John. 1992. "Goody and the Implosion of the Literacy Thesis." *Man* n.s. 27: 301–17.

—. 1994. "Oral and Written Gospel: A Critique of Werner Kelber." *NTS* 40: 180–95.

Hammer, Reuven. 1991. "What Did They Bless? A Study of Mishnah Tamid 5.1." *JQR* 81: 305–24.

Hanhart, R. 1984. "Die Bedeutung der Septuaginta in neutestamentlicher Zeit." *ZTK* 81: 395–416.

Hanson, Anthony Tyrrell. 1974. *Studies in Paul's Technique and Theology*. Grand Rapids: Eerdmans.

Harl, M. 1993. "Le grand cantique de Moïse en Deutéronome 32: quelques traits originaux de la version grecque des Septante." Pages 183–201 in *Rashi, 1040–1990: Hommage à Ephraim E. Urbach*. Edited by G. Sed-Rajna. Paris: Cerf.

—. 1995. "L'originalité lexicale de la version grecque du Deutéronome (LXX) et la 'paraphrase' de Flavius Josèphe (AJ IV 176–331)." Pages 1–20 in *VIII Congress of the International Organization for Septuagint and Cognate Studies*. Atlanta: Scholars Press.

Harnack, Adolf von. 1912. *Bible Reading in the Early Church*. Trans. J. R. Wilkinson. Crown Theological Library 36. London: Williams & Norgate.

—. 1995. "The Old Testament in the Pauline Letters and in the Pauline Churches." Pages 27–49 in Rosner 1995. ET of "Das Alte Testament in den paulinischen Briefen und in den paulinischen Gemeinden." *Sitzungsberichte der Preußischen Akademie der Wissenschaften* (1928): 124–41.

Harrington, Daniel J. 1970. "The Original Language of Pseudo-Philo's *Liber Antiquitatum Biblicarum*." *HTR* 63: 503–14.

—. 1971. "The Biblical Text of Pseudo-Philo's 'Liber Antiquitatum Biblicarum'." *CBQ* 33: 1–11.

—. 1973. "Interpreting Israel's History: The Testament of Moses as a Rewriting of Deut 31–34." Pages 59–70 in *Studies on the Testament of Moses*. Edited by G. W. E. Nickelsburg. SBLSCS 4. Cambridge, MA: Harvard University Press.

—. and Maurya P. Horgan. 1986. "Palestinian Adaptations of Biblical Narratives and Prophecies." Pages 239–58 in *Early Judaism and Its Modern Interpreters*. Edited by Robert A. Kraft and G. W. E. Nickelsburg. Philadelphia: Fortress. Atlanta: Scholars.

Harris, William V. 1989. *Ancient Literacy*. Cambridge, Mass: Harvard University Press.

Hatina, Thomas R. 1999. "Intertextuality and Historical Criticism in New Testament Studies: Is There a Relationship?" *BibInt* 7: 28–43.

Hay, David. 1991. "References to Other Exegetes." Pages 81–97 in *Both Literal and Allegorical. Studies in Philo of Alexandria's Questions and Answers on Genesis and Exodus*. Edited by D. M. Hay. Atlanta: Scholars Press.

Hays, Richard B. 1989. *Echoes of Scripture in the Letters of Paul*. New Haven: Yale University Press.

—. 1996. "The Role of Scripture in Paul's Ethics." Pages 30–47 in *Theology and Ethics in Paul and His Interpreters*. Edited by E. H. Lovering, Jr. and J. L. Sumney. Nashville: Abingdon Press. Repr. in Hays 2005: 143–62.

—. 2005. *The Conversion of the Imagination: Paul as Interpreter of Israel's Scripture*. Grand Rapids: Eerdmans.

—. 2007. "Paul's Hermeneutics and the Question of Truth." *ProEccl* 16: 126–33.

Hecht, Richard D. 1981. "Scripture and Commentary in Philo." Pages 129–64 in *The Society of Biblical Literature 1981 Seminar Papers*. SBLSP 20. Chico, CA: Scholars.

Heil, John Paul. 2005. *The Rhetorical Role of Scripture in 1 Corinthians*. Studies in Biblical Literature 15. Leiden: Brill.

Heinemann, J. 1968. "The Triennial Lectionary Cycle." *JJS* 19: 41–48.

Hempel, Charlotte. 1998. *The Laws of the Damascus Document: Sources, Tradition and Redaction*. STDJ 29. Leiden: Brill.

Hendrickson, G. L. 1929. "Ancient Reading." *CJ* 25: 182–96.

Hengel, Martin. 1971. "Proseuche und Synagoge. Jüdische Gemeinde, Gotteshaus und Gottesdienst in der Diaspora und in Palästina." Pages 157–84 in *Tradition und*

Glaube: Festgabe für Karl Georg Kuhn zum 65. Geburtstag. Edited by G. Jeremias, H.-W. Kuhn and H. Stegemann. Göttingen: Vandenhoeck & Ruprecht. Reprinted as pages 171–95 in his *Judaica et Hellenistica: Kleine Schriften I.* WUNT 90. Tübingen: Mohr Siebeck, 1996.

—. 1974. *Judaism and Hellenism: Studies in their Encounter in Palestine during the Early Hellenistic Period.* 2 vols. Translated by John Bowden. Philadelphia: Fortress. Reprinted: Eugene, OR: Wipf and Stock, 2003.

—. 1977. *Crucifixion In the Ancient World and the Folly of the Message of the Cross.* Translated by John Bowden. Philadelphia: Fortress.

—. 1983. "Between Jesus and Paul: The 'Hellenists', the 'Seven' and Stephen (Acts 6.1–15; 7.54–8.3)." Pages 1–29, 133–56 in *Between Jesus and Paul: Studies in the Earliest History of Christianity.* Translated by John Bowden. London: SCM Press.

—. 1989. *The 'Hellenization' of Judaea in the First Century After Christ.* Translated by J. Bowden. London: SCM and Philadelphia: Trinity Press International.

—. 2005. "The Beginning of Christianity as a Jewish-Messianic and Universalistic Movement." Pages 85–100 in *The Beginnings of Christianity.* Edited by Jack Pastor and Menachem Mor. Jerusalem: Yad Ben-Zvi Press.

—. in collaboration with Roland Deines. 1991. *The Pre-Christian Paul.* Translated by J. Bowden. London: SCM and Philadelphia: Trinity Press International.

—. and Anna Maria Schwemer. 1997. *Paul Between Damascus and Antioch: The Unknown Years.* Translated by J. Bowden. Louisville: Westminster John Knox.

Héring, Jean. 1958. *La seconde Épitre de Saint Paul aux Corinthiens.* CNT 8. Neuchâtel and Paris: Delachaux & Niestlé.

—. 1959. *La première Épitre de Saint Paul aux Corinthiens.* 2nd ed. CNT 7. Neuchâtel and Paris: Delachaux & Niestlé.

Hezser, Catherine. 1997. *The Social Structure of the Rabbinic Movement in Roman Palestine.* TSAJ 66. Tübingen: Mohr Siebeck.

—. 2001. *Jewish Literacy in Roman Palestine.* TSAJ 81. Tübingen: Mohr Siebeck.

Himbaza, Innocent. 2002. "Le Décalogue de Papyrus Nash, Philon, 4QPhyl G, 8QPhyl 3 et 4QMez." *RevQ* 79: 411–28.

Hock, Ronald F. 2003. "Paul and Greco-Roman Education." Pages 198–227 in *Paul in the Greco-Roman World: A Handbook.* Edited by J. Paul Sampley. Harrisburg, London and New York: Trinity Press International.

Hody, Humphrey. 1705. *De bibliorum textibus originalibus.* Oxford: Oxford University Press.

Hofius, Otfried. 2002a. " 'Einer ist Gott – Einer ist Herr': Erwägungen zu Struktur und Aussage des Bekenntnisses 1 Kor 8,6." Pages 167–80 in his *Paulusstudien II.* WUNT 143. Tübingen: Mohr Siebeck.

—. 2002b. "Christus als Schöpfungsmittler und Erlösungsmittler: Das Bekenntnis 1 Kor 8,6 im Kontext der paulinischen Theologie." Pages 181–92 in his *Paulusstudien II.* WUNT 143. Tübingen: Mohr Siebeck.

Hofmann, Norbert Johannes. 2000. *Die Assumptio Mosis: Studien zur Rezeption massgültiger Überlieferung.* JSJSup 67. Leiden: Brill.

—. 2003. "Die Rezeption des Dtn im Buch Tobit, in der Assumptio Mosis und im 4. Esrabuch." Pages 311–42 in *Das Deuteronomium.* Edited by George Braulik. Österreichische Biblische Studien 23. Frankfurt am Main: Peter Lang.

Holtz, T. 1995. "The Question of the Content of Paul's Instructions." Pages 51–71 in Rosner 1995. ET of "Zur Frage der inhaltlichen Weisungen bei Paulus." *TLZ* 106 (1981): 385–400.

Hooker, Morna. 1975. "In His Own Image?" Pages 28–44 in *What About the New Testament? Essays in Honour of Christopher Evans*. Edited by Morna Hooker and Colin Hickling. London: SCM.

Hopkins, Keith. 1991. "Conquest by Book." Pages 133–58 in *Literacy in the Roman World*. Edited by J. H. Humphrey. Journal of Roman Archaeology Supplementary Series 3. Ann Arbor, MI: University of Michigan Press.

Horbury, William. 1985. "Extirpation and Excommunication." *VT* 35: 13–38. Reprinted as pages 43–66 in his *Jews and Christians in Contact and Controversy*. Edinburgh: T. & T. Clark, 1998.

—. 1997. "Septuagintal and New Testament Conceptions of the Church." Pages 1–17 in *A Vision for the Church: Studies in Early Christian Ecclesiology*. Edited by M. Bockmuehl and M. B. Thompson. Edinburgh: T&T Clark. Reprinted as pages 255–72 in his *Messianism Among Jews and Christians: Biblical and Historical Studies*. London: T&T Clark, 2003.

—. 2000. Review of Birger Gerhardsson, *The Shema in the New Testament: Deut. 6:4–5 in Significant Passages*. *JTS* 51: 239–41.

—. 2003. "Moses and the Covenant in *The Assumption of Moses* and the Pentateuch." Pages 191–208 in *Covenant as Context: Essays in Honour of E. W. Nicholson*. Edited by A. D. H. Mayes and R. B. Salters. Oxford: Oxford University Press. Reprinted as pages 34–46 in his *Herodian Judaism and New Testament Study*. WUNT 193. Tübingen: Mohr Siebeck.

Horrell, David G. 1996. *The Social Ethos of the Corinthian Correspondence: Interests and Ideology from 1 Corinthians to 1 Clement*. SNTW. Edinburgh: T. & T. Clark.

Horsley, Richard A. 1998. *1 Corinthians*. ANTC. Nashville: Abingdon.

Howard, George E. 1973. "The 'Aberrant' Text of Philo's Quotations Reconsidered." *HUCA* 44: 197–209.

Hübner, Hans. 1973. "Gal 3,10 und die Herkunft des Paulus." *KD* 19: 215–31.

—. 1984. *Gottes Ich und Israel. Zum Schriftgebrauch des Paulus in Römer 9–11*. FRLANT 136. Göttingen: Vandenhoeck and Ruprecht.

—. 1993. *Die Theologie des Paulus und ihre neutestamentliche Wirkungsgeschichte*. Band 2 of *Biblische Theologie des Neuen Testament*. Göttingen: Vandenhoeck and Ruprecht.

Hughes, Philip Edgcumbe. 1962. *Paul's Second Epistle to the Corinthians*. NICNT. Grand Rapids: Eerdmans.

Hurtado, Larry W. 1988. *One God, One Lord: Early Christian Devotion and Ancient Jewish Monotheism*. Philadelphia: Fortress.

—. 1997. "Greco-Roman Textuality and the Gospel of Mark: A Critical Assessment of Werner Kelber's *The Oral and the Written Gospel*." *BBR* 7: 91–106.

—. 2006. *The Earliest Christian Artifacts: Manuscripts and Christian Origins*. Grand Rapids: Eerdmans.

Hüttenmeister, G. 1977. *Die antiken Synagogen in Israel. Teil 1: Die jüdischen Synagogen, Lehrhäuser und Gerichtshöfe*. Wiesbaden: L. Reichert.

Hvalvik, Reidar. 2006. "Christ Proclaiming His Law to the Apostles: The *Traditio Legis*-Motif in Early Christian Art and Literature." Pages 405–37 in *The New Testament and Early Christian Literature in Greco-Roman Context: Studies in Honor of David E. Aune*. Edited by John Fotopoulos. NovTSup 122. Leiden and Boston: Brill.

Inowlocki, Sabrina. 2005. "'Neither Adding nor Omitting Anything': Josephus' Promise not to Modify the Scriptures in Greek and Latin Context." *JJS* 56: 48–65.

Instone Brewer, David. 1992. "1 Corinthians 9.9–11: A Literal Interpretation of 'Do Not Muzzle the Ox'." *NTS* 38: 554–65.

Irwin, William. 2004. "Against Intertextuality." *Philosophy and Literature* 28: 227–42.

Ito, A. 1995. "Romans 2: A Deuteronomistic Reading." *JSNT* 59: 21–37

Jacobson, Howard. 1989. "Biblical Quotation and Editorial Function in Pseudo-Philo's *Liber Antiquitatum Biblicarum*." *JSP* 5: 47–64.

—. 1994. Review of *Pseudo-Philo. Rewriting the Bible* by F. J. Murphy. *JJS* 45: 302–311.

Jaffee, Martin S. 1994. "Figuring Early Rabbinic Literary Culture: Thoughts Occasioned by Boomershine and J. Dewey." *Semeia* 65: 67–73.

Jellicoe, S. 1968. *The Septuagint and Modern Study*. Oxford: Clarendon.

Jeremias, J. 1964. "ἄβυσσος." *TDNT* 1.9–10.

—. 1969a. "Paulus als Hillelit." Pages 88–94 in *Neotestamentica et Semitica: Studies in Honour of Matthew Black*. Edited by E. E. Ellis and M. Wilcox. Edinburgh: T. & T. Clark.

—. 1969b. *Jerusalem in the Time of Jesus: An Investigation into Economic and Social Conditions during the New Testament Period*. Translated by F. H. and C. H. Cave. London: SCM.

Jewett, Robert. 2007. *Romans: A Commentary*. Hermeneia. Minneapolis: Fortress.

Johnson, William A. 1994. "The Function of the Paragraphus in Greek Literary Prose Texts." *ZPE* 100: 65–68.

Kahana, Menahem. 2002. "The Tannaitic Midrashim." Pages 59–73 in *The Cambridge Genizah Collections: Their Contents and Significance*. Edited by Stefan C. Reif. Cambridge: Cambridge University Press.

Kahle, Paul. 1959. *The Cairo Geniza*. 2nd ed. Oxford: Basil Blackwell.

Kaiser, W. 1978. "The Current Crisis in Exegesis and the Apostolic Use of Deuteronomy 25:4 in 1 Corinthians 9:8–10." *JETS* 21: 3–18.

Kamesar, Adam. 1997. "The Literary Genres of the Pentateuch as Seen from the Greek Perspective: The Testimony of Philo of Alexandria." *SPhilo* 9: 143–89.

Kamlah, E. 1974. "Frömmigkeit und Tugend. Die Gesetzesapologie des Josephus in cAp II, 145–295." Pages 220–32 in *Josephus-Studien. Untersuchungen zu Josephus, dem antiken Judentum und dem Neuen Testament. Otto Michel zum 70. Geburtstag gewidmet*. Edited by Otto Betz, Klaus Haacker and Martin Hengel. Göttingen: Vandenhoeck & Ruprecht.

Kant, L. H. 1987. "Jewish Inscriptions in Greek and Latin." Pages 671–713 in *ANRW* 2.20.2. Edited by W. Haase. Berlin and New York: de Gruyter.

Käsemann, Ernst. 1969. "Sentences of Holy Law in the New Testament." Pages 66–81 in *New Testament Questions of Today*. Philadelphia: Fortress.

—. 1980. *Commentary on Romans*. Translated by G. W. Bromiley. Grand Rapids: Eerdmans.

Katz, Peter. 1950. *Philo's Bible. The Aberrant Text of Bible Quotations in Some Philonic Writings and Its Place in the Textual History of the Greek Bible*. Cambridge: Cambridge University Press.

Kaufman, Stephen A. 1985. "On Methodology in the Study of the Targums and their Chronology." *JSNT* 23: 117–24.

Kedar, Benjamin. 1988. "The Latin Translations." Pages 299–338 in Mulder 1988.

Kee, H. C. 1990. "The Transformation of the Synagogue After 70 C.E.: Its Import for Early Christianity." *NTS* 36: 1–24.

—. 1994. "The Changing Meaning of Synagogue: A Response to Richard Oster." *NTS* 40: 281–83.

—. 1995. "Defining the First-Century CE Synagogue: Problems and Progress." *NTS* 41: 481–500.

Kelber, Werner H. 1987. "Biblical Hermeneutics and the Ancient Art of Communication: A Response." *Semeia* 39: 97–105.

—. 1997. *The Oral and the Written Gospel: The Hermeneutics of Speaking and Writing in the Synoptic Tradition, Mark, Paul, and Q*. Bloomington and Indianapolis: Indiana University Press. Originally Minneapolis: Fortress, 1983.

Kellermann, Ulrich. 2001. "Der Dekalog in den Schriften des Frühjudentums: Ein Überblick." Pages 147–226 in *Weisheit, Ethos und Gebot: Weisheits- und Dekalogtraditionen in der Bibel und im frühen Judentum*. Edited by Henning Graf Reventlow. Biblisch-theologische Studien 43. Neukirchen-Vluyn: Neukirchener.

Kelsey, David H. 1999. *Proving Doctrine: The Uses of Scripture in Modern Theology*. Harrisburg, PA: Trinity Press International. Originally 1975.

Kenyon, Frederic G. 1951. *Books and Readers in Ancient Greece and Rome*. 2nd ed. Oxford: Clarendon.

Kiel, Micah D. 2008. "Tobit and Moses Redux." *JSP* 17: 83–98.

Kilpatrick, G. D. 1971. "The Cairo Papyrus of Genesis and Deuteronomy (P. F. Inv. 266)." *EPap* 9: 221–26.

Klauser, Theodor. 1966. *Frühchristliche Sarkophage in Bild und Wort*. Beiheft zur Halbjahresschrift Antike Kunst 3. Olten: Urs Grav-Verlag.

Klein, R. W. 1973. "The Text of Deuteronomy Employed in the Testament of Moses." Page 78 in *Studies on the Testament of Moses*. Edited by G. W. E. Nickelsburg. SCS 4. Cambridge, MA: Harvard University Press.

Klijn, A. F. J. 1977. "A Library of Scriptures in Jerusalem?" *TU* 124: 265–72.

Kloppenborg Verbin, John S. 2000. "Dating Theodotus (*CIJ* II 1404)." *JJS* 51: 243–80.

Knibb, Michael A. 1976. "The Exile in the Literature of the Intertestamental Period." *HeyJ* 17: 253–79.

—. 1987. *The Qumran Community*. Cambridge Commentaries on Writings of the Jewish and Christian World 200 BC to AD 200, 2. Cambridge: Cambridge University Press.

Knight, G. A. F. 1995. *The Song of Moses: A Theological Quarry*. Grand Rapids: Eerdmans.

Knox, B. M. W. 1968. "Silent Reading in Antiquity." *GRBS* 9: 421–35.

—. and P. E. Easterling. 1985. "Books and Readers in the Greek World." Pages 1–41 in *The Cambridge History of Classical Literature I: Greek Literature*. Edited by P. E. Easterling and B. M. W. Knox. Cambridge: Cambridge University Press.

Knox, W. L. 1940. "A Note on Philo's Use of the Old Testament." *JTS* 41: 30–34.

Koch, Dietrich-Alex. 1986. *Die Schrift als Zeuge des Evangeliums: Untersuchungen zur Verwendung und zum Verständnis der Schrift bei Paulus*. BHT 69. Tübingen: Mohr Siebeck.

Kolenkow, Anitra Bingham. 1973. "The Assumption of Moses as a Testament." Pages 71–77 in Nickelsburg 1973.

Kooij, Arie van der. 1994. "The Ending of the Song of Moses: On the Pre-Masoretic Version of Deut 32:43." Pages 93–100 In *Studies in Deuteronomy. In Honour of C. J. Labuschagne*. Edited by F. García Martínez, A. Hilhorst, J. T. A. G. M. van Ruiten, and A. S. van der Woude. VTSup 53. Leiden: Brill.

Korpel, Marjo C. A. 2000. "Introduction to the Series Pericope." Pages 1–50 in *Delimitation Criticism: A New Tool in Biblical Scholarship*. Edited by Marjo C. A. Korpel and

Josef M. Oesch. Pericope: Scripture as Written and Read in Antiquity 1. Assen: Van Gorcum.

Kraabel, A. T. 1979. "The Diaspora Synagogue: Archaeological and Epigraphic Evidence since Sukenik." Pages 477–510 in *ANRW* 2.19.1. Berlin and New York: de Gruyter.

Kraft, Robert A. 2002. "Exploring Early Jewish Greek Literary Practices." Pages 673–76 in *Bible and Computer: The Stellenbosch AIBI-6 Conference*. Edited by Johann Cook. Leiden and Boston: Brill.

—. 2003. "The 'Textual Mechanics' of Early Jewish LXX/OG Papyri and Fragments." Pages 51–72 in *The Bible as Book: The Transmission of the Greek Text*. Edited by S. McKendrick and O. A. O'Sullivan. London: The British Library and Oak Knoll Press in Association with The Scriptorium: Center for Christian Antiquities.

—. 2005. "Philo's Bible Revisited: The 'Aberrant Texts' and Their Quotations of Moses." Pages 237–53 in *Interpreting Translation: Studies on the LXX and Ezekiel in Honour of Johan Lust*. Edited by F. García Martínez and M. Vervenne. Bibliotheca ephemeridum theologicarum lovaniensium 192. Leuven: Leuven University Press.

—. 2007. "Files and Information on Early Jewish and Early Christian Copies of Greek Jewish Scriptures." http://ccat.sas.upenn.edu/rs/rak/jewishpap.html. Accessed 3 June 2009.

Kristeva, Julia. 1969. *Semeiotikè: Recherches pour une Sémanalyse*. Paris: Éditions du Seuil.

—. 1974. *La révolution du langage poétique*. Paris: Éditions du Seuil.

—. 1980. *Desire in Language: A Semiotic Approach to Literature and Art*. Oxford: Basil Blackwell.

—. 1984. *Revolution in Poetic Language*. Translated by Margaret Waller. New York: Columbia University Press.

—. 1986. *The Kristeva Reader*. Edited by Toril Moi. Oxford: Basil Blackwell.

Lagrange, M.-J. 1950a. *Saint Paul, Épitre aux Galates*. 2nd ed. Études bibliques. Paris: Gabalda. Originally 1925.

—. 1950b. *Saint Paul, Épitre aux Romains*. Études Bibliques. Paris: Gabalda. Originally 1931.

Lambert, David. 2006. "Did Israel Believe that Redemption Awaited Its Repentance? The Case of *Jubilees* 1." *CBQ* 68: 631–50.

Lang, Friedrich. 1994. *Die Briefe an die Korinther*. NTD 7. Göttingen and Zürich: Vandenhoeck & Ruprecht.

Lange, Armin. 2006. "The Qumran Dead Sea Scrolls – Library or Manuscript Corpus?" Pages 177–93 in *From 4QMMT to Resurrection: Mélanges qumraniens en homage à Émile Puech*. Edited by F. García Martínez, A. Steudel and E. Tigchelaar. STDJ 61. Leiden and Boston: Brill.

Laubscher, F. du Toit. 1980. "Notes on the Literary Structure of 1QS 2:11–18 and its Biblical Parallel in Deut. 29." *JNSL* 8: 49–55.

Leaney, A. R. C. 1966. *The Rule of Qumran and Its Meaning: Introduction, Translation and Commentary*. NTL. London: SCM.

—. 1976. "Greek Manuscripts from the Judaean Desert." Pages 283–300 in *Studies in New Testament Language and Text: Essays in Honour of George D. Kilpatrick on the Occasion of His Sixty-Fifth Birthday*. Edited by J. K. Elliott. NovTSup 44. Leiden: Brill.

Leenhardt, F.-J. 1957. *L'épitre de Saint Paul aux Romains*. CNT 6. Neuchâtel and Paris: Delachaux & Niestlé.

Légasse, S. 1995. "Paul's Pre-Christian Career According to Acts." Pages 365–90 in *The Book of Acts in Its Palestinian Setting*. Edited by R. Bauckham. Vol. 4 of *The Book of Acts in Its First Century Setting*. Grand Rapids and Carlisle: Eerdmans and Paternoster.

Lentz, J. C. 1993. *Luke's Portrait of Paul*. SNTSMS 77. Cambridge: Cambridge University Press.

Leonhardt, Jutta. 2001. *Jewish Worship in Philo of Alexandria*. TSAJ 84. Tübingen: Mohr Siebeck.

Levine, B. A. 1973. "Damascus Document IX, 17–22: A New Translation and Comments." *RevQ* 8: 195–96.

Levine, Etain B. 1978. "Anexo III: Parallels to Deuteronomy of Pseudo-Jonathan and Neophyti 1." Pages 575–629 in Alejandro Díez Macho, *Neophyti 1: Targum Palestinense MS de la Biblioteca Vaticana, Tomo V: Deuteronomio*. Madrid: Consejo Superior de Investigaciones Científicas.

Levine, Lee I., ed. 1981. *Ancient Synagogues Revealed*. Jerusalem: Israel Exploration Society.

—. 1987. "The Second Temple Synagogue: The Formative Years." Pages 7–31 in *The Synagogue in Late Antiquity*. Edited by Lee I. Levine. Philadelphia: American Schools of Oriental Research.

—. 2005. *The Ancient Synagogue: The First Thousand Years*. 2nd ed. New Haven and London: Yale University Press.

Levinson, Bernard M. 1997. *Deuteronomy and the Hermeneutics of Legal Innovation*. Oxford and New York: Oxford University Press.

Lichtenberger, H. 2004. *Das Ich Adams und das Ich der Menschheit: Studien zum Menschenbild in Römer 7*. WUNT 164. Tübingen: Mohr Siebeck.

Lierman, John. 2004. *The New Testament Moses: Christian Perceptions of Moses and Israel in the Setting of Jewish Religion*. WUNT 2/173. Tübingen: Mohr Siebeck.

Lietzmann, Hans. 1949. *An die Korinther I/II*. 4th ed. HNT. Tübingen: Mohr Siebeck.

—. 1971. *An die Galater*. 4th ed. HNT 10. Tübingen: Mohr Siebeck.

Lim, Timothy H. 1991. "Attitudes to Holy Scripture in the Qumran Pesharim and Pauline Letters." D.Phil. Thesis. University of Oxford.

—. 1993. "The Wicked Priests of the Groningen Hypothesis." *JBL* 112: 415–25.

—. 1997. *Holy Scripture in the Qumran Commentaries and Pauline Letters*. Oxford: Clarendon.

—. 2007. "Deuteronomy in the Judaism of the Second Temple Period." Pages 6–26 in Moyise and Menken 2007.

Lincicum, David. 2006. Review of Christopher D. Stanley, *Arguing with Scripture: The Rhetoric of Quotations in the Letters of Paul*. *JETS* 49: 429–31.

—. 2008a. "Paul's Engagement with Deuteronomy: Snapshots and Signposts." *CBR* 7: 37–67.

—. 2008b. "Scripture and Apotropaism in the Second Temple Period." *BN* 138: 63–87.

—. 2008c. "Paul and the *Testimonia*: Quo Vadimus?" *JETS* 51: 297–308.

—. 2008d. "The Epigraphic Habit and the Biblical Text: Inscriptions as a Source for the Study of the Greek Bible." *BIOSCS* 41: 84–92.

—. 2009. "Paul and the Temple Scroll: Reflections on a Shared Engagement with Deuteronomy." *Neot* 43: 69–92. Also to appear in *"What Does the Scripture Say?" Studies in the Function of Scripture in the Gospels and Letters of Paul*. Edited by C. A. Evans and D. Zacharias. SSEJC 16. London and New York: T. & T. Clark, 2010.

Lindemann, Andreas. 2000. *Der Erste Korintherbrief.* HNT 9/1. Tübingen: Mohr Siebeck.

Lipton, Sara. 1999. *Images of Intolerance: The Representation of Jews and Judaism in the* Bible moralisée. Berkeley and Los Angeles: University of California Press.

Llewelyn, S. R. 1994. "The Development of the Codex." Pages 249–56 in *A Review of the Greek Inscriptions and Papyri Published in 1982–83.* Edited by S. R. Llewelyn. Vol. 7 of *New Documents Illustrating Early Christianity.* Macquarie University: The Ancient History Documentary Research Centre.

Lohse, Eduard. 1997. "Kümmert sich Gott etwa um die Ochsen?" *ZNW* 88: 314–15.

Longenecker, Richard N. 1990. *Galatians.* WBC 41. Dallas: Word.

Lübbe, John. 1986. "A Reinterpretation of 4 Q Testimonia." *RevQ* 12: 187–97.

Lührmann, Dieter. 1989. "Paul and the Pharisaic Tradition." *JSNT* 11: 75–94.

Luyten, Jos. 1985. "Primeval and Eschatological Overtones in the Song of Moses (Dt 32,1–43)." Pages 341–347 in *Das Deuteronomium: Entstehung, Gestalt und Botschaft.* Edited by Norbert Lohfink. Leuven: Leuven University Press.

Luz, Ulrich. 1985. "Wirkungsgeschichtliche Exegese: Ein programmatischer Arbeitsbericht mit Beispielen aus der Bergpredigtexegese." *BTZ* 2: 18–32.

—. 1994. *Matthew in History: Interpretation, Influence, Effects.* Minneapolis: Fortress.

Mack, Burton. 1984. "Philo Judaeus and Exegetical Traditions in Alexandria." Pages 227–71 in *ANRW* 2.21.1. Berlin and New York: de Gruyter.

Magness, Jodi. 2002. *The Archaeology of Qumran and the Dead Sea Scrolls.* Grand Rapids: Eerdmans.

Maher, Michael. 1994. "Targum Pseudo-Jonathan of Deuteronomy 1.1–8." Pages 264–90 in *The Aramaic Bible: Targums in Their Historical Context.* Edited by D. R. G. Beattie and M. J. McNamara. JSOTSup 166. Sheffield: JSOT Press.

Mann, Jacob. 1927. "Changes in the Divine Service of the Synagogue due to Religious Persecutions." *HUCA* 4: 241–310.

—. 1971. *The Bible as Read and Preached in the Old Synagogue: A Study in the Cycles of the Readings from the Torah and the Prophets, and in the Structure of the Midrashic Homilies.* 2 vols. Library of Biblical Studies. New York: Ktav. Orig. Cincinnati, 1940 and New York, 1966.

Maori, Yeshayahu. 1998. "The Relationship Between the Peshitta Pentateuch and the Pentateuchal Targums." Pages 57–73 in *Targum Studies. Vol. 2: Targum and Peshitta.* Edited by Paul V. M. Flesher. South Florida Studies in the History of Judaism 165. Atlanta: Scholars.

Martens, J. W. 1991. "Philo and the 'Higher' Law." Pages 309–22 in *The Society of Biblical Literature 1991 Seminar Papers.* Society of Biblical Literature Seminar Papers 30. Atlanta: Scholars Press.

—. 2003. *One God, One Law: Philo of Alexandria on the Mosaic and Greco-Roman Law.* SPAMA 2. Ancient Mediterranean and Medieval Texts and Contexts. Boston and Leiden: Brill.

Martin, Dale. 1995. *The Corinthian Body.* New Haven and London: Yale University Press.

—. 2001. "Review Essay: Justin J. Meggitt, *Paul, Poverty and Survival.*" *JSNT* 84: 51–64.

Martin, Matthew J. 2000. "Philo's Interest in the Synagogue." *ANES* 37: 215–23

Martyn, J. L. 1997. *Galatians: A New Translation with Introduction and Commentary.* AB 33A. New York: Doubleday.

—. 2006. "Francis Watson, *Paul and the Hermeneutics of Faith.*" *SJT* 59: 427–38.

Matera, Frank J. 2003. *II Corinthians: A Commentary*. NTL. Louisville, KY: Westminster John Knox.

Matlock, R. Barry. 1996. *Unveiling the Apocalyptic Paul: Paul's Interpreters and the Rhetoric of Criticism*. JSNTSup 127. Sheffield: Sheffield Academic Press.

McBride, Sean Dean. 1987. "Polity of the Covenant People: The Book of Deuteronomy." *Int* 41: 229–44.

McCartney, Eugene S. 1948. "Notes on Reading and Praying Audibly." *CP* 43: 184–87.

McConville, J. Gordon. 2000. "Deuteronomy: Torah for the Church of Christ." *EuroJTh* 9: 33–47.

—. 2002. *Deuteronomy*. Downers Grove: InterVarsity Press.

McCormick, M. 1985. "The Birth of the Codex and the Apostolic Life-Style." *Scriptorium* 39: 150–158.

McDonough, Sean. 2005. "Competent to Judge: The Old Testament Connection Between 1 Corinthians 5 and 6." *JTS* n.s. 56: 99–102.

McKay, Heather. 1994. *Sabbath and Synagogue: The Question of Sabbath Worship in Ancient Judaism*. RGRW 122. Leiden, New York, Köln: Brill.

Meeks, Wayne A. 1982. "'And Rose Up to Play': Midrash and Paraenesis in 1 Corinthians 10:1–22." *JSNT* 16: 64–78.

Meggitt, J. 1999. *Paul, Poverty and Survival*. SNTW. Edinburgh: T. & T. Clark.

—. 2001. "Response to Martin and Theissen." *JSNT* 84: 85–94.

Mendelson, Alan. 1997. "Philo's Dialectic of Reward and Punishment." *SPhilo* 9: 104–25.

Metso, Sarianna. 1997. *The Textual Development of the Qumran Community Rule*. STDJ 21. Leiden: Brill.

—. 1998. "The Use of Old Testament Quotations in the Qumran Community Rule." Pages 217–31 in *Qumran Between the Old and New Testaments*. Edited by Frederick H. Cryer and Thomas L. Thompson. JSOTSup 290. Copenhagen International Seminar 6. Sheffield: Sheffield Academic Press.

—. 2002. "Biblical Quotations in the Community Rule." Pages 81–92 in *The Bible as Book: The Hebrew Bible and the Judaean Desert Discoveries*. Edited by Edward D. Herbert and Emanuel Tov. London: The British Library. New Castle, DE: Oak Knoll Press.

Metzger, B. M. 1994. *A Textual Commentary on the Greek New Testament*. 2nd ed. New York: United Bible Societies.

Meyers, E. M. 1992. "Synagogue." *ABD* 6:251–60:

—. 1999. "The Torah Shrine in the Ancient Synagogue: Another Look at the Evidence." Pages 201–23 in *Jews, Christians, and Polytheists in the Ancient Synagogue: Cultural Interaction During the Greco-Roman Period*. Edited by S. Fine. London and New York: Routledge.

Michel, O. 1929. *Paulus und seine Bibel*. Gütersloh: C. Bertelsmann. Reprinted: Darmstadt: Wissenschaftliche Buchgesellschaft, 1972.

Milik, J. T. 1957. "Le Travail de l'édition des manuscrits du Désert de Juda." Pages 17–26 in *Volume du congrès: Strasbourg 1956*. VTSup 4. Leiden: Brill.

Millard, Alan. 2000. *Reading and Writing in the Time of Jesus*. Biblical Seminar 69. Sheffield: Sheffield Academic Press.

Mink, Hans-Aage. 1987. "The Use of Scripture in the Temple Scroll and the Status of the Scroll as Law." *SJOT* 1: 20–50.

Mitchell, Margaret M. 1991. *Paul and the Rhetoric of Reconciliation: An Exegetical Investigation of the Language and Composition of 1 Corinthians.* HUT 28. Tübingen: Mohr Siebeck.

Moo, Douglas J. 1996. *The Epistle to the Romans.* NICNT. Grand Rapids: Eerdmans.

Moore, Carey A. 1977. *Daniel, Esther, and Jeremiah: The Additions.* AB 44. Garden City, NY: Doubleday.

—. 1996. *Tobit: A New Translation with Introduction and Commentary.* AB 40A. New York: Doubleday.

Morgan, Teresa. 1998. *Literate Education in the Hellenistic and Roman Worlds.* Cambridge Classical Studies. Cambridge: Cambridge University Press.

Moritz, Thorsten. 1996. *A Profound Mystery: The Use of the Old Testament in Ephesians.* NovTSup 85. Leiden, New York, Köln: Brill.

Morris, Leon. 1964. *The New Testament and the Jewish Lectionaries.* London: Tyndale.

Morris, Nathan. 1937. *The Jewish School: An Introduction to the History of Jewish Education.* London: Eyre and Spottiswoode.

Moyise, Steve. 2008a. "Quotations." Pages 15–28 in *As It Is Written: Studying Paul's Use of Scripture.* Edited by Stanley E. Porter and Christopher D. Stanley. SBLSymS 50. Atlanta: Society of Biblical Literature.

—. 2008b. *Evoking Scripture: Seeing the Old Testament in the New.* London: T. & T. Clark.

—. and M. J. J. Menken, eds. 2007. *Deuteronomy in the New Testament.* The New Testament and the Scriptures of Israel. LNTS 358. London: T. & T. Clark International.

Mulder, M. J., ed. 1988. *Mikra: Text, Translation, Reading and Interpretation of the Hebrew Bible in Ancient Judaism and Early Christianity.* CRINT 2/1. Assen: Van Gorcum. Philadelphia: Fortress.

Müller, Karlheinz. 2008. "Neutestamentliche Wissenschaft und Judaistik." Pages 32–60 in *Judaistik und neutestamentliche Wissenschaft. Standorte – Grenzen – Beziehungen.* Edited by Lutz Doering, Hans-Günther Waubke and Florian Wilk. FRLANT 226. Göttingen: Vandenhoeck & Ruprecht.

Müller, M. 1996. *The First Bible of the Church: A Plea for the Septuagint.* JSOTSup 206. Sheffield: Sheffield Academic Press.

Murphy, F. J. 1993. *Pseudo-Philo. Rewriting the Bible.* New York and Oxford: Oxford University Press.

Murray, John. 1968. *The Epistle to the Romans.* NICNT. 2 vols. in 1. Grand Rapids: Eerdmans.

Mussies, G. 1987. "Greek in Palestine and the Diaspora." Pages 1040–64 in *The Jewish People in the First Century: Historical Geography, Political History, Social, Cultural and Religious Life and Institutions.* Edited by S. Safrai and M. Stern. CRINT 1/2. Assen and Maastricht: Van Gorcum. Philadelphia: Fortress.

Najman, Hindy. 1999. "The Law of Nature and the Authority of Mosaic Law." *SPhilo* 11: 55–73.

—. 2003a. "A Written Copy of the Law of Nature: An Unthinkable Paradox?" Pages 54–63 in *Laws Stamped with the Seals of Nature: Law and Nature in Hellenistic Philosophy and Philo of Alexandria.* Edited by D. T. Runia, G. E. Sterling and H. Najman. *SPhilo* 15. BJS 337. Providence: Brown University.

—. 2003b. *Seconding Sinai: The Development of Mosaic Discourse in Second Temple Judaism.* JSJSup 77. Leiden: Brill.

Neill, Stephen and N. T. Wright. 1988. *The Interpretation of the New Testament, 1861–1986.* 2nd ed. Oxford and New York: Oxford University Press.

Nelson, Richard D. 2002. *Deuteronomy: A Commentary*. OTL. Louisville: Westminster John Knox.

Neusner, J. 1973." 'By the Testimony of Two Witnesses' in the Damascus Document IX, 17–22 and in Pharisaic-Rabbinic Law." *RevQ* 8: 197–217.

—. 1985. *The Memorized Torah: The Mnemonic System of the Mishnah*. BJS 96. Chico, CA: Scholars Press.

—. 2004. *Judaism and the Interpretation of Scripture: Introduction to the Rabbinic Midrash*. Peabody, MA: Hendrickson.

—. 2005. "How Important Was the Destruction of the Second Temple in the Formation of Rabbinic Judaism? Some Reconsiderations." Pages 77–93 in *"The Words of a Wise Man's Mouth Are Gracious" (Qoh 10,12): Festschrift for Günter Stemberger on the Occasion of His 65th Birthday*. Edited by Mauro Perani. SJ 32. Berlin and New York: Walter de Gruyter.

Nicholson, Ernest. 1998. *The Pentateuch in the Twentieth Century: The Legacy of Julius Wellhausen*. Oxford: Clarendon.

Nickelsburg, G. W. E., ed. 1973. *Studies on the Testament of Moses*. SCS 4. Cambridge, MA: Society of Biblical Literature.

—. 2001. *1 Enoch 1: A Commentary on the Book of 1 Enoch: Chapters 1–36; 81–108*. Hermeneia. Minneapolis: Fortress.

—. 2005. *Jewish Literature Between the Bible and the Mishnah*. 2nd ed. Philadelphia: Fortress.

—. 2006. "Torah and the Deuteronomic Scheme in the Apocrypha and Pseudepigrapha: Variations on a Theme and Some Noteworthy Examples of Its Absence." Pages 222–35 in *Das Gesetz im frühen Judentum und im Neuen Testament. Festschrift für Christoph Burchard zum 75. Geburtstag*. Edited by D. Sänger and M. Konradt. NTOA/SUNT 57. Göttingen: Vandenhoeck & Ruprecht. Fribourg: Academic Press.

Niebuhr, K.-W. 1987. *Gesetz und Paränese: Katechismusartige Weisungsreihen in der frühjüdischen Literatur*. WUNT 28. Tübingen: Mohr Siebeck.

Nikiprowetzky, V. 1977. *Le commentaire de l'Écriture chez Philon d'Alexandrie: son caractère et sa portée, observations philologiques*. Leiden: Brill.

Nodet, Étienne. 1996. *La Bible de Josèphe I: Le Pentateuque de Flavius Josèphe*. Paris: Cerf.

O'Brien, Kelli S. 2006. "The Curse of the Law (Galatians 3.13): Crucifixion, Persecution, and Deuteronomy 21.22–23." *JSNT* 29: 55–76.

Oepke, Albert. 1965. "κρύπτω, κτλ." *TDNT* 3: 957–78.

Olson, Dennis T. 1994. *Deuteronomy and the Death of Moses: A Theological Reading*. OBT. Minneapolis: Fortress.

Ong, Walter J. 1986. "Writing Is a Technology that Restructures Thought." Pages 23–50 *The Written Word: Literacy in Transition*. Edited by in Gerd Baumann. Wolfson College Lectures 1985. Oxford: Clarendon.

—. 1987. "Text as Interpretation: Mark and After." *Semeia* 39: 7–26.

—. 2002. *Orality and Literacy: The Technologizing of the Word*. London and New York: Routledge. Originally: London: Methuen, 1982.

Oropeza, B. J. 1998. "Laying to Rest the Midrash: Paul's Message on Meat Sacrificed to Idols in Light of the Deuteronomic Tradition." *Bib* 79: 57–68.

Orr, William F. and James Arther Walther. 1976. *1 Corinthians: A New Translation*. AB 32. Garden City, New York: Doubleday.

Oster, Richard. 1993. "Supposed Anachronism in Luke-Acts' Use of ΣΥΝΑΓΩΓΗ: A Rejoinder to H. C. Kee." *NTS* 39: 178–208.

Otzen, Benedikt. 2002. *Tobit and Judith*. Guides to Apocrypha and Pseudepigrapha. Sheffield: Sheffield Academic Press.

Passoni Dell'Acqua, Anna. 2003. "Upon Philo's Biblical Text and the Septuagint." Pages 25–52 in *Italian Studies on Philo of Alexandria*. Edited by F. Calabi. Ancient Mediterranean and Medieval Texts and Contexts 1. Leiden and Boston: Brill.

Pearce, Sarah. 1995a. "Josephus as Interpreter of Biblical Law: The Representation of the High Court of Deut 17:8–12 according to Jewish Antiquities 4.218." *JJS* 46: 30–42.

—. 1995b. "The Representation and Development of Deuteronomic Law in Jewish Writings after Deuteronomy and before the Mishnah with reference to Selected Passages in Deut. 16–19." D.Phil. Thesis. University of Oxford.

Pelletier, A. 1962b. *Flavius Josèphe adaptateur de la Letter d'Aristée. Une réaction atticisante contre la Koinè*. Études et Commentaires 45. Paris: Klincksieck.

—. 1989. "Josephus, the Letter of Aristeas, and the Septuagint." Pages 97–115 in *Josephus, the Bible and History*. Edited by L. H. Feldman and Gohei Hata. Detroit: Wayne State University Press.

Perona, Edwin G. 2005. "The Presence and Function of Deuteronomy in the Paraenesis of Paul in 1 Corinthians 5:1–11:1." Ph.D. Dissertation. Trinity Evangelical Divinity School.

Perrot, Charles. 1969. "Petuhot et setumot: Étude sur les alinéas du Pentateuque." *RB* 76: 50–91.

—. 1973. *La lecture de la Bible dans la synagogue: Les anciennes lectures palestiniennes du Shabbat et des fêtes*. Collection Massorah I/1. Hildesheim: H. A. Gerstenberg.

—. 1984. "La lecture de la Bible dans la Diaspora hellénistique." Pages 109–34 in *Études sur le Judaïsme hellénistique: congrès de Strasbourg 1983*. Edited by R. Arnaldez, R. Kuntzmann, and J. Schlosser. LD 119. Paris: Cerf.

—. 1988. "The Reading of the Bible in the Ancient Synagogue." Pages 137–59 in Mulder 1988.

Pietersma, Albert. 1974. "F. G. Kenyon's Text of Papyrus 963 (Numbers and Deuteronomy)." *VT* 24: 113–18.

Pike, Dana M. 1996. "The Book of Numbers at Qumran: Texts and Context." Pages 166–93 in *Current Research and Technological Developments on the Dead Sea Scrolls*. Edited by Donald W. Parry and Stephen D. Ricks. STDJ 20. Leiden: Brill.

Porter, J. R. 1963. "The Pentateuch and the Triennial Lectionary Cycle: An Examination of a Recent Theory." Pages 163–74 in *Promise and Fulfillment: Essays Presented to Professor S. H. Hooke in Celebration of His Ninetieth Birthday*. Edited by F. F. Bruce. Edinburgh: T. & T. Clark.

Porter, Stanley E. 1997a. "The Greek Papyri of the Judaean Desert and the World of the Roman East." Pages 293–316 in *The Scrolls and the Scriptures: Qumran Fifty Years After*. Edited by Stanely E. Porter and Craig A. Evans. JSPSup 26. RILP 3. Sheffield: Sheffield Academic Press.

—. 1997b. "The Use of the Old Testament in the New Testament: A Brief Comment on Method and Terminology." Pages 79–96 in *Early Christian Interpretation of the Scriptures of Israel*. Edited by C. A. Evans and J. A. Sanders. JSNTSup 148. SSEJC 5. Sheffield: Sheffield Academic Press.

—. 2006. "Further Comments on the Use of the Old Testament in the New Testament." Pages 98–110 in *The Intertextuality of the Epistles: Explorations of Theory and Prac-*

tice. Edited by Thomas L. Brodie, Dennis R. MacDonald, and Stanley E. Porter. NTM 16. Sheffield: Sheffield Phoenix Press.

—. 2008. "Allusions and Echoes." Pages 29–40 in *As It Is Written: Studying Paul's Use of Scripture*. Edited by Stanley E. Porter and Christopher D. Stanley. SBLSymS 50. Atlanta: Society of Biblical Literature.

—. and AndrewW. Pitts. 2008. "Paul's Bible, His Education and His Access to the Scriptures of Israel." *Journal of Greco-Roman Christianity and Judaism* 5: 9–41.

Pouilly, J. 1976. *La Règle de la Communauté de Qumrân: Son Évolution Littéraire*. CahRB 17. Paris: Gabalda.

Puech, Émile. 1997b. "Notes sur 11Q19 LXIV 6–13 et 4Q524 14,2–4: À propos de la crucifixion dans le Rouleau du Temple et dans le Judaïsme ancien." *RevQ* 18: 109–24.

—. 2001. "Identification de Nouveaux Manuscrits Bibliques: *Deutéronome* et *Proverbes* dans les Débris de la Grotte 4." *RevQ* 20: 121–28.

Quesnel, Michel. 2003. "La figure de Moïse en Romains 9–11." *NTS* 49: 321–335

Rabinowitz, Louis Isaac. 2007a. "Mezuzah." *EncJud*. 2nd ed. 14:156–57.

—. 2007b. "Tefillin." *EncJud* 2nd ed. 19:577–80.

Rainbow, Paul. 1987. "Monotheism and Christology in I Corinthians 8.1–6." D.Phil. Thesis. University of Oxford.

Räisänen, Heikki. 1992a. "The 'Hellenists': A Bridge Between Jesus and Paul?" Pages 149–202 in *Jesus, Paul and Torah: Collected Essays*. Translated by David E. Orton. JSNTSup 43. Sheffield: Sheffield Academic Press.

—. 1992b. "The 'Effective History' of the Bible: A Challenge to Biblical Scholarship." *SJT* 45: 303–24.

Rajak, Tessa. 2002. *Josephus: The Historian and His Society*. 2nd ed. London: Duckworth.

Ramsay, William M. 1915a. "The Old Testament in the Roman Phrygia." *ExpT* 26: 168–74.

—. 1915b. *The Bearing of Recent Discovery on the Trustworthiness of the New Testament*. London: Hodder and Stoughton.

Rappaport, Salomo. 1930. *Agada und Exegese bei Flavius Josephus*. Vienna: Alexander Kohut Memorial Foundation.

Reinbold, Wolfgang. 1995. "Israel und das Evangelium: Zur Exegese von Römer 10,19–21." *ZNW* 86: 122–129.

Reinmuth, E. 1985. *Geist und Gesetz: Studien zu Voraussetzungen und Inhalt der paulinischen Paränese*. TA 44. Berlin: Evangelische Verlagsanstalt.

Rendtorff, Rolf. 1996. "Is It Possible to Read Leviticus as a Separate Book?" Pages 22–35 in *Reading Leviticus: A Conversation with Mary Douglas*. Edited by J. F. A. Sawyer. JSOTSup 227. Sheffield: Sheffield Academic Press.

Rese, Martin. 1997. "Intertextualität: Ein Beispiel für Sinn und Unsinn 'neuer' Methoden." Pages 431–39 in *The Scriptures in the Gospels*. Edited by C. M. Tuckett. Leuven: Leuven University Press.

Revell, E. J. 1971–72. "The Oldest Evidence for the Hebrew Accent System." *BJRL* 54: 214–22.

—. 1976. "Biblical Punctuation and Chant in the Second Temple Period." *JSJ* 7: 181–98.

Richardson, Ernest Cushing. 1914. *Biblical Libraries: A Sketch of Library History From 3400 B.C. to A.D. 150*. Princeton: Princeton University Press.

Richardson, Peter. 1980. " 'I Say, Not the Lord': Personal Opinion, Apostolic Authority and the Development of Early Christian Halakah." *TynBul* 31: 65–86.

Ridderbos, Herman N. 1953. *The Epistle of Paul to the Churches of Galatia.* NICNT. Grand Rapids: Eerdmans.

Riesner, Rainer. 1995. "Synagogues in Jerusalem." Pages 179–211 in *The Book of Acts in Its Palestinian Setting.* Edited by Richard Bauckham. Vol. 4 of *The Book of Acts in Its First Century Setting.* Grand Rapids: Eerdmans. Carlisle: Paternoster.

—. 1998. *Paul's Early Period: Chronology, Mission Strategy, Theology.* Translated by D. Scott. Grand Rapids and Cambridge: Eerdmans.

Rinaldi, Giancarlo. 1998. *La Bibbia dei pagani. II. Testi e Documenti.* EDB. Bologna: Centro editoriale dehoniano.

Robert, L. 1940–1965. *Hellenica. Recueil d'épigraphie de numismatique et d'antiquités grecques.* 13 vols. Paris: Adrien-Maisonneuve.

Roberts, Colin H. 1979. *Manuscript, Society and Belief in Early Christian Egypt.* Schweich Lectures 1977. Oxford: Oxford University Press.

—. and T. C. Skeat. 1983. *The Birth of the Codex.* Oxford: Oxford University Press.

Rofé, Alexander 2002. "The End of the Song of Moses (Deuteronomy 32.43)." Pages 47–54 in *Deuteronomy: Issues and Interpretation.* London: T. & T. Clark.

Rosner, Brian S. 1991. "Moses Appointing Judges: An Antecedent to 1 Cor 6,1–6?" *ZNW* 82: 275–78

—. 1994. *Paul, Scripture, and Ethics: A Study of 1 Corinthians 5–7.* AGJU 22. Leiden: Brill. Reprinted: Grand Rapids: Baker, 1999.

—. ed. 1995. *Understanding Paul's Ethics: Twentieth Century Approaches.* Grand Rapids: Eerdmans. Carlisle: Paternoster.

—. 2007. "Deuteronomy in 1 and 2 Corinthians." Pages 118–35 in Menken and Moyise 2007.

Rosso, Liliana. 1977. "Deuteronomio 21,22. Contributo del Rotolo del Tempio alla valutazione di una variante medievale dei Settanta." *RevQ* 9: 231–236.

Rothschild, Clare K. 2009. *Hebrews as Pseudepigraphon: The History and Significance of the Pauline Attribution of Hebrews.* WUNT 235. Tübingen: Mohr Siebeck.

Runesson, Anders. 2003. "Persian Imperial Politics, the Beginnings of Public Torah Readings, and the Origins of the Synagogue." Pages 63–89 in *The Ancient Synagogue from Its Origins until 200 C.E.* Edited by Birger Olsson and Magnus Zetterholm. ConBNT 39. Stockholm: Almqvist & Wiksell International.

—. 2004. "The Origins of the Synagogue in Past and Present Research: Some Comments on Definitions, Theories, and Sources." *ST* 58: 60–76.

Runesson, Anders, D. Binder and B. Olsson, eds. 2008. *The Ancient Synagogue from Its Origins to 200 C.E.* AJEC 72. Leiden and Boston: Brill.

Runia, David T. 1991. "Secondary Texts in Philo's *Quaestiones*." Pages 47–79 in *Both Literal and Allegorical. Studies in Philo of Alexandria's Questions and Answers on Genesis and Exodus.* Edited by D. M. Hay. Atlanta: Scholars Press.

Ryle, H. E. 1895. *Philo and Holy Scripture, Or: The Quotations of Philo from the Books of the Old Testament.* London and New York: Macmillan. Electronically updated at: http://ccat.sas.upenn.edu/rs/rak/courses/999/RYLE1.htm by Robert Kraft. Accessed 3 June 2009.

Saenger, P. 1997. *Space Between Words: The Origin of Silent Reading.* Stanford: Stanford University Press.

Safrai, S. 1976. "Religion in Everyday Life." Pages 793–833 in *The Jewish People in the First Century: Historical Geography, Political History, Social, Cultural and Religious Life and Institutions.* Edited by S. Safrai and M. Stern. CRINT 1/2. Assen and Amsterdam: Van Gorcum. Philadelphia: Fortress.

—. 1987a. "Education and the Study of the Torah." Pages 945–70 in *The Jewish People in the First Century: Historical Geography, Political History, Social, Cultural and Religious Life and Institutions*. Edited by S. Safrai and M. Stern. CRINT 1/2. Assen and Maastricht: Van Gorcum. Philadelphia: Fortress.

—. 1987b. "The Synagogue." Pages 908–44 in *The Jewish People in the First Century: Historical Geography, Political History, Social, Cultural and Religious Life and Institutions*. Edited by S. Safrai and M. Stern. CRINT 1/2. Assen and Maastricht: Van Gorcum. Philadelphia: Fortress.

Salvesen, Alison. 1991. *Symmachus in the Pentateuch*. Journal of Semitic Studies Monograph 15. Manchester: University of Manchester Press.

Samely, Alexander. 2002. *Rabbinic Interpretation of Scripture in the Mishnah*. Oxford: Oxford University Press.

Sanders, E. P. 1983. *Paul, the Law and the Jewish People*. Philadelphia: Fortress.

Sandmel, S. 1979. *Philo of Alexandria: An Introduction*. New York and Oxford: Oxford University Press.

Sandnes, Karl Olav. 1991. *Paul – One of the Prophets? A Contribution to the Apostle's Self-Understanding*. WUNT 2/43. Tübingen: Mohr Siebeck.

—. 2009. *The Challenge of Homer: School, Pagan Poets and Early Christianity*. ECC. LNTS 400. London and New York: T. & T. Clark.

Sänger, Dieter. 2001. "Tora für die Völker – Weisungen der Liebe. Zur Rezeption des Dekalogs im frühen Judentum und Neuen Testament." Pages 97–146 in *Weisheit, Ethos und Gebot: Weisheits- und Dekalogtraditionen in der Bibel und im frühen Judentum*. Edited by Henning Graf Reventlow. BTS 43. Neukirchen-Vluyn: Neukirchener.

Sarna, Nahum. 1989. *Ancient Libraries and the Ordering of the Biblical Books: A Lecture Presented at the Library of Congress, March 6, 1989*. The Center for the Book Viewpoint Series 25. Washington D. C.: Library of Congress.

Schäfer, P. 2005. "Martin Hengel at Seventy." Pages 21–34 in *The Beginnings of Christianity*. Edited by Jack Pastor and Menachem Mor. Jerusalem: Yad Ben-Zvi Press.

Schearing, Linda S. and Steven L. McKenzie, eds. 1999. *Those Elusive Deuteronomists: The Phenomenon of Pan-Deuteronomism*. JSOTSup 268. Sheffield: Sheffield Academic Press.

Schenck, Kenneth. 2005. *A Brief Guide to Philo*. Louisville: Westminster John Knox.

Schiffman, Lawrence H. 1975. "The Qumran Law of Testimony." *RevQ* 8: 603–12.

—. 1983. *Sectarian Law in the Dead Sea Scrolls: Courts, Testimony and the Penal Code*. BJS 33. Chico, CA: Scholars Press.

—. 1989. "The Temple Scroll and the Systems of Jewish Law of the Second Temple Period." Pages 239–55 in Brooke 1989.

—. 1990. "Miqsat Ma'aseh Ha-Torah and the Temple Scroll." *RevQ* 14: 435–57.

—. 1992. "The Deuteronomic Paraphrase of the *Temple Scroll*." *RevQ* 60: 543–67.

—. 1994. "The Theology of the Temple Scroll." *JQR* 85: 109–23.

—. 1999. "The Early History of Public Reading of the Torah." Pages 44–56 in *Jews, Christians, and Polytheists in the Ancient Synagogue: Cultural Interaction During the Greco-Roman Period*. Edited by S. Fine. London and New York: Routledge.

—. 2000a. "Halakhah and Sectarianism in the Dead Sea Scrolls." Pages 123–42 in *The Dead Sea Scrolls in their Historical Context*. Edited by Timothy H. Lim. Edinburgh: T. & T. Clark.

—. 2000b. "Phylacteries and Mezuzot." *EDSS* 2:675–77.

Schmidt, Hans Wilhelm. 1972. *Der Brief des Paulus an die Römer.* 3rd ed. THNT 6. Berlin: Evangelische Verlagsanstalt.

Schneider, Heinrich. 1959. "Der Dekalog in den Phylakterien von Qumrân." *BZ* 3: 18–31.

Schnelle, Udo. 2005. *Apostle Paul: His Life and Theology.* Translated by M. Eugene Boring. Grand Rapids: Baker Academic.

Schrage, W. 1971. "συναγωγή, κτλ." *TDNT* 7: 798–841.

Schreiner, Thomas R. 1984. "Is Perfect Obedience to the Law Possible? A Reexamination of Galatians 3:10." *JETS* 27: 151–60.

—. 1998. *Romans.* BECNT. Grand Rapids: Baker.

Schürer, Emil. 1973–1987. *The History of the Jewish People in the Age of Jesus Christ (175 B.C. – A.D. 135).* Revised English version by Geza Vermes, Fergus Millar and Martin Goodman. 3 vols. in 4. Edinburgh: T. & T. Clark.

Schwartz, Daniel R. 1990. *Agrippa I: The Last King of Judaea.* TSAJ 23 Tübingen: Mohr Siebeck.

—. 1998. "On Something Biblical about 2 Maccabees." Pages 223–32 in *Biblical Perspectives: Early Use and Interpretation of the Bible in Light of the Dead Sea Scrolls. Proceedings of the First International Symposium of the Orion Center for the Study of the Dead Sea Scrolls and Associated Literature, 12–14 May 1996.* Edited by M. E. Stone and E. G. Chazon. STDJ 28. Leiden: Brill.

Schweizer, E. 1974. " 'Der Jude im Verborgenen..., dessen Lob nicht von Menschen, sondern von Gott kommt.' Zu Röm 2,28 f. und Matt 6,1–18." Pages 115–24 in *Neues Testament und Kirche für Rudolph Schnackenburg.* Edited by J. Gnilka. Freiburg: Herder.

Scott, James M. 1993a. "For As Many As Are of Works of the Law Are Under a Curse (Galatians 3:10)." Pages 187–221 in *Paul and the Scriptures of Israel.* Edited by Craig A. Evans and James A.Sanders. JSNTSup 83. SSEJC 1. Sheffield: JSOT Press.

—. 1993b. "Paul's Use of Deuteronomistic Tradition." *JBL* 112: 645–65.

—. 1993c. "Restoration of Israel." Pages 796–805 in *Dictionary of Paul and His Letters.* Edited by G. F. Hawthorne and R. P. Martin. Downers Grove, IL: InterVarsity.

Segal, Alan F. 1986. *Rebecca's Children: Judaism and Christianity in the Roman World.* Cambridge, MA: Harvard University Press.

Segal, Michael. 2007. *The Book of Jubilees: Rewritten Bible, Redaction, Ideology and Theology.* JSJSup 117. Leiden and Boston: Brill.

Sevenster, J. N. 1968. *Do You Know Greek? How Much Greek Could the First Jewish Christians Have Known?* NovTSup 19. Leiden: Brill.

Shanks, Hershel, ed., with notes and comments by Ronny Reich. 2004. *The City of David: Revisiting Early Excavations. English Translations of Reports by Raymond Weill and L.-H. Vincent.* Washington, D.C.: Biblical Archaeology Society.

Shemesh, Aharon and Cana Werman. 1998. "Hidden Things and Their Revelation." *RevQ* 18: 409–27.

Shroyer, Montgomery J. 1936. "Alexandrian Jewish Literalists." *JBL* 55: 261–84.

Shum, Shiu-Lun. 2002. *Paul's Use of Isaiah in Romans: A Comparative Study of Paul's Letter to the Romans and the Sibylline and Qumran Sectarian Texts.* WUNT 2/156. Tübingen: Mohr Siebeck.

Siegert, Folker. 1996. "Early Jewish Interpretation in a Hellenistic Style." Pages 130–98 in *Hebrew Bible/Old Testament: The History of Its Interpretation. Volume I: From the Beginnings to the Middle Ages (Until 1300).* Edited by Magne Sæbø. Göttingen: Vandenhoeck & Ruprecht.

Silva, Moisés. 2001. "The Greek Psalter in Paul's Letters: A Textual Study." Pages 277–88 in *The Old Greek Psalter: Studies in Honour of Albert Pietersma*. Edited by Robert J. V. Hiebert, Claude E. Cox and Peter J. Gentry. JSOTSup 332. Sheffield: Sheffield Academic Press.

—. 2007. "Galatians." Pages 785–812 in *Commentary on the New Testament Use of the Old Testament*. Edited by G. K. Beale and D. A. Carson. Grand Rapids: Baker Academic.

Skeat, T. C. 2004a. "Irenaeus and the Four-Gospel Canon." Pages 73–78 in Skeat 2004g.

—. 2004b. "Roll versus Codex – A New Approach?" Pages 71–72 in Skeat 2004g.

—. 2004c. "The Length of the Standard Papyrus Roll and the Cost-advantage of the Codex." Pages 65–70 in Skeat 2004g.

—. 2004d. "The Origin of the Christian Codex." Pages 79–87 in Skeat 2004g.

—. 2004e. "Two Notes on Papyrus: I. Was Re-Rolling a Papyrus Roll an Irksome and Time-consuming Task?" Pages 60–63 in Skeat 2004g.

—. 2004f. "Was Papyrus Considered as 'Cheap' or 'Expensive' in the Ancient World?" Pages 88–105 in Skeat 2004g.

—. 2004g. *The Collected Biblical Writings of T. C. Skeat*. Edited by J. K. Elliott. NovTSup 113. Leiden and Boston: Brill.

Skehan, P. 1954. "A Fragment of the 'Song of Moses' (Deut 32) from Qumran." *BASOR* 136: 12–15.

—. 1993. "The Structure of the Song of Moses in Deuteronomy (32:1–43)." Pages 156–68 in *A Song of Power and the Power of Song: Essays on the Book of Deuteronomy*. Edited by Duane L. Christensen. Winona Lake: Eisenbrauns. Originally: *CBQ* 13 (1951): 153–63.

Slusser, Michael. 1992. "Reading Silently in Antiquity." *JBL* 111: 499.

Small, Jocelyn Penny. 1997. *Wax Tablets of the Mind: Cognitive Studies of Memory and Literacy in Classical Antiquity*. London and New York: Routledge.

Snyder, H. Gregory. 2002. Review of *Jewish Literacy in Roman Palestine* by Catherine Hezser. *JBL* 121: 559–62.

Soards, Marion L. 1999. *1 Corinthians*. NIBC. Peabody, MA: Hendrickson. Carlisle, UK: Paternoster.

Soll, W. 1989. "Misfortune and Exile in Tobit: The Juncture of a Fairy Tale Source in Deuteronomic Theology." *CBQ* 51: 209–231.

Sprinkle, Preston M. 2008. *Law and Life: The Interpretation of Leviticus 18:5 in Early Judaism and in Paul*. WUNT 2/241. Tübingen: Mohr Siebeck.

Stanley, Christopher D. 1990. " 'Under a Curse': A Fresh Reading of Galatians 3.10–14." *NTS* 36: 481–511.

—. 1992. *Paul and the Language of Scripture: Citation Technique in the Pauline Epistles and Contemporary Literature*. SNTSMS 74. Cambridge: Cambridge University Press.

—. 2004. *Arguing with Scripture: The Rhetoric of Quotations in the Letters of Paul*. New York and London: T. & T. Clark International.

—. 2006. "A Decontextualized Paul? A Response to Francis Watson's *Paul and the Hermeneutics of Faith*." *JSNT* 28: 353–62.

Starr, Raymond J. 1991. "Reading Aloud: *Lectores* and Roman Reading." *CJ* 86: 337–343.

Steck, Odil H. 1993. *Das apokryphe Baruchbuch: Studien zu Rezeption und Konzentration "kanonischer" Überlieferung*. FRLANT 160. Göttingen: Vandenhoeck & Ruprecht.

Stegemann, H. 1988. "The Origins of the Temple Scroll." Pages 235–56 in *Congress Volume: Jerusalem 1986*. Edited by J. A. Emerton. VTSup 40. Leiden: Brill.

—. 1989. "The Literary Composition of the Temple Scroll and Its Status at Qumran." Pages 123–48 in Brooke 1989.

Stegner, William Richard. 1992. "The Rebuke Tradition in the Targums and the Narrative of the Temptation." Pages 33–59 in *Textual and Contextual Studies in the Pentateuchal Targums*. Edited by Paul V. M. Flesher. Targum Studies 1. Atlanta: Scholars.

Stemberger, Günter. 1989. "Der Dekalog im frühen Judentum." *JBTh* 4: 91–103.

—. 1996. *Introduction to the Talmud and Midrash*. 2nd ed. Translated and Edited by Markus Bockmuehl. Edinburgh: T. & T. Clark.

—. 2005. "The Pre-Christian Paul." Pages 65–81 in *The Beginnings of Christianity*. Edited by Jack Pastor and Menachem Mor. Jerusalem: Yad Ben-Zvi Press.

—. 2008. "Judaistik und neutestamentliche Wissenschaft." Pages 15–31 in *Judaistik und neutestamentliche Wissenschaft. Standorte – Grenzen – Beziehungen*. Edited by Lutz Doering, Hans-Günther Waubke and Florian Wilk. FRLANT 226. Göttingen: Vandenhoeck & Ruprecht.

Stendahl, K. 1962. "Hate, Non-Retaliation, and Love: 1QS x,17–20 and Rom. 12:19–21." *HTR* 55: 343–55.

Steyn, Gert Jacobus. 2002. "A Quest for the *Vorlage* of the 'Song of Moses' (Deut 32) Quotations in Hebrews." *Neot* 34: 263–272.

Stone, Michael. E. 1990. *Fourth Ezra*. Hermeneia. Minneapolis: Fortress.

Strachan, R. H. 1935. *The Second Epistle to the Corinthians*. MNTC. London: Hodder and Stoughton.

Strecker, Georg. 1992. "Die Legitimität des Paulinischen Apostolates nach 2 Korinther 10–13." *NTS* 38: 566–86.

Street, Brian V. 1984. *Literacy in Theory and Practice*. Cambridge: Cambridge University Press.

Strubbe, J. H. M. 1994. "Curses Against Violation of the Grave in Jewish Epitaphs of Asia Minor." Pages 70–128 in *Studies in Early Jewish Epigraphy*. Edited by Jan Willem van Henten and Pieter W. van der Horst. AGJU 21. Leiden, New York, Köln: Brill.

Strugnell, John. 1970. "Notes en marge de volume V des 'Discoveries in the Judaean Desert of Jordan.'" *RevQ* 7: 163–276.

—. 1990. "Moses-Pseudepigrapha at Qumran. 4Q375, 4Q376, and Similar Works." Pages 221–234 in *Archaeology and History in the Dead Sea Scrolls. The New York University Conference in Memory of Yigael Yadin*. Edited by L. H. Schiffman. JSPSup 8. JSOTSup / ASOR Monographs 2. Sheffield: JSOT Press.

—. 1994. "MMT: Second Thoughts on a Forthcoming Edition." Pages 57–73 in *The Community of the Renewed Covenant: The Notre Dame Symposium on the Dead Sea Scrolls*. Edited by E. Ulrich and J. VanderKam. Notre Dame: Notre Dame University Press.

Stuhlmacher, Peter. 1994. *Paul's Letter to the Romans: A Commentary*. Translated by S. J. Hafemann. Louisville, KY: Westminster John Knox.

Suggs, M. Jack. 1967. "'The Word Is Near You:' Romans 10:6–10 within the Purpose of the Letter." Pages 289–312 in *Christian History and Interpretation: Studies Presented to John Knox*. Edited by W. R. Farmer, C. F. D. Moule, and R. R. Niebuhr. Cambridge: Cambridge University Press.

Sukenik, E. L. 1934. *Ancient Synagogues in Palestine and Greece*. Schweich Lectures 1930. London: Oxford University Press.

Swanson, Dwight D. 1995. *The Temple Scroll and the Bible: The Methodology of 11QT*. STDJ 14. Leiden, New York, Köln: Brill.

Swete, Henry Barclay. 1914. *An Introduction to the Old Testament in Greek*. Revised by R. R. Ottley. Edited by H. St. J. Thackeray. Cambridge: At the University Press.

Tabor, James D. 1989. " 'Returning to the Divinity': Josephus's Portrayal of the Disappearances of Enoch, Elijah, and Moses." *JBL* 108: 225–38.

Talmon, Shemaryahu. 1962. "The Three Scrolls of the Law that Were Found in the Temple Court." *Textus* 2: 14–27.

—. 1991. "Oral Tradition and Written Transmission, Or the Heard and Seen Word in Judaism of the Second Temple Period." Pages 121–58 in *Jesus and the Oral Gospel Tradition*. Edited by Henry Wansbrough. JSNTSup 64. Sheffield: Sheffield Academic Press.

Tassin, Claude. 1996. "Paul dans le monde juif du Ier siècle." Pages 171–93 in *Paul de Tarse*. Edited by J. Schlosser. Lectio Divina 165. Paris: Cerf.

Thackeray, H. St. John. 1923. *The Septuagint and Jewish Worship: A Study in Origins*. Schweich Lectures 1920. 2nd ed. London: Oxford University Press.

Theissen, Gerd. 1982. *The Social Setting of Pauline Christianity: Essays on Corinth*. Translated by John H. Schütz. Philadelphia: Fortress.

—. 2001. "The Social Structure of Pauline Communities: Some Critical Remarks on J. J. Meggitt, *Paul, Poverty and Survival*." *JSNT* 84: 65–84.

Thielman, Frank. 1989. *From Plight to Solution: A Jewish Framework for Understanding Paul's View of the Law in Galatians and Romans*. NovTSup 61. Leiden: Brill.

Thompson, M. 1991. *Clothed with Christ: The Example and Teaching of Jesus in Romans 12.1–15.13*. JSNTSup 59. Sheffield: JSOT Press.

Thornton, T. 1996. "Anti-Samaritan Exegesis Reflected in Josephus' Retelling of Deuteronomy, Joshua, and Judges." *JTS* 47: 125–30.

Thrall, M. E. 2000. *The Second Epistle to the Corinthians*. 2 vols. ICC. London and New York: T. & T. Clark International.

Tiede, D. L. 1973. "The Figure of Moses in the Testament of Moses." Pages 86–92 in *Studies on the Testament of Moses*. Edited by G. W. E. Nickelsburg. SCS 4. Cambridge, MA: Harvard University Press.

Tigay, Jeffrey H. 1979. "On the Term Phylacteries (Matt 23:5)." *HTR* 72: 45–53.

—. 1982. "On the Meaning of *t(w)t'pt*." *JBL* 101: 321–31.

—. 1996. *Deuteronomy*. JPS Torah Commentary. Philadelphia: Jewish Publication Society.

Tomson, Peter J. 1990. *Paul and the Jewish Law: Halakhah in the Letters of the Apostle to the Gentiles*. CRINT 3/1. Assen and Maastricht: Van Gorcum. Minneapolis: Fortress.

Tov, E. 1992. *Textual Criticism of the Hebrew Bible*. 2nd ed. Minneapolis: Fortress. Assen and Maastricht: Van Gorcum.

—. 1995. "Excerpted and Abbreviated Biblical Texts from Qumran." *RevQ* 16: 581–600.

—. 1997. "*Tefillin* of Different Origin from Qumran?" Pages 44*–54* in *A Light for Jacob. Studies in the Bible and the Dead Sea Scrolls in Memory of Jacob Shalom Licht*. Edited by Y. Hoffman and F. H. Polak. Jerusalem: The Bialik Institute.

—. 2000. "The Background of the Sense Divisions in the Biblical Texts." Pages 312–50 in *Delimitation Criticism: A New Tool in Biblical Scholarship*. Edited by Marjo C. A. Korpel and Josef M. Oesch. Pericope: Scripture as Written and Read in Antiquity 1. Assen: Van Gorcum.

—. 2001a. "Scribal Features of Early Witnesses of Greek Scripture." Pages 125–48 in *The Old Greek Psalter: Studies in Honour of Albert Pietersma*. Edited by Robert J. V. Hiebert, Claude E. Cox and Peter J. Gentry. JSOTSup 332. Sheffield: Sheffield Academic Press.

—. 2001b. "The Nature of the Greek Texts from the Judean Desert." *NovT* 43: 1–11.

—. 2002. "The Biblical Texts from the Judaean Desert." Pages 165–202 in *The Texts from the Judaean Desert: Indices and an Introduction to the Discoveries in the Judaean Desert Series*. Edited by E. Tov. DJD 39. Oxford: Clarendon.

—. 2003a. "The Greek Biblical Texts from the Judean Desert." Pages 97–122 in *The Bible as Book: The Transmission of the Greek Text*. Edited by S. McKendrick and O. A. O'Sullivan. London: The British Library and Oak Knoll Press in Association with The Scriptorium: Center for Christian Antiquities.

—. 2003b. "The Text of the Hebrew/Aramaic and Greek Bible Used in the Ancient Synagogues." Pages 237–59 in *The Ancient Synagogue from Its Origins until 200 C.E.* Edited by Birger Olsson and Magnus Zetterholm. ConBNT 39. Stockholm: Almqvist & Wiksell International.

—. 2004. *Scribal Practices and Approaches Reflected in the Texts Found in the Judean Desert*. STDJ 54. Leiden and Boston: Brill.

Townsend, John T. 1968. "1 Cor 3:15 and the School of Shammai." *HTR* 61: 500–504.

Trebilco, Paul R. 1991. *Jewish Communities in Asia Minor*. SNTSMS 69. Cambridge: Cambridge University Press.

Treu, Kurt. 1973. "Die Bedeutung des Griechischen für die Juden im Römischen Reich." *Kairos* 15: 123–44.

Tuckett, Christopher M. 1986. "Deuteronomy 21:23 and Paul's Conversion." Pages 345–50 in *L'Apôtre Paul: Personalité, Style et Conception du Ministère*. Edited by A. Vanhoye. BETL 73. Leuven: Leuven University Press.

—. 1997. "Scripture and Q." Pages 3–26 in *The Scriptures in the Gospels*. Edited by C. M. Tuckett. Leuven: Leuven University Press.

—. 2000. "Paul, Scripture and Ethics. Some Reflections." *NTS* 46: 403–24.

Turner, E. G. 1977. *The Typology of the Early Codex*. Philadelphia: University of Pennsylvania Press.

—. 1987. *Greek Manuscripts of the Ancient World*. 2nd ed. by P. J. Parsons. London: University of London Institute of Classical Studies.

Ulrich, E. C. 1984. "The Greek Manuscripts of the Pentateuch from Qumrân, Including Newly-Identified Fragments of Deuteronomy (4QLXXDeut)." Pages 71–82 in *De Septuaginta: Studies in Honour of John William Wevers*. Edited by A. Pietersma and C. Cox. Mississauga, Ontario: Benben.

—. 1992. "The Septuagint Manuscripts from Qumran: A Reappraisal of Their Value." Pages 49–80 in *Septuagint, Scrolls and Cognate Writings: Papers Presented to the International Symposium on the Septuagint and Its Relations to the Dead Sea Scrolls and Other Writings*. Edited by G. J. Brooke and B. Lindars. SCS 33. Atlanta: Scholars.

Urbach, Ephraim E. 1990. "The Role of the Ten Commandments in Jewish Worship." Pages 161–89 in *The Ten Commandments in History and Tradition*. Edited by B. Z. Segal. English version edited by G. Levi. Jerusalem: Magnes Press.

Urman, Dan. 1995. "The House of Assembly and the House of Study: Are They One and the Same?" Pages 232–55 in vol. 1 of Urman and Flesher 1995.

—. and P. V. M. Flesher, eds. 1995. *Ancient Synagogues: Historical Analysis and Archaeological Discovery*. 2 vols. SPB 47. Leiden, New York, Köln: Brill.

Vahrenhorst, Martin. 2005. "Paulus und das pharisäische Judentum." Pages 49–67 in *Paulus der Jude: Seine Stellung im christlich-jüdischen Dialog heute*. Edited by Sung-Hee Lee-Linke. Frankfurt am Main: Verlag Otto Lembeck.

van der Horst, Pieter W. 1991. *Ancient Jewish Epitaphs: An Introductory Survey of a Millennium of Jewish Funerary Epigraphy (300 B.C.E. – 700 C.E.)*. CBET 2. Kampen: Kok Pharos.

—. 1999. "Was the Synagogue a Place of Sabbath Worship Before 70CE?" Pages 18–43 in *Jews, Christians, and Polytheists in the Ancient Synagogue: Cultural Interaction During the Greco-Roman Period*. Edited by S. Fine. London and New York: Routledge.

van Haelst, Joseph. 1989. "Les Origenes du Codex." Pages 13–35 in *Les Débuts du Codex*. Edited by A. Blanchard. Bibliologia 9. Brepols: Turnhout.

van Unnik, W. C. 1949. "De la règle μήτε προσθεῖναι μήτε ἀφελεῖν dans l'histoire du canon." *VC* 3: 1–36. Reprinted as pages 123–56 in *Sparsa Collecta: The Collected Essays of W. C. van Unnik*. NovTSup 30/2. Leiden: Brill, 1980.

—. 1962. *Tarsus or Jerusalem. The City of Paul's Youth*. Translated by G. Ogg. London: Epworth. Reprinted as pages 259–320 in *Sparsa Collecta: The Collected Essays of W. C. van Unnik I*. NovTSup 29. Leiden: Brill 1973.

—. 1973. "Once Again: Tarsus or Jerusalem." Pages 321–27 in *Sparsa Collecta: The Collected Essays of W. C. van Unnik I*. NovTSup 29. Leiden: Brill.

van Vliet, H. 1958. *No Single Testimony: A Study in the Adoption of the Law of Deut 19:15 par. into the New Testament*. STRT 4. Utrecht: Kemink & Zoon.

VanderKam, James C. 1994. "The Theology of the Temple Scroll: A Response to Lawrence H. Schiffman." *JQR* 85: 129–35.

—. 2000. "Studies on the Prologue and *Jubilees* 1." Pages 266–79 in *For a Later Generation: The Transformation of Tradition in Israel, Early Judaism, and Early Christianity*. Edited by R. A. Argall, B.A. Bow, and R. A. Werline. Harrisburg, PA: Trinity Press International.

—. 2008. "Recent Scholarship on the Book of Jubilees." *CBR* 6: 405–31.

Vanhoozer, Kevin J. 2008. "The Apostolic Discourse and Its Development." Pages 191–207 in *Scripture's Doctrine and Theology's Bible: How the New Testament Shapes Christian Dogmatics*. Edited by Markus Bockmuehl and Alan Torrance. Grand Rapids: Baker.

Verbruggen, Jan L. 2006. "Of Muzzles and Oxen: Deuteronomy 25:4 and 1 Corinthians 9:9." *JETS* 49: 699–711.

Vermes, G. 1959. "Pre-Mishnaic Jewish Worship and the Phylacteries from the Dead Sea." *VT* 9: 65–72.

—. 1973. *Scripture and Tradition in Judaism: Haggadic Studies*. 2nd ed. SPB 4. Leiden: Brill.

—. 1975. "The Decalogue and the Minim." Pages 169–77 in his *Post-Biblical Jewish Studies*. SJLA 8. Leiden: Brill.

—. 1982. "A Summary of the Law by Flavius Josephus." *NovT* 24: 289–303.

Verseput, Donald. 1997. "James 1:17 and the Jewish Morning Prayers." *NovT* 39: 177–91.

Via, Dan O. 1974. "A Structuralist Approach to Paul's Old Testament Hermeneutic." *Int* 28: 201–20.

Vos, J. S. 1992. "Die Hermeneutische Antinomie bei Paulus (Galater 3:11–12; Römer 10:5–10)." *NTS* 38: 254–70.

Vouga, François. 1998. *An die Galater*. HNT 10. Tübingen: Mohr Siebeck.

Waaler, Erik. 2008. *The Shema and the First Commandment in First Corinthians: An Intertextual Approach to Paul's Re-reading of Deuteronomy.* WUNT 2/253. Tübingen: Mohr Siebeck.

Wacholder, B. Z. 1961. "Greek Authors in Herod's Library." *Studies in Bibliography and Booklore* 5: 102–09.

—. 1983. *The Dawn of Qumran: The Sectarian Torah and the Teacher of Righteousness.* MHUCA 8. Cincinnati: Hebrew Union College Press.

—. 1989. "Rules of Testimony in Qumranic Jurisprudence: CD 9 and 11Q Torah 64." *JJS* 40: 163–74.

Wagner, J. Ross. 2002. *Heralds of the Good News: Isaiah and Paul in Concert in the Letter to the Romans.* NovTSup 101. Leiden: Brill.

Wakefield, Andrew H. 2003. *Where to Live: The Hermeneutical Significance of Paul's Citations from Scripture in Galatians 3:1–14.* Academia Biblica 14. Atlanta: Society of Biblical Literature.

Walser, Georg. 2001. *The Greek of the Ancient Synagogue: An Investigation on the Greek of the Septuagint, Pseudepigrapha and the New Testament.* Studia Graeca et Latina Lundensia 8. Lund: Almqvist and Wiksell International.

—. 2003. "The Greek of the Ancient Synagogue." Pages 260–76 in *The Ancient Synagogue from Its Origins until 200 C.E.* Edited by Birger Olsson and Magnus Zetterholm. ConBNT 39. Stockholm: Almqvist & Wiksell International.

Ward, Richard F. 1994. "Pauline Voice and Presence as Strategic Communication." *Semeia* 65: 95–107.

Wasserstein, Abraham and David J. Wasserstein. 2006. *The Legend of the Septuagint: From Classical Antiquity to Today.* Cambridge: Cambridge University Press.

Waters, Guy Prentiss. 2006. *The End of Deuteronomy In the Epistles of Paul.* WUNT 2/221. Tübingen: Mohr Siebeck.

Watson, Duane F. and Alan J Hauser. 1994. *Rhetorical Criticism of the Bible: A Comprehensive Bibliography With Notes on History and Method.* Leiden: Brill.

Watson, Francis. 2004. *Paul and the Hermeneutics of Faith.* London and New York: T. & T. Clark International.

—. 2006a. "A Response from Francis Watson." *SJT* 59: 461–68.

—. 2006b. "Paul and the Reader: An Authorial Apologia." *JSNT* 28: 363–73.

—. 2007. "Response to Richard Hays." *ProEccl* 16: 134–40.

Watt, Jonathan M. 2003. "Language Pragmatism in a Multilingual Religious Community." Pages 277–97 in *The Ancient Synagogue from Its Origins until 200 C.E.* Edited by Birger Olsson and Magnus Zetterholm. ConBNT 39. Stockholm: Almqvist & Wiksell International.

Wedderburn, A. J. M. 1988. *The Reasons for Romans.* Edinburgh: T. & T. Clark.

Weill, Raymond. 1920. *La cité de David. Compte rendu des fouilles executées, à Jérusalem, sur le site de la ville primitive: campagne de 1913–1914.* Paris: Librairie Paul Geuthner.

Weinfeld, Moshe. 1972. *Deuteronomy and the Deuteronomic School.* Oxford: Clarendon.

—. 1986. *The Organizational Pattern and the Penal Code of the Qumran Sect.* Fribourg and Göttingen: Vandenhoeck & Ruprecht.

—. 1992a. "Grace After Meals in Qumran." *JBL* 111: 427–40.

—. 1992b. "Prayer and Liturgical Practice in the Qumran Sect." Pages 241–58 in *The Dead Sea Scrolls: Forty Years of Research.* Edited by D. Dimant and U. Rappaport. STDJ 10. Leiden: Brill.

—. 1992c. "God Versus Moses in the Temple Scroll: 'I Do Not Speak on My Own Authority But on God's Authority' (*Sifrei Deut.* Sec. 5; *John* 12, 48f)." *RevQ* 15: 175–80.

Weise, M. 1961. *Kultzeiten und kultischer Bundesschluss in der Ordensregel vom Toten Meer.* SPB 3. Leiden: Brill.

Weitzman, Stephen. 1996. "Allusion, Artifice, and Exile in the Hymn of Tobit." *JBL* 115: 49–61.

Welborn, L. L. 1995. "The Identification of 2 Corinthians 10–13 with the 'Letter of Tears'." *NovT* 37: 138–53.

Wendel, Carl. 1950. *Der Toraschrein im Altertum.* Hallische Monographien 15. Halle: Max Niemeyer. Reprinted as pages 108–43 in his *Kleine Schriften zum antiken Buch- und Bibliothekswesen.* Edited by W. Krieg. Köln: Greven, 1974.

Wernberg-Møller, P. 1957. *The Manual of Discipline: Translated and Annotated with an Introduction.* STDJ 1. Leiden: Brill.

Wevers, John William. 1977a. "The Attitude of the Greek Translator of Deuteronomy towards his Parent Text." Pages 498–505 in *Beiträge zur Alttestamentlichen Theologie. Festschrift für W. Zimmerli zum 70. Geburstag.* Edited by H. Donner, R. Hanhart and R. Smend. Göttingen: Vandenhoeck & Ruprecht.

—. 1977b. "The Earliest Witness to the LXX Deuteronomy." *CBQ* 39: 240–44.

—. 1978. *Text History of the Greek Deuteronomy.* Abhandlungen der Akademie der Wissenschaften in Göttingen, Philologisch-Historische Klasse 3.106. MSU 13. Göttingen: Vandenhoeck & Ruprecht.

—. 1994. "Yahweh and Its Appositives in LXX Deuteronomium." Pages 269–80 in *Studies in Deuteronomy.* Edited by F. García Martínez, et al. VTSup 53. Leiden: Brill.

—. 1995. *Notes on the Greek Text of Deuteronomy.* SBLSCS 39. Atlanta: Scholars Press.

—. 1997. "The LXX Translator of Deuteronomy." Pages 57–89 in *IX Congress of the International Organization for Septuagint and Cognate Studies. Cambridge, 1995.* Edited by Bernard A. Taylor. SBLSCS 45. Atlanta: Scholars Press.

White, Sidnie Ann. 1990a. "4QDt[n]: Biblical Manuscript or Excerpted Text?" Pages 13–20 in *Of Scribes and Scrolls.* Edited by H. W. Attridge et al.. College Theology Society Resources in Religion 5. Lanham: University Press of America.

—. 1990b. "The All Souls Deuteronomy and the Decalogue." *JBL* 109: 193–206.

Wilcox, Max. 1977. " 'Upon the Tree': Deut 21:22–23 in the New Testament." *JBL* 96: 85–99.

Williams, David S. 2003. "Recent Research in 2 Maccabees." *CBR* 2: 69–83.

Williams, Sam K. 1988. "Promise in Galatians: A Reading of Paul's Reading of Scripture." *JBL* 107: 709–20.

Willis, W. 1985. "An Apostolic Apologia? The Form and Function of 1 Corinthians 9." *JSNT* 24: 33–48

Wilson, A. and L. Wills. 1982. "Literary Sources of the Temple Scroll." *HTR* 75: 275–88.

Wisdom, Jeffrey R. 2001. *Blessing for the Nations and the Curse of the Law: Paul's Citations of Genesis and Deuteronomy in Gal 3:8–10.* WUNT 2/133. Tübingen: Mohr Siebeck.

Wise, Michael O. 1990. *A Critical Study of the Temple Scroll From Qumran Cave 11.* SAOC 49. Chicago: The Oriental Institute of the University of Chicago.

Witherington III, Ben. 1995. *Conflict and Community in Corinth: A Socio-Rhetorical Commentary on 1 and 2 Corinthians.* Grand Rapids: Eerdmans.

Wittstruck, T. 1976. "The So-called Anti-Anthropomorphisms in the Greek Text of Deuteronomy." *CBQ* 38: 29–34.

Wright, G. Ernest. 1962. "The Lawsuit of God: A Form-Critical Study of Deuteronomy 32." Pages 26–67 in *Israel's Prophetic Heritage. Essays in Honor of James Muilenburg.* Edited by Bernard W. Anderson and Walter Harrelson. New York: Harper & Brothers.

Wright, N. T. 1992. *The Climax of the Covenant: Christ and the Law in Pauline Theology.* Minneapolis: Fortress. Originally: T. & T. Clark, 1991.

—. 1997. *What St. Paul Really Said.* Oxford: Lion.

Yadin, Y. 1966. *Masada: Herod's Fortress and the Zealots' Last Stand.* London: Weidenfeld and Nicolson.

—. 1971. "Pesher Nahum (4QpNahum) Reconsidered." *IEJ* 21: 1–12.

York, Anthony D. 1974. "The Dating of Targumic Literature." *JSJ* 5:49–62.

—. 1979 "The Targum in the Synagogue and in the School." *JSJ* 10: 74–86.

Young, Frances M. 1997. *Biblical Exegesis and the Formation of Christian Culture.* Cambridge: Cambridge University Press.

Ziesler, John. 1988. "The Role of the Tenth Commandment in Romans 7." *JSNT* 33: 41–56.

—. 1989. *Paul's Letter to the Romans.* TPI New Testament Commentaries. London: SCM. Philadelphia: Trinity Press International.

Zimmerman, Jens. 2004. "*Quo Vadis*? Literary Theory Beyond Postmodernism." *Christianity and Literature* 53: 495–519.

Zimmermann, Johannes. 1998. *Messianische Texte aus Qumran. Königliche, priesterliche und prophetische Messiasvorstellungen in den Schriftfunden von Qumran.* WUNT 2/104. Tübingen: Mohr Siebeck.

Index of Ancient Sources

1. Hebrew Bible and Septuagint

2. New Testament

3. Old Testament Pseudepigrapha

4. Dead Sea Scrolls

5. Philo of Alexandria

6. Josephus

7. Targums

8. Mishnah

9. Tosefta

13. Other Ancient Christian Writings

14. Classical Greek and Latin Sources

15. Manuscripts

16. Inscriptions

Index of Modern Authors

Index of Subjects